NEUTERING THE CIA

NEUTERING THE CIA

WHY US INTELLIGENCE VERSUS TRUMP HAS LONG-TERM CONSEQUENCES

JOHN A. GENTRY

ARMINLEAR

Library of Congress (LOC): 2023935465

ISBN (hardback): 978-1-956450-68-2
ISBN (paperback): 978-1-956450-69-9
ISBN (eBook): 978-1-956450-70-5

Armin Lear Press Inc
215 W Riverside Drive, #4362
Estes Park, CO 80517

*To the many fine people of the Central Intelligence Agency
who still produce, unseen by outsiders and quietly, apolitical
intelligence in support of American national decision-makers.*

CONTENTS

PREFACE

ALTHOUGH THE EVENTS THAT TRIGGERED the writing of this book began in mid-2016, my interest in the intersection of politics and intelligence began in 1986 when, as an intelligence analyst at the Central Intelligence Agency (CIA), I personally experienced a variant of the "politicization" of intelligence by intelligence professionals, which traditionally is defined as the injection of political or ideological perspectives into intelligence analyses in order to advance personal, political, or organizational goals. My primary responsibility then was analyzing the East German economy. It was an interesting and challenging account. After following the German Democratic Republic for several years, I was under no illusions about the many negative and few good aspects of the country's communist regime, not least the omnipresence of its internal security service, the Stasi, and its close association with the Soviet Union as a member of the Warsaw Pact. My assessments reflected these characteristics, as did those of colleagues who followed other East European communist countries. Yet in 1986 my division chief, Steve K., began to insist that his analysts make the countries we followed look worse than they were, mainly by adding pejorative adjectives in our analytic papers. My immediate supervisor, branch chief Barry B., made sure that I, like all other analysts in the branch, got the word.

Steve and Barry told us that Robert Gates, who then headed CIA's Directorate of Intelligence (DI, now re-named the Directorate of Analysis, DA), wanted such language in CIA reports.[1] We were given the impression that Gates wanted to curry favor with anti-communist "hard-liners" of the Reagan administration. Interested in pleasing their bosses, Steve and Barry were happy to comply. Drafts were re-written; we were told what types of language were acceptable. Additional pejorative adjectives were seen as desirable. Analysts in other DI offices, I learned later, received similar directives. In retrospect, the politicization was mild, but it was very unusual given CIA's organizational culture of the time, and it produced some unpleasant conversations. Steve and Barry insisted that we violate a core organizational norm—analytic objectivity. These unpleasant conversations were a major reason I took another job at CIA soon thereafter and eventually left the CIA in 1990 after twelve years there.

It was not hard, therefore, for me to go to the Senate Select Committee on Intelligence (SSCI) in the fall of 1991 when it was considering Gates's nomination to be Director of Central Intelligence (DCI). Like several dozen analysts who had experienced politicization in other DI offices, I told SSCI staffers that Gates had politicized intelligence. But, because I had not myself heard him direct the politicization, I was not asked to testify in public sessions. Years later, after learning more about the situation, I concluded that Gates probably had not directly demanded the politicization I experienced, that it almost certainly was initiated by the late George Kolt, our office director, who was widely known

---

1 For some of many references to this episode in the literature, see: Hutchings, "Introduction," 13, Gentry, *Lost Promise*.

internally to have had strongly anti-Soviet views. But Gates remains culpable, in my judgment, for establishing a climate in which this kind of politicization could occur.

Gates survived a tumultuous confirmation process and, to his credit, as DCI addressed the politicization issue directly, making clear that he opposed politicization.[2] The case continues to be a prominent part of CIA analysts' cultural tradition and still is frequently cited in the intelligence literature as a prominent case of politicization from the political Right. No senior intelligence officer since has acted as forthrightly against politicization as Gates did in 1991-1993.

My experiences in 1986 and the revelations of Gates's 1991 confirmation hearings led to my continuing interest in the intersection of intelligence and politics, what is known as intelligence "producer-consumer relations," and especially the politicization of intelligence by professional intelligence personnel. The politicization I experienced was a prominent topic in my *Lost Promise: How CIA Analysis Misserves the Nation*, published in 1993, and in later articles after I returned to studying the US Intelligence Community (IC), and intelligence more generally, as an academic. I tracked the modest but growing literature on the subject, published mainly in the United States, the United Kingdom, and Israel. This literature is virtually unanimous in viewing the politicization of intelligence by intelligence officers—of any kind and in any way—as inappropriate for the intelligence services of democracies. The portion of this literature addressing US intelligence similarly concludes that politicization of the sort I experienced is incompatible with the stated and implied purposes of US intelligence and damages the perceived objectivity, credibility, trustworthiness, and therefore the usefulness, of intelligence. Because memories of intelligence failures, especially, are long, even small instances of politicization

---

2   Gates, "Guarding against Politicization."

endure in memories for extended periods of time, often decades, generating a variety of negative consequences, especially a loss of trust in intelligence by senior leaders. This analytic judgment is widely held by knowledgeable students of intelligence and consumers of intelligence. It appreciably informs my assessment of the political activism of intelligence professionals in recent years and to a considerable degree shapes the research questions and analytic approach of this book. However, for intellectual completeness, to be fair to the political activists who politicize US intelligence, and to recognize that societies evolve and the lessons of intelligence history do, too, I also examine activists' assertions that their activism is a civic responsibility in extraordinary times and that the activism of recent years is temporary, harmless, or even a net positive development for the IC and the country.

In later years I rejoined the IC in other capacities. First, in 2000-2001, while employed by the MITRE Corporation, I worked for the intelligence policy office of the Assistant Secretary of Defense for Command, Control, Communications, and Intelligence, the predecessor of today's Under Secretary of Defense for Intelligence (USD(I)). And, beginning in 2010, I taught at the Defense Intelligence Agency's training center before joining the National Intelligence University (NIU), which provides a year-long master's-level program on strategic intelligence for US government personnel, most of whom are currently serving intelligence officers. I left NIU in late 2015, after two and a half years there. In these roles in recent years, I taught several hundred students from virtually all IC agencies and interacted regularly with many other intelligence personnel from several agencies. These people, at junior and middle grades and at all stages of careers, gave me insights into many aspects of the IC, including appreciation for how different the agencies of the IC are and how differently the IC operated then compared to my time at CIA in the 1980s. These experiences prompted, and partly enabled, me to write several journal articles and a book on intelligence topics, some of which directly addressed cultural and managerial aspects of then-contemporary IC. These writings and experiences remain, to the best of my knowledge, accurate although incomplete reflections of the practices and organizational cultures of some IC agencies, giving me first-hand knowledge of structural, leadership, and cultural situation at the time. While I saw evolution in the organizational cultures of IC agencies, my view was that the traditional, core IC ethic of apolitical public service remained strong.

Therefore, when former intelligence officers loudly broke many of the traditional norms of behavior of intelligence officers by attacking Donald Trump, beginning immediately after he secured the Republican presidential nomination in mid-2016, I like many others was surprised. The activism represented a radically different variant of politicization than I experienced and was then assessed in the intelligence literature. In the past in the United States and in most other countries, intelligence loyally served legitimate national leaders even when leader-intelligence relationships were not close. While intelligence occasionally has been involved in coups against leaders, never in the history of any country until 2016 (and since) had intelligence personnel acted in opposition to a duly elected national leader for such an extended period without generating a strenuous response by the leader—often a purge of offending personnel or even of entire agencies.[3] This anti-Trump politicization potentially has much greater ramifications for the IC and the United States as a whole than the relatively tame politicization I experienced in 1986.

It was therefore immediately clear to me that this new

---

3   Gentry, "Purges of Intelligence Services."

phenomenon warranted special, focused scholarly attention. Three related research questions quickly arose as important topics of inquiry: (1) What activities and attitudes are new, and at which IC agencies? (2) Why and how did the changes occur? And (3), what are the immediate and long-term implications of the politicization of intelligence for specific intelligence agencies and the IC as a whole, for senior national policy-makers including the president, and for the country in general? Answering these questions is the purpose of this book. While divining the depths of the world of intelligence is never easy, the literature relevant to my questions is considerable, reputable, and growing, and my long tenure in and around the IC has given me both insights and contacts with knowledgeable people who have been helpful in many ways. I therefore think the analytic methods used in this book are appropriate, my sources are credible, and my conclusions are defensible. The activism receded markedly soon after Joe Biden became president in 2021, making even clearer that the politicization of intelligence was aimed at Trump. While it is in remission, the changes in the political culture of some IC agencies that triggered the attacks on Trump remain intact, available for re-activation in the event of another serious candidacy by Trump or the election of another Republican president. Hence, it is important to see Trump as the first target of the IC's new political activists, meaning the full implications of the IC's bout of political activism from 2016 to 2021 may not be apparent for years. The findings of this book therefore surely will be, and should be, seen as preliminary conclusions to be re-examined over time by other scholars, journalists, citizens generally, and professional intelligence officers.

By focusing on the political activities of current and former intelligence officers in relation to President Trump, this book purposely does not address other activities of intelligence officials, including: writings on national security issues generally; former officials running for public office on their own merits and political philosophies; and all non-political activities. The boundaries between various categories of activities are sometimes gray, however, especially for political candidates. My main criterion for including the public commentary and written analyses of current and former intelligence officials in this book is that the officials engaged in political activity focused on a sitting president or his senior appointees while invoking their intelligence careers as legitimizing their politically partisan comments or activities. I define commentary and actions as partisan if they invoke a party affiliation, attack a party platform, or criticize political candidates and elected or appointed US government officials based on their personal characteristics or political views. By this definition, many intelligence persons' attacks on Trump were partisan.

Therefore, Donald Trump is *not* the focus of this book. He appears inevitably because the overwhelming majority of political activism by intelligence persons in 2016-2021 was directed against him. This book does not defend Trump or assess his presidency. It is about the causes and consequences of politically motivated attitudes and actions of intelligence officers, then-current and former. This scope limit is my way of trying to keep this book as analytically objective as possible and to avoid, to the extent I can, the emotion Donald Trump often elicits. Because many intelligence officers' anti-Trump activities reflect a fundamental change in political aspects of the organizational cultures of some IC agencies, which seems likely to recur, I see the IC-Trump conflict as the first in a series of ideology-based struggles. This book therefore is an effort to understand a phenomenon that we will see again.

Numerous people helped this project, including: Richard K. Betts, David Bush, Daniel Byman, Peter Clement, Steve Coll, William Costanza, Andrew Defty, Charles Sam Faddis, Peter D. Feaver, Thomas Fingar, Burton Gerber, Dan Gressang, Elizabeth Grimm, Glenn Hastedt, Bruce Hoffman, Loch K. Johnson, Mark M. Lowenthal, Joseph Maccone, David R. Mandel, Stephen Marrin, John McLaughlin, Christopher Moran, Alexa O'Brien, Edward (Ned) Price, Brian Powers, Bruce Riedel, Michael Robinson, Luis Rodriguez, James Simon, Kenneth L. Stiles, Gregory F. Treverton, Richard Valcourt, Philip Zelikow, and Barry Zulauf. I especially thank Nicholas Dujmović, Susan Gentry, Jan Goldman, the late Robert Jervis, and David G. Muller, Jr., who read earlier versions of the entire manuscript and provided helpful comments and detailed suggestions. Dave Muller also provided many information sources I might have missed. Many other people who wish to remain anonymous contributed information, perspectives, and analytical ideas. A few people declined to provide me their views on this subject, and others did not respond to my requests for discussions.

My requests for insights focused mainly on former intelligence officers and scholars of intelligence with whom I shared the three main research questions cited above. Parts of the book reflect information and opinions of then-serving government employees and intelligence contractors with whom I have personal relationships, who offered unsolicited views relevant to this book. I have continuing contacts with many such people and did not ask anyone to compromise a confidentiality agreement. I tried to discuss these issues with people from a wide variety of backgrounds, including agency, functional roles as intelligence officers, seniority, time within the IC, and degrees of political activism, including both harsh critics of President Trump and critics of those critics. I purposefully sought input with people from a wide variety of political orientations if I knew or suspected them, including partisan Democrats and partisan Republicans, but I do not know the political affiliations of many of my interlocutors.

I also thank Maryann Karinch and her staff at Armin Lear. Maryann was an early believer in this project and has been instrumental in enabling its publication in this form. Others found the approach I have tried to take as either politically incorrect or not adequately supportive of Donald Trump. I am grateful.

This book contain material adapted from four of my published articles: "'Truth' as a Tool of the Politicization of Intelligence," *International Journal of Intelligence and CounterIntelligence* 33:2 (May 2019): 217-249; "An INS Special Forum: US Intelligence officers' involvement in political activities in the Trump era," *Intelligence and National Security* 35:1 (2020): 1-19; "The New Politicization of the U.S. Intelligence Community," *International Journal of Intelligence and CounterIntelligence* 33:4 (2020): 639-665; and "Trump-Era Politicization: A Code of Civil-Intelligence Behavior Is Needed," *International Journal of Intelligence and CounterIntelligence* 34:4 (2021):757-786. This material is used with the permission of Taylor & Francis, for which I am grateful.

As a former intelligence officer, I am required to submit my writings to government security reviewers before they are published. This book was reviewed by the CIA's Prepublication Classification Review Board (PCRB), which approved its text without change. The PCRB requires the following statement:

> *All statement of fact, opinion, or analysis expressed are those of the author and do not reflect the official positions or views of the Central Intelligence Agency (CIA) or any other U.S. Government agency. Nothing in the contents should*

be construed as asserting or implying U.S. Government authentication of information or CIA endorsement of the author's views. This material has been reviewed by the CIA to prevent the disclosure of classified information. This does not constitute an official release of CIA information.

ABBREVIATIONS

★

ANGLE	Agency Network for Gay, Lesbian, Bisexual, and Transgender Officers and Allies (CIA)
BIG	Blacks in Government
CIA	Central Intelligence Agency
C/NIC	chairman of the National Intelligence Council
CPUSA	Communist Party of the United States of America
CRT	critical race theory
CT	counterterrorism
DA	Directorate of Analysis (CIA)
DCI	Director of Central Intelligence
DCIA	Director of the Central Intelligence Agency
DDI	Deputy Director for Intelligence (CIA)
DEA	Drug Enforcement Administration
DEI	diversity, equity, and inclusion
DI	Directorate of Intelligence (CIA)
DIA	Defense Intelligence Agency
DNI	Director of National Intelligence

DO	Directorate of Operations (CIA)
DOD	Department of Defense
DOJ	Department of Justice
EEO	equal employment opportunity
EO	executive order
EPA	Environmental Protection Agency
EU	European Union
FBI	Federal Bureau of Investigation
FEC	Federal Election Commission
GAO	Government Accountability Office
GRU	*Glavnoye razvedyvatel'noye upravleniye*, or foreign military-intelligence agency of the General Staff of the Armed Forces (USSR and Russia)
HBCU	Historically Black Colleges and Universities
HPSCI	House Permanent Select Committee on Intelligence
IC	Intelligence Community
ICA	Intelligence Community Assessment
IC CAE	Intelligence Community Centers for Academic Excellence
ICD	Intelligence Community Directive
ICIG	Intelligence Community Inspector General
IG	inspector general
INR	Bureau of Intelligence and Research, Department of State

IRTPA	Intelligence Reform and Terrorism Prevention Act of 2004
IT	information technology
KGB	*Komitet Gosudarstvennoy Bezopasnosti*, or Committee for State Security (USSR)
LGBT	lesbian, gay, bisexual, transgender
NASIC	National Air and Space Intelligence Center
NATO	North Atlantic Treaty Organization
NCMI	National Center for Medical Intelligence
NCTC	National Counterterrorism Center
NGA	National Geospatial-Intelligence Agency
NIC	National Intelligence Council
NIE	national intelligence estimate
NIM	national intelligence manager
NIMA	National Imagery and Mapping Agency
NIO	national intelligence officer
NIO/W	national intelligence officer for warning
NIPF	National Intelligence Priorities Framework
NIU	National Intelligence University
NKVD	*Naródnyy Komissariát Vnútrennikh Del*, or People's Commissariat for Internal Affairs (USSR)
NPR	National Public Radio
NSA	National Security Agency
NSC	National Security Council

ODNI	Office of the Director of National Intelligence
ODNI/AIS	Office of the Director of National Intelligence, Analytic Integrity and Standards
ONE	Office of National Estimates
OPA	Office of Public Affairs (CIA)
OSS	Office of Strategic Services
PCRB	Prepublication Classification Review Board (CIA)
PDB	*President's Daily Brief*
PDDNI	Principal Deputy Director of National Intelligence
PRB	Publications Review Board (CIA)
SAT	structured analytic technique
SEAL	Sea, Air, Land (US Navy special operations personnel)
SNIE	special national intelligence estimate
SOVA	Office of Soviet Analysis (CIA)
SSCI	Senate Select Committee on Intelligence
UCMJ	Uniform Code of Military Justice
USD(I)	Undersecretary of Defense for Intelligence
WMD	weapons of mass destruction

1
INTRODUCTION: WHY THIS BOOK?

There is no phase of the intelligence business which is more important than the proper relationship between intelligence itself and the people who use its product. Oddly enough, this relationship, which one would expect to establish itself automatically, does not do this. It is established as a result of a great deal of persistent conscious effort, and is likely to disappear when the effort is relaxed.

Proper relationship between intelligence producers and consumers is one of utmost delicacy. Intelligence must be close enough to policy, plans and operations to have the greatest amount of guidance, and must not be so close that it loses its objectivity and integrity of judgment.[1]

—SHERMAN KENT

---

[1] Kent, *Strategic Intelligence for American World Policy,* 180. While this is the general view, Robert Jervis frequently noted that one of the best services intelligence can provide is to increase the uncertainty of decision-makers who are unduly confident.

US INTELLIGENCE EXISTS TO HELP DECISION-MAKERS make better decisions, often by reducing their uncertainties about important world events.[2] If decision-makers find intelligence collection deficient, its analytic quality poor, or its objectivity suspect, leading them to seek information and analytic support elsewhere, intelligence is worthless. For many years the US intelligence community (IC) worked hard to make its intelligence products valuable to national leaders, generally achieving this despite some distrust and occasional animosity by presidents such as Richard Nixon, Jimmy Carter, and Bill Clinton. When presidents showed some distrust and dislike of the intelligence they received, intelligence professionals consistently strove to adjust to make their work useful to them.[3] Intelligence officers at the Central Intelligence Agency (CIA) and elsewhere knew and accepted that their successes were usually unpublicized, that their relatively small number of major failures usually became public knowledge, and that one of their jobs was to take the fall for presidents when their policies went bad. Reflecting this view, an old IC saying is, "There are policy successes and intelligence failures."

That perspective changed radically in 2016, however. Several former senior American intelligence officers, or "formers," entered partisan politics by prominently endorsing Hillary Clinton's presidential bid and harshly criticizing candidate and then President Donald Trump—for his political views and for his character.[4] Some of the attacks were very personal in nature. The formers rationalized their actions in new ways—frequently by claiming to have moral obligations to defend truth or democracy or, as

---

2   Fingar, *Reducing Uncertainty*.

3   For example, Smith, *The Unknown CIA*; Helms, *A Look Over My Shoulder*; Cline, *The CIA Under Reagan, Bush & Casey*; Phillips, *The Night Watch*.

4   For debates among former intelligence officers about the propriety of public attacks on Trump, see Adam Entous, "John Brennan's Choice to Confront Trump," *The New Yorker*, August 20, 2018, https://www.newyorker.com/news/news-desk/john-brennans-choice-to-confront-trump.

intelligence professionals, a duty to warn of an impending or ongoing domestic political calamity.[5] At the same time, press organizations began to report significant opposition to Trump among serving intelligence officers and a surge in leaks of intelligence material damaging to Trump. While most of the leaks were evidently of accurate information, some were apparently purposefully untrue; they were what intelligence officers call "disinformation"—narratives containing intentional gaps and/or errors designed to mislead audiences. Some of the formers, the press, and serving intelligence officers reported significant increases in anti-Trump banter in government work spaces, especially at the CIA and the Office of the Director of National Intelligence (ODNI). These politically motivated comments and practices continued to the end of Trump's term in office in January 2021 and beyond. They remain unprecedented in their substance, tone, and volume.

Long-time observers of US intelligence therefore began to wonder in 2016 if the CIA's once-firm prohibition on partisan politics had changed and to ponder whether a new kind of politicization of intelligence had arisen: institutionally embedded, partisan bias.[6] If so, the implications seemed potentially serious. While the activist formers and their backers within the IC rationalized their actions as warranted given Trump's allegedly severe deficiencies, more neutral observers wondered whether the former officials, especially, had instead damaged the intelligence institutions they claimed to be protecting by diminishing the perceived usefulness of intelligence to senior US foreign policy decision-makers—and thence to the nation as a whole.

This radical change in behavior, which required the overturning of a once-firmly held cultural norm at the CIA, especially,

---

5   Gentry, "'Truth' as a Tool of the Politicization of Intelligence."
6   Gentry, "A New Form of Politicization?"

begs for an explanation. Was it, as some of Trump's supporters argued, an attempt by the bureaucratic "Deep State" to overthrow an elected president, to stage a coup?[7] Or was it, as many of Trump's critics averred, a one-time set of criticisms of a uniquely unattractive president designed to help the country avert disaster? Or something else? Whatever the case, other questions abound. How, when, where, and why did these political and normative changes occur? Was something else at work? Given the importance of trust in the president-intelligence relationship, did this antagonism affect President Trump's and his senior advisors' (and their successors') confidence in, and therefore use of, intelligence? Does his alone or mutual belligerence explain Trump's skepticism of some of the IC's analytical judgments? Did the activism end when Trump left office, or is it a permanent new characteristic of the IC? If the behavior of intelligence personnel in 2016-2021 is a problem, as many observers believe, what might any president—Joe Biden or a successor—do about the situation? With what additional consequences? The goal of this book is to begin to answer these questions.

The book focuses on the causes and consequences of changes in the organizational cultures of IC agencies and on the effects of IC agency leaders' policies on the development of the political activism by some intelligence professionals from 2016 to 2021. The overt activism of the Trump years subsided in 2021, but by many accounts the organizational cultures of some IC agencies, especially the CIA, remain politicized, meaning that understanding the lessons of 2016-2021 is essential for appreciating the fundamental changes in US intelligence agencies that make a resurgence of political activism likely if a president again appears

---

7   For example, Chaffetz, *The Deep State*; Jarrett, *Witch Hunt*, 132-179.

to intelligence officers to act in ways inconsistent with their desires and expectations.

Intelligence by historical definition in the United States works for presidents, meaning intelligence and decision-makers perform very different functions. Correspondingly, traditional standards for judging the behavior of each, appropriately in my view, have been very different. In taking this stance this book, which mainly focuses on the actions of intelligence during the Trump-intelligence conflict of 2016-2021, assesses each in historically conventional ways. Descriptions and analyses are as objective and non-partisan as possible, recognizing the difficulty of trying to be objective in a period of American history characterized by intense political polarization. The book does not assess, critique, or defend the Trump presidency—tasks already done by many other writers. President Trump was unusually confrontational and controversial, and I have little doubt that most reputable historians will judge his presidency to have been seriously troubled.

Traditionally, the politicization of intelligence by professional intelligence officers has been widely regarded as normatively inappropriate, and the record fairly clearly shows that it is dysfunctional in many ways. I share these views. Although some may call it a bias, I view it as a sound, widely shared, evidence-based professional judgment. Trump's intelligence critics knew this background, too, and claimed to share traditional norms, which is why they universally refused to call their words and actions politicization. Instead, they talked of the severe abnormality that the Trump presidency allegedly was. Because intelligence critics of Trump came overwhelmingly from the Left half of the political spectrum, my assessment of their words and actions as being forms politicization will mistakenly be seen by some as partisanship in favor of Trump. There is little I can do about this except to present all sides of the issue as objectively as I can while clearly identifying my own judgments as such.

LEGACY FROM WHICH THE CRITICS EMERGED

To understand the degree of novelty and the significance of recent political activism by American intelligence professionals, it helps to know how intelligence normally serves policymakers and the ways thoughtful people in the United States— intelligence professionals and others—have traditionally seen the proper relationship between intelligence personnel and the leaders they support. In these views, intelligence exists to support authorized national-level policy-makers such as the president and cabinet officers, military commanders, and lesser executive branch officials who use intelligence to make decisions about diplomatic strategies, military procurements, and many other issues.[8] Intelligence also supports the Congress, which has significant decision-making and oversight responsibilities.[9]

American intelligence therefore always supports Democrats, Republicans, and apolitical civil servants. Intelligence personnel and agencies, by longstanding tradition, are expected to support *all* decision-makers to the best of their abilities without injecting organizational or personal political views into intelligence products. That is, they provide apolitical intelligence support to the US government in general. Since the creation of the modern American IC after World War II, the vast majority of intelligence professionals have tried to provide accurate collection and sound, objective intelligence analyses to all decision-makers.[10] They

---

8   Intelligence agencies also produce products that are designed for public consumption. The CIA's annual *World Factbook*, for example, is used widely by the public.

9   For examples of congressional use of intelligence and intelligence oversight, see Ott, "Partisanship and the Decline of Intelligence Oversight;" Kibbe, "Congressional Oversight of Intelligence."

10   Rare exceptions are discussed in chapter 2.

usually have succeeded, some major analytic failures and a few episodes of politicization notwithstanding. Deviations from the norm were individual in nature—not organizational—and were small in magnitude and importance.

The eighteen agencies of the IC specialize but serve overlapping sets of decision-makers. By law, tradition, and presidential directives, the CIA primarily serves presidents and other senior national decision-makers in Washington. The CIA has a large and capable staff, is the IC's primary analytic agency, and often is seen as the "face" of US intelligence. When candidate and then President Trump developed an adversarial relationship with intelligence in 2016, the CIA soon appeared prominently as both the target of Trump's criticisms and as the organization whose current and former employees were most visibly critical of him.

When intelligence is good enough to support national decision-making, it inevitably has ramifications within domestic politics. Leaders use intelligence routinely to "get smart" about international affairs, indirectly assisting their decision-making processes.[11] They use current intelligence reporting and analyses directly in their decision-making processes, especially during crises, rightly believing that intelligence can help them devise plausible courses of action and make wiser or more effective decisions, thereby advancing national interests and their own political agendas and legacies.[12] They frequently also use intelligence to discredit political opponents' views and to foster public support for their policies. These practices occur routinely when there is no politically-motivated effort to shape the content of intelligence analyses by intelligence professionals.

The intelligence literature long has examined many political

---

11   This function is sometimes known as providing policymakers with "decision advantage." See Sims, "Foreign Intelligence Liaison."

12   Steinberg, "The Policymaker's Perspective."

aspects of intelligence and synthesized them into two general forms of "politicization:" (1) "cooking the books" by intelligence professionals—typically analysts or their managers—by selecting, omitting, shaping, or altering intelligence in ways designed to further personal or organizational political, ideological, or bureaucratic interests;[13] and (2) outsiders' efforts to manipulate or use intelligence selectively to affect policy debates.[14] The first type of politicization, which is the only one intelligence personnel directly influence, is widely viewed as inappropriate behavior inconsistent with the purposes and cultural norms of US intelligence—especially those of the CIA.[15] Sometimes called "bottom-up" politicization, it is the focus of this book.[16]

The second type is inevitable if intelligence is in fact useful to decision-makers, as it usually is, and hence is untroublesome in principle if not in all forms of practice. It is sometimes called "top-down" politicization, but is more appropriately viewed as the "politics of intelligence," which is the term used in this book.[17] This type of politicization occurs in many ways, has occurred repeatedly over time by all presidents including Trump, is well addressed in the literature, and is *outside the scope of this book*.

But intelligence politicization and the politics of intelligence are not as clearly distinguishable in practice as the generic types noted above suggest. Glenn Hastedt of James Madison University proposed a typology that adds important nuance to the issue.[18]

---

13   Examples include Gates, "Guarding against Politicization;" Gentry, *Lost Promise*; Westerfield, "Inside ivory bunkers: CIA analysts resist managers' 'pandering' - part II;" Rubin, "The Temptation of Intelligence Politicization to Support Diplomacy."

14   Perhaps the best example of this genre is Rovner, *Fixing the Facts*. See also Hastedt, "Public intelligence;" Rovner, "Is Politicization Ever a Good Thing?"

15   Gates, "The CIA and American Foreign Policy," 227.

16   Betts, *Enemies of Intelligence*; Bar-Joseph, "The Politicization of Intelligence;" Gentry, "The intelligence of fear."

17   For other discussions of this function, see Betts, *Enemies of Intelligence*; Warner, "The Use and Abuse of Intelligence in the Public Square;" Lucas, "Recognizing Politicization;" Woodard, "Tasting the Forbidden Fruit."

18   Hastedt, "The Politics of Intelligence and the Politicization of Intelligence;" Nye, *Soft Power*.

He argued that politics and intelligence can be seen as involving three groups of actors: intelligence officers, political leaders, and the general public. Hastedt asserted that politicization can be of two varieties: hard and soft, which are both used by intelligence agencies and intelligence consumers. The "hard" form is the one commonly discussed; its core feature is coercion, by policymakers or senior intelligence officials, which limits acceptable analytic approaches and may specify ideologically appropriate analytic conclusions. This occurs rarely in blatant forms. President Lyndon Johnson, for example, reportedly asked the CIA in 1965 to produce an intelligence report that he could use to publicly justify the military intervention in the Dominican Republic that he had already begun.[19] Former director of central intelligence (DCI) William Casey (1981-1987) has been accused of hard politicization within CIA on flimsier factual grounds.[20]

The "soft" variety, adapted from Joseph Nye's concept of "soft power," denotes influence on analytic judgments that derive from intelligence organizations' culture-based assumptions that underlie analyses, decision rules about how analysis is conducted, and the institutional settings within which analyses are conducted.[21] Soft politicization is subtle and may not be done consciously. The worldviews of intelligence organizations and senior intelligence officials often are embedded in organizational cultures, sometimes biasing analyses in politically significant ways even unconsciously.[22] This kind of politicization may have increased in recent years.

Worldviews are a prominent topic of discussion in this book. If the organizational cultural changes that permitted,

---

19   Jeffreys-Jones, *CIA & American Democracy*, 149-150.

20   Hänni, "When Casey's blood pressure rose."

21   Hastedt, "The Politics of Intelligence and the Politicization of Intelligence," 10.

22   Robert Jervis and David Muller make similar points. For example, see Jervis, "Why Intelligence and Policymakers Clash;" Jervis, "Why Intelligence and Policymakers Clash Reexamined," Muller, "Intelligence Analysis in Red and Blue." For an example of the influence of such cultures, see Stevens, "The SAM Upgrade Blues."

encouraged, and enabled the partisan outburst of 2016 also influenced the selection of relevant intelligence topics, the ways they are addressed, and standards of accuracy conceived as analytical "truth," then the changes may have more influence, quietly, than the most belligerent words of former senior intelligence officers talking on cable news shows.[23] Assessing the magnitude and impact of such bias is difficult but not impossible for government watchdogs who have access to the full range of published intelligence products.[24] Outsiders will have to wait for declassification processes to work, which could take many years. If organizational worldviews are strong enough to systematically bias analyses in significant ways, they could pose major threats to sound senior decision-making and thence have significant implications for the enduring usefulness of US intelligence.

Hastedt assessed how his variables interacted in several prominent episodes in American intelligence history, ranging from the "bomber gap" and "missile gap" controversies of the 1950s to allegations that the George W. Bush administration politicized intelligence to justify an aggressive war against Iraq in 2003 to the Congress, the American people, the United Nations Security Council, and world opinion generally.[25] In the latter case, policymakers wanted intelligence support for chosen policies, "cherry picked" useful intelligence information for public release, and may have (this claim remains disputed) put undue pressure on analysts to provide politically helpful analyses. More certainly, Democratic senators on the Senate Select Committee on Intelligence (SSCI) in early September 2002, after the Bush administration had decided to attack Iraq, asked for a national intelligence estimate (NIE) on Iraqi weapons of mass destruction

23   Gentry, "An INS Special Forum," 9-10.
24   Marrin, "Evaluating the Quality of Intelligence Analysis."
25   Jervis, "Reports, Politics, and Intelligence Failures."

(WMD) with the goal of either embarrassing the Bush administration or giving themselves political cover for voting to authorize
the war. The authorization vote occurred in October 2002. The
rapidly written NIE contained only information and judgments
the IC had reported earlier in other formats, which were available
to the senators.

In the event, the IC's understanding of events in Iraq was
seriously deficient, leading to erroneous judgments about Iraqi
WMD that led Democrats to accuse Bush of politicizing intelligence, to White House accusations of IC ineptitude and perhaps
politicization, and to considerable soul-searching within the
IC.[26] The extensive record of these events contains very different
emphases in various renditions. While Trump remembered the
well-established intelligence errors and saw them as cause for
skepticism about the competence of IC agencies, intelligence
people claimed the internal reforms they made after 2003 made
their views entirely accurate—and thereby worthy of unquestioning respect during the Trump years.

In all of Hastedt's cases, politicization was designed to
support the policy objectives of political leaders or tangible organizational interests of an intelligence service. For example, US
Air Force intelligence argued in the 1950s that the Soviet bomber
fleet, and then the Soviets' intercontinental ballistic missile forces,
substantially exceeded those of the United States—hence the
"gaps" in capabilities.[27] The then-alleged, later disproven, US
inadequacies helped rationalize the Air Force's requests for larger
budgets. In none of Hastedt's cases did the personal political
or ideological leanings of any individual intelligence officer, or
group of intelligence personnel, factor in the politicization. Hence,

---

26   Jervis, *Why Intelligence Fails*, chapter 3.
27   Jeffreys-Jones, *CIA & American Democracy*, 109-110, 112, 114.

Hastedt did not address the issue of intelligence officers overtly attacking the political views of presidents they do not like—the situation when Trump was president.

Joshua Rovner, in one of the most detailed recent treatments of politicization, focused primarily on the politics of intelligence.[28] Rovner discussed three previously identified causes of influence of policymakers on intelligence analysis: (1) the "proximity" of intelligence officers to consumers, who may coopt intelligence if intelligence gets too close to policymaking, which was Sherman Kent's big worry, as noted in the epigraph of this chapter; (2) organizational proximity in which large organizations such as military services direct their subordinate intelligence units to produce biased intelligence useful for budgetary or other reasons, such as the Air Force episodes noted above; (3) and organizational dependence, in which policymakers threaten agencies with sanctions if they do not produce desired intelligence.[29] These are fairly standard explanations.

Rovner also offered a domestic politics-focused theory of politicization.[30] In such cases, policymakers seek to influence the content of intelligence to help support their domestic political agendas. Intelligence becomes an instrument of public relations. This is a variant of "top-down" politicization. Some anti-Trump formers claimed that Trump and his appointees politicized this way when they objected to CIA's recurrent claims that Russia aided Trump politically in 2016, something Trump clearly did not like. But CIA analysts appear to have repetitively pushed such stories at Trump to annoy him, another matter entirely. A far better recent example of top-down politicization was President

---

28   Rovner, *Fixing the Facts*; Wirtz, "The Politicization Paradox."

29   Rovner, *Fixing the Facts*, 8-11.

30   Ibid., 11.

Barack Obama's effort to change the demographics of the IC in politically salient ways, discussed in chapter 3.

Rovner accepted that intelligence agencies and individual personnel sometimes politicize intelligence, but gave this phenomenon little space. In Rovner's view, intelligence can "subvert" political leaders' policies in two ways, both of which occurred in recent years. Intelligence can: (1) provide biased information and analyses, and (2) leak information detrimental to administration policies.[31] The latter may be effective because intelligence is generally seen as having credibility about such things. In fact, the *Washington Post* and *New York Times* long have had intelligence sources who regularly leak information that appears on their front pages. In years past, these leaks occurred on many issues, but after 2016 they centered on Trump's perceived character deficiencies and his policies. By multiple accounts, the number of leaks grew substantially in number. In Rovner's accurate view, "[t]he fear of subversion, no less than subversion itself, contributes to intelligence-policy dysfunction."[32] Unlike in recent years, when management was complicit in the politicization, the CIA formally conducted an investigation of politicization after Robert Gates's brutal 1991 confirmation hearings to be DCI, which concluded that intelligence personnel can, and sometimes do, politicize intelligence.[33] Partisan political activism by current and former intelligence officials since 2016 surely has included forms of leaking, but the extent to which analyses have been biased is much less clear.

As Rovner recognized, a significant focus of the intelligence literature is the interaction of intelligence personnel and the decision-makers they support, or the "intelligence producer-consumer

---

31   Ibid., 32.

32   Ibid.

33   Gates, "Guarding Against Politicization."

relationship." A key variable in this discussion is the optimal physical and organizational "distance" intelligence is from policymakers.[34] Sherman Kent argued that the distance should be considerable, that if intelligence is "too close" it would become ensnared in decision-making processes and lose its objectivity.[35] CIA headquarters' location in the woods of northern Virginia helps ensure both varieties of distance. But others, such as Willmoore Kendall[36] and Robert Gates,[37] argued that excessive distance keeps intelligence from knowing policymakers' needs, risking the irrelevance of intelligence. Gates argued that intelligence should be close to policymakers while maintaining its analytic objectivity.

These authors did not address the possibility that intelligence could come to actively oppose a president, thereby coming "too close" to policy in a previously unanticipated way—hostility. A recent example is the prominent CIA "whistleblower" who complained in August 2019 about Trump's policies concerning Ukraine, thereby contributing directly to Trump's first impeachment in late 2019. This aspect of the "distance" discussion was minimally relevant in the Trump years except in the "whistleblower" case, but could become more important if another president acts against IC political activism by removing intelligence officers from sensitive positions in the White House, a possibility discussed in detail in chapter 7.[38] The literature also did not address the idea that intelligence could stay so distant from senior consumers that it came to value independence over service, to become a "Deep State."

Whatever the proximity of intelligence producers to consumers, the relationship is always unequal. As Mark Lowenthal, a former senior intelligence officer and prominent academic student

---

34   Marrin, "At Arm's Length or at the Elbow?" 402-408.
35   Kent, *Strategic Intelligence for American World Policy.*
36   Kendall, "The Function of Intelligence."
37   Gates, "The CIA and American Foreign Policy."
38   Schmidt, *Donald Trump v. The United States*, 381-389.

of US intelligence, has remarked, presidents can live without intelligence but the opposite is never true.[39] Making the point in personal terms, former DCI Richard Helms (1966-1973), who was fired by President Nixon, recalled that he was "the easiest man in Washington to fire. I have no political, military, or industrial base."[40] Accepting that the public gives intelligence some deference in matters of foreign policy, the Lowenthal and Helms observations, which remain sound, and the rise of overt and covert but obvious efforts to "subvert" or "resist" Trump, lead to questions explored below in detail: Why and how did intelligence officers come to perceive their relationship with the president differently than before—that they were morally superior to a president they did not like? Why did many of Trump's overt critics, at least, think they could bring Trump down without damaging their institutions and perhaps themselves? And how did the anti-Trump press convince the public that intelligence officers were so uniquely and credibly insightful that they would be useful in the media's anti-Trump campaign?

Combining concerns about intelligence officers' biases and leaks, senior career officials involved in sensitive, intelligence-supported policy-making have made similar points about the importance of discretion for intelligence analysts. For example, former Ambassador Robert Blackwill, who was a senior policy-maker in Republican administrations, recounted that intelligence analysts sometimes were policy-prescriptive in his presence.[41] In an interview published in CIA's internally-focused journal *Studies in Intelligence*, Blackwill advised intelligence officers who hoped to gain the trust of, and access to, senior policy-makers, to resist

---

39   Lowenthal, *Intelligence*, 2-6; Roberts and Saldin, "Why Presidents Sometimes Do Not Use Intelligence Information."

40   As quoted in Jervis, *Why Intelligence Fails*, 157.

41   Davis, "A Policymaker's Perspective on Intelligence Analysis," 12. Blackwill, a career Foreign Service officer, was also a policymaker for President Reagan and both Presidents Bush.

urges to leak to the press information about sensitive deliberations to derail policies they do not like.[42] James Steinberg, a senior policymaker in Democratic administrations, added that intelligence must recognize that policymakers expect career bureaucrats to help them succeed and that the credibility of intelligence depends on its ability to withstand tough questioning by skeptical policymakers.[43] Mark Lowenthal wrote:

> ... the idea that intelligence is distinct from policy does not mean that intelligence officers do not care about the outcome and do not influence it. One must differentiate between attempting to influence (that is, inform) the process by providing intelligence, which is acceptable, and trying to manipulate intelligence so that policymakers make a certain choice, which is not acceptable.[44]

And Thomas Fingar, who headed the State Department's Bureau of Intelligence and Research (INR) before becoming a senior official in the ODNI in 2005, wrote that discreet analysts should not share privileged conversations with consumers about decision-making deliberations even with fellow intelligence officers.[45]

Like Fingar, CIA people study the consumers of their work and long have also sought to identify "proper" roles of intelligence officers in dealing with policymakers, the general public, and fellow intelligence officers. For example, the late Jack Davis, a long-time, well-respected CIA analyst, addressed analysts'

---

42   Ibid., 9.
43   Steinberg, "The Policymaker's Perspective."
44   Lowenthal, *Intelligence*, 5.
45   Fingar, *Reducing Uncertainty*, 43-45; Fingar e-mail to author, December 22, 2017.

periodic concerns that policymakers try to pressure them into reaching judgments consistent with their policy views. Davis explained, long before 2016, that policymakers have every right to ask difficult questions of analysts—and to ask them frequently.[46] He made the point clearly in several widely cited articles.[47] He too observed that policymakers' trust in intelligence, and thereby the usefulness of intelligence, depends on the unquestioned integrity and non-partisanship of intelligence analysts.[48] Davis also said analysts' common belief that their own analyses are free from bias is a "conceit."[49] More recently, it has been called arrogance.[50] Other prominent CIA analysts have made similar points.[51]

Robert Gates, whose 1991 confirmation as DCI was almost derailed by charges of politicization against him, as DCI spoke eloquently about, and took tangible steps to prevent, politicization. He was aided by new legislation, including the creation at CIA of a politicization ombudsman to whom analysts concerned about politicization by consumers or agency managers could turn. Gates also emphasized the importance of the agency's "review process," the steps CIA managers and expert analysts take to transform an analyst's draft into a CIA publication by reviewing drafts for clarity, accuracy, and political neutrality, as critical to preventing politicization.[52] These processes and norms long were prominent in the culture of CIA analysts, although they too faded in the

---

46   Davis, "Analytic Professionalism and the Policymaking Process," 2-8.
47   Davis, "Intelligence Analysts and Policymakers;" Davis, "A Policymaker's Perspective on Intelligence Analysis."
48   Davis, "Paul Wolfowitz on Intelligence Policy-Relations," 35-42.
49   Davis, "Intelligence Analysts and Policymakers," 1001.
50   Gentry, "'Truth' as a Tool of the Politicization of Intelligence," 222, 238; Simon, "Intelligence Analysis as Practiced by the CIA," 646; Lowenthal, "Intelligence is NOT About 'Telling Truth to Power,'" 797-798.
51   For example, Petersen, "What I learned in 40 Years of Doing Intelligence Analysis for US Foreign Policymakers."
52   Gentry, "Managers of Analysts," 161-163.

Trump years. These institutional protections are much less useful if analysts' managers also are politicization culprits.

Despite these warnings, after 2016, intelligence personnel began to claim that they consistently knew "truth" that Trump did not know, pushed that "truth" at him, and argued that presidential questioning of their judgments and public criticism of intelligence was inappropriate. No insightful observers of US intelligence ever before argued that intelligence officers deserve respect as a right. All made clear that respect is earned, has a short half-life, and can be quickly and enduringly lost if decision-makers lose their trust in intelligence. These hard-earned lessons were discarded in 2016.

When intelligence officers violate established norms, senior decision-makers sometimes exclude intelligence people from decision-making processes. Intelligence personnel know that senior decision-makers can use any information sources they choose and can reject intelligence when they disagree with it, which happens periodically. They recognize that presidents sometimes have better information sources than analysts do—including personal relationships with foreign leaders—and that leaders' analytic judgments sometimes are better than those of intelligence analysts. They also know that presidents reject even good intelligence as they see fit—for good reasons if domestic political or other factors compel a suboptimal policy decision, and sometimes because they have already made up their minds about a policy issue. Intelligence people also traditionally have recognized that historians and voters, not intelligence personnel, appropriately judge the wisdom of such decisions. Most intelligence critics of Trump put these useful insights aside in 2016 and later.

Well-informed intelligence professionals know that all presidents, even experienced ones such as Dwight Eisenhower, who as a senior general used intelligence extensively during World

War II, enter the White House ignorant of some intelligence processes, capabilities, and limitations, and that they learn over time to varying degrees and at different speeds. In years past, they saw educating new presidents as a core responsibility and did not attack new presidents' use or misuse of intelligence.[53] This, too, changed in 2016.

Historian of intelligence Rhodri Jeffreys-Jones argued that the effectiveness of the CIA, and implicitly of other US intelligence agencies—defined as the willingness of senior decision-makers to use intelligence in their decision-making—depends on its "standing," which he believed to be a function of several factors: institutional legitimacy; the credibility of its estimates; its prestige, which affects its political acceptability in Washington and more broadly; and the respect it enjoys among the bureaucracy and with presidents.[54] The literature on politicization normally is more narrowly focused on the objectivity of analyses and the relationship intelligence has with presidents, its most important consumer and direct boss. The latter can be summarized in the word "trust." The politicization of 2016 and later radically altered the "standing" of the CIA in new ways.

Henry Kissinger, like his also very knowledgeable boss President Nixon, frequently criticized the quality of CIA analyses. But Kissinger also wrote about the importance of intelligence to him in his first role in the Nixon administration as assistant to the president for national security affairs:

> It is to the Director [of Central Intelligence] that the assistant first turns to learn the facts in a crisis and for analysis of events, and since decisions turn the perception

---

53   Helgerson, *Getting to Know the President*, 2nd ed.; Wilder, "An Educated Consumer."

54   Jeffreys-Jones, *The CIA & American Democracy*, 5-6.

of the consequences of actions the CIA assessment can almost amount to a policy recommendation.[55]

Kissinger added that DCI Richard Helms, who worked for President Nixon and for him, performed this function well. Kissinger wrote of Helms:

> Disciplined, meticulously fair and discreet, Helms performed his duties with a total objectivity essential to an effective intelligence service. I never knew him to misuse his intelligence or his power. He never forgot that his integrity guaranteed his effectiveness, that his best weapon with presidents was a reputation for reliability....[56]

But Nixon fired Helms because he did not respond to Nixon's order to shrink the CIA's staff and make it more responsive to White House needs.[57] Helms himself wrote that he thought his successor's instructions were "... to shake up the Agency, trim it down, and rid it of what Nixon perceived to be the existing regime of anti-Nixon Georgetown dilettantes and free-range liberals."[58] Helms did not want to do so and therefore was quietly but clearly insubordinate. Insubordination became more much more apparent in 2016 and later. But it did not begin in 2016, and it is important to understand how the CIA became an insular organization that went from looking after its parochial interests quietly in the Nixon years to one that came close to overtly attacked a sitting president.

John Helgerson, a retired senior CIA officer who has written

---

55   Kissinger, *White House Years*, 37.

56   Ibid., 487.

57   Moran, "Nixon's Axe Man."

58   Helms, *A Look Over My Shoulder*, 423; Freedman, "The CIA and the Soviet Threat," 135.

on the IC's (mainly CIA's) experiences in briefing presidential candidates and presidents-elect on important intelligence issues, noted that the four former presidents he interviewed for his books all said it was important for presidents to have "an intelligence director in whom he has confidence and with whom he feels comfortable."[59] Helgerson added that a key lesson of his study is that "… the president must be comfortable with his director, trust him implicitly, be associated with him politically, and, above all, give him routine access."[60] This key point is made in different ways throughout this book: presidential *trust* in intelligence agencies and their leaders is an essential element of effective intelligence support to national-level policy-makings.[61] Indeed, if there is a single factor that determines the value of intelligence to decision-makers, it is decision-makers' *trust* in intelligence. This book correspondingly devotes much attention to the impact of recent partisanship on the level and type of presidential trust in intelligence—in the Trump years and thereafter. The history Helgerson and others have recounted also establishes plainly that memories of intelligence failures and lapses in intelligence analysts' objectivity are long.

Hence, there long has been good understanding of the nature of the intelligence producer-consumer relationship within the IC, from both normative and historical perspectives, by intelligence officers, consumers, and knowledgeable outside observers. But these norms of appropriate intelligence behavior, and collective memories of the importance of trust in the history of producer-consumer relations, slowly dissolved within some agencies, especially the CIA, as new norms developed over an extended

---

59   Helgerson, *Getting to Know the President, 2ⁿᵈ ed.*, 182.

60   Ibid., 184.

61   Miller, "US Strategic Intelligence Forecasting," 690; Omand, "Reflections on Intelligence Analysts and Policymakers," 480.

period of time. They burst forth dramatically and very publicly in 2016 only when Trump became a serious presidential candidate, surprising many observers.

The basic concepts discussed thus far, politicization by practitioners and the politics of intelligence, do not refer to a chronic characteristic of US government organizations in general, which include parochially-motivated rivalries with other agencies and sometimes vicious bureaucratic in-fighting over budgets, roles and missions (or "turf" in Washington-speak), and kudos, or praise for good performance.[62] Similar fights frequently also occur between strong-willed persons within agencies. Battles within what some have called the "permanent government" are long-standing and, although important to bureaucrats, often rightly seem petty to outsiders. These fights focus primarily on other bureaucrats, meaning they do not reflect partisan political or ideological agendas and do not attack political leaders defined as elected or appointed decision-making officials in personal terms. Hence, they are not similar to the attacks of anti-Trump activists since 2016, except in that a major sub-theme of the attacks on Trump was defense of the organizational interests of IC agencies and their employees. The attacks thus raise another important discussion question: do the attacks represent the emergence of a "Deep State" that resists the president for ideological or other political reasons, or are the activities just slight variants of the old intramural battles of the government agencies?

Therefore, nothing in the large literature on intelligence anticipated what happened in 2016—decisions by a significant number of people closely associated with the national intelligence community to attack politically the president, whom intelligence ostensibly serves. In no other case, anywhere in the world, has

---

62   Jeffreys-Jones, *The CIA & American Democracy*, x.

something close to this set of events occurred. Elsewhere, intelligence personnel occasionally have participated in coup attempts and sometimes shown disloyalty to specific leaders. But in all such cases national political leaders have acted promptly to solve the problem, normally though variants of purge, usually done quickly, sometimes violently.[63] The extended period of conflict between parts of the IC and Trump, as well as its nature and intensity, thus also is unique.

Early efforts to describe and understand this new intelligence relationship with a president include works by serving intelligence officers, other government officials, and academics. For example, Peter Usowski, the director of CIA's Center for the Study of Intelligence, published "Former CIA Officers Writing about Intelligence, Policy, and Politics, 2016-2017" in September 2018 in *Studies in Intelligence*.[64] Usowski studiously avoided assessing the implications of the new politicization, but he put it in context and addressed his analysis to intelligence professionals, the primary readers of *Studies*.[65] Others also examined the situation and are continuing to do so.[66] It promises to remain a topic of serious study for years to come as well as a topic of shrill charges and countercharges by partisans.

PLAN OF THE BOOK

The rest of the book proceeds as follows. Chapter 2 describes key elements of IC history relevant to the issue of politicization. The chapter mainly discusses the CIA and ODNI for three

---

63   Gentry, "Purges of Intelligence Services."

64   Usowski, "Former CIA Officers Writing about Intelligence, Policy, and Politics, 2016-2017."

65   Gentry, "A New Form of Politicization?"

66   Warner, "The Use and Abuse of Intelligence in the Public Square;" Rogg, "The U.S. Intelligence Community's 'MacArthur Moment;'" O'Brien and Rodriguez, "By the Numbers;" Gentry, "An INS Special Forum."

major reasons: (1) these are the most important intelligence organizations supporting presidents; (2) they were hotbeds of opposition to President Trump; and (3) the largest literature is on the CIA, meaning we can better track its organizational evolution than that of any other IC agency. Shorter coverage of several other agencies makes clear that they differ sharply from the CIA and ODNI and helps explain why they were not sources of political activism. To set the stage for later discussions, this chapter discusses the importance of worldviews as causes of bias in intelligence analyses and the appreciable extent to which presidents before Donald Trump also were sometimes unhappy with their intelligence services.

Chapter 3 describes the development of six major factors, identified initially in chapter 2, which led to the outburst of 2016. Beginning in the 1990s, these changes accelerated in 2009-2017 when Barack Obama was president. Obama clearly instigated some of the changes purposefully, aided by important subordinate leaders at the ODNI and CIA. These factors all remain influences on the IC organizational cultures and may trigger new outbursts in the future.

Chapter 4 identifies major aspects of President Trump's policies and character that were unpalatable to many intelligence officers, and which they identified as substantive reasons to oppose Trump. The chapter does not defend Trump, his comments, or his actions. Rather, it identifies characteristics that largely provoked the reactions discussed in chapter 5.

Chapter 5 focuses on IC persons' reactions to Trump, his policies, and his rhetoric, including public comments by former IC leaders and the more difficult to identify and assess attitudes and actions of serving officers, which include leaks, internally-focused political commentary, and the use of "formers" as public mouthpieces for their views.

The strong criticism of Trump by many government employees, including intelligence officers, led Trump's supporters and some politically neutral observers to assail an alleged "Deep State" that was determined to destroy Trump's presidency. Others decried such characterizations as baseless attacks on selfless public servants. Chapter 6 examines this controversy, first defining "Deep State" and then assessing whether events of 2016-2021 were consistent with a Deep State as it is traditionally defined or as it is now commonly viewed in the American political context. The chapter also considers whether a different variant of the "permanent government" arose and was active—or whether something else existed.

Chapter 7 identifies implications of recent events, focusing on: immediate and long-term consequences of recent events for the IC as a whole and for specific agencies; implications for senior-level national decision-making, including that of President Trump and his successors; and implications for the country as a whole.

Based on the judgment of chapter 7 that political activism by intelligence officers has indeed been damaging in many ways, chapter 8 discusses remedial actions that might alter the attitudes and activities of IC personnel. None of these is likely to significantly affect the IC's institutional biases any time soon. Hence, the chapter also offers suggestions for structural changes that could minimize recalcitrant agencies and subcomponents thereof.

Finally, chapter 9 summarizes the book's findings and speculates about the future of politicization in the IC. Renewed activism seems likely if even a traditional Republican again becomes president.

2

THE IC'S TRADITIONAL ROLE IN AMERICAN POLITICS

★

TO UNDERSTAND THE MAGNITUDE and significance of the cultural changes of recent years, it is necessary to appreciate the longstanding, once-solid institutional foundations that some IC leaders worked hard to change. This chapter therefore discusses the historical roles and cultures of intelligence agencies, identifying key traits of the major agencies, including collective "worldviews" that historically generated institutional biases that were modest by recent standards. IC agencies, like most organizations, developed distinctive ways of seeing the world and of addressing intellectual challenges, which sometimes led to analytical errors and varieties of political sensitivities despite institutionalized attempts to minimize them. These perspectives often reflected subconscious biases, but as parts of the cultures of insular organizations they replicated and were enduring. The chapter also demonstrates that several presidents before Donald Trump sometimes found the performance of intelligence to be weak or objectionable for many reasons. This history makes clear that Trump's critics' allegations that he was uniquely critical of the IC are incorrect.

The Roles and Cultures of Intelligence Agencies

Intelligence is a big part of the US government. It directly and indirectly affects national security decision-making in many ways that also make it politically important. First, intelligence agencies' sheer size makes them important claimants on the federal budget and objects of budgetary debates in Congress and among themselves. Second, the agencies have distinctive organizational cultures that reflect both bureaucratic interests and the worldviews of their leaders and workforces, which have given some IC agencies reputations for variously being intellectually and politically "liberal" or "conservative." These cultures are largely responsible for some agencies' post-2016 political activism—and lack thereof. Third, organizational differences produce varying sets of priorities and perspectives that chronically distinguish them from agencies with different worldviews. "Competitive analyses" among agencies counter these biases to some extent, but they also foster watered-down, compromise language in NIEs, warning failures, and advocacy of parochial interests. Worldviews help shape concepts of truth and rationalize the alleged responsibility of intelligence personnel to speak "truth to power"—in recent years defined as their concepts of truth in opposition to Trump's power. Fourth, occasional but often prominent failures of IC agencies make them sources of controversy, especially during intelligence-fueled debates about major policy issues. Fifth, the factors above, combined with generally good analytic performance, chronically make intelligence both useful to, and a source of frustration and skepticism for, senior decision-makers including presidents. Doubts typically center on the competence and objectivity of analysis—the final stage of the process of collecting information and converting it into finished intelligence. The record is clear that some presidents have been as skeptical of US intelligence as was Donald Trump, albeit generally in different, less publicly harsh ways.[1]

These factors form the institutional context in which the overt political activism of 2016 developed. They are important variables to consider when assessing the activism's immediate and long-term implications for the IC and for decision-makers. They form the context in which the activism is seen by intelligence professionals and politicians in Washington.

SIZE AND STRUCTURE OF THE IC

The small intelligence units of the Army, Navy, Federal Bureau of Investigation (FBI), and State Department in 1941 grew dramatically during World War II. The intelligence failure at Pearl Harbor, chronic squabbling among the intelligence services, and then the emerging Cold War overcame President Harry Truman's aversion to creating a peacetime civilian intelligence structure that risked becoming an "American Gestapo," leading him in 1946 to establish a small "central" entity to coordinate intelligence support for him and his White House staff.[2] Congress then created the CIA as part of the National Security Act of 1947, which also created the Department of Defense, the National Security Council (NSC), and the US Air Force. Advocates for creation of the CIA overcame the fierce opposition of the four existing intelligence-related agencies,

---

1   Priess, *The President's Book of Secrets*; Andrew, *For the President's Eyes Only*; Helgerson, *Getting to Know the President*.

2   Andrew, *For the President's Eyes Only*, 149-198.

which did not want another competitor for intelligence turf, funds, and kudos. Truman established the National Security Agency (NSA) in November 1952 by secret executive order to try to overcome the chronic bickering over control of signals intelligence (SIGINT) by the Army, Navy, and Air Force. NSA since then has been partly successful at unifying the national SIGINT effort.[3] The growing constellation of post-war intelligence agencies soon came to be called an "intelligence community," or IC, ostensibly headed by the director of central intelligence (DCI), which continued to grow and evolve over the years. Some government departments—such as the Department of Energy, which tracks nuclear weapons-related intelligence—built intelligence elements within themselves. Other organizations with intelligence units, such as the Department of Homeland Security, were created recently. Still other intelligence agencies are products of the amalgamation and/or renaming existing organizations; the National Geospatial-Intelligence Agency (NGA) is the result of several mergers and a name change, for example.

The terrorist attacks of 2001 led to appreciable changes in US intelligence. Reviews by special commissions and much public and congressional debate led Congress to enact the Intelligence Reform and Terrorism Prevention Act of 2004 (IRTPA), which created the director of national intelligence (DNI), a supporting office (the ODNI), and the National Counterterrorism Center (NCTC). After yet more changes, the IC in 2023 is a complex of eighteen agencies nominally led by the DNI. The al-Qaeda attacks of September 11, 2001 (9/11) also led to substantially increased funding for intelligence—continuing the American practice of rewarding government agencies for their failures. For fiscal year

---

3   Johnson, *American Cryptology During the Cold War 1945-1989.*

2019, Congress appropriated $81.7 billion for intelligence, the largest amount ever.[4] The Trump administration requested $85.75 billion for fiscal year 2020 and $85.0 billion for FY 2021.[5] These large figures include both the National Intelligence Program and the Military Intelligence Program. Trump's large budget requests were consistent with the growth of previous years but sharply inconsistent with the prominent complaint of Trump's critics that he conducted a systematic "assault on intelligence."[6] The IC's budgets have grown more in the Biden years.[7]

"Intelligence Community" is a misnomer because the agencies are largely independent and IRTPA gave the DNI little power to direct the agencies or, more importantly, to control their funding—the major source of bureaucratic power in Washington. Secretary of Defense Donald Rumsfeld in 2004 mobilized his congressional allies to ensure that IRTPA did not appreciably degrade his control over DOD's intelligence agencies and their large share of the IC's overall budget. The IC now is comprised of the ODNI and its subordinate NCTC, one independent actor (the CIA), and sixteen agencies that report in varying degrees to department secretaries—about half of them to the secretary of defense. They act in concert when they want to do so consistent with their own ideas about national intelligence needs and organizational interests, which means they cooperate to a limited degree most of the time. Hence, the IC is more a confederation of self-interested agencies than an integrated community.

---

4   See ODNI website, https://www.dni.gov/index.php/what-we-do/ic-budget. Publicly released figures do not indicate budgets of individual agencies or general functions, which are known as "programs."

5   Federation of American Scientists intelligence site, https://fas.org/irp/budget/.

6   For example, the title of Michael Hayden's book, *The Assault on Intelligence*.

7   Director of National Intelligence, "U.S. Intelligence Community Budget," https://www.dni.gov/index.php/what-we-do/ic-budget.

Intelligence professionals therefore frequently refer to the DNI's job as one of "herding cats."[8]

While the DNI's executive power is modest due to the limited legal and budgetary powers of the position, the substantial independence of the CIA, most agencies' subordination to departmental secretaries, and their simple refusal to be controlled, the DNI has several roles important for this book. For example, the DNI is a statutory advisor to the National Security Council, meaning she or he often directly advises the president; hence, the personal chemistry between presidents and the DNI is an important generator of the trust presidents have in intelligence generally. A DNI who is not trusted by a president virtually by definition is ineffective. The DNI declassifies and releases intelligence assessments selectively to the public, making the DNI a public face of intelligence. The DNI issues some policy directives applicable to the agencies, which sometimes reflect personal views or presidential guidance; these include the intelligence variants of government-wide personnel policies ordered by President Obama that are an important part of the explanation of the IC's politicization, and resulting attacks on Trump. Often, however, the DNI issues policy statements only after the agencies have debated and agreed to the specific language of the policies—a sometimes long process that is key evidence that the IC is more of a confederation than an integrated whole. These documents are called Intelligence Community Directives (ICDs). And, not least, the DNI directly controls the ODNI, whose roughly 3,000 relatively senior personnel monitor the IC agencies, report to the White House and to Congress, and supervise drafting of national intelligence estimates. He or she has considerable leeway on structuring the ODNI and naming its senior personnel.

---

8   Author's personal experience. See also Brennan, *Undaunted*, 165-166.

Consistent with American bureaucratic traditions, major intelligence agencies squabble with each other in ways that have political ramifications. Prominent, enduring adversaries have been CIA and the FBI over counterintelligence issues and control of overseas operations, and CIA and the Defense Intelligence Agency (DIA) over analytic issues, especially military-related issues.[9] These rivalries reflect conflicting bureaucratic interests, the influence of strong personalities such as the FBI's J. Edgar Hoover, insular organizational cultures, memories of historical inter-agency animosity such as FBI efforts to prevent creation of the CIA and the Defense Department's chronic efforts[10] to control CIA, and standard bureaucratic competition for control of turf and resources as well as the assignment of kudos and blame.

A prominent perceived lesson of the 9/11 attacks was that the attacks might have been prevented if IC agencies, especially CIA and the FBI, had shared information more effectively. The IRTPA therefore demands better inter-agency cooperation, and successive DNIs have pushed for more and better IC "integration," with some success but at the cost of what some observers consider to be an excessively large and expensive bureaucracy in the form of the ODNI.[11] The IC's agencies appear to work together a bit better than before, but most still do so eagerly only when it is organizationally advantageous to do so.[12] Common publicly stated or de facto goals therefore are signs that there may be close inter-agency cooperation on some issues. These goals may be politically innocuous and useful—as efforts to combat global terrorism—or controversial if they are politically sensitive. The push for integration and Obama's personnel-focused executive orders helped

---

9   Jeffreys-Jones, *The CIA & American Democracy*, 212, 242.

10   Oakley, *Subordinating Intelligence*.

11   Hulnick, "Intelligence Reform 2007," 580.

12   Gentry, "Has the ODNI Improved U.S. Intelligence Analysis?" 654.

DNIs establish IC-wide personnel management policies, which played an important role in generating the 2016 outburst against Trump. Some of Trump's supporters still in 2023 allege that some CIA and FBI officials conspired to damage Trump—cooperation of a sort that historically has been rare.

While some professional intelligence officers laud improved cooperation, others complain about how limited the "progress" has been. Still others worry that the slightly more unified confederation has created an allegedly stronger "national security state," composed largely of the intelligence services and DOD, which threatens Americans' freedoms and even American democracy. President Eisenhower famously warned in his farewell address of the power of the emerging military-industrial complex. Civil libertarians long have warned of threats to freedom posed by security services' surveillance. Recently, Michael Glennon, applying to the US government a theory Walter Bagehot developed in the mid-nineteenth century to explain the evolution of the British government, argued that the complex of military-intelligence-diplomatic agencies comprise a second or "Double Government."[13] Other analysts call the bureaucracy the "permanent government" or, increasingly, a "Deep State." This government, Glennon argued, is composed of a few hundred "Trumanite" leaders of the security agencies that President Truman fostered, who are gradually taking power from constitutional, or "Madisonian," institutions such as the presidency, Congress, and the Supreme Court. "Trumanite" leaders, who form a nebulous, collaborative group, ostensibly subservient to elected officials, in fact make policies that presidents and the Congress largely accept. This phenomenon largely explains, Glennon argued, the substantial similarity of the national security policies of President Obama, who as candidate

---

13   Glennon, *National Security and Double Government.*

had promised significant changes in the policies of his predecessor, George W. Bush, and Bush's policies. Former CIA and NSA director Michael Hayden used similar language to describe the perspectives of former senior intelligence officers—what Hayden called a "common worldview and shared life experiences"—which he claimed explain their similar criticisms of Trump, a man who appeared to want to change policies the "Trumanites" valued.[14]

Glennon did not address (except briefly in an afterward to his book) the post-2016 political activism of intelligence officers. He, too, evidently was surprised by the partisan outburst. But Glennon's concept of "Double Government" is relevant to assessing competing post-2016 claims that intelligence formed a "Deep State" opposed to President Trump and often vehement denials of such charges and counter-claims that "Deep State" accusations were cheap shots at legitimate critics of the president and protestations that Trump's targets were really only hard-working public servants.

The organizational history of the US government suggests that agencies become politically active, or not, based largely on the leadership and organizational cultures of each agency independently. Hence, an intelligence-wide "Deep State" comprised of all IC agencies would require eighteen largely independent collective decisions to act in a coordinated manner. Because the DNI has modest powers over the individual agencies, any DNI can appreciably influence agencies only if the agencies are receptive to them. The degree of receptivity to DNI policies, and of opposition to Trump, has varied considerably across agencies. Chapter 6 examines whether former (and perhaps current) senior intelligence officials who opposed Trump comprised a group consistent with Glennon's concept of "Trumanite" leaders of the Double Government, a Deep State, or something else.

---

14   Hayden, *Assault on Intelligence*, 247-248.

The Importance of Organizational Cultures

Like all bureaucracies, IC agencies have distinctive cultures. There is little movement of employees from agency to agency, even after the IRTPA encouraged more short-term "rotations" of workers among agencies. People who like different kinds of work self-select into agencies with different missions. The most important agency for this discussion is the CIA, which has prominent collection, covert action, and analytic responsibilities, and which works directly for the president as opposed to a departmental secretary. The FBI has a police-like focus on arresting criminals and winning convictions in court, which it largely retains despite having domestic counterintelligence responsibilities and heightened emphasis after 2001 on intelligence-led counterterrorism. The FBI prominently displays a strong sense of organizational self-interest, a legacy of Hoover's long directorship. Military intelligence elements reflect the military service cultures of which they are parts.[15] And the new ODNI makes and coordinates IC-wide policies while continuing to develop its own organizational culture. It also is the IC element most responsive to external pressures, including ones emanating from the White House and Congress. The other agencies operate in their own ways but are less important for this story.

CIA's Cultures

The distinctive organizational cultures of the CIA's two major components, the operations and analysis directorates, reflect skills, roles, history, and personality types relevant to the rise of political activism in 2016. The early CIA adopted the cultural

---

15   Hutchings, "Introduction," 12.

norms of parts of the Office of Strategic Services (OSS), which operated from 1942-1945. The OSS was staffed largely by East Coast professionals and academics, most of whom were politically liberal Caucasian men. Focused on winning the war against Germany, OSS chief William Donovan hired people he thought could help. He initially was not worried about Soviet espionage against the United States—the USSR was a wartime ally—and knowingly hired communist veterans of the Spanish Civil War whose fighting skills would, he thought, be useful against Germany.[16] Before OSS security improved late in the war, the external arm of the Soviet civilian intelligence service, the NKVD, a predecessor of the KGB, recruited at least twenty-two OSS officers, including an aide to Donovan, Army Major Duncan Lee.[17] The Army's Venona Project, which later decrypted part or all of some 2,900 Soviet intelligence cables written during World War II, proved conclusively that the OSS was riddled with Soviet agents.[18] In those days Americans worked for the Soviet Union mainly for ideological reasons, not money. In addition, by one estimate, fifty to one hundred OSS employees may have been members of the Communist Party of the United States of America (CPUSA), which was loyal to, and took orders, from Stalin's Soviet Union.[19] When it was created in 1947, the CIA hired many OSS veterans. About one-third of employees of the new CIA reportedly had worked for the OSS.[20] CIA components' cultures evolved after 1947,

---

16 Bradley, *A Very Principled Boy*, 88, 90, 205.

17 No byline, "Venona decrypts and Soviet Penetration of the OSS," *Open Geography*, August 28, 2013, https://opengeography.wordpress.com/2013/08/28/venona-decrypts-and-soviet-penetration-of-the-oss/; Bradley, *A Very Principled Boy*, 66.

18 Sulick, *Spying In America*, 176.

19 Bradley, *A Very Principled Boy*, 66.

20 Ibid., 204.

but the CIA retained a workforce collectively more politically liberal than most IC agencies.

Operations

Officers of the Directorate of Operations (DO), which in the past has had several names, recruit and manage spies and conduct covert and paramilitary operations abroad. For the DO, a key cultural characteristic is what Charles Cogan, a former senior operations officer, called the "manipulation imperative."[21] Case officers recruit people, sometimes under misleading or deceptive circumstances, and they deal with people who are committing treason in their own countries. This role appeals to, and attracts, only certain types of people. Self-selection makes operations officers as a whole an unusual group of people. Operations officers' traits are useful for domestic operations as well. DCIs and operations officers long have used "tradecraft" skills to advance CIA's interests by influencing the domestic press and Congress, especially. Indeed, as a former staffer of the SSCI once said, he felt that the CIA case officers with whom he dealt were always trying to recruit him to be an asset for CIA.[22]

Manipulation of people often is closely linked with the manipulation of information. Intelligence people know that information operations facilitate deception, which typically features creative combinations of carefully selected facts and lies, leading targets to misunderstand an issue of importance—the purpose of disinformation. The CIA learned to conduct disinformation operations abroad in the 1950s and 1960s as part of its covert political actions.[23] While Congress sharply restricted its activities

---

21   Cogan, "The in-culture of the DO," 81.
22   Personal communication.
23   Rid, *Active Measures*, 61-100.

in this arena in the 1970s, CIA people monitored Soviet "active measures," which prominently employed disinformation, and they still apply the techniques periodically to foreign and domestic enemies, including operations against DCIs in the 1970s and Donald Trump.[24] The subtitle of former director of the CIA (DCIA) John Brennan's memoir is *My Fight against America's Enemies at Home and Abroad.*[25] "Enemies" at home!

Operators' work typically is tactical and tangible in nature.[26] Case officers focus on recruiting persons with desired information, and then on working with and protecting their assets. Paramilitary operators fight designated national enemies. Officers who conduct covert action missions focus on mission accomplishment abroad, typically caring for US domestic politics only to the extent that their orders are legal and that they will not be hauled before congressional investigating committees or the courts for doing jobs the president asked them to do. Operations officers mainly work abroad, away from Washington—the location of what many of them view as the stifling bureaucracy of headquarters. Hence, field operators rarely are caught up in Washington politics. Therefore, by many accounts, operations officers tend to be less liberal and less politically active than employees who work mainly in the Washington area, especially analysts.[27] But some operations people, especially those in headquarters elements of the DO, and former operations officers surely were politically active against Trump.

Early in the CIA's history, operations officers also developed a strong culture of secrecy. They frequently did not tell even immediate family members where they worked. Leaking or, as

---

24   Wettering, "(C)overt Action."
25   Brennan, *Undaunted.*
26   For example, London, *The Recruiter.*
27   For example, Ismael Jones, "The real CIA," *American Thinker*, October 4, 2019, https://www.americanthinker.com/blog/2019/10/the_real_cia.html.

a retired or former intelligence officer, writing articles and books critical of US intelligence or kiss-and-tell memoirs was rare.[28] There was considerable social pressure against discussing any intelligence-related matter in public, let alone free-lance leaking by unauthorized officers.[29] Because writing for external audiences was uncommon, in its early years the CIA did not conduct pre-publication reviews of the few manuscripts its employees tried to publish, which initially were generally flattering of the CIA. The interests of the agency, it was thought, were best served by maintaining strict secrecy. An important legacy of this tradition is that a large share of former CIA officers, including many senior officers, still do not talk publicly about intelligence in any way, even to criticize those who violate what many still consider to be a near-sacred obligation to maintain secrecy.

But operations officers typically also were keenly interested in securing, and advancing, the agency's organizational interests—and their own—a trait other CIA officers also long have displayed. When secrecy seemed to be inconsistent with its organizational interests, the CIA at times promoted memoir writing, usually by senior officers and always favorable in tone and message: intelligence helps the country and CIA does a good job of it! Memoirs did not criticize political leaders or their policies; they described and explained how CIA served both well.

A good example of this genre is DCI Allen Dulles's (1953-1961) memoir, *The Craft of Intelligence*, originally published in 1963, in which he memorialized the CIA and the intelligence profession but did not criticize his political masters, Presidents Eisenhower and John Kennedy, both of whom made appreciable

---

28   Moran, *Company Confessions*.
29   Email communication to author from Burton Gerber, August 12, 2019. Gerber was a CIA operations officer from 1955-1995.

intelligence-related mistakes.[30] It would have been especially easy for Dulles, then retired, to have remarked on Kennedy's blunders concerning the Bay of Pigs invasion of 1961, which also featured serious CIA mistakes, and Kennedy's repeated orders to the CIA to assassinate Cuban leader Fidel Castro, which CIA officials were not keen about doing and which they could not do.[31] Instead, Dulles like many CIA officers later, even during the painful congressional hearings on questionable CIA activities in 1975-1976, took the blame for the assassination attempts, shielding President Kennedy and his brother, Attorney General Robert Kennedy, who also wanted badly to have Castro killed.[32] Kennedy fired Dulles several months after the Bay of Pigs debacle, adding a personally unpleasant element to the relationship. But unlike the FBI's James Comey and Andrew McCabe, both of whom Trump fired, Dulles did not publish a personally oriented, complaining memoir that criticized the president.[33]

Dulles cultivated the press, a skill CIA people retain. He "leaked" information favorable to the CIA to journalists and had publicly well-known relationships with executives of the *Washington Post*, who in the 1950s gave the CIA generally favorable treatment.[34] Other senior CIA officers also socialized with prominent journalists, who reciprocated by writing mostly favorable stories.[35] The CIA's Office of Public Affairs (OPA), under other names in years past, gave briefings on background to selected journalists. The mission now, as then, according to a senior OPA official in 2019, is to give journalists information favorable

---

30   Dulles, *The Craft of Intelligence*; Andrew, *For the President's Eyes Only*, 199-306; Thomas, *The Very Best Men*.
31   Husain, "Covert Action and US Cold War Strategy in Cuba, 1961-1962," 43.
32   Ibid.
33   Comey, *A Higher Loyalty*; McCabe, *The Threat*.
34   Moran, *Company Confessions*, 78-79, 85-88, 133-134.
35   Ibid., 78-79.

to the agency and to help ensure that erroneous information is not reported.[36] In the early 1980s, these backgrounders totaled about 400 per year; they now are fewer in number and focus more on selected journalists, who sometimes are briefed by several analysts.[37] Over the years, other CIA officers followed Dulles's example, creating contacts that could easily be resurrected when they became "formers" critical of Trump. And working officers regularly leaked to sympathetic journalists who historically, as now, prominently included staff of the *Washington Post* and *New York Times*.

In the 1970s, the number of critical comments about the CIA from former officers grew. Victor Marchetti[38] and Frank Snepp[39] criticized CIA's management, its operations, and its policies. But these authors, too, did not criticize presidents. Historian Christopher Moran has noted that the increasing number of memoirs critical of CIA over the years prompted agency concerns.[40] CIA created its Publications Review Board (PRB) in 1977 to screen manuscripts for classified information before they went to publishers. (The PRB's name changed to Prepublication Classification Review Board in 2020.) As Moran noted, the PRB frequently was biased in its reviews; favorable manuscripts generally were processed quickly with few required deletions of passages, or "redactions" in intelligence vernacular, while critical manuscripts were processed slowly and savaged with excessive redactions of innocuous, publicly available information, sometimes including authors' own names. The agency thus was able to control public perceptions of it to a considerable degree while annoying many

---

36   CIA briefing for Agency retirees and their families, July 25, 2019.
37   Ibid.
38   Marchetti and Marks, *The CIA and the Cult of Intelligence*.
39   Snepp, *Decent Interval*.
40   Moran, *Company Confessions*.

current and former employees who wanted prompt reviews of their uncontroversial work.[41]

Objective truth in the drafts it reviews has never been a concern of the PRB. Facilitating favorable impressions of the agency in its early years and, chronically and more reasonably, protection of sources and methods of intelligence information are. This history is one of several threads of evidence relevant for assessing claims of Trump's critics that US intelligence officers devote themselves exclusively to finding objective truth and do in fact find it, unlike Trump.

Moran argued that critiques of presidents by current and former CIA officers did not begin until the early 2000s.[42] In one of the first of these, Michael Scheuer, who led the DO unit following Osama bin Laden in the late 1990s and early 2000s, wrote *Imperial Hubris* (initially under the name "Anonymous"), which criticized President George W. Bush's policies on Iraq and attacked policies of other administration officials, including Secretary of Defense Rumsfeld.[43] Others criticized management, protested interrogation techniques, and wrote roughly fact-based tales of experiences in exotic places that appealed to readers of adventure stories.[44] But even these books focused on policy aspects of intelligence-related issues the authors were knowledgeable about and thought unwise or objectionable in some way. They did not address domestic political issues or attack political leaders in partisan ways.

---

41   Personal note: the PRB generally has been fair and prompt in reviewing my work, over 30 manuscripts of various sorts since 1992. The PCRB took only nine days to clear this manuscript. But many people have had worse experiences than mine. Current staff face more stringent review than do former employees; they are ongoing representatives of the agency and potentially of its views.

42   Moran, *Company Confessions.*

43   Anonymous (Michael Scheuer), *Imperial Hubris.*

44   For example, Carle, *The Interrogator.*

Moran argued that former DCI Richard Helms's memoir, *A Look Over My Shoulder*, co-authored by William Hood late in Helms's life when he was ailing, is more critical of President Nixon personally than Helms originally intended, a reflection of Hood's anti-Nixon views.[45] Perhaps so, but it is mild in comparison to the strongly anti-Trump books published in 2018 and later by former senior intelligence officials John Brennan, James Clapper, James Comey, Michael Hayden, and Andrew McCabe.[46]

The Dulles memoir and selected information releases to journalists set a precedent that remains valid: it was perfectly acceptable to release information to the public that protected or advanced CIA's organizational interests, even if it meant manipulating people, especially in the press. It would be nice if the public relations efforts were factually accurate, but favorable half-truths and misrepresentations were acceptable to advance or protect organizational interests. General public release of the information was fine, but even better was passage of information of special institutional value to sympathetic journalists.

The relationships reporters and executives of media companies have had with intelligence people varied considerably over the years. Sometimes, as in the Dulles era, relationships were close, friendly, and mutually beneficial. But usually the press has been harshly critical of intelligence, frequently for ideological or other political reasons. Press reporting on intelligence issues often has been factually incorrect. The Soviets chronically fed truthful information damaging to the CIA as well as disinformation about the CIA to the American press, some of which was published. In response to such attacks, intelligence has tended to return to its cultural roots of secrecy. In recent years, a new community

---

45   Moran, *Company Confessions,* 238-242.
46   Clapper, *Facts and Fears*; Brennan, *Undaunted*; Comey, *A Higher Loyalty*; Hayden, *Assault on Intelligence*; McCabe, *The Threat.*

of interest—opposition to Trump—has led to unusually close but probably temporary alliances between journalists and intelligence officers.

In the past, while most intelligence officials remained silent when presidents criticized their work or made questionable policy decisions, some intelligence officers (apparently) independently leaked information to the press to attack DCIs and sometimes specific policies of presidents. For example, CIA analysts opposed to the war in Vietnam leaked assessments in 1964 that prospects for a successful outcome to the war were not good, evidently hoping to influence President Johnson to withdraw from Vietnam.[47] Seymour Hersh, in researching his explosive exposé on the CIA's "Family Jewels" compilation of questionable agency operations, a project initiated by DCI James Schlesinger, which was published in the *New York Times* in December 1974, received tips from "troubled employees in many places."[48]

Leaks prominently accompanied events closest to purges in the history of the modern IC—DCI Schlesinger's firing of some operations personnel in 1973 and DCI Stansfield Turner's decision in 1977 to again reduce the size of CIA's operations directorate.[49] President Nixon, by many accounts, did not like CIA and its people, and he distrusted CIA analyses because he thought, sometimes for good reasons, that they were either substantively weak or were efforts by liberals to influence his policies.[50] When Nixon told DCI Helms that he wanted the agency reduced in size and made more responsive to the White House, CIA personnel

---

47   Handel, "Intelligence and the Problem of Strategic Surprise," 259; Smith, *The Unknown CIA*, 217-219.

48   Prados, *The Family Jewels*, 23.

49   Moran, "Nixon's Axe Man," 95-121.

50   Warner, "The Use and Abuse of Intelligence in the Public Square," 17; Kissinger, *White House Years*, 11, 36.

were well aware of his wishes.[51] Helms, a CIA careerist, resisted the directive by dragging his feet on implementing it, a common form of bureaucratic insubordination in which civil servants delay work on implementing instructions they do not like, hoping to wait out political appointees or elected officials. Nixon saw through the tactic, leading him to replace Helms with Schlesinger, who had done a study of CIA in 1971 that found serious problems at the agency. Schlesinger's marching orders were to "clean house." Christopher Moran has argued that Schlesinger did so with gusto, firing and retiring what is variously reported to have been about seven percent of the agency's workforce—some 630 to nearly 2,000 people, depending on account—mainly from the operations directorate.[52] Moran argued that the main target, though, was the operations personnel's culture—one of secrecy, independence, and a "can-do" spirit that Nixon and Schlesinger disliked, especially given then-fresh memories of the Bay of Pigs debacle.[53]

In turn, many agency personnel disliked Nixon and Schlesinger for their disdain of CIA people and their culture, the staff reductions, and the reduced freedom of action for career senior managers they imposed.[54] Employees were so unhappy that the agency's Office of Security assigned extra bodyguards to Schlesinger and placed a closed circuit television camera to watch his official portrait at CIA headquarters—both designed to protect against possible attacks by irate CIA employees.[55] Schlesinger remains one of agency persons' least favorite directors—one who was problematic because he insisted on being in charge and told the bureaucracy to do things differently. This issue arose again in 2016

---

51   Whipple, *Spy Masters*, 34.
52   Moran, "Nixon's Axe Man."
53   Ibid., 98, 101.
54   Garthoff, *Directors of Central Intelligence*, 131-148.
55   Ibid., 96.

for a much less substantive reason—the *possibility* of change.[56] For all his bluster, Trump unlike Nixon never tried to change the inner workings of any IC agency. More generally, according to CIA's chief historian David Robarge, "The agency has always been suspicious of outsiders.... They're always brought in after periods of problems and difficulties. So you kind of get your hair up, watching for signs that this person is not your friend."[57] Similarly, former senior case officer Robert Baer said, "In the CIA, like in most places, blood's thicker than common sense."[58]

In the fall of 1977, in the immediate aftermath of the Vietnam War, where many CIA paramilitary operations officers served, DCI Turner restructured the DO somewhat and reduced headcount. The DO then reportedly had 4,730 employees, down from a peak of about 8,000 during the war; Turner cut 820 positions by firing seventeen people, mandating 147 early retirements, and letting normal attrition take care of the rest over the next two years.[59] None of the positions eliminated was an overseas position, no managers were released, and all personnel fired had low scores on performance appraisals. With the war over, the directorate itself reportedly had planned to reduce headcount by a similar number, but more slowly. Press reports at the time claimed the 820 positions comprised about eight percent of CIA's workforce.[60] As in 1973, many CIA people were outraged and some reportedly "retired in protest." Others resorted to an old CIA tradition—leaking both accurate and inaccurate information to friendly journalists to discredit opponents, in this case Turner. Prominent journalist William Safire obligingly reported

---

56   Rogg, "The U.S. Intelligence Community's 'MacArthur Moment.'"

57   Whipple, *Spy Masters*, 54.

58   Baer, *The Fourth Man*, 41.

59   Jeffreys-Jones, *The CIA & American Democracy*, 218; Turner, *Secrecy and Democracy*, 196-197, 203.

60   Moran, *Company Confessions*, 162.

incorrectly that Turner had "destroyed the clandestine service."[61] The claim is still commonly cited. Loch Johnson, a long-time student of US intelligence, noted in reporting his 1991 interview with Turner that DO personnel are "well-trained in retaliating against enemies at home and abroad."[62] Turner said in his interview with Johnson that his intent was solely to improve the management of the directorate, and he said he thought his actions did improve the agency's performance.[63]

Leaking increased again in 2004-2005 as current and former CIA officials criticized personnel moves DCI Porter Goss made to help correct what Goss, a former CIA case officer and former chairman of the House Permanent Select Committee on Intelligence (HPSCI), and President Bush considered to be CIA's collection and analytic deficiencies.[64] The number of leaks rose again sharply in the Trump era.

In recent years, by many accounts, the DO (like the agency in general) has become more risk averse. This was in part a defense mechanism designed to shield the agency from new episodes of the significant external criticism it received for alleged failures such as the Aldrich Ames spy case, discovered in 1994, and the 9/11 attacks.[65] According to retired case officer Douglas London, CIA's leaders sanctioned officers who objected to the agency's endorsement of the President George W. Bush's rosy views of the prospective success of the US invasion of Iraq in 2003, thereby politicizing intelligence.[66] This change, which London asserts continued after 2003, reportedly made CIA personnel chronically

61   Johnson, "In remembrance: Admiral Stansfield Turner," 593.

62   Ibid., 587.

63   Ibid., 593.

64   Douglas Jehl, "C.I.A. Deputy for Analysis Is Being Removed, *New York Times*, December 29, 2004, http://www.nytimes.com/2004/12/29/us/cia-deputy-for-analysisis-being-removed.html.

65   London, *The Recruiter*, 31-32.

66   Ibid., 12., 34.

more responsive to the political and other personal views of agency leaders, a change that would have a different kind of significance during the Obama years and later. And former case officer Robert Baer wrote that expertise and intellectual depth were enemies of bureaucratic ambition.[67] As in the analysis directorate, organizational incentives in recent years favored generalist career tracks.

In sum, the operations culture contributes four major elements of the story of this book. First, most operators are largely apolitical, but not all of them. Second, those who are politically inclined know how to conduct information operations, including against domestic enemies in Washington, within and outside the agency—skills that they passed to other CIA personnel, including analysts. Third, operators, like analysts, are keenly interested in protecting the perceived interests of the agency and themselves, and they are willing to attack domestic enemies who threaten, or might threaten, their culture and interests. And fourth, risk aversion, self-protection, and low-level politicization variously have long existed and were on the rise before Trump appeared on the national political scene.

Analysis

CIA's early analysis organization, like its operational units, quickly established norms of appropriate behavior and standards of desirable performance. A key builder of CIA's analytic culture was Sherman Kent, who was a professor of history at Yale University before World War II and an analyst in the wartime OSS. After a short break from intelligence, during which he wrote his now-classic *Strategic Intelligence for American World Policy*, he joined the CIA in 1950, working most of his CIA career as head of the Board of National Estimates

---

67   Baer, *The Fourth Man*, 87.

(1952-1967) and its subordinate Office of National Estimates (ONE), which produced NIEs.[68] The Board initially had an excellent reputation for producing quality analysis but also was widely known for being, in the words of former chairman of the National Intelligence Council (C/NIC) Robert Hutchings, "a haven for liberal East Coast academics."[69] The CIA protected its people from Senator Joseph McCarthy's inquiries into Soviet intelligence penetration of the US government in the early 1950s, making it attractive for left-leaning people—in some cases literally as a haven. CIA's widespread reputation as a collectively liberal organization dates to this period.

Kent made many contributions to intelligence analysis. He established CIA's initially in-house and still largely classified *Studies in Intelligence*, the first journal focused on the serious study of intelligence. *Studies* published its first issue in 1955. Kent asserted that the profession of intelligence, like all professions, needed a scholarly literature. He argued persuasively that analysts had clearly defined roles vis-a-vis policymakers. Analysts should be "close" enough to policy to know decision-makers' intelligence needs but not so close that they lost their analytic objectivity. They were to help improve decision-making processes without suggesting or advocating specific policies. This meant without saying that intelligence did not second-guess or criticize executives' decisions or the executives personally. Much more recently Mark Lowenthal argued, using an oft-cited metaphor, that a "semi-permeable membrane" separates policymakers and intelligence officers: "policymakers can and do cross over into the intelligence sphere, but intelligence officers cannot cross over into the policy sphere."[70]

---

68   Kent, *Strategic Intelligence for American World Policy.*
69   Hutchings, "Introduction," 7.
70   Lowenthal, *Intelligence*, 5.

The early CIA analytic corps, like its OSS predecessor, consisted largely of former professors. While there have always been Republicans in American intelligence agencies, the Research and Analysis element of the OSS, the predecessor of CIA's current Directorate of Analysis (DA), was "moderately liberal" in aggregate and it contained some hard leftists, in the view of OSS and CIA veteran Ray Cline.[71] Former chief of CIA counterintelligence Michael Sulick observed that many Ivy League intellectuals of the 1930s, and the OSS analysts some of them became, were infatuated with the deceptive promises of Soviet communism.[72] The NKVD recruited at least four analysts employed by Research and Analysis.[73] And some of President Franklin Roosevelt's New Dealers pointedly tried to place like-minded people, including "smart young Harvard Law School products," throughout the government.[74] Retired CIA officer Benjamin Fischer quoted an unnamed, evidently knowledgeable observer of US intelligence, as saying about CIA: "I never met a stupid person in the agency. Or an assassin. Or a Republican."[75]

While they brought liberal political perspectives to the CIA, OSS veterans also believed that methodologically sound research was essential in intelligence analysis. Because they recognized that intelligence is always about the future, meaning relevant reporting is always incomplete, often unreliable, and subject to deception, analysts did not seek perfect knowledge, predictive accuracy, or absolute "truth." Instead, the goal in the early years always was

---

71   Cline, *The CIA Under Reagan Bush & Casey*, 98.

72   Sulick, *Spying In America*, 166, 186.

73   No byline, "Venona decrypts and Soviet Penetration of the OSS," *Open Geography*, August 28, 2013, https://opengeography.wordpress.com/2013/08/28/venona-decrypts-and-soviet-penetration-of-the-oss/; Bradley, *A Very Principled Boy*, 66.

74   Ibid., 60.

75   Fischer, "An Agency Insider's View of the World," 388.

objective analysis and service to presidents.[76] If analyses were objective and rigorous, truth as best it could be determined and better support to decision-making processes would result. The early analysts did not assert a mission to, or an ability to, speak "truth to power," which in the 1960s became a favorite phrase of aggressive, politically motivated analysts. These analysts often were world-class experts on their subjects, in the view of the late Columbia University professor and long-time student of US intelligence Robert Jervis, something that Jervis believed is no longer the case.[77]

Consistent with its origins and early reputation, the CIA still is widely seen within the IC as a whole as having collective perspectives—worldviews—that are politically more left-leaning than the Defense agencies but a bit less liberal than State/INR.[78] Unconscious biases reflecting organizational worldviews seem to account for most of this slant given that the agency long has recognized the dangers of political biases and employs formal mechanisms to try to excise all forms of bias that may enter analytic drafts. Former senior CIA executive James Simon, an analyst early in his career, argued that *intellectual* diversity is needed to "avoid that greatest of analytic perils: 'group think.'"[79] This useful kind of diversity is not always present, however, and has been discouraged in recent years in favor of more politically attractive beliefs, arguably reified in recent years into an ideology that instead values demographic diversity, which in turn generated new biases that are largely responsible for the activism against Trump.[80]

---

76   Cline, *The CIA Under Reagan, Bush, & Casey*; Smith, *The Unknown CIA*; Ford, "The US government's experience with intelligence analysis," 36.

77   Personal communication with Jervis, 2019.

78   For example, Richard Betts's observations in Gentry, "An INS Special Forum," 4; Gentry, "Managers of Analysts."

79   Simon, "Intelligence Analysis as Practiced by the CIA," 646.

80   Gentry, "Demographic Diversity in U.S. Intelligence Personnel."

The CIA's liberal reputation within the IC is widely shared by people in Washington, including presidents and Congress people of both parties.[81] But few hard data exist to demonstrate this point. Intelligence agencies do not survey the political views of their employees. Federal Election Commission (FEC) data on campaign contributions by serving and former intelligence officers indicate that large majorities of contributions (in both number and monetary value) by current and former CIA people over the years were to Democrats, although sample sizes are small; few serving CIA officers contribute to political candidates or organizations.[82] Of perhaps greater importance given their seniority and abilities to both influence organizational worldviews and promote like-minded people into leadership positions, FEC data show that two former heads of CIA's analysis directorate, Winston Wiley (2000-2002) and Jami Miscik (2002-2005), contributed to Democratic candidates after they retired from the CIA. After she retired, Miscik also served on President-elect Obama's 2008 transition team.[83] FEC data show that Mary Beth Manion Morell, the wife of former deputy CIA director Michael Morell, who headed the analysis directorate in 2008-2010 and became a prominent Trump critic, gave $7,900 to the Democratic National Committee on August 24, 2020 and a total of $19,100 to two Joe Biden presidential campaign funds in seven separate contributions in June-August 2020.[84] These contributions slightly concealed Morell's partisanship when he worked for CBS News and was supposed to be politically neutral. In late August 2020, Morell

---

81 Jeffreys-Jones, *The CIA & American Democracy*, 7, 33, 62, 64, 70, 76, 89, 173, 230, 233; Gentry, "An INS Special Forum," 3-5, 9-10.

82 Federal Election Commission, https://www.fec.gov/data/receipts/individual-contributions/?two_year_transaction_period=2020&min_date=01%2F01%2F2019&max_date=12%2F31%2F2020.

83 Brennan, *Undaunted*, 179.

84 FEC database.

asked friends to contribute to the Biden campaign and to attend with him an online fundraiser for Biden to be held on September 1, 2020.[85] No head of the analysis directorate since Robert Gates, who left that position in 1986, gave money to a Republican.[86]

My discussions with former analyst colleagues, now freed from previous restrictions on political talk, are consistent with the stereotypical view. Of roughly 30 former analysts whose political leanings I did not know while we worked at CIA but learned later, four people in recent years explicitly stated to me their Republican affiliation or expressed views generally consistent with Republican positions on major issues. The rest said enough to indicate explicitly or strongly suggest that they are Democrats. None expressed support for Trump.

Recognition that derivation of truth in the intelligence business is both impossible and an unreasonable goal led to adoption of a "batting average" metaphor for analytic performance, usually applied to judgmental accuracy. Princeton University professor and CIA advisor Klaus Knorr coined the term in 1964 to reflect the fact that even good intelligence services are not "right" all the time, just as good batters in baseball do not always get hits.[87] Columbia University professor Richard Betts later popularized the concept.[88] But the definition of a good "batting average" for intelligence analysis has never been determined, and rarely even suggested, primarily for the excellent reason that determining accuracy is hard, cannot always be done quickly, and may be influenced by policy actions taken in response to intelligence warnings.[89] In a rare such comment, a then-chief of the National

---

85   Personal communication with a knowledgeable person.

86   FEC database.

87   Knorr, "Failures in National Intelligence Estimates," 460.

88   Betts, "Analysis, War, and Decision," 85.

89   For example, the "paradox of warning" refers to the fact that prescient warnings of emerging events of importance appear to be inaccurate if they persuade policymakers to take effective actions to deter the warned-about events. See Gentry and Gordon, *Strategic Warning Intelligence*, 19-21, 43.

Foreign Assessment Center (the Carter administration's name for the current Directorate of Analysis), Bruce Clarke, in early 1980 told a congressional hearing that it would be an "unexpected achievement" if the CIA at any time in its history had been right "50 percent of the time."[90] This responsibly modest view of CIA's ability to consistently divine "truth" about the uncertain future changed dramatically in 2016, when IC personnel claimed possession of truth that Trump did not have. In 2021, Mark Lowenthal sharply criticized intelligence officers' claims in recent years that they know truth, appropriately calling them "arrogant."[91]

CIA analysis from the 1950s through the 1970s generally reflected the institutional values established by Kent and other early analysts.[92] Research and expertise remained valued, and objective analysis that helped decision-makers make better decisions, not acquisition of truth, was the goal.[93] Analysts still tried to leave their politics at home. By the 1970s and 1980s, analysts often had master's degrees but doctorates and Ivy League pedigrees were fewer than before. The agency expanded its recruiting efforts to hire more women and people from throughout the country. In this early search for "diversity," the goal was to hire good people with intellectual diversity—people who would be good at government jobs—whatever their background and wherever they could be found. Analysts held spirited debates about major intelligence issues of the day that often were anything but politically correct but always aimed to understand world affairs better.[94] Analysts typically had thick skins and were not bothered by minor linguistic slights. This was the intellectually vigorous environment I joined in 1978.

---

90   As cited in Jeffreys-Jones, *The CIA & American Democracy*, 226.
91   Lowenthal, "Intelligence is NOT About 'Telling Truth to Power,'" 797-798.
92   For example, Smith, *The Unknown CIA*; Cline, *The CIA Under Reagan, Bush & Casey*.
93   Marrin, "Evaluating the Quality of Intelligence Analysis," 897-899.
94   Firehock, Gentry, Rogers, and Simon, "Negotiating the Review Process;" Simon, "Intelligence Analysis as Practiced by the CIA."

Lapses in adhering to these standards occurred periodically, however, especially during the American war in Vietnam, when some CIA personnel actively opposed the policies of Presidents Johnson and Nixon. For example, some CIA analysts lamented the agency's acquiescence to the Defense Department's politicization of a 1967 special NIE (SNIE) on the military situation in Vietnam, which published estimated enemy force levels lower than the analysts believed were accurate; the military demanded lower numbers to support their claims that they were winning the war.[95] A few outraged CIA analysts claimed it was their duty to speak their view of truth even though their own order-of-battle (OB) numbers were widely recognized as soft.[96] That is, they reflected incomplete and sometimes inconsistent data whose validity could not be determined persuasively. Then-head of the analysis directorate Russell Jack Smith later wrote, "The zealots in our midst wanted us to rush into battle and carry the fight for Eternal Truth right up to the front steps of the White House."[97] Smith and DCI Richard Helms instead compromised on the SNIE's language while making sure senior officials, including President Johnson and key NSC staffers, knew CIA's views on the issue. CIA also continued to express these perspectives in its own publications. "Zealots" such as Sam Adams nevertheless claimed that Helms politicized intelligence by dropping the issue during SNIE coordination sessions.[98] The "truth to power" mantra became temporarily popular at this time as analyst "zealots" used it to justify their challenges to a DCI they believed politicized intelligence and a president whose policies they did not like. The slogan faded away when the war ended, but it and zealotry

---

95   Wirtz, "Intelligence to Please."
96   Smith, *The Unknown CIA*, 224.
97   Ibid., 225-227.
98   Adams, *War of Numbers*; Hiam, *Who the Hell Are We Fighting*.

reemerged in 2016 in force as part of the rhetorical assault on Trump. James Clapper added it to the IC's mission statement just before leaving office, very late in his long tenure as DNI, fairly obviously for political reasons.

We know now that some CIA analysts as individuals went much further in 1971 than zealots like Sam Adams when they "cooked the books" about North Vietnamese supply routes into South Vietnam to try to thwart President Nixon's planned invasion of the eastern part of Cambodia—an effort designed to destroy communist sanctuaries and supply depots there.[99] CIA analysts claimed that most supplies entered South Vietnam by land via Laos and the "Ho Chi Minh Trail," not by sea to Cambodia, making the planned invasion needless. The invasion occurred anyway, and Nixon soon learned that CIA analysts gave him biased intelligence, contributing to his already low opinion of CIA people.[100] The politicization occurred despite CIA's review processes, perhaps because managers also opposed the war and agreed with the analysts' message. To his credit, when he learned that CIA clandestine reporting confirmed that his analysts were mistaken about the relative importance of the various communist supply routes into South Vietnam and that the Cambodian port of Sihanoukville was a major entry point, DCI Helms immediately told the White House.[101]

In 1985-1986, when strongly anti-communist William Casey was DCI, there was pressure on some analysts, including me, to make communist states look even worse than they were.[102] This issue plagued Robert Gates, head of CIA's analysis directorate

---

99   Ahern, *Good Questions, Wrong Answers,* 43-45; Warner, "The Use and Abuse of Intelligence," 18-19.

100   Andrew, *For the President's Eyes Only,* 350-396.

101   Helms, *A Look Over My Shoulder,* 389-392.

102   Gentry, *Lost Promise.*

in 1982-1986, at his DCI confirmation hearings in 1991 because several dozen analysts, mainly, took their concerns to the SSCI and a few testified openly against Gates.

These episodes of politicization from both the political Left and Right were relatively minor, but they precipitated much introspective discussion and still are widely cited—evidence that the traditional culture that emphasized the importance of analytical objectivity remains fairly strong in older intelligence officers, at least, and that memories of politicization are long. Casey's views or the widely known anti-communist views of some members of the Reagan administration evidently led to politicization from within CIA by senior officers who wanted to please them. But there also were some unusually strong misrepresentations of Casey's views by people with strongly left-wing political views such as Melvin Goodman, who was a severe public critic of Gates at his DCI confirmation hearings and who wrote a book titled *Whistleblower at the CIA*—a self-characterization.[103] In retrospect, Goodman was a harbinger of the activism of 2016 and later. He criticized CIA management, and the broader US government, from a radical political perspective and displayed certainty that he knew the truth about CIA activities, their meanings, and their consequences that others did not. In 2016 and later, the focus of the erstwhile truth-tellers was again ideological, this time focused on Donald Trump and his appointees.

By 1990, a few prominent exceptions notwithstanding, CIA's analytic culture had changed little from previous years. An anonymous analyst described the DI's culture in a *Studies in Intelligence* article, emphasizing that an organizational culture often manifests itself in "a distinct professional personality" consisting

---

103   Goodman has written several other strongly anti-CIA articles and books.

of "common work norms, attitudes, and behaviors."[104] The author cited prominent personality characteristics of the analytic corps:

> In the [Directorate of Intelligence], we take great pride in our ability to think critically about issues, to ask the right questions, to be objective, to see issues from a number of perspectives, and to marshal evidence in support of our conclusions. We also pride ourselves on being intellectually honest. We call the shots as we see them, regardless of any partisan political considerations or pressures. As a group, we are a tough-minded and critical lot, always ready to do battle with words and ideas. We are as quick to challenge anyone else's conclusions and arguments as we are to defend our own. While we see ourselves as open-minded empiricists, at times we can also be defensive, intellectually arrogant, and overly cynical. We often find it easier to be neutral or negative than to be upbeat and optimistic. To survive in this culture, intellectual robustness, self-confidence, resiliency, and assertiveness are essential.[105]

The combativeness long has varied by functional responsibility, or by the specialist subsets of the corps of analysts. Robert Vickers, a retired senior military analyst who was twice a national intelligence officer (NIO) and directed CIA's Office of Imagery Analysis, explained:

> Political analysts are more biased and liberal, perhaps because that is the dominant culture in academic

---

104   Anonymous, "The DI's Organizational Culture," 21.
105   Ibid., 22.

political science departments. They thrive on making judgments of foreign government intentions. Military and scientific analysts focus on capabilities and pride themselves on lack of political bias. These subcultures still persist and will likely survive Trump.[106]

The analytic culture generally was quite functional, in my experience, a few notable exceptions notwithstanding. The combative spirit and firmness of conviction about analytic issues had one prominent dysfunction, however. As the anonymous analyst suggested, when analysts and analytical units developed firm views on an issue, a reflection of a collective organizational worldview, they sometimes strongly resisted new information, which occasionally led to analytical mistakes. They collectively displayed what psychologists call cognitive closure. To combat this, the IC sometimes promoted "competitive analyses" between IC agencies. On some issues senior officials sometimes employed national intelligence officers as checks on cognitive closure within the line analytic units. For example, former C/NIC John Gannon (1997-2001) observed this phenomenon repeatedly and used his NIO for Warning (NIO/W), Robert Vickers, to both prod line units and to provide alternative analyses.[107] Cognitive closure and the related phenomenon of confirmation bias can occur on many subjects. It is a chronic danger in hierarchical, insular organizations such as intelligence agencies but is not the same as "groupthink," with which it is commonly confused.[108] Both were evident in Trump's critics. All of Trump's words and actions seemed to confirm his evilness.

In the early 1990s, the earlier strong emphasis on research

---

106   Robert Vickers email to author, November 26, 2019.

107   Gentry and Gordon, *Strategic Warning Intelligence*, 83.

108   Groupthink is a small-group phenomenon. See Janis, *Victims of Groupthink*.

gradually diminished. Then-chief of the DI Douglas MacEachin, reflecting the perceived wishes of President Clinton, shifted the focus of CIA analysis toward current intelligence. This meant that the ability to quickly convert incoming reports into a short intelligence product that could smoothly sail through the review process became an even more highly valued skill.

Occasional episodes of intelligence conflict with presidents recurred, albeit in new ways. For example, new President Clinton, unfamiliar with foreign affairs and intelligence, in 1993 objected strongly to a NIE that characterized former Haitian President Jean Bertrand Aristide as a mentally unstable tyrant, among other things.[109] Clinton publicly attacked the estimate, leading to a months-long, nasty public relations campaign that charged that CIA's collection was biased and its analyses were racist and incompetent.[110]

Clinton reportedly was unhappy with CIA about other issues as well. In response, MacEachin reorganized the DI and reportedly told analysts, "Analysts must recognize that if they give a briefing which deviates too much from official policy, they may be accused by Clinton administration officials of being disloyal."[111] MacEachin's actions and comments reflected politicization of a sort Kent warned about—getting too close to policy-makers. But no analysts resigned in protest over Clinton's repeatedly inaccurate

---

109   Director of Central Intelligence, NIE 93–2, "Haiti over the Next Few Months," January 1993, https://www.cia.gov/library/readingroom/docs/DOC_0000652921. pdf.

110   David Lauter, "Clinton Meets With Aristide, Haiti Premier," *Los Angeles Times*, December 7, 1993, http://articles.latimes.com/1993-12-07/news/mn-64873_1_ aristide-clinton-haiti; Prados, *Safe for Democracy*, 595; Omestad, "Psychology and the CIA," 104–122; author's personal discussion with a lawyer doing public relations work in support of Aristide for the Congressional Black Caucus.

111   Center for Security Policy, "'SAY IT AIN'T SO, JIM': IMPENDING REORGANIZATION OF CIA LOOKS LIKE SUPPRESSION, POLITICIZING OF INTELLIGENCE," Publication No. 94-D74, July 15, 1994, https://centerforsecuritypolicy.org/say-it-aint-so-jim-impending-reorganization-of-cia-looks-like-suppression-politicizing-of-intelligence-2/.

and inflammatory public attacks on the CIA, however. Clinton was a Democrat whose political philosophy was widely shared by CIA people. No one leaked criticisms of Clinton, although one former analyst involved in the controversy later said the experience was "very unpleasant."[112] The "truth to power" slogan did not reappear. DCI James Woolsey backed the estimators against White House pressure, but MacEachin did not.[113] No latter-day "zealots" chastised MacEachin for politicizing intelligence. When I suggested in 2017 to someone close to the Haiti NIE controversy that he publish his account of the episode, he demurred, saying the episode remained too painful. I take the person at his word but do not rule out the possibility that he wanted to protect Clinton, just as CIA people protected President Kennedy for years after his death by accepting sole responsibility for the assassination attempts on Fidel Castro that Kennedy personally, directly, and repeatedly ordered.

Apparently partly in response to Clinton's complaints about the Haiti NIE, MacEachin dramatically cut back long-term research, emphasized short papers, and de-emphasized the acquisition of expertise by analysts. Soon the analyst culture changed appreciably again. Rob Johnston, a CIA officer trained as an anthropologist, conducted a large-scale survey of IC analysts in the early 2000s that concluded that journalism was a good comparison for much of what IC analysts did—a radically different perspective than those of analysts of the OSS and the early CIA, which were much more scholarly in nature.[114] This emphasis on the short-term has continued, leading many observers to lament the loss of expertise at CIA and at other IC agencies.[115] Many

---

112   Personal communication.

113   Ibid.

114   Johnston, *Analytic Culture in the U.S. Intelligence Community.*

115   George, "Reflections on CIA Analysis;" Gentry, "The 'Professionalization' of Intelligence Analysis."

wrote, "intelligence failure in the strategic analysis realm should be judged, not primarily on abstract prediction, but on whether we rigorously mined the best information and expertise available at the time of dissemination."[124]

At the CIA's Office of Soviet Analysis (SOVA) in the 1980s, office directors killed papers they thought might be unwelcome by Reagan administration officials. For example, a director of SOVA told an analyst who initiated a study that suggested a slowdown in the growth of Soviet military capabilities might be occurring that his paper would not be published because its message would not be welcome "downtown"—a CIA euphemism for the White House and senior cabinet officials.[125] Later, another SOVA director killed a paper concerning East European countries' relationships with the USSR because he said he believed the Reagan White House would not be receptive to it. To make clear that politicization was his motive, the director said he regarded the paper as a good one and said it would be counted in the analyst's tally of "production" when annual performance appraisal time came around.[126] This politicization was done to avoid alienating administration officials—which may occasionally have happened in the Trump years.

Pressures to please consumers by producing favorable language also occurred regularly over the years, but probably in small numbers and magnitude of importance. But before the 9/11 attacks, as the IC was working to identify Iraqi weapons of mass destruction, the CIA completed a study that CIA's "seventh floor"—the DCI's office—found too weak. According to a former CIA analyst familiar with the study, DCI George Tenet's staff re-wrote part of the study to make the CIA appear more confident

---

124   Gannon, "A New Global Agenda, 1997-2001," 74.

125   Personal communication with the analyst, July 25, 2019.

126   Personal communication with the former CIA analyst who experienced this policy, May 2019.

of its findings than the analysts who wrote the original study believed was warranted.[127] This issue haunted Tenet later, when he was accused of being inappropriately over-confident in assessments about the existence of Iraqi WMD embedded in a 2002 NIE on the subject.[128]

Occasionally, intelligence analysts have transparently liked or opposed political leaders despite the cultural norm that analysts leave their personal political views at home. CIA analysts "festooned" the walls of CIA office spaces with anti-Nixon "propaganda," according to Robert Gates, who joined CIA just before Nixon became president.[129] This practice seems to have been especially prominent in the Nixon years. I do not recall any instance of it in my twelve years (1978-1990) at the agency and many career CIA people with whom I have spoken about this issue do not report such political sensitivities at other times. But retired CIA operations officer Ken Stiles recounted an anecdote that suggests institutional bias.[130] In 2004 Stiles received a message from CIA administrators asking him to remove a yard sign endorsing Republican George W. Bush for reelection as president, which was inside his automobile in the parking lot at CIA headquarters. The sign was visible through the car's windows to passersby, as Stiles intended. Someone had complained, he was told. Stiles asked if management had asked owners of all cars in the parking lot sporting other candidates' bumper stickers to remove them. The answer was "no." At that point Stiles refused to comply with the request and agency officials backed down. In fact, such visual indications of political opinion on vehicles are not violations of federal law or government-wide policy.

127   Personnel communication with a retired CIA analyst, July 2019.

128   George Tenet devotes considerable space to this issue in his memoir. See Tenet, *At the Center of the Storm*, 359-368.

129   Gates, *From the Shadows*, 30.

130   Author discussion with Ken Stiles, July 10, 2019.

The evolving culture of CIA analysts is an important part of this story. Analysts' traditionally liberal worldviews have been evident but generally suppressed as popular and unpopular presidents came and went, and as presidential policies were more or less congruent with the interest-based and ideological wishes of CIA employees. Analysts and managers tried to minimize the effects of political bias on agency analyses. Nevertheless, as the anonymous analyst wrote in 1990, analysts tend to be excessively confident in the correctness of their views, are self-centered, and sometimes are arrogant.[131] Even former DCIA John Brennan, a strong advocate of the agency and its people, wrote in his memoir that in his CIA career he often encountered "pockets of insularity, parochialism, and arrogance."[132] These traits emerged publicly in powerful new ways in 2016, largely for new reasons discussed in chapter 3.

THE ODNI

Created by the IRTPA in late 2004, the ODNI began to operate in April 2005 with personnel seconded from many of the IC's agencies. It also inherited the DCI's Community Management Staff, a small version of what ODNI became. Over time, the ODNI developed its own hiring practices and career services and began to develop its own culture. It hired lots of lawyers and brought in senior personnel from outside the IC on short-term assignments.[133]

Because it is still new, little has been written on the ODNI's organizational culture. But the ODNI workforce is widely viewed

---

131 Anonymous, "The DI's Organizational Culture." For similar views, see Simon, "Intelligence Analysis as Practiced by the CIA," 646; Nolan, "Information Sharing and Collaboration in the United States Intelligence Community," 71.

132 Brennan, *Undaunted*, 298.

133 For example, historian Richard Immerman, a professor at Temple University, served as Assistant Deputy Director of National Intelligence for Analytic Integrity and Standards from September 2007 to January 2009. Nancy Bernkopf Tucker, a history professor at Georgetown University, previously held the same position.

within the IC as collectively left-leaning. FEC data show that over 90 percent of the small number of ODNI employees who contributed to political campaigns in recent years gave to Democrats.[134] David Muller, who worked there in the late Bush and early Obama years, reported that the ODNI's culture then did not include a prohibition on internal political banter, as CIA's culture once had, and that many ODNI employees were outspoken Democrats.[135]

For many years the NIC worked for DCIs and was staffed mainly by CIA officers, but per IRTPA it became an ODNI element, working for DNIs. Former NIC chairmen Robert Hutchings and Gregory Treverton provide to discerning readers in *Truth to Power*, a history of the post-Cold War NIC, evidence that the leaders of one of the IC's premier analytic elements have generally been Democratic leaning in recent decades, even in Republican administrations.[136] The job is important and influential. NIC chairs select or approve topics the NIC analyzes, advise senior NSC staffers, review NIC written products, and play a major role in selecting the NIOs and their deputies, who draft and approve NIE drafts and interact with line analytic units and senior intelligence consumers. Because they have considerable power to shape the IC's analytic agenda and collective worldview of the NIC, presidents sometimes have killed planned hiring of NIOs who had views perceived to be undesirable. For example, in 2002 President George W. Bush's NSC staff did not like C/NIC John Helgerson's choice to be the NIO covering China and persuaded

---

134   FEC database.

135   Author discussion with David Muller, July 11, 2019.

136   Hutchings and Treverton, *Truth to Power*. The title is instructive, given the history noted here—that the term normally is code for opposition to a president. Co-editor Treverton said he does not believe that intelligence is in fact in the "truth" business.

DCI George Tenet to tell Helgerson to find someone else to fill the vacancy.[137]

In 2009, DNI Dennis Blair prevented C/NIC Christopher Kojm and the NIO for South Asia from preparing an NIE on the situation in Afghanistan because, according to Kojm, Blair thought the estimate would inevitably be seen as "grading the military's performance."[138] A retired admiral, Blair evidently wanted to protect the US military from yet more criticism, given that the war obviously was not going well. He may have recalled that the annual SNIEs on the military situation in Vietnam in the 1960s were contentious, and the military was willing to politicize the 1967 version to make it appear the war was going better than CIA more accurately thought it was. Kojm gave no hint that pressure in this case came from the White House or Pentagon, which clearly influenced the political/bureaucratic viability, tone, and conclusions of other NIEs.

Of eight former NIC chairmen who contributed narratives of their tenures to *Truth to Power*, only career intelligence officers Thomas Fingar, John Gannon, and John Helgerson do not provide clear evidence of their partisan beliefs, and Fingar describes himself elsewhere as a liberal.[139] President Clinton's first two NIC chairs, Richard Cooper and Joseph Nye, were political appointees in the Carter administration.[140] Robert Hutchings, appointed by President George W. Bush, admitted that he came to the job opposed to Bush's war in Iraq and remained concerned about developing intelligence to help mitigate the effects of the Bush administration's perceived policy errors.[141] Hutchings thereby

---

137   Helgerson. "The Trauma of 9/11," 94.

138   Kojm, "Intelligence Integration and Reform: 2009-2014," 166.

139   Fingar, *Reducing Uncertainty*, 45.

140   Nye, "Estimative Intelligence after the Cold War, 1993-1994," 27; Cooper, "Controlling Controversy: 1995-1997, 43-44.

141   Hutchings, "America at War: 2003-2005," 105, 112-113.

gave additional credence to the charges by some Bush administration officials and outside observers that there was a major
White House-IC feud over Iraq policy during the Bush years. In
addition, in oral comments at a signing of *Truth to Power* at the
Center for Strategic and International Studies in Washington on
July 16, 2019, Hutchings scathingly criticized Trump. Christopher
Kojm, President Obama's first C/NIC, was an Obama campaign
official in 2008.[142] Treverton, also an Obama appointee, made clear
that he opposed Trump and left the job rather than work for
Trump.[143] Helgerson believed most of the personnel on the NIC
staff when he was chairman (2001-2002) opposed President Bush's
then-anticipated war on Iraq.[144] In addition, Peter Lavoy, who was
C/NIC in 2008-2009, gave $500 to the reelection campaign of
Representative Elissa Slotkin (D-MI), who formerly was a CIA
analyst, in October 2020.[145]

The ODNI has major responsibilities to oversee the agencies
and submits most of the IC's required reports to Congress.
Among its units are two diversity offices, the significance of which
is discussed below. One administers diversity policies within the
ODNI. The other oversees diversity policy implementation in
the agencies and is a greater contributor to the politicization of
intelligence in recent years.

FEDERAL BUREAU OF INVESTIGATION (FBI)

The FBI has a strong organizational culture that is relevant
to the politicization story in different ways than CIA's
directorate-based cultures. Founded in 1908 as the Bureau
of Investigation, it received its current name in 1935. Led by

---

142 Kojm, "Intelligence Integration and Reform: 2009-2014," 187.
143 Treverton, "From Afghanistan to Trump: 2014-2017, 196.
144 Ibid., 100.
145 FEC database.

the legendary J. Edgar Hoover for forty-eight years (1924–1972), the Bureau is primarily a law enforcement agency with an appended responsibility for counterintelligence activities within the United States. The FBI's major components are its fifty-six field offices, each led by a "special agent in charge" (SAC) who largely controls the priorities and operations of his or her office. Headquarters has modest influence on the day-to-day operations of the field offices. The FBI had some foreign intelligence responsibilities during World War II and after 9/11 it has dealt more with US externally-focused intelligence agencies and other countries' internal security services concerning terrorism-related issues.[146] The Congress tasked the FBI with working more closely with other US intelligence agencies as a perceived lesson of the 9/11 intelligence failure, and it appears to be doing so to some extent.

By many accounts, the FBI's first and major mission long has been the protection and advancement of its organizational interests. Concerns about protecting and advancing FBI interests match or exceed those of CIA people. "Don't embarrass the Bureau" was a de facto requirement Hoover placed on all FBI employees.[147]

Special agents, for whom putting criminals in prison is the main organizational goal, historically have run the organization. Most special agents, like CIA's operations officers, like to work in the field, which is where most of the criminals are.

The FBI is an aggressive bureaucratic infighter against other intelligence agencies and politicians who threaten the Bureau's interests. Director Hoover is widely believed to have spread rumors in Washington that contributed to President Truman's

---

146   Tromblay, *The FBI Abroad.*
147   Weiner, *Enemies,* 117.

decision to abolish the OSS in September 1945, and Hoover vehemently opposed creation of the CIA in 1947.[148]

The FBI long has been a notoriously cantankerous IC "partner" and generally is still regarded as such, despite some improvement since 2001.[149] It is still learning to work with other intelligence agencies, according to former FBI Deputy Director Andrew McCabe who, like most FBI people, is a strong advocate for the FBI's organizational interests.[150] McCabe added that the agency's culture is "paramilitary" in nature and that its people experience "groupthink."[151] Former senior FBI counterintelligence officer Peter Strzok concurred, calling the FBI a "deeply hierarchical bureaucracy" subject to the dangers of groupthink.[152] The FBI under Hoover spied on Americans including presidents, fought other agencies, and quarreled with the Justice Department, its departmental overseer, all of which later came to be seen widely as inappropriate.[153] The FBI's Hoover problems allegedly were "fixed" in 1976, soon after his death, yet many others developed and the FBI's focus on protecting its interests clearly remains.[154] For example, the FBI for many years ignored organized crime because it produced few arrests, and thus was not bureaucratically rewarding.[155] It largely ignored immigration laws for the same reason, helping to create the immigration policy mess the United States now faces.[156] And, according to former Attorney General William Barr and others, the FBI, recalling that it received some

---

148 Andrew, *For the President's Eyes Only*, 156-161; Andrew, "American presidents and their intelligence communities."
149 Riebling, *Wedge*.
150 McCabe, *The Threat*, 20, 137, 261.
151 Ibid., 31, Riebling, *Wedge*.
152 Strzok, *Compromised*, 88.
153 McCabe, *The Threat*, 181.
154 Ibid., 209.
155 Ibid., 36.
156 Ibid., 69.

of its worst public criticism when it targeted leftist groups in the 1960s, has continued to focus mainly on right-wing groups.[157] It thereby skews its reporting, and public perceptions, of ideology-based threats to national security. McCabe acknowledged that the FBI and CIA often have not gotten along and recognized that the FBI bears responsibility for at least some of the animosity.[158] Yet McCabe also argued when Trump was president that the FBI deserved complete independence because it served only truth and the Constitution. Both claims were and remain factually incorrect.

The FBI long has had a reputation within the IC for recruiting politically conservative people.[159] This is unsurprising given the dominant law-enforcement mission of the Bureau and Hoover's conservative personal politics and personal ethics, such as his strongly anti-communist views and his aversion to homosexuality.[160] Hence, the political color of the FBI's organizational culture has been more akin to that of the military than to CIA or INR analysts, meaning there is little commonality in the ideological opposition to Trump between the two entities. However, as in all large organizations, there are exceptions to general rules. For example, Peter Strzok stated repeatedly in his memoir that he liked Hillary Clinton and loathed Trump, and he reported that when Trump announced his candidacy for president in June 2015, he was troubled by Trump's rhetoric, which he called "[d]og whistles to racists and conspiracy theorists."[161]

The 9/11 attacks changed a lot in the US government, including increasing the importance of counterterrorism to the FBI. Director Robert Mueller (2001-2013) made organizational

---

157 Barr, *One Damn Thing After Another*, 485-486.
158 McCabe, *The Threat*, 109, 113, 117, 140; Baer, *The Fourth Man*.
159 Personal experience. See also Nolan, "Information Sharing and Collaboration in the United States Intelligence Community," 73-74.
160 Riebling, *Wedge*, 122, 124-125; Weiner, *Enemies*, 23-45, 106-107, 123.
161 Strzok, *Compromised*, 65.

changes designed to improve the FBI's counterterrorism efforts, which by several accounts both failed and had significantly negative organizational cultural implications. Former FBI special agent and manager James Gagliano has argued that the Bureau in the Mueller years centralized control at headquarters in Washington, where many experienced field agents did not want to work, opening the way for ambitious, politically attuned young personnel to move into upwardly mobile positions.[162] Among them, he claimed, was agent Andrew McCabe, who once worked for Gagliano and who as deputy director became a major actor in the post-2016 politicization controversy at the FBI. Gagliano said of McCabe:

> Imbued with healthy amounts of intellectual curiosity and naked ambition, McCabe expertly read the writing on the wall. Recognizing that Mueller was bent on reconstituting an FBI HQ that [former FBI Director Louis] Freeh had summarily dismantled, McCabe made his move.[163]

McCabe spent much of his FBI career at headquarters and the Washington field office, where Gagliano said politically sensitive people such as the controversial Peter Strzok also worked. Gagliano added about McCabe:

> Once leaving New York, he made a life inside the [Washington] Beltway. He shuttled back and forth between FBI HQ and the Washington field division

---

162 James A. Gagliano, "Outgoing FBI deputy director Andrew McCabe owes us some answers," *The Hill,* January 18, 2018, https://thehill.com/opinion/white-house/371384-outgoing-fbi-deputy-director-andrew-mccabe-owes-us-some-answers.

163 Ibid.

— commonplace for ladder-climbers interested in hastening their ascent in the midlevel and senior executive ranks.

And with James Comey's arrival on the scene as FBI chief in September 2013, he found a kindred spirit in McCabe.

Comey was personally responsible for quickly guiding McCabe through a number of senior-level positions. As some FBI bystanders groused — these "blue-flamers" are put into positions long enough for a cup of coffee; just enough time to touch the base and move up.[164]

Darren Tromblay, a government analyst who knows the FBI well, similarly believes the reforms of Mueller and Comey changed structures and organizations' names but little affected the organizational culture of the FBI or its weak analytic abilities.[165] While the FBI increased its intelligence work after 9/11, analysts remained second-class employees. A common saying at the FBI reportedly is, "If you're not an Agent, you're furniture."[166] Tromblay argued in 2019 that the Bureau retained its reactive, case-focused approach and remained collectively unable to think in ways needed to anticipate and prevent the emergence of threats, not just catch perpetrators after crimes have been committed.[167] For this reason, Tromblay argued that the Bureau was failing to perform

---

164 Ibid.

165 Tromblay, *Spying*; Tromblay, "The Threat Review and Prioritization Trap;" Tromblay, "Information Technology (IT) Woes and Intelligence Agency Failures."

166 Nolan, "Information Sharing and Collaboration in the United States Intelligence Community," 73.

167 For devastating critiques of the FBI's analytical savvy, see Zegart, *Spying Blind* and Tromblay "The Threat Review and Prioritization Trap."

key elements of its national security responsibilities, which are set by executive policy, not statute; the FBI has no legal charter.[168] Strzok admitted as much, saying for example that he and the rest of the Bureau were caught off guard in late 2016 by Russian use of social media for political purposes despite knowing about at least some of the long history of Soviet and Russian "active measures" in the United States and the publication of characteristics of "social media intelligence" in academic journals as early as 2012.[169]

In sum, the FBI's organizational and cultural traits differ sharply from all other IC agencies except the Drug Enforcement Administration, another primarily police agency that also is part of the Justice Department. The FBI evidently is not composed of large numbers of people who opposed Trump on ideological grounds, unlike the CIA, ODNI, and INR. What the entities share is a strong commitment to organizational self-advancement, which Trump activated by his critical comments about intelligence in general, about the FBI's investigation of him and his campaign, about Comey and McCabe, and about his desire to "drain the swamp" of bureaucratic Washington. Trump thereby helped create a presumably temporary community of interest among anti-Trump intelligence officers across the IC: the enemy of my enemy is my friend. In recent years senior formers have frequently defended other agencies, and their friends in the other agencies, against Trump's alleged predations—not a common historical occurrence.

STATE DEPARTMENT'S BUREAU OF INTELLIGENCE AND RESEARCH (INR)

INR is a small but important analytic agency. With 313 employees in 2019, including about 200 analysts, and an

---

168 Tromblay, *Spying*, 36, 38, 42, 44, 79, 81, 87, 209.
169 Strzok, *Compromised*, 176-177; Omand, Bartlett, and Miller, "Introducing Social Media Intelligence (SOCMINT)."

annual budget of $59 million, INR's main mission is to provide intelligence support to US diplomacy.[170] It is widely regarded throughout the US government as a quality organization and its products are read by many senior policymakers. INR, like the State Department as a whole, long has had a reputation as a liberal bastion.[171] Secretary of State (and former DCIA) Mike Pompeo told then-national security advisor John Bolton in 2019 he thought about 90 percent of Foreign Service officers had voted for Hillary Clinton in 2016.[172] A standard vignette is that in inter-agency debates about political-military issues, while the military agencies are likely to take a "hard" line, INR is likely to take a "soft" line, with CIA often in the middle. INR did not significantly grow during the post-9/11 hiring binge of most IC agencies. Also unlike them, it retained a view that analyst expertise is a good thing. Former Assistant Secretary of State for Intelligence and Research Thomas Fingar said that in 2005, his last year as INR chief, over half of INR analysts had doctorates and the average length of time analysts then worked their accounts was almost sixteen years.[173] Hence, INR analysts tend to be older and more experienced than those of other agencies, meaning not least that fewer of them received the indoctrination in critical race theory and other Marxism-based perspectives on domestic social/political issues that became common in public schools and universities in recent years and that the influx of young employees after 9/11 brought to other agencies. The result is that INR's culture and workforce

---

170 Mission statement, INR webpage, https://www.state.gov/bureaus-offices/bureaus-and-offices-reporting-directly-to-the-secretary/bureau-of-intelligence-and-research/, and an INR official.

171 Federal Election Commission data show overwhelming majorities of contributions to political campaigns by State personnel are to Democrats or Democrat-supporting organizations such as ActBlue.

172 Bolton, *The Room Where It Happened*, 455.

173 Gentry, "Has the ODNI Improved U.S. Intelligence Analysis?", 650.

have been more stable and traditional than those of most IC agencies. While worldview-generated politicization issues surely are present at INR, its continuing commitment to expert analyses makes significant changes in organizational culture more difficult to engineer in the short-term than elsewhere in the IC. INR analysts also work more closely with policymakers than do analysts of other agencies—their offices are down the hall—making intelligence producer/consumer discussions much more personal in nature than for CIA analysts, who are cloistered in a complex surrounded by forests several miles from downtown Washington and whose managers generally represent CIA to senior policymakers. INR people tend not to use the term "truth to power," a slogan coined and much more commonly used at the CIA. The result is that INR is relatively immune to the politicization the CIA experienced.

OTHER AGENCIES

The other US intelligence agencies are less involved in national-level politics for several reasons. First, the defense agencies, although located in the Washington area, have large military components, are typically led by apolitical military officers on short tours, and are focused on missions and audiences that include support to "warfighters"—troops in the field. Second, the six military service intelligence elements focus mainly on tactical intelligence of use to their own services; they rarely participate in the drafting of NIEs or otherwise coordinate on analyses of primarily political issues, except when politics affects potential threat-countries' military budgets and programs.[174] Even then, issues seldom are overtly partisan in nature. Third, other elements of the IC are relatively small support

---

174 These are the Army, Navy, Air Force, Marine Corps, the Coast Guard, a part of the Department of Homeland Security during peacetime, and the Space Force, which became a member of the IC on January 8, 2021.

components of much larger civilian organizations; they take orders and organizational cultural cues from these larger units and therefore cannot be independent agents of politicization, although some employees as individuals surely have taken political stances at the office in recent years.[175] Hence, only the DIA, NSA, and NGA are discussed further here.

Defense Intelligence Agency

The DIA is a national-level agency that has collection and all-source analytic elements that focus primarily on defense policy- and military intelligence-related issues. Like NSA and NGA, it is a designated Defense Department "combat support agency," meaning it has a formal responsibility to support US troops in the field. DIA therefore does less political analysis than the CIA or INR. Despite its greater ability to contribute to the *President's Daily Brief* (*PDB*) in recent years thanks to IRTPA, by many accounts DIA analysts write few of the articles published in the *PDB*. It is a fairly big agency, with "more than 16,500" employees, as reported consistently on its website for several years.[176] Occasionally, as for a time in the 1980s, DIA has sought to beat CIA at providing support broadly to senior policy-makers, including the president. More commonly, as in recent years, DIA has perceived its job more narrowly as supporting Defense Department intelligence needs, including writing and coordinating on military-related NIEs. Over the years DIA's directors, who for decades have been military three-star officers from all of the military services on (typically) three-year assignments that generally are their last tours before they retire, usually aspire to put their personal stamps on the

---

175 For example, an employee of the National Air and Space Intelligence Center in Dayton, Ohio, the Air Force element of the IC, told me he has seen a spike in partisan talk by both Trump critics and defenders within NASIC in recent years.

176 DIA website, https://www.dia.mil/About/FAQs/, last accessed May 15, 2022.

agency in modest ways, often by articulating slightly different mission statements. DIA's 2018 strategy document, the product of its then-commander, Army Lieutenant General Robert Ashley, says:

> The Defense Intelligence Agency (DIA) fulfills a unique mission at the intersection of the Department of Defense (DoD) and the Intelligence Community (IC). Warfighters, policymakers, and acquisition leaders rely on us for foundational intelligence on foreign militaries and the operating environment that only we provide.[177]

LTG Ashley, as many directors before him, also identified a set of principles that he wanted to see "represented throughout the DIA enterprise:"

> We strive to be great teammates.
> We challenge the status quo, respectfully.
> We listen first.
> We move at the speed of relevance.
> We must be accountable for our own behavior.
> We value people.
> We complete the run together.[178]

Ashley added, "I challenge each of you to play an active part in achieving this culture in every action you take."[179]

These statements of mission and principles reflect fairly traditional IC and military values. They are not highly political

---

177 Defense Intelligence Agency, Strategic Approach, September 2018, https://www.dia.mil/Portals/27/Documents/About/DIA_Strategic_Approach.pdf.

178 Ibid.

179 Ibid.

or Washington-centric in focus and do not strongly emphasize demographic diversity in personnel policies, which by 2018 were firmly established as core organizational goals at the ODNI and CIA. DIA created a "diversity and inclusion" program, but it retained a focus on achieving operationally useful diversity of experience and thinking, not politically important domestic demographic diversity.[180] DIA's collectors, like CIA's, seem to prefer to avoid Washington politics. While DIA's staff is primarily civilian, employees reflect military traditions to a considerable degree, as Ashley intended. DIA personnel, in my experience, like INR people generally do not use the "truth to power" slogan.

The DIA, like the other defense agencies, retains significant autonomy while also reporting to the secretary of defense. These cats do not like to be herded by any DNI or even the secretary of defense. A personal anecdote illustrates this point: In 2000, while employed by the MITRE Corporation, I worked for the intelligence policy office of the secretary of defense at the Pentagon. On the occasion of a technical problem at one of the Defense agencies, I worked with colleagues to make sure the problem would not occur elsewhere, including at DIA. While discussing the issue with DIA officials, the senior DIA officer present told us that DIA would not do as we asked because DIA did not recognize the secretary of defense's authority; DIA worked for the DCI, we were told. My government colleagues (and I) smothered smiles and explained curtly that this attitude was unacceptable. But we also knew it had become commonplace: Defense intelligence agencies claim to work for either the secretary of defense or the DCI/DNI when it supports the real goal of maintaining maximum institutional autonomy. To make sure that DIA did not again try

---

180   DIA website on diversity and inclusion, https://www.intelligencecareers.gov/dia/diadiversity.html.

to evade Pentagon guidance on this issue, we drafted a formal policy document that ordered DIA to comply with the remedy we recommended. The deputy secretary of defense signed the document. DIA did in fact comply.

DIA's adherence to traditional goals and values led former DCIA Michael Hayden, a retired US Air Force four-star general who also headed the NSA, to refer to DIA as a "blue collar" agency.[181] This was not a snub, apparently, but rather was a reference to the fact that although it plays intra-IC bureaucratic politics like other agencies, DIA focuses on Pentagon decision-makers and "warfighters" as its primary intelligence consumers.[182] It does foundational work assembling information on foreign military establishments but little engages senior civilian Washington political officials, including the president. DIA people therefore have little reason to be concerned about non-Defense policy issues of any administration, including Trump's.

Unlike former CIA personnel, few DIA alumni write of their experiences or about intelligence issues generally. None "resigned in protest" of Trump or became a television talking head in the Trump years. None wrote a book or an op-ed article complaining about Trump. One prominent alumnus, former director Lieutenant General Michael Flynn (2012-2014), is one of the few senior intelligence officers who have spoken positively about Trump. Flynn also (in)famously led chants of "lock her up" at the 2016 Republican national convention, referring to the controversy surrounding Hillary Clinton's use of personal email servers for official business when she was secretary of state. But, unlike many of the anti-Trump activist formers, Flynn did not invoke his intelligence credentials to rationalize his political activism.

---

181   Hayden, *Assault on Intelligence*, 63.
182   Others are more critical. See Nolan, "Information Sharing and Collaboration in the United States Intelligence Community," 74-75.

Flynn was relieved of command at DIA in August 2014, short of the end of his normal three-year tour, by DNI Clapper and Under Secretary of Defense for Intelligence Michael Vickers, evidently over a dispute about DIA's collection activities.[183] Flynn was energetic but not very effective at DIA and was not well regarded by DIA people when he was director; he was even more unpopular with many current and former intelligence officers elsewhere in the IC, especially at CIA, during and after his directorship at DIA.[184] Leakers took revenge on Flynn in 2016 (discussed below) and the FBI targeted him over his discussions with the Russian ambassador to Washington in late 2016, leading to a confession of lying to the FBI that Flynn later recanted. Trump pardoned him in late 2020.[185] Although remaining politically active, he still does not claim that his intelligence career entitles him to domestic political opinions. He therefore is mentioned infrequently in this book.

National Security Agency

The NSA is a technical collection agency. Many of its personnel are engineers, mathematicians, computer specialists, and linguists. NSA analysts focus fairly narrowly on the meaning of NSA-collected information. By presidential order they do not perform all-source analysis.[186] But NSA analysts often help write and more commonly coordinate NIE drafts because of

---

183   Greg Miller and Adam Goldman, "Head of Pentagon intelligence agency forced out, officials say, *Washington Post*, April 30, 2014, https://www.washingtonpost.com/world/national-security/head-of-pentagon-intelligence-agency-forced-out-officials-say/2014/04/30/ec15a366-d09d-11e3-9e25-188ebe1fa93b_story.html.

184   Personal experience of author at National Intelligence University, which then was located at DIA headquarters.

185   Marty Lederman, "Understanding the Michael Flynn Case: Separating the Wheat from the Chaff, and the Proper from the Improper," *Just Security*, May 20, 2020, https://www.justsecurity.org/70431/understanding-the-michael-flynn-case-separating-the-wheat-from-the-chaff-and-the-proper-from-the-improper/.

186   Executive Order 12333.

the frequently major role NSA plays in collection on important issues. Even less so than DIA analysts, NSA analysts tend not to focus on intelligence related to political controversies in Washington.

Dan Gressang, who retired from NSA in 2018, described the political leanings of NSA personnel:

> [NSA] employees, and most employees of other agencies I had the opportunity to interact with, represented the gamut of political orientation. I know Republicans, Democrats, and Independents, liberals and conservatives, and largely apolitical types in the Intelligence Community. As a group, however, most of those I interacted with tended to be middle of the road politically, although with the 2016 campaign and subsequent election of Donald Trump, that seemed to drift a bit toward the liberal end of the spectrum. Politics, however, was never a major concern for those I know, as mission and mission fulfillment was of greater concern. Reaction to campaigns and policies was largely a rational approach of if-then mission consideration (e.g. how will this affect the Agency's ability to do X? Will we be able to continue Y? If the president does this, what would we need to do to do Z?).[187]

NSA's director since 2018 has been Army General Paul Nakasone, who is dual-hatted as commander of US Cyber Command, a war-fighting command. He runs NSA as the "combat support agency" that, by Defense Department directive, it is. Like his predecessors, he appears not to be particularly

---

187   Dan Gressang email to author, July 28, 2019.

focused on domestically important political issues. Said a former subordinate of Nakasone:

> "He's 100 percent warfighter-centric. He understands warfighter needs because he's been on the sharp end. Most intel folks haven't. When you have it changes your perspective."[188]

These accounts largely explain the near absence of NSA people among the IC's prominent anti-Trump activists.

National Geospatial-Intelligence Agency

Like NSA, NGA is technically focused. But unlike NSA, NGA is an analytic organization, conducting imagery and geospatial analyses based primarily on evaluations of satellite imagery. It does not do broadly-focused all-source analysis. As a combat support agency, it supports military units but also assists other IC agencies by providing geospatial intelligence that complements other varieties of collection and analysis. NGA maintains support cells at military combatant commands and other IC agencies, which have reputations for being very helpful.[189] While imagery-based analysis often complements other forms of analysis, it is a primary form of analysis on a relatively narrow set of topics, which generally do not include issues of domestic political importance. Hence, NGA is an unusually cooperative, non-confrontational government agency. Perhaps even more so than DIA and NSA personnel, NGA personnel tend to avoid political controversies.

---

188   Andy Greenberg, "The Next NSA Chief Is More Used to Cyberwar than Spy Games," *Wired*, April 3, 2018, https://www.wired.com/story/paul-nakasone-nsa-cyber-command/.

189   NGA website, https://www.nga.mil/ProductsServices/Pages/default.aspx.

NGA people were absent from the crowd of anti-Trump formers until 2020, when Robert Cardillo, a civilian who was director from 2014 to 2019, joined the group.[190] In mid-2020 he co-authored an anti-Trump op-ed in the *Washington Post* with Michael Hayden and Michael Leiter, a former director of NCTC, who both had previously written anti-Trump op-eds.[191] It is not clear what, if any, effects Cardillo's political views had on his management of NGA.

Cardillo's successor, Navy Vice Admiral Robert Sharp, in May 2020 issued a conventional mission statement which, like those of DIA and NSA, has little politically meaningful content.[192] This mission statement does not refer to politically sensitive personnel management policies, unlike recent such ODNI and CIA statements.[193] Evidently Sharp, like other military commanders of intelligence agencies, worked to keep NGA apolitical. Vice Admiral Frank Whitworth succeeded Sharp in 2022.

THE IMPACT OF WORLDVIEWS AND BUREAUCRATIC INTERESTS ON ESTIMATES AND POLICY

Intelligence officers and intelligence agencies have worldviews that shape their personal and group identities and their identification of intelligence challenges, help them select appropriate analytical methods, and influence their concepts of effective intelligence analysis and even of truth. The purposeful

---

190   Most NGA directors have been active duty military officers. Cardillo was Clapper's Deputy Director of National Intelligence for Intelligence Integration (2010-2014) and before that was a senior DIA career analyst.

191   Michael Leiter, Michael Hayden, and Robert Cardillo, "We've briefed many presidents. Uncertainty comes with the job." *Washington Post*, July 7, 2020, https://www.washingtonpost.com/opinions/2020/07/06/weve-briefed-many-presidents-uncertainty-comes-with-job/.

192   NGA website, https://www.nga.mil/MediaRoom/PressReleases/Pages/intent.aspx.

193   NGA website, https://www.nga.mil/ProductsServices/Pages/default.aspx.

reengineering of the organizational cultures of some IC agencies in recent years changed their collective worldviews. This section helps set the stage for discussion of the effects of the worldview changes and politicization of recent years, discussed in chapters 6 and 7, by discussing the nature and effects of agencies' historical organizational cultures.

To make the point glaringly, there is little doubt that Adolf Hitler, Josef Stalin, Mother Teresa, and Osama bin Laden did not see the world the same way. Their ideological and theological beliefs shaped how they saw the world and how they assessed events in it. Their beliefs influenced their concepts of reality and of truth, which affected decisions they made. Worldviews also affect intelligence analysts, frequently subconsciously, and they sometimes generate analytical errors. Because worldviews are largely products of culture, knowing IC agencies' organizational cultures, and trends in their evolution, can help observers understand how the institutional engineering efforts of recent years may have affected analytical biases.

American intelligence officers are well aware that IC agencies have reputations for collective, institutional biases, while typically being sure they are not themselves biased. For example, the relatively liberal collective political orientations of CIA and State/INR often lead them to see other countries as less potentially or actually threatening than Defense agencies do, and to be less eager to issue threat warning messages. While bureaucratic interests sometimes lead to exaggerated Defense perceptions of adversaries' capabilities and intentions, beliefs about their missions also influence military intelligence analyses. Military personnel who see their role as protecting the nation against external physical threats tend to make worst case assumptions about actual and potential adversaries, something that both biases their analyses and can be self-defeating by encouraging security dilemma situations, needless or excessive spending, and the "cry wolf syndrome"—the situation in which consumers disappointed by forecasts that turn out to be wrong view intelligence as less credible and therefore ignore future, accurate warnings.[194]

These worldview-generated perspectives appear in the following fake "footnote" to a NIE, written out of boredom during one of the lengthy coordination meetings of the 1976 version of the annual estimate on Soviet strategic programs and Soviet strategic goals (designated NIE 11-3/8) by a CIA representative to the coordination process, military analyst Boyd S.[195] The humor to intelligence insiders is its application of internally widely held, stereotypical worldviews and parochial interests of IC agencies to an NIE footnote format—differences that also should be obvious to casual lay readers. These general perspectives have not changed much since Boyd wrote, a testament to the enduring nature of the organizational cultures, once established, of insular intelligence bureaucracies:

> The State Department, Bureau of Intelligence and Research believes the Soviet Union has no ability to take over the world and wouldn't even if they could. The Central Intelligence Agency believes that the Soviet Union might want to take over the world if it could, but currently lacks the capability to do so. The Defense Intelligence Agency and the Assistant Chief of Staff for Intelligence, US Army believe the Soviet

---

194   For example, Betts, "Analysis, War, and Decision," 65-66, 74-75, 88; Handel, "Intelligence and the Problem of Strategic Surprise," 247-248; Herman, "Intelligence and the assessment of military capabilities," 773-782; Kent, "A Crucial Estimate Relived," 116; Hutchings, "Introduction," 12, 15.

195   The NIE "footnote" was literally a footnote in NIEs in which agencies expressed opinions dissenting from the main text of the estimates. NIE formats now are different, meaning the "footnote" is less important.

Union is actively building the weapons systems that will allow it to take over the world in the near future. The Director of Naval Intelligence believes the debate over Soviet intentions to take over the world is distracting the community from more important issues like their intention to build a blue water navy and large-deck aircraft carriers. The National Security Agency cannot reveal what it knows about Soviet leadership intentions because it would endanger sensitive sources and methods. Finally, the Assistant Chief of Staff for Intelligence, US Air Force believes that the Soviet Union already has taken over the world and is running the US Intelligence Community.[196]

More seriously, Luke Benjamin Wells has argued that American concepts of the Soviet threat in the 1950s led to assumptions about Soviet intentions that contributed to the "bomber gap" controversy of the late 1950s in the United States while British intelligence, working from different assumptions based on different worldviews but using virtually the same, shared intelligence information, reached a much more accurate and benign assessment than did US intelligence: the Soviets did not then have a bomber force that significantly threatened the West.[197] Consistent with Boyd's fictional footnote, the Defense agencies, CIA, and INR still frequently differ on such issues based on perceived missions, parochial interests, organizational cultures, and worldviews. While sometimes biases are obvious, more commonly, as in Wells' account, they are hard to spot until later—if ever.

---

196   Thanks to David Bush for this joke. Bush email to author, June 20, 2020.
197   Wells, "The 'bomber gap'," 979-981.

Mistaken collective perspectives periodically have caused US intelligence to make other appreciable analytic errors. For example, Melanie Brand described how US intelligence analysts developed a "mindset" that the Soviets and their Warsaw Pact allies would not crush the communist liberalization in Czechoslovakia, known as the "Prague Spring," leading to a major warning failure when the invasion occurred in August 1968.[198] Once cognitive closure occurred, Brand argued, new information was not given the weight it deserved. Cynthia Grabo, a career DIA warning analyst who worked the Czechoslovakia case, generally agreed with Brand's assessment of the failure, although she used different terms.[199] Grabo was so frustrated by the experience that she wrote a now-classic book on strategic warning, which she hoped would help prevent such failures in the future.[200]

DCI William Colby (1973-1976) saw a worldview, or what he like Grabo and others called a collective "mindset," in the Board of National Estimates, which damaged its performance so badly that he abolished the Board in 1973. Colby explained:

> I had sensed an ivory-tower mentality in the Board; its composition had tended to shift to a high proportion of senior analysts who had spent most of their careers at [CIA] and who had developed a "mindset" about a number of the issues in opposition to the views of the Pentagon and because of the way [President Richard] Nixon and [National Security Advisor Henry] Kissinger had excluded them from the White House's

---

198 Brand, "Mind Games."
199 Grabo, *Handbook of Warning Intelligence*; Grabo, "Soviet Deception in the Czechoslovak Crisis."
200 Grabo, *Handbook of Warning Intelligence.*

more sensitive international dealings… Thus, I created the positions of National Intelligence Officers.[201]

Former chairmen of the NIC repeatedly saw the presence, and effects, of biases in general, some of which were caused by worldviews, and sought to diversify their staff members intellectually as a counter. For example, Robert Hutchings noted that in 2003 he was able to recruit an excellent group of NIOs with different perspectives who "helped the NIC avoid the grooved thinking that often afflicts organizational cultures."[202] In the 1990s, roughly half of NIOs were retired senior State Department officials, senior military officers, and academics. The rest were career intelligence officers. But in January 2017, due to changing security procedures and NIO selection criteria, former C/NIC Greg Treverton (2014-2017) reported that only two of his seventeen NIOs were outsiders.[203] The risk of bias driven by organizational worldviews had risen. Treverton reported that he recurrently encountered biases in his efforts to help the Obama administration forge policies regarding Afghanistan and Syria. Said Treverton:

> Whether intelligence should have foreseen Russia's move into Crimea, then Ukraine, continued to hang over us, as we tried to anticipate Russian behavior in Syria. I was impressed, as always, by the challenge posed by mindsets. We were aware by the late spring of 2015 that Russia was likely to up the ante in Syria. But we expected more of the same, more weapons, more aid.

---

201   Colby and Forbach, *Honorable Men*, 351, 353.
202   Hutchings, "America at War," 108.
203   Treverton, "From Afghanistan to Trump: 2014-2017," 190.

> We did not anticipate—a mind-set again—a significant movement of Russia's forces into Syria.[204]

Since the 1990s, and especially after 2001, senior CIA officers repeatedly have been accused of a different kind of mindset—risk aversion as a way of deflecting potential damage to the agency and to themselves.[205] This evidently sometimes entailed avoiding antagonizing the White House even in the Trump years.[206]

Blatant parochialism by intelligence agencies sometimes combines with worldview-generated biases. While military services most frequently display this trait, former C/NIC Joseph Nye provided a good example of a non-Defense agency doing the same thing. In the early 1990s, an NIE on narcotics drafted by the Drug Enforcement Administration (DEA) contained impressive data on the quantities of drugs the DEA had seized, but no information about retail drug prices in American cities, which Nye saw as a much better measure of the effectiveness of law enforcement agencies in eliminating illegal narcotics from American society.[207] Per basic economic logic, low street prices would indicate ready availability of drugs, high prices that drugs were scarce. DEA and other participating agencies resisted, however, evidently understanding that including price data in the NIE would undercut their claims of operational effectiveness. Nye persisted, the draft was reworked several times, and price data were included in the final estimate. More generally, even when analytical objectivity and integrity are held to high standards, managers want to make themselves look good for organizational and personal reasons.[208]

---

204   Ibid., 181.
205   For example, London, *The Recruiter*, 292-294; Baer *The Fourth Man*, 245.
206   London, *The Recruiter*, 294.
207   Nye, "Estimating Intelligence After the Cold War, 1993-1994," 37.
208   Gentry, "Managers of Analysts."

Said a retired NSA careerist about CIA and NSA, "managers in both agencies are willing to frame analyses and positions to ensure favorable consideration of programs and budget allocations."[209]

Robert Jervis, who learned a great deal about intelligence while consulting for the CIA and who was an expert on psychological aspects of foreign policy decision-making, argued that political orientations are biases that always influence analysis:

> *With some reason, [Republicans] see intelligence analysts as predominantly liberals.* Their suspicions that intelligence has sought to thwart and embarrass the administration are *usually* false, but to the extent that the worldviews of most intelligence officers are different from those of the *Republicans*, the latter *are justified in being skeptical of IC analysis on broad issues.* For their part, intelligence analysts, like everyone else, underestimate the degree to which their own interpretations of specific bits of evidence are *colored by their general predispositions* and so consider the leaders' rejection of their views closed-minded and ideological. Although not all people are equally driven by their theories about the world, there is a *degree of legitimacy to the leaders' position that members of the IC often fail to grasp.* President Ronald Reagan and his colleagues, including DCI Bill Casey, probably were right to believe that the IC's assessments that the Soviet Union was not supporting terrorism and was not vulnerable to economic pressures were more a *product of the IC's liberal leanings than of the evidence.* They therefore felt justified in ignoring the IC when

---

209   Personal communication, July 2019.

they did not put pressure on it, which in turn led to charges of politicization (emphasis added).[210]

Jervis's observations are relevant to this book in several respects. First, as a self-described liberal[211] and a keen observer, he long has seen Democratic biases in the serving CIA workforce and explained how worldviews color intelligence analyses even when analysts and managers try to be objective. Collective worldviews at CIA seem to have moved leftward in aggregate since he wrote, suggesting the bias may now be more pronounced.

Second, Jervis argued plausibly that political biases reflect worldviews that are hard to see and may not be apparent to analysts and managers once they have become embedded in organizational cultures. And he confirmed that they cause intelligence failures. Even sub-units of analytic offices sometimes develop organizational positions on issues that they are loath to review or reconsider, leading to costly analytic errors. For example, in late 1967 CIA analyst Joseph Hovey, working in Saigon, accurately forecast the purpose and consequences of what we now call the Tet Offensive of January-February 1968, but CIA analysts working Vietnam issues at headquarters from a different collective viewpoint rejected Hovey's analysis.[212] And, the CIA's Office of Near East and South Asia (NESA), which had a good reputation within CIA in the 1980s for the quality of its analyses, concluded in 1990 that Iraq's squabble with Kuwait was over money and that a military attack on Kuwait was unlikely.[213] The result in each case was an appreciable intelligence failure in the form of a surprise military attack.

---

210   Jervis, "Why Intelligence and Policymakers Clash," 199-200.
211   Jervis, *Why Intelligence Fails*, 8, 12.
212   Wirtz, *The Tet Offensive*, 172-179.
213   Brennan, *Undaunted*, 83.

Third, the now-public Democratic leanings of some former senior officials suggest that they communicated such views during their time at the CIA and NIC, that they appreciated similar political perspectives when reviewing articles for publication, and that they embedded such judgments in their assessments of the analytic abilities of employees and managers while serving on promotion boards. It is well established that the ability to get one's papers through the review process smoothly is key to promotion success.[214] Offering versions of "truth" congruent with reviewers' beliefs can be a good way to do so. Analysts keenly observe senior managers' preferences on many subjects; after all, they are paid to study people and make judgments about their attitudes. Some even have created "dictionaries" of reviewers' personal linguistic preferences, which sometimes reveal political views.[215] Now that some former leaders have revealed their political views, analysts can reasonably assume that the leaders these people chose to succeed them share their general perspectives, providing a continuing guide for appropriate analytic perspectives in the form of bureaucratic incentives.

In addition, while observers of US intelligence long have noted such institutional biases, the Marxian post-modern and "critical" theoretical perspectives emphasize the importance of language and power on the derivation of collective perspectives. Post-modern philosophers such as Michel Foucault distinguish analytic from ideological truth, and Marxian "critical" theorists similarly have developed "theories" labeled as truth that are actually (often) overtly designed to further Marxist ideological agendas. Critical theory holds that there is no such thing as objective truth (except its own), that reality is socially constructed,

---

214 Gentry, "Managers of Analysts."
215 Firehock et al., "Negotiating the Review Process."

and that language shapes perceptions of reality. It is, according to critical theorists, both acceptable and desirable to reframe, lie about, or simply make up history and current events to help achieve political goals.

In the United States critical theory penetrated universities massively in the 1990s and later and produced widely accepted sub-variants, including critical legal studies and critical race theory (CRT), which influenced many students, radicalizing some, and is clearly an influence on the "diversity and inclusion," and especially the later "diversity, equity, and inclusion" (DEI) programs of the Democratic Party.[216] Marxists designed "critical pedagogy" in the 1980s to teach teachers how to indoctrinate their students on such perspectives.[217] As an ideology, CRT has obviously informed President Obama's and President Biden's personnel policies. One of Biden's first executive orders undid a belated Trump EO on race training in the federal government and Trump's 1776 Commission, which was a rejoinder to the *New York Times*'s 1619 Project, thereby satisfying demands of the Marxian leaders of the Black Lives Matter movement.[218] CRT clearly influences the political views of many intelligence officers, especially younger ones. The extent to which these ideological leanings affect analysis is not yet clear.

Critical theory has been applied to some degree to thinking specifically about intelligence issues. For example, Gunilla Eriksson of the Swedish Defence University argued that Swedish intelligence is affected by a collective perspective, or worldview, that is realist in nature and defines "what ... intelligence analysis holds as being important objects of knowledge."[219] But analysts,

---

216   For example, Bean, "Rhetorical and Critical/Cultural Intelligence Studies."
217   For example, Darder et al., *The Critical Pedagogy Reader*.
218   Gonzales, *BLM*, 78, 192-193.
219   Eriksson, "A theoretical reframing of the intelligence–policy relation," 555.

she argued, do not recognize that realism is the frame of organizational analysis.[220] She added:

> Hence, the assumptions underlying the intelligence analysis are not argued, discussed or defined; rather they might be conceived as complying with an established way of thought – a tradition of conceptualizing. This underlying and immanent worldview guides the choice of relevant actors and problems, and functions as a frame of interpretation. The intelligence worldview defines how the intelligence service conceptualizes its representation and defines the problem horizon and interpretative horizon. In short, this worldview affects which information is sought, selected and used and influences all interpretations, thereby structuring and defining the meaning of the objects of knowledge in the intelligence discourse.

> Rather than an explicit reliance on a defined worldview, what matters is the emphasis on seeking consistency and continuity within the established 'style of thought'. The drive for continuity and consistency in the intelligence–knowledge discourse dominates the analytical distinction between assumptions, arguments and conclusions. The arguments and facts used for substantiating the analysis are not distinctly separated from assumptions and valuations. Hence, the intelligence knowledge discourse suggests a reproducing of knowledge rather than a creation of new insights. That is, in intelligence estimates, the assessments and conclusions

---

220   Ibid.

are substantiated through statements. These statements are partly argued using facts and factual underpinnings, and partly argued using assumptions and valuations articulated as facts. The former are argued according [sic] an expected line of reasoning based on the intelligence worldview.[221]

Intelligence operators frequently try to construct or alter perceived realities in ways favorable to them through disinformation or the more nuanced technique of "framing"—selectively using facts (and sometimes disinformation) to alter perceptions of issues, states, and personalities—and truth.[222] Philosophers, journalists, and intelligence officers also long have known that even blatant lies, repeated often enough, frequently morph into perceived truths. The battle over definitions of truth and possession of it in the intelligence-Trump conflict was another case of this general phenomenon.

The literature on constructivism in political science also offers insights about ways to evaluate the IC's cultures. The constructivist school argues that reality is "socially constructed" and that choices about the use of language can significantly affect meaning—an insight intelligence people who conduct information operations long have known.[223] Constructivists also argue that organizational cultures produce *constituent* norms—which help form and specify personal and organizational identities—and *regulative* norms—which identify types of appropriate and inappropriate

---

221   Ibid., 555-556.
222   Lillbacka, "Realism, Constructivism, and Intelligence Analysis."
223   Rid, *Active Measures*.

behavior. Other people have made similar points.[224] As discussed in chapter 3, anti-Trump political activism at CIA and ODNI, especially, reflected the evolution of both types of norms.

PRESIDENTS' FREQUENTLY NEGATIVE VIEWS OF INTELLIGENCE

Presidents also have mindsets and biases, and they often do not appreciate different ones in their intelligence officers. Ignorance of the actual workings of intelligence also has given presidents excessive expectations, disappointments when expectations were unfulfilled, and unwarranted suspicions. These factors, and the sheer difficulty of intelligence work, has led to recurrent presidential unhappiness with the performance of intelligence, sometimes for good reasons, sometimes not. Presidents periodically have been pointedly critical of intelligence, especially the CIA, and they sometimes were more hostile to the IC than President Trump was. Former DCI Robert Gates, who worked for eight presidents, reported that all of them occasionally disagreed with their advisors, including intelligence advisors, ignored their advice, and acted on their own beliefs.[225] Gates added that there is "usually an undercurrent of discord (and sometimes open conflict)" between the White House on the one hand and the departments and agencies of government on the other.[226] Former Principal Deputy DNI Sue Gordon similarly said that all five of the presidents she briefed sometimes did not like the briefings they received; Trump was just more

---

224 Ford, "The US government's experience with intelligence analysis," 51; Hastedt, "The Politics of Intelligence and the Politicization of Intelligence: The American Experience," 9; Kahana, "Early warning versus concept," 81-104.

225 Gates, *Exercise of Power*, 61.

226 Ibid., 62.

public about his dislikes than the others.[227] Gates's and Gordon's perspectives and the anecdotes that follow are relevant to assessments of IC persons' frequent complaints about Trump's allegedly uniquely unfair critiques of, and disrespect for, IC agencies, including his purported "assault on intelligence."

Presidents and lesser officials often enter office with limited knowledge of the strengths, weaknesses, and limitations of intelligence, and they often do not have time or inclination to seriously study intelligence when in office. Hence, intelligence officers know that one of their most important responsibilities is to educate incoming senior officials, especially the president, about intelligence.[228] This is a never-ending task given the speed with which policy-makers rotate into and out of Washington. Put differently, intelligence officers traditionally have understood and accepted that new (and not-so-new) presidents often have incomplete or jaundiced views of intelligence and have seen working through these challenges as a core responsibility of intelligence officers, not presidents.

All presidents have learned, at varying speeds and to different degrees, to accept, trust, and use intelligence. Knowledgeable observers generally regard Presidents Eisenhower, George H.W. Bush, and George W. Bush as particularly well-informed and appreciative consumers of intelligence. Eisenhower used intelligence extensively during his military career and was an avid user and supporter of intelligence as president; he was instrumental in supporting the development of the U-2 spy plane and

---

227   David Welna, "Exclusive: After Quitting Last Year, Senior U.S. Intelligence Official Now Talks," *NPR*, August 13, 2020, https://www.npr.org/2020/08/13/902345240/exclusive-after-quitting-last-year-senior-u-s-intelligence-official-now-talks.

228   For example, Helgerson, *Getting to Know the President*; Wilder, "An Educated Consumer."

reconnaissance satellites, for example.[229] The first President Bush is the only president to have served as DCI or DNI (for about a year in 1976-1977) and as president unsurprisingly was both knowledgeable about, and appreciative of, the intelligence support he received.[230] He is widely thought to have encouraged his son to trust and use intelligence, and George W. Bush is generally regarded as having been a strong supporter of intelligence despite IC-White House tensions over Iraq policy and even though he was unhappy with a 2007 NIE on the status of Iran's nuclear weapons program.[231] Also unhappy that the contents of his *PDB* briefings quickly appeared in the *New York Times*, Bush reportedly once snapped at a *PDB* briefer:

> Since whatever you tell me in the PDB is in the *New York Times* two or three days later, why don't we just cut out this middle stage? Just give it directly to the *Times* and I'll find out about it my morning press briefing.[232]

Other presidents were more skeptical, hostile, or sharply critical of intelligence at various times, sometimes making charges that in retrospect are, and often then were known to be, flatly incorrect. Skepticism of intelligence frequently led to modest use of intelligence in formulating presidential policies.[233]

Some presidents also have demanded personal loyalty from intelligence officers. For example, President Johnson became quite unhappy with DCI John McCone, whom he inherited from President Kennedy, when McCone told him in 1964 that CIA

---

229 Andrew, *For the President's Eyes Only*, 199-256.

230 Ibid., 503-536; Priess, *The President's Book of Secrets*.

231 Helgerson, *Getting to Know the President*; Warner, "The Use and Abuse of Intelligence in the Public Square."

232 Draper, *Dead Certain*, 262.

233 Immerman, "Intelligence and Strategy."

analysts thought the war Johnson was managing in Vietnam was going poorly and was unlikely to get better. Wanting good news, he lost confidence in McCone and excluded him from White House meetings, leading McCone to resign in early 1965. Johnson then named an old friend from Texas, retired Navy Vice Admiral William Raborn, to replace him. Raborn had no intelligence background and by most accounts was among the least effective DCIs. He resigned in June 1966 after fourteen months on the job.[234] Former national security advisor John Bolton, who reported that Trump also valued loyalty, wrote that Trump once quoted President Johnson as allegedly saying of an aide:

> I want real loyalty. I want him to kiss my ass in Macy's window at high noon and tell me it smells like roses.[235]

Former DCI Helms quoted Johnson as stating his view of intelligence in a similarly earthy way at a White House dinner:

> Let me tell you about these intelligence guys. When I was growing up in Texas, we had a cow named Bessie. I'd go out early and milk her. I'd get her in the stanchion, seat myself and squeeze out a pail of fresh milk. One day I'd worked hard and gotten a full pail of milk, but I wasn't paying attention, and old Bessie swung her shit-smeared tail through the bucket of milk. Now, you know that's what these intelligence guys do. You work hard and get a good program or policy going, and they swing a shit-smeared tail through it.[236]

Richard Nixon probably was the president most consistently

---

234 Andrew, *For the President's Eyes Only*, 323-327.
235 Bolton, *The Room Where It Happened*, 7.
236 Ibid., 323.

critical of US intelligence, and especially of the CIA. Nixon certainly but evidently erroneously believed the CIA had worked to aid Senator Kennedy in the presidential election campaign of 1960, but he more accurately distrusted CIA for being composed of Ivy League liberals and the "Georgetown set" who did not like him personally, did not like his policies, and whose analyses frequently were biased or just not very good. The latter point is understandable given that Nixon and his national security advisor, Henry Kissinger, were among the most knowledgeable foreign policy decision-makers in American history. Nixon (in)famously wondered aloud within the White House, not publicly, what "those clowns out at Langley" were doing when they failed to warn him of the fall of the Sihanouk government in Cambodia in 1970.[237] The quip still is frequently cited.

Governor Jimmy Carter ran on an anti-CIA platform in his 1976 presidential campaign, erroneously charging that the CIA killed President Salvador Allende of Chile in 1973—a tale that Soviet KGB disinformation specialists successfully peddled globally.[238] Unusually naïve for a president, only late in his term did he discover that the Soviets really were not his friends. He then authorized some covert actions against the USSR, especially after their invasion of Afghanistan, something he had eschewed earlier. Carter's grasp of world affairs and intelligence was so obviously weak that Soviet leader Leonid Brezhnev and KGB chief Yuri Andropov believed the Soviet Union could manipulate him, and used disinformation to do so repeatedly, including on arms control issues such as negotiations over deployments of intermediate range nuclear weapons in Europe.[239] In addition, Andropov in the early 1970s used disinformation to make Romanian President Nicolae Ceaușescu appear to Westerners to be an "independent"

---

237 Jeffreys-Jones, *The CIA and American Democracy*, 177.
238 Gustafson and Andrew, "The Other Hidden Hand," 407-421.
239 Rid, *Active Measures*, 257-259; Pacepa and Rychlak, *Disinformation*, 325.

communist leader in Eastern Europe, thereby weakening accurate charges that the Soviets ran a monolithic empire from Moscow.[240] By 1978, this effort had also fooled Carter, and the Soviets gave Ceaușescu the task of convincing Carter that the United States should establish diplomatic relations with one of Moscow's favorite revolutionaries, Yasser Arafat.[241] Immediately after Carter kissed Ceaușescu in the Oval Office in April 1978, Ceaușescu splashed alcohol on his face and called the one-time peanut farmer Carter "Peanut-head" in disgust.[242] But Ceaușescu accomplished his mission. On May 1, 1978 the Palestine Information Office opened in Washington. Trump's domestic critics would accuse him, with considerably less reason and with no comparisons to Carter, of being manipulated by the Russians.

Perhaps the presidential episode most comparable to Trump's derisive comments about the IC was President Clinton's attack on the 1993 NIE on Haiti, briefly mentioned above. He quickly injected domestic politics into his relationship with the IC by bowing to pressure from the Congressional Black Caucus, whose members were outraged that the NIE contained an uncomplimentary assessment of former Haitian President Jean-Bertrand Aristide. In response, over many months the White House orchestrated a highly critical public relations campaign against the NIE and CIA as a whole, in which Clinton and Vice President Al Gore participated significantly. Clinton repeatedly, pointedly charged that CIA's collection was biased and its analysts were racist and incompetent. Publicly available evidence since suggests that the NIE was in fact generally accurate. Clinton never acknowledged that he was wrong. His attacks were notable for another reason;

---

240   Pacepa and Rychlak, *Disinformation*, 298; Golitsyn, *New Lies For Old*, 183-194.
241   Pacepa and Rychlak, *Disinformation*, 325-326.
242   Ibid., 298. Pacepa witnessed this event.

he spoke critically of the CIA as the NIE's author, not the IC as a whole, showing his ignorance of intelligence processes.[243] Since the early 1970s NIEs have been products of the IC as a whole, not the CIA.

Clinton, focused mainly on domestic matters, initially cared so little about intelligence that his first DCI, James Woolsey, quit in 1995 after chronically finding it hard to get time on Clinton's calendar.[244] It was not so much that Woolsey had a bad relationship with Clinton as that he had no relationship with the president worth mentioning. After a small plane landed on the White House lawn without permission in September 1994, wags in Washington joked that the pilot was Woolsey trying to get in to see the president.[245] Woolsey resigned soon thereafter. Trump never cut off his DCIAs or *PDB* briefers.

Later, a scandal tainted CIA operatives who had ties to Guatemalan military officers who allegedly killed (in 1992 or 1993) a captured communist guerilla whose wife, Jennifer Harbury, was an American lawyer and human rights activist with connections to members of Congress. In response to Harbury's complaints, Clinton and DCI John Deutch (1995-1996) ordered CIA officers to have nothing to do with "bad" people, crippling human intelligence collection for a time and leading operations officers who worried that the Clinton administration later would charge them with crimes for performing missions they had been authorized to

---

243 David Lauter, "Clinton Meets With Aristide, Haiti Premier," *Los Angeles Times*, December 7, 1993, http://articles.latimes.com/1993-12-07/news/mn-64873_1_aristide-clinton-haiti; Prados, *Safe for Democracy*, 595; Omestad, "Psychology and the CIA," 104-122; author's personal discussion with a lawyer doing public relations work in support of Aristide for the Congressional Black Caucus.

244 Jeffreys-Jones, *The CIA & American Democracy*, 146-147.

245 Personal experience. See also Brennan, *Undaunted*, 104.

conduct to buy insurance against potential legal defense fees.[246] Their worries centered initially on Clinton and the anti-CIA attitudes of some Congressional Democrats, but a senior intelligence officer told me in 2015 that he still bought such insurance. Such concerns changed dramatically in 2016 when many CIA officers emerged as political allies in the Democrats' fight against Trump.

President Obama, while politically and personally attractive to some in the IC, was sometimes very critical of intelligence. Hayden believed Obama was "always a bit distant" and "wasn't above a little hanging the IC out to dry for personal political cover," such as when he publicly defended his inaction against the Islamic State by claiming the IC had underestimated the movement.[247] According to Obama's first secretary of defense, Robert Gates, Obama and his staff regularly were at odds with the national security establishment as a whole, including the State and Defense Departments, the chairman of the Joint Chiefs of Staff, the DNI, and the CIA.[248]

Of these presidents only two tried to significantly change the inner workings of the IC—Nixon and Obama. Nixon's failed effort was the short tenure of DCI Schlesinger, which CIA people bitterly opposed. Schlesinger left few influences on the agency. In sharp contrast, many CIA officers, especially, embraced Obama and his policies warmly, particularly the political agenda embedded in his 2011 executive order on "diversity and inclusion" and its implementation in practice. His impact was large and enduring.

---

246   R. Jeffrey Smith, "Worried CIA Officers Buy Legal Insurance," *Washington Post*, September 11, 2006, http://www.washingtonpost.com/wp-dyn/content/article/2006/09/10/AR2006091001286.html; Shane Scott, "In Legal Cases, C.I.A. Officers Turn to Insurer," *New York Times*, January 20, 2008, http://www.nytimes.com/2008/01/20/washington/20lawyers.html?_r=0, accessed 28 February 2015; Guy Dinmore, "CIA agents 'refused to operate' at secret jails," *Financial Times*, September 21, 2006.

247   Hayden, *Assault on Intelligence*, 34.

248   Gates, *Exercise of Power*, 306.

PUTTING THE PIECES TOGETHER

The organizational histories and cultures noted in this chapter help explain the overt political activism by intelligence officers against Trump in 2016. In summary, organizational cultures shape persons' behavior and intelligence services' collective attitudes to a large degree. The early mission-oriented emphasis on secrecy at CIA gradually changed as the agency learned to actively defend and advance its interests. The various IC agency cultures differ, based on missions and the actions of strong leaders of agencies; the FBI's Hoover left arguably the largest personal impact on any agency. Leaders can, and do, occasionally try to shift organizational cultures; effects of these usually are marginal but can be significant when pushed by aggressive leaders. External events affect intelligence agencies, but internal change usually occurs slowly. Change can, however, be accelerated or thwarted by reasons of leadership emphasis, organizational interests, or societal change. The next chapter discusses ways the general "model" suggested here developed in actual detail in recent years, and how they produced the specific causes of the outburst of 2016.

3

HOW THE CURRENT SITUATION DEVELOPED

SEVERAL FACTORS CONTRIBUTED to a significant shift in the traditional organizational cultures and worldviews of some IC agencies, described in chapter 2, which by 2016 were incompatible with the political views of candidate and then President Trump, leading directly to the outburst of political activism against him. Some of these changes reflected evolutionary societal developments, some were unintended consequences of actions taken for other purposes. But the most important factors were products of politically-motivated policies, meaning the partisanship, if not the specific charges hurled at Trump, were the result of purposeful re-engineering of the federal workforce and its culture. Although they started in the 1990s and were still developing during the George W. Bush administration (2001-2009), President Barack Obama (2009-2017) and his appointees made and institutionalized significant changes, largely by creating new structures, policies, and incentives designed to alter organizational cultures in ways congruent with Obama's political agenda. They restructured the federal bureaucracy in ways that emphasized employment of members of the Democratic coalition and thereby shifted leftward the collective, politically salient worldview of the intelligence bureaucracy. These efforts particularly affected the CIA and the ODNI, elements of the IC that deal closely with the White House and whose leaders embraced Obama's agenda enthusiastically. In this sense Trump was a victim; he was the first Republican president to come along after a series of events that re-shaped the political culture of the IC in ways that effectively oppose Republicans generally. But Trump's personal quirks surely amplified the effects.

While they overlap and have reinforcing effects, six major factors account for much of the change in the institutions. They occurred independently in some cases; in others they are causally related. They are not equally important. Actions taken by Obama administration officials are most important. The socialization effects of standardized training (item #3 below) are more speculative, but they link the 9/11-related demographic changes to the political changes of the Obama years. The factors listed here in summary are in rough chronological order of their appearance and prominent development:

1. Adoption of the "First Customer" doctrine at CIA in late 1990s led to excessive focus on serving presidents, which became debilitating when many intelligence personnel came to dislike President Trump.

2. Changes in demographics following the 9/11 terrorist attacks indirectly affected traditional norms. Large numbers of young and inexperienced people entered

most IC agencies in the years immediately following
9/11 as part of President George W. Bush's "global
war on terrorism." Ongoing societal changes and
the radical shift leftward in the politics of American
university campuses in recent decades brought to the
IC large numbers of people whose views influenced
collective IC perspectives on politically important
issues such as respect for traditional norms of secrecy
and perceived rights to public expression of partisan
political views. Not least, many were indoctrinated by
teachers with increasingly left-wing politics who, like
them, desired to spread the word.

3. Lengthy training formats for CIA analysts that
began in 2000, which were designed to provide
basic training given the diminished emphasis on
expertise and graduate educations that occurred in
the 1990s, helped to standardize the organizational
culture of CIA's analysis directorate. Other agencies
later developed formal training programs using
standardized curricula, which communicated
organizational standards in skills such as writing
styles but also conveyed and reinforced evolving
cultural norms that had political aspects.

4. Affirmative action programs, first initiated in
the 1980s, dramatically increased in the Obama
years under the rubric of "diversity and inclusion,"
which reflected Obama's desire to make the federal
workforce "look like America." These policies added
to the workforce appreciable numbers of people

from demographic groups known to have collectively left-of-center political views, especially minorities and lesbian, gay, bisexual, and transgender (LGBT) people. In pushing his political agenda within the federal government generally, Obama also injected domestic politics into the management of the intelligence services, which created cleavages within the agencies between opponents and supporters of his reforms. Some of the latter group actively opposed Trump.

5. To help implement his program in the IC, Obama appointed leaders of some IC elements who had personal political views congruent with his own, which they made clear to the workforce through speeches, policy statements, organizational structures, and revisions in institutional incentives. DNI James Clapper and DCIA John Brennan especially strongly pushed Obama's "diversity and inclusion" agenda. A significant share of the CIA workforce came to embrace Obama's political agenda, including the Democratic Party's identity politics—a radical change from the largely apolitical nature of the intelligence business in years past.

6. Obama's policies led to demographic changes in the IC, new internal organizations, and associated political efforts by ideological leftists and members of demographic special interest groups that benefited from the changes. These groups reacted, sometimes publicly, when candidate Trump emerged

as a possible threat to their political views and institutional interests, and they lashed out at Trump even more strongly after he was elected. The activism of former FBI officials had more personal origins—especially anger at Trump's firing of Director James Comey and Deputy Director Andrew McCabe. Other agencies were much less affected.

Methodologically, this argument is presented as a variant of process tracing. Evidence for my hypotheses is considerable but not conclusive in all respects. Some of these hypotheses are tested in later chapters.

THE FIRST CUSTOMER DOCTRINE

In the late 1990s John Gannon, then chief of CIA's analysis directorate, decided to concentrate his analysts' work on serving President Clinton.[1] This decision followed a lengthy internal debate about the best way to support decision-makers, especially presidents. Some intelligence personnel held to Sherman Kent's argument that intelligence distance from policy-making, and the objectivity it allegedly fosters, are essential. Others, following DCI Robert Gates (1991-1993) and Willmoore Kendall earlier, argued that analysts need to be close to presidents to understand their needs well enough to ensure that intelligence remains relevant.[2] Gannon's predecessor, Douglas MacEachin, had moved in the Gatesian direction by shifting the focus of his analysts toward current intelligence and away from research studies, a move that senior policy officials clearly appreciated. Gannon completed the transition.

---

1   Priess, *The President's Book of Secrets*, 207-208.
2   Kendall, "The Function of Intelligence;" Gates, "The CIA and American Foreign Policy."

CIA's leaders had not newly discovered that they worked for presidents. Rather, they decided to emphasize analyses for the president even more, especially production of the *President's Daily Brief.* CIA thereby effectively de-emphasized its support to other intelligence consumers, who the IC incongruously came to call "customers." To institutionalize his goal, Gannon launched an internal campaign to make analysts and their managers view the president as their "First Customer," leading analytic units to emphasize writing for the *PDB*, which is designed narrowly to satisfy presidential desires.[3] Focus on the *PDB*, which is a current intelligence publication, accelerated the de-emphasis on expertise that MacEachin initiated. Presidents' reactions to *PDB* articles became more important determinants of bureaucratic success. Receiving "kudos" from the president or other senior officials for current intelligence articles became even more highly career enhancing. While this change had the advantage of making intelligence more responsive to presidents' needs, it also enhanced incentives for politicizing by trying to please presidents, increased the importance of managers in their roles as reviewers of analysts' drafts, and made presidential rejection of analytic judgments more painful for analysts and their agencies.[4] The old ethic of analytical objectivity initially remained strong, however. Through leadership exhortation and bureaucratic incentives such as outsized rewards for publishing one's work in the *PDB*, the First Customer doctrine entered CIA's analytic culture.

The First Customer notion became even more important for some IC elements as a result of enactment of the IRTPA. In addition to restructuring the IC by creating the ODNI and other changes, the IRTPA opened the *PDB* further to input by

---

3   Priess, *The President's Book of Secrets,* 208.
4   Gentry, "Managers of Analysts;" London, *The Recruiter,* 292, 294.

agencies other than the CIA, encouraging them to compete for the limited space in each edition of the *PDB*. It also directed the NIC to more directly support the NSC staff, which works directly for presidents, while still supervising the preparation of NIEs and other duties.[5] By many accounts serving the White House became a preoccupation at CIA and a huge consumer of analysts' and managers' time.[6]

This cultural change meant that rejection by presidents hurt more. Historically, especially during the Nixon years, rejection led to three reactions. First, most intelligence officers worked still harder to serve the president well. Second, intelligence worked more for other senior and mid-level officials, recognizing that important national policies are made by many officials and organizations and that they could inform presidents indirectly through lesser officials, including their staff officers. Third, a few intelligence people blamed the president's ideology or venality or ignorance of intelligence or lack of caring about intelligence for the reaction, denying they had failed to perform adequately. David Priess, who wrote a well-regarded history of the *PDB*, has argued that CIA analysts at first displayed the third reaction to Obama's initially cool reaction to his intelligence briefings. Priess wrote:

> Some analysts and managers, especially at the CIA, find it difficult to avoid feeling rejected when a president gives the impression that he just isn't that into the PDB. ODNI and CIA leaders who put heavy emphasis on the PDB magnify the effect.[7]

---

5   Treverton, "From Afghanistan to Trump," 183-184.

6   George, "Reflections on CIA Analysis," 74-77.

7   Treverton, "From Afghanistan to Trump," 282.

Although many intelligence officers later warmed to Obama, the third reaction also applied, especially strongly, to Trump for his entire presidency.

Despite occasional problems, Gannon's initiative generally worked well for nearly two decades. President Clinton was more receptive to intelligence in his later years than he was initially. President Bush was by many accounts a keen and attentive student of intelligence, which intelligence officers liked, even though many of them reportedly opposed Bush administration policies regarding Iraq, especially.[8]

President Obama's relationship with the IC reveals a lot about why the IC's relationship with Trump was rocky. Obama initially was less taken by intelligence than Bush but, in Priess's view, later was a roughly average presidential user of intelligence.[9] Obama sometimes treated intelligence agencies harshly, as over the enhanced interrogation program CIA started at Bush's request soon after 9/11.[10] Earlier, although he was not on the Senate intelligence committee, then-chairman of the SSCI Senator Chuck Hagel invited Senator Obama to join him on some foreign trips, during which Obama impressed many CIA field personnel as being smart.[11] Intelligence people by many accounts also generally liked him. For example, former CIA analyst and manager Nicholas Dujmović believes Obama generated "rock star hero worship" in many CIA employees, especially younger people.[12] He shared

8   Ibid., 223-251.
9   Priess, *The President's Book of Secrets*, 273-286. This fairly common view contrasts with that of Clapper, who unconvincingly claimed that Obama knew where intelligence "came from" better than any other president. See Clapper, *Facts and Fears*, 244.
10   Hayden, *Playing to the Edge*, 354-355, 357-358, 378-396, 410. According to former intelligence people, there were numerous tense meetings between intelligence officials and Obama administration officials in this period.
11   Author discussion with a former CIA officer, 2019.
12   Author discussion with Nicholas Dujmović, June 19, 2019; Panetta, *Worthy Fights*, 221.

their politics. Another former CIA officer said there was "a lot of sub-rosa support for Obama" during the 2008 election campaign.[13] Former DCIA Hayden agreed that intelligence people generally had a "positive" view of Obama.[14] Hence, at CIA, despite some tensions, widespread affection for Obama was both personal and political—sharply different in both ways from their feelings about Trump.

The "First Customer" doctrine also enhanced a vulnerability. Per Sherman Kent, efforts to please presidents increased the risk that intelligence would become too close to policy, risking politicization, which developed during Obama's second term in ways virtually identical to Kent's warning. Hayden reported, for example, that CIA analysts' liking of Obama, whom they perceived to want better relations with Moscow, led to less careful analysis of Russia and thence to belated recognition of Russian information operations targeting the United States in 2015; it also led analysts to agree with Obama's nuclear deal with Iran, not just support the development of his policy.[15] Easing of the Kentian admonition to avoid moving "too close" to policy they liked in the Obama years made it easier for analysts to move "away" from policies they did not appreciate in the Trump years.

In sharp contrast to George W. Bush but like Obama, Trump initially displayed little interest in, or knowledge of, intelligence. In contrast to Obama, he was not well liked. But like Presidents Kennedy, Johnson, Nixon, Carter, and Clinton,

---

13   Private conversation, 2019.

14   Hayden, *Assault on Intelligence*, 33-38.

15   Ibid., 36-37, 196. See also Brennan, *Undaunted*, 269-271. And former national security advisor Lieutenant General H.R. McMaster wrote that when he was posted to Kabul in 2011 he forwarded to Washington a paper forecasting that a resurgent al-Qaeda in Iraq would defeat Iraqi security forces. In response, "senior intelligence officials" in Washington had a "tepid" response because the paper's "predictions did not conform to U.S. leaders' self-delusion" that the war was going well. See McMaster, *Battlegrounds*, 255.

he held some aspects of intelligence history—such as the flawed 2002 NIE on Iraqi WMD—in low regard. Like Carter, Clinton, and occasionally Obama, he sometimes said so publicly in harsh ways. Hence, the by-now strong institutional focus on the "First Customer" meant hard work to satisfy an unattractive president. Trump's initial rejection of the IC's assessment that Russia meddled in the 2016 presidential campaign, his occasionally disparaging comments about intelligence, and his unappealing politics combined to magnify some analysts' disappointment with him.[16] Together with analysts' chronically excessive confidence in the wisdom of their own analyses, solid evidence that Russia did in fact try to influence the election campaign, and the weakly based but psychologically satisfying belief of Clinton supporters that Russia unfairly tipped a close election in Trump's favor,[17] it became easier to fault Trump for a variety of knowledge- and political philosophy-based reasons, only some of which had good empirical grounding. He seemed to some intelligence officers to be a flawed president unworthy of the IC's excellent intelligence support. This perception in turn helped rationalize aggressive, anti-Trump actions by some intelligence officers in 2016 and later.

DEMOGRAPHIC CHANGES

The IC grew dramatically after the 9/11 attacks. President Bush ordered the CIA to increase its corps of analysts and operators by 50 percent.[18] Later, the CIA evidently grew still more. Most

---

16   Intelligence Community Assessment, "Assessing Russian Activities and Intentions in Recent US Elections," January 6, 2017, https://www.dni.gov/files/documents/ICA_2017_01.pdf.

17   Rid, *Active Measures*, 407-408; McCombie, et al. "The US 2016 presidential election & Russia's troll farms," 96, 101-108; Shimer, *Rigged*, 223; Jamieson, *Cyberwar*.

18   Walter Pincus, "Bush Orders the CIA to Hire More Spies," *Washington Post*, November 24, 2004, A4.

other agencies, but not State/INR, which chose to remain small and focus on traditional issues of interest to the State Department rather than chase terrorists, over time grew similarly. Bush articulated gross hiring numbers, but the agencies decided whom to hire. New employees at CIA included many young people right out of college.[19] These people were products of their educations, which unlike the educations of intelligence officers a generation older, frequently featured large doses of radical indoctrination about politically important social issues, including race, ethnicity, gender, and sexual orientation.

At DIA, new employees in the 2010-2012 period whom I met personally were mostly young, little experienced, and modestly educated. That is, DIA hired a lot of people in their early 20s, right out of college. Most had only bachelors' degrees, some had masters' degrees, and only a few possessed terminal degrees.[20] A relative lack of foreign travel made security processing easier. Given the emphasis on current intelligence and the denigration of expertise that had become common in the IC in the 1990s, again except at INR, such young people were satisfactory employees.[21] They also could be hired at low pay grades, making them financially inexpensive until excessively rapid promotion rates raised rank structures—and entitlement expectations.

The large number of new hires dramatically changed the age profile of IC agencies. Given the dearth of hiring in the 1990s, when the intelligence workforce shrank appreciably as a result of the budget cuts that generated part of the post-Soviet "peace dividend," the IC by 2005 was composed of large numbers of

---

19   Communication with a former CIA officer familiar with CIA training programs.

20   Comments of many IC people and author discussions with several hundred DIA employees in training courses in 2010-2012. CIA evidently hired somewhat more educated, experienced people than did DIA in these years.

21   Gentry, "'Professionalization' of Intelligence Analysis."

young people, a relatively small number of mid-career people hired in the 1990s, and a larger group, hired in the 1970s and 1980s, nearing and then reaching retirement age.[22] The IC workforce in aggregate became much younger.

Mark Lowenthal summarized the demographic changes, "The net result is an analyst corps that is younger and less experienced than before. Former CIA Deputy Director of Intelligence (DDI) Jami Miscik captured the fact when she observed that 40 percent of the analysts in the directorate of intelligence had worked for only one DCI, George Tenet, who resigned after exactly seven years."[23] The dearth of mid-career people meant that the old system of on-the-job training, complemented by significant mentorship by senior analysts and junior managers, no longer worked well.[24] The new employees, by many accounts, got less guidance by colleagues and supervisors and relied more extensively on formal government training courses and the values they brought with them from college, including politically salient views about social issues. CIA Deputy Director Vaughn Bishop said in July 2019 that 77 percent of CIA's then-current workforce had entered on duty after 9/11 and about 20 percent had been hired since the CIA reorganized into mission centers in May 2015.[25]

The post-9/11 influx and retirements left the IC short on experienced leadership, including people who knew and respected the old norms. Sue Gordon, a career CIA officer who then was Principal Deputy DNI, in April 2018 told a gathering:

---

22 According to David Priess, the number of CIA analysts declined 17 percent from 1990 to 1995; see Priess, *The President's Book of Secrets*, 209. James Clapper reported that during the 1990s the number of analysts in the IC shrank by one-third and the number of human intelligence collectors declined by a quarter; see Clapper, *Facts and Fears*, 87.

23 Lowenthal, "Intelligence Analysis," 231; Gentry, "The 'Professionalization' of Intelligence Analysis."

24 Bakos, *The Targeter*.

25 Bishop comments to CIA retirees and their families, July 25, 2019.

We have had a demographic shift of people leaving our organizations that were wise. We have mission growth where we have had people sucked up into leadership positions without all the experiences. Their presence has been good, but now, when we need to find differential value, they are struggling to know how to take an idea and turn it into an action. We are going to have to get back to that.[26]

Gordon diffusely made a point that others frequently state more explicitly. Many old-timers, especially, think that while there are many fine people in the IC, the overall quality of the workforce, including its leadership, declined after the 1990s.[27]

By many accounts, the new employees were appreciably different than those hired in the 1980s and before. In constructivist language, they held different constituent and regulative norms. Their personal values differed from those of older employees on many issues. Greg Lukianoff and Jonathan Haidt, a lawyer and social psychologist, respectively, in an essay entitled "The Coddling of the American Mind" and published in 2015, asserted that students increasingly demand protection from thoughts and words they do not like, which they argued is disastrous for both education and students' mental health.[28] Some such troubled students become intelligence officers, and these pathologies sometimes appear in peculiar, intelligence-related ways. For example, younger people have less regard for traditional intelligence cultural norms, including respect for secrecy and apolitical conduct in government workplaces. David Muller, a retired US Navy intelligence

---

26   *The Cipher Brief,* "Sue Gordon on Speaking Truth to Power, Including the President," July 30, 2019, https://www.thecipherbrief.com/column_article/sue-gordon-speaking-truth-power-including-president.

27   Gentry, "The 'Professionalization' of Intelligence Analysis."

28   Lukianoff and Haidt, "The Coddling of the American Mind."

officer working as a contractor for the ODNI, described how he first became aware of the change: at an ODNI off-site meeting in 2007, many middle ranking and junior officers talked openly in highly political, pro-Democratic ways that once would have been severely chastised as inappropriate behavior in a government meeting.[29] Senior personnel present did nothing to suppress the partisan talk, however. This experience led Muller to publish in 2008 a still-relevant discussion of the importance of worldview in shaping the conduct of intelligence analysis.[30] In contrast to the palpable politicization at the ODNI, Muller says there was no such activity at NCTC, where he went soon thereafter and remained until he finally retired in 2014.[31] NCTC for many years employed large numbers of people on short-term assignments from other agencies, retarding its ability to build an independent organizational culture.[32]

Dan Gressang, who was an analyst and manager at NSA from 1987-2018, described the group hired after 2001:

> The hiring surge seemed to foster a subtle shift in the culture of the IC workforce. While mission was still paramount for both long-time employees and new hires, the newer generation seemed to pay a bit more attention to career building and development, albeit not at the expense of mission. It could be that shift was a result of generational differences or the result of increased emphasis by the human resources offices

---

29 Author discussion with David Muller, July 11, 2019.

30 Muller, "Intelligence Analysis in Red and Blue."

31 Author discussion with David Muller, July 11, 2019. An academic who was a junior NCTC analyst in 2006-2009 reports the same apolitical work environment; email to author, September 15, 2019.

32 Betsy Woodruff Swan, "A top terrorism fighter's dire warning," *Politico*, July 10, 2020, https://www.politico.com/news/2020/07/09/travers-terrorism-warning-355734.

in ensuring employees knew of, understood, and posi-
tioned themselves to take advantage of career building
opportunities and benefits, or some combination of
both. I do feel that career opportunities, work life
balance, and employment benefits were stressed more
in the later part of my time at the Agency.[33]

Edward (Ned) Price, born in 1982, who was an analyst and
then public affairs officer at the CIA from 2006-2017, also thinks
his generation is different. The climate of the times accounts for
part of it, he said.[34] His generation has "more ego." He said young
people internalized the "need to share" paradigm that temporarily
replaced the longstanding "need to know" standard for information
exchanges as a perceived lesson of the 9/11 attacks, a characteristic
intelligence veterans Mark Lowenthal and Margaret Marangione
also noted.[35]

Older observers think the younger generation generally
has an entitlement ethic that leads young employees to expect
rapid promotions without a need for doing the "grunt work" of
developing expertise or otherwise earning respect, as a former
CIA officer described the attitude.[36] They allegedly want rapid
promotion based only on production of current intelligence
articles. This attitude reflects in part the generous promotion
practices in the financially flush years immediately following
9/11 as well as societal changes. The perception of entitlement
extends to the perceived quality of work intelligence officers do:

---

33   Dan Gressang email to author, July 28, 2019.

34   Author discussion with Ned Price, July 30, 2019.

35   Ibid.; Mark Lowenthal email to author, August 13, 2019; Marangione,
     "Millennials."

36   Author conversation with a retired CIA officer who wishes to remain anonymous,
     summer 2019; George "Reflections on CIA Analysis," 77; Marangione,
     "Millennials," 367-368.

their work always is good and any criticism of it is unfair, wrong, or discriminatory, especially if the discussion concerns persons from favored demographic groups. Barry Zulauf, who was then the Intelligence Community Analytic Ombudsman, a senior ODNI position, observed in October 2020:

> I have seen in the comments brought to my attention as Analytic Ombudsman where analysts confuse editing or constructive criticism as politicization. I am afraid we have a whole generation now in the workforce who have never had a harsh word spoken to them or never had any criticism expressed to them in college as they express their "feelings" on issues. Such snowflake treatment does not prepare them well for the kind of give-and-take needed to make for rigorous analysis.[37]

Margaret Marangione, a former CIA analyst, cited surveys indicating that the Millennial generation is also different in other respects. She noted that 58 percent of college students scored higher on a narcissism test in 2009 than did students in 1982 and that narcissistic personality disorder is nearly three times higher in Millennials than in persons over sixty-five years of age.[38] CIA psychologist Ursula Wilder observed that the combination of senses of entitlement and narcissism is strongly associated with leaking by intelligence personnel.[39] Similarly, former CIA security officer Terence Thompson argued that narcissism and disgruntlement are abetted by three phenomena that recently have become more prominent in the intelligence workforce: "grandiose needs for recognition," a "culture of non-restraint," and anonymity—until

---

37   Zulauf email to author, October 11, 2020.
38   Marangione, "Millennials," 356.
39   Wilder, "The Psychology of Espionage and Leaking in the Digital Age," 24-27.

leakers wish to become public figures.[40] All of these traits became more visible in 2016 and later. Former assistant DCI for administration James Simon pointed to the influence of activist groups and the disinformation programs of Russia and other countries as causes of some of the evolution in the IC's cultures.[41]

These patterns reflect cultural changes that increasingly also appear in the commercial world. Survey research shows that younger workers want their employers' political values to be consistent with their own and frequently insist that executives change corporate policies to match those of employees.[42] Silicon Valley firms such as Google and Meta have prominently vocal workforces whose collective politics have been distinctly left-of-center and which have demanded that corporate leaders adopt their politically controversial views, many of them on social issues.[43] In March 2022, more than 100 LGBT and other employees of Disney staged a walkout to protest the company's response to a bill under consideration by the Florida legislature concerning transgender people and public schools.[44] Disney management eventually took actions consistent with employee demands, generating a major fight with the Governor Ron DeSantis and the legislature of Florida, where its large Disney World asset is located. Such employee activism has been encouraged in varying degrees

---

40   Thompson, "A Psycho-Social Motivational Theory of Mass Leaking," 116, 119.

41   James Simon, email to author, June 20, 2020. For similar arguments, see Rid, *Active Measures;* Pacepa and Rychlak, *Disinformation;* Gonzales, *The Plot to Change America;* Gentry, "Belated Success."

42   Rachel Feintzeig, Charity L. Scott, and Sharon Terlep, "More Workers Speak Out Against Their CEOs," *Wall Street Journal,* February 3, 2020, B4.

43   Ibid.

44   Kiara Alfonseca, "Disney employees stage walkout to demand action against 'Don't Say Gay' bill, ABC News, March 22, 2022, https://abcnews.go.com/Business/disney-employees-plan-walkout-demand-action-dont-gay/story?id=83585126.

by evolving societal norms, the media, and radical professors who have indoctrinated students and urged political activism.[45]

In the business world, such activism is sometimes led by, but more often abetted by, corporate leaders with left-wing, not liberal, political views. Examples of politically aggressive chief executives include Meta's Mark Zuckerberg, Twitter's Jack Dorsey, Apple's Tim Cook, and Larry Fink of BlackRock, who have extensively politicized their organizations.[46] Obama's IC leaders, especially Brennan and Clapper, were political entrepreneurs of only slightly different sorts; they acted a lot like these men.

The sharing, and foisting, of opinions is abetted by new information technologies, with which most young people are familiar. Edward Snowden and Bradley/Chelsea Manning, who claimed their leaks were altruistically motivated, are prime examples of the phenomenon. Ned Price said his colleagues generally were appalled by the actions of Snowden and Manning; their claims of being whistleblowers were unpersuasive because they did not use any of the complaint mechanisms available to them. But a former senior CIA official said Snowden and Manning were worrisome because they conveyed to intelligence officers that it was acceptable to decide on one's own what could be released to the public.[47] DCIA Pompeo in 2017 similarly blamed Snowden and the WikiLeaks culture for the apparently growing number of leaks by intelligence officers.[48] Snowden's autobiography, published in 2019, makes clear that he then still considered himself to be a moral

---

45 Kimball, *Tenured Radicals;* Gonzales, *BLM*, 149-168, 173-174; Hegseth with Goodwin, *Battle for the American Mind;* Murray, *The War on the West*, 18, 24-25, 52-58, 267; Soukup, *The Dictatorship of Woke Capital.*

46 Soukup, *The Dictatorship of Woke Capital.*

47 Author discussion with Ned Price, July 30, 2019; separate conversation with another former CIA person.

48 Rebecca Morin, "CIA director says intelligence leaks have 'accelerated'," *Politico*, June 24, 2017, https://www.politico.com/story/2017/06/24/cia-pompeo-leaks-intelligence-accelerated-239931.

whistleblower; he released classified material because he knew the truth about the evils of government surveillance that the US and other governments would not accept and that citizens needed to know.[49] Then-NSA linguist Reality Winner used similar logic to rationalize leaking anti-Trump intelligence material to a news website in June 2017.[50] Perhaps not coincidentally, a CIA review made public in 2020 blamed the theft and release to WikiLeaks in 2016 of the "Vault 7" documents on CIA hacking tools on a "woefully lax" security environment within CIA.[51]

As is well documented, young people collectively are politically more left-leaning than older Americans.[52] They have recently been in colleges and universities, most of which have become conspicuously illiberal and intolerant of diverse viewpoints given the strongly leftist outlooks of many faculty and administrators. Many universities impose degrees of ideological orthodoxy on students, faculty, and guest speakers by establishing restrictive speech codes that, critics argue, violate constitutional guarantees of free speech.[53] Believing these restrictions are good, some schools chronically and clearly tell students and faculty (including me) that intolerance of some historically reputable political perspectives is good if it prevents offending ethnic minorities and favorite

---

49   Snowden, *Permanent Record*, 3, 238–239, 243, 251, 262.

50   David Choi, "'I felt really hopeless': NSA leak suspect Reality Winner explains why she smuggled a classified report," *Business Insider*, September 28, 2017, http://www.businessinsider.com/reality-winner-nsa-leaker-fox-news-al-jazeera-pantyhose-2017-9.

51   Dustin Volz, "Weak CIA Security Blamed for Theft," *Wall Street Journal*, June 17, 2020, A7.

52   For example, Susan Milligan, "Young Voters Support Democratic Socialist Policies," *U.S. News & World Report*, October 29, 2018, https://www.usnews.com/news/national-news/articles/2018-10-29/harvard-poll-young-voters-support-democratic-socialist-policies.

53   Frederick M. Hess and Grant Addison, "Colleges Should Protect Speech–or Lose Funds," *Wall Street Journal*, October 31, 2017, A17; Anthony Kronman, "The Downside of Diversity," *Wall Street Journal*, August 3–4, 2019, C1. The BIG website is at http://www.bignet.org/.

political orthodoxies.[54] In 2014, the Higher Education Research Institute at UCLA found that 60% of university professors self-identified as "liberal" or "far-left," up from 42% in 1990, while in the same period "moderates" declined from 40% to 27% and "conservatives" declined from about 18% to about 12%.[55] By the 2020s, national teachers' unions were among the most left-leaning in the country. Reflecting these trends, a YouGov poll conducted in 2019 found that 36% of Millennials (then persons aged 23 to 38) approved of communism, up from 28% in 2018, and 70% were extremely or slightly likely to vote for a socialist candidate in the future.[56] Some graduates of these institutions become government employees.[57] Some of them unsurprisingly found Obama's views attractively consistent with those of their leftist professors and themselves. In contrast, Trump's views and those of Trump appointees such as DCIA Mike Pompeo were objectionable and worthy of protesting, as they had done on campus.

David Muller argued in 2008, before Obama administration initiatives changed the IC's demography more dramatically, that demographics already had played a role in the changed collective outlook of intelligence analysts and therefore in the IC's analytic products:

---

54   Personal experience.

55   Christopher Ingraham, "The dramatic shift among college professors that's hurting students' education," *Washington Post*, January 16, 2016, https://www. washingtonpost.com/news/wonk/wp/2016/01/11/the-dramatic-shift-among-college-professors-thats-hurting-students-education/. See also Jon A. Shields, "The Disappearing Conservative Professor," *National Affairs*, Fall 2018, https:// nationalaffairs.com/publications/detail/the-disappearing-conservative-professor.

56   Shawn Langlois, "More than a third of millennials polled approve of communism," *MarketWatch*, November 2, 2019, https://www.marketwatch. com/story/for-millennials-socialism-and-communism-are-hot-capitalism-is-not-2019-10-28.

57   A former intelligence officer, now a university professor, who shares this view notes that students with far left perspectives tend to be repulsed by the idea of working for an intelligence service, so this generalization applies mainly to students with liberal, center-left political philosophies.

Consider a typical intelligence analyst: 30-something years old, single or recently married with no children, as likely to be female as male, living in the Eastern urban environment of greater Washington, the recent product of a university social sciences department, without military experience, secularly minded, who reads the *Washington Post* every morning. This is a quintessentially Blue [Democratic] demographic profile. Greater diversity in worldview is found at the middle and senior levels, and in the military organizations, but the Blue worldview dominates the civilian organizations all the way to the top, based on my unsystematic but long-term observations.[58]

Other veteran intelligence officers made similar points to me in private conversations. Therefore, it is unsurprising that many young intelligence officers, leaning Democratic and hoping for a Clinton win in 2016, repulsed by Trump's ideas and personality and believing that sharing their obviously wise views was both desirable and perfectly acceptable, expressed their disparaging opinions about Trump via leaks, Facebook posts, office banter, and comments to former intelligence officers such as Michael Hayden and Michael Morell, who reported them to the world.[59]

New Training Institutions

The influx of young, relatively unskilled employees after 2001 overpowered the ability of IC's old analyst mentoring systems, which formerly ensured that analysts learned to think clearly, analyze rigorously, and write to agency standards consistent

---

58   Muller, "Intelligence Analysis in Red and Blue," 9-10.
59   For numerous such references, see Hayden, *Assault on Intelligence*.

with objectivity norms. Instead, new analysts increasingly took courses that imparted basic information about the IC and its organizational processes, agency ways of doing things, writing styles, and some standard analytic techniques helpful for beginner analysts. The CIA was the first of the agencies to develop a comprehensive training course that all new analysts must attend. The Career Analyst Program (CAP), established in 2000, was developed largely to meet a perceived need to redress the deficiencies in analytic skills brought about by Douglas MacEachin's denigration of expertise and emphasis on current intelligence, versus research, in the 1990s.[60] The now 16-week course still teaches new analysts how to write to CIA standards and conveys analytic "tradecraft" skills.[61] It inevitably also imparts organizational cultural norms by following a standard curriculum and making budding analysts work together in prescribed, "collaborative" ways. These influences in turn help standardize thought processes. Young employees fresh from colleges that pushed the same ideological agendas undoubtedly find comfort in meeting people of similar minds, reinforcing such views. In contrast, the mentoring of new analysts by many managers and veteran analysts with varied educational backgrounds and experiences previously led to a more intellectually diverse workforce.

The CAP teaches many things, but it emphasizes what have become known as structured analytical techniques (SATs), which are standard methods for addressing various kinds of analytic challenges. Former CIA operations officer Richards Heuer in the 1970s became interested in the causes of analytic errors and wrote a series of articles published in *Studies in Intelligence*, which the

---

60   Marrin, "Training and Educating U.S. Intelligence Analysts;" Marrin, "CIA's Kent School."

61   For a student's view of the course in its early years, see Bakos, *The Targeter*, 46-60.

CIA compiled and published as a book in 1999.[62] Heuer convinced many intelligence officers (and later scholars) that "mindsets and biases" are major obstacles to sound analysis and should be targets of specialized analytic techniques designed to overcome them. Since then, several dozen SATs have been developed to improve thinking processes, mainly by devising ways to avoid easily avoidable errors—useful aids for less well-educated analysts. Universities' graduate-level courses on social science research techniques convey similar ideas more rigorously. Former national intelligence officer for warning (NIO/W) Mary McCarthy in 1999 suggested that the IC develop techniques that would amount to "social science for dummies,"—that is, for people who had not taken graduate-level methodology courses.[63] SATs do just that.

But SATs have not been demonstrated to work and they suggest an orthodoxy of analytic approaches, which in turn imposes forms of intellectual rigidity. Most importantly for this study, prominent psychologist Philip Tetlock of the University of Pennsylvania and his colleagues, who worked for the IC's Intelligence Advanced Research Projects Activity (IARPA) for several years on psychological aspects of intelligence analysis, noted that political bias creeps into the SATs that most IC agencies now also teach new analysts:

> Analysts may also actively expand the original conceptual framework of a favored hypothesis to accommodate new evidence (whereas confirmation bias shoehorns evidence into the hypothesis). Thus, it is not the *most accurate* hypothesis that emerges as the *most likely* from an SAT framework, but the hypothesis that is *most*

---

62   Heuer, *Psychology of Intelligence Analysis*.

63   Marrin, *Improving Intelligence Analysis*, 31.

ideologically consistent with an analysts' preconceived notions—a problem known as "conceptual stretching" or "elastic redefinition."[64]

This situation becomes more important when organizational cultures evolve to reflect ideological preferences as "preconceived notions," or worldviews, and analysts' managers accept and reward these views.

DIA followed CIA's lead in 2013 when it began to teach its Professional Analyst Career Education (PACE) program. DIA's then-director, Lieutenant General Michael Flynn, told his training unit to ensure the course instilled the DIA "brand" in new employees.[65] CIA's CAP effectively does the same without claiming to do so. While agency "brands" prominently reflect loyalty to agencies and understanding of the forms and styles of agency publications, they also reflect and are designed to influence organizational cultural norms. These in turn can reflect bureaucratically innocuous imperatives or communicate worldviews that have analytic and perhaps political significance. The Defense Department as a whole formally recognized its skills deficit problem in its intelligence personnel, and in 2012 initiated a program of "professionalization" of the Defense intelligence workforce as a whole via certification that is rudimentary and is unlikely to help create a capable workforce.[66]

DIA also established an orientation program called Touchstone, which is required of all new government employees (not contractors):

---

64   Chang, Berdini, Mandel, and Tetlock, "Restructuring structured analytic techniques in intelligence," 344.

65   Author discussion with DIA training officers.

66   Gentry, "The 'Professionalization' of Intelligence," 653.

The **Touchstone Program** introduces new government employees and military members to DIA's culture and mission, while emphasizing each new employee's role as a DIA Officer. Touchstone familiarizes students with the DIA strategy, the DIA core values (Teamwork, Integrity, Excellence, and Service), and enables them to create effective teams and maintain a network of professional colleagues. The intent of the program is to promote a culture that supports DIA's goal of "Committed to Excellence in Defense of the Nation." In addition, Touchstone delivers essential training and provides the opportunity and assistance necessary for new employees and military members to navigate through the security and onboarding process at DIA.[67]

This program, with its emphasis on organizational mission and basic data, is much less likely to lead to analytic biases than the introductory analyst courses.

Dan Gressang, the NSA officer who was involved with training at NSA and was for several years on the faculty of the National Intelligence University (NIU), described the impact of new training institutions at NSA:

At the Agency, my sense is that the training of analysts did much to help standardize culture. I'm not sure that's as desirable as usually assumed, though. In analytic skills training, emphasis was placed on ICD 203 (Analytic Standards), particularly through the application of structured methods of analysis (SATs)

---

67   DIA website, https://www.dia.mil/Careers/Touchstone-Orientation-for-New-Employees/.

and the emphasis on rigor. While both are commendable, the application, as I experienced it, was rigid in its adherence to the notion that SATs were the *sine qua non* of acceptable practice. That rigidity forced an emphasis on the "science" of analysis without due consideration of the "art" of analysis. The result, too often, was an analyst so fixated on applying the "school house approach" that ambiguity, uncertainty, and inflexibility hindered the actual analytic process.[68]

Hence, training programs provide basic skills and convey organizational cultural norms, but they do not alone make good analysts. They also can create rigidities that are sometimes dysfunctional and establish politically-salient worldviews as parts of agency branding processes that have repeatedly led to analytic errors. These programs became especially important socialization tools when senior managers tried pointedly to alter organizational cultures.

THE "DIVERSITY AND INCLUSION" AGENDA

A major cause of the collectively changing political views of parts of the IC was a purposeful effort to alter its demographic composition through hiring, promotion, and personnel management policies framed under the banner of "diversity and inclusion." These efforts were independent of the hiring surge after 9/11, but were enabled to a considerable degree by it. There were many new positions to fill, even into the Obama years.

The US government and the IC long have sought to expand employment opportunities for all Americans. For many years, this was done under the rubric of equal employment opportunity

---

68   Dan Gressang email to author, July 28, 2019. For information on ICD 203, see https://www.dni.gov/files/documents/ICD/ICD%20203%20Analytic%20 Standards.pdf.

(EEO), and there were EEO offices in all major agencies, which had several motives for embracing this policy. First, it was government policy. Second, intelligence people knew that the IC had hired relatively few women and minorities in years past and wanted to expand hiring opportunities for these groups. Third, intelligence people well understood that diversity of outlook—of mental perspective—and a variety of ethnic backgrounds, experiences, and cultural awareness were critical to effective operational performance. Hence, intelligence agencies embraced operationally useful demographic diversity.

The early IC had a long way to go. As has been frequently complained about, the OSS and the early CIA were composed largely of East Coast professional men. In the national emergency that was World War II, the leaders of the OSS sought the best people they could quickly find, who often were Ivy League university graduates and professors they knew personally. That demographic changed appreciably by the 1970s, however, as CIA managers recognized that capable people come from all corners of the country and that the human intelligence collection mission of the operations directorate, which by then focused globally and not just on the European theater of war, as the intelligence arm of the OSS generally did, needed broader ethnic and cultural diversity to both know and blend into the many environments in which operations officers worked.[69] Analysts, too, now tracked events globally and needed broadly focused cultural awareness. There also was increased political pressure to increase the number of women at the CIA. Activists claimed that employment statistics demonstrated sex discrimination while largely ignoring the substantial differences in the gender make-up of professions and vocations in the American economy.[70] Agency managers

---

69   Durbin, "Addressing 'This Woeful Imbalance.'"
70   Gentry, "Demographic Diversity in U.S. Intelligence Personnel."

went along, recognizing the obvious fact that women, too, can be capable intelligence officers.[71]

Hence, IC managers adopted the view that hiring qualified people, whatever their demographic profile, was desirable. Yes, there was affirmative action, but demographics were only part of the picture. Diversity of backgrounds and outlooks and rigorous qualifications remained essential. Sherman Kent in 1949 put the traditional view well, noting the need for organizational tolerance for the analytic "queer bird and the eccentric with a unique talent," even if such people sometimes produce "crackpot findings."[72] No bureaucracy gives wholly free rein to imagination, but CIA gave employees considerable opportunities for initiative and insightful creativity. While the number of women at CIA and NSA grew steadily over the years, critics chronically complained that women were inappropriately under-represented in senior positions.[73] While being sure to provide equal opportunity, the dominant philosophy for many years remained that hiring and promotions should generally be merit-based and race- and gender-blind even while giving women and minorities modest advantages in the form of "affirmative action."

President Clinton altered the "equal opportunity" ethic of earlier years, emphasizing "affirmative action" more strongly.[74] This amounted, at the time, to purposefully hiring more women and minorities, especially blacks, into government. For Democrats such as Clinton, this policy served the additional useful purpose of providing jobs to people from key Democratic constituencies. African-Americans soon became, and remain, substantially

---

71   Crosston, "Petticoat Promise: Gender and the CIA in the #MeToo Era."

72   Kent, *Strategic Intelligence for American World Policy*, 74.

73   Durbin, "Addressing 'This Woeful Imbalance;'" Callum, "The Case for Cultural Diversity in the Intelligence Community;" Chin, "Diversity in the Age of Terror."

74   For Clinton's reasoning, see his speech of July 19, 1993, "The Job of Ending Discrimination in this Country is Not Over," https://www.washingtonpost.com/wp-srv/politics/special/affirm/docs/clintonspeech.htm.

over-represented in the federal workforce, although they tend to occupy lower-skilled, lower paying positions—reflections of their continuing collective lack of education and skills needed for more senior positions. President George W. Bush's administration stuck to what had become the traditional approach to "equal opportunity" hiring and did not change hiring practices appreciably. Clinton-era racial and gender preferences remained in place.

In 2005, Congress directed the IC to work to increase minority representation in the IC by creating the IC Centers of Academic Excellence (IC CAE) program, which funded intelligence-related courses at colleges and universities with large minority populations. The idea was that the program would encourage minorities to become interested in intelligence work and apply to the agencies, thereby enhancing minority hiring.

Barack Obama, the first African-American president, had a much more ambitious demographic plan for the federal government as a whole, which in his years in the White House became known as "diversity and inclusion." Obama's Executive Order (EO) 13583 of August 18, 2011, "Establishing a Coordinated Government-wide Initiative to Promote Diversity and Inclusion in the Federal Workforce," summarized his agenda.[75] This document generalized previous Obama executive orders and less formal directives that mandated hiring more veterans (EO 13518) and persons with physical handicaps (EO 13548), and it emphasized the continuing applicability of Clinton-era EOs on hiring disabled persons. Later, Obama made the hiring of LGBTQ+ persons a priority. The first part of EO 13583 repeated the "equal opportunity" language of old, but soon largely dropped it in favor of indicating that hiring people of favored domestic demographic groups was his primary goal. The order applied to all

---

75   Available at https://obamawhitehouse.archives.gov/the-press-office/2011/08/18/
      executive-order-13583-establishing-coordinated-government-wide-initiativ.

executive agencies and specified reporting requirements. Hence, it paid no attention to the specific operational needs of any federal agency—including the IC's special needs for expertise in *foreign* languages and cultures and an ability to operate effectively in *foreign* environments. Obama's focus was *domestic* and his motive clearly was political. John Brennan, who was a special assistant to Obama in the White House in 2009-2013 and by many accounts was a close aide, asserted in his book that Obama aimed to change the country in an evolutionary, not revolutionary, manner.[76] Given its many influences on the country as a whole, engineering demographic and political change in the federal workforce was a good place to start. EO 13583 was a valuable tool.

Obama's order had the dual advantages, for a Democrat, of benefitting core constituency groups and reshaping the federal workforce politically in a "progressive" way. By focusing on demographic groups with known collective political leanings, the move enabled purposeful political restructuring of the federal workforce without asking individuals their political views—an action widely viewed as inappropriate, especially since it also was banned by the Civil Service Reform Act of 1978. Civil service laws outlawed political favoritism of the sort Franklin Roosevelt's administration practiced, which also prompted the Hatch Act of 1939 that outlawed partisan political activity by civil servants. Obama found a way to get around these laws.

EO 13583 required development of demographic diversity-focused hiring and promotion plans as well as new offices within the agencies to implement the policies. Agencies were held accountable for implementing the order. There was no statement of what constituted enough diversity; the order simply mandated more hiring of persons belonging to favored demographic

---

76   Brennan, *Undaunted*, 251.

groups—effectively all people who were not Caucasian, male, heterosexual, and healthy. When they felt a need to do so, agencies and leaders variously cited many measures of allegedly inadequate diversity to justify increased hiring and promotion of favored demographic groups.

IC Leaders Did Obama's Bidding

Obama made clear that he wanted the IC, like the rest of the civilian part of the federal government, to "look like America," a term President Clinton used that became much more prominent in the Obama years.[77] But he needed agency executives to turn his goals into reality. At Obama's behest, in the name of his "diversity and inclusion" agenda some of his appointees politicized the IC in ways and to an extent that never existed before. IC agencies, like the military, long had been granted exemptions from many civil service regulations, reflecting congressional recognition that intelligence work was unique and should not be burdened by the rigid Civil Service rules applicable to domestic agencies. Obama's appointees voluntarily abandoned many of their Civil Service exemptions, choosing to accept Obama's policies for the government as a whole, and swept away much of the tradition of keeping partisan politics from their work spaces.[78]

While most IC leaders altered their agencies' organizational cultures at least a little in politically significant ways, leaders of two especially important elements of the IC—the ODNI and the CIA—played key roles in significantly politicizing their organizations. Retired Air Force Lieutenant General James Clapper was

---

77   No byline, "Clinton's National Security Team," *Baltimore Sun*, December 23, 1992, http://www.baltimoresun.com/news/bs-xpm-1992-12-23-1992358039-story. html.

78   Gentry, "The 'Professionalization' of Intelligence Analysis," 662.

DNI for nearly seven years (2010-2017), substantially affecting the ODNI directly and the broader IC to a lesser extent. At the CIA, DCIA John Brennan (2013-2017) embraced diversity policies strenuously and both generated and institutionalized policy changes that shifted collective worldviews in ways that achieved Obama's goals while also fostering an organizational culture that opposed Trump vigorously.

ODNI POLICY INITIATIVES

Obama's directives covered the entire government, meaning the DNI and his office, the ODNI, had major roles to play in implementing them in the IC—even given the DNI's limited ability to control agencies' specific policies. Obama's first DNI, retired Admiral Dennis Blair (January 2009-May 2010), did little in this arena. But Clapper, Obama's second and last DNI, actively promoted Obama's agenda. Under Clapper's direction and oversight, the ODNI and some agencies created diversity offices headed by senior officials with activist agendas that replaced the old EEO offices. The ODNI in fact has two diversity offices comprised of several persons each, each headed by senior executives to give the offices clout. One manages the diversity program within ODNI. The other monitors those of other IC agencies and hectors recalcitrant agencies if necessary. At most IC elements, these offices were and are staffed overwhelmingly by women and minorities, many of whom are candid about their gender- and race-oriented political agendas. A common pejorative quip that was not politically incorrect given Obama's policies was that federal employees collectively were still "too male, pale, and stale." Demographic engineering would fix that problem!

Clapper's political views matched Obama's closely. Clapper recounted in his book that he was pleased by Obama's election in

2008.[79] While he had a reputation in parts of the IC as being a largely apolitical, even conservative military officer, his speeches as DNI and his memoir make clear that he agreed with Obama on most domestic political issues, and he said later that he wanted Hillary Clinton to win in 2016.[80] Indeed, the public record of his actions as DNI should dispel any doubts that he was fully on the "diversity and inclusion" team. As he wrote, these views drove actions when he held positions as director of DIA (1992-1995), director of NGA (2001-2006), and Undersecretary of Defense for Intelligence (USD(I)) (2007-2010).[81] For example, as director of DIA, Clapper created a senior-level "equal opportunity and inclusion officer whose job was to root out and deal with issues of inclusion."[82] He received a meritorious service award from the National Association for the Advancement of Colored People in 1994, evidently partly for this work.[83] When the National Imagery and Mapping Agency (NIMA), which he headed, was to be re-named the National Geospatial Intelligence Agency (NGIA), black employees complained to Clapper about how the new agency's acronym might be pronounced, so Clapper added a hyphen, creating NGA.[84]

Clapper strongly supported gay employees. As DNI, he spoke at government-funded conferences of LGBT people and said he was "proud" that gays had established an inter-agency "fly team" to help other gays employed by IC agencies come out.[85]

---

79   Clapper, *Facts and Fears*, 120.

80   Shimer, *Rigged*, 179.

81   Clapper, *Facts and Fears*, 70-71.

82   Ibid., 70.

83   Ibid., 71.

84   Ibid., 96. Another story commonly asserted in the IC for the name change at the time was that Clapper allegedly wanted to head a three-letter agency, which among Washington bureaucrats is more prestigious than NGIA or NIMA as four-letter agencies. Clapper presumably would be less likely to admit to this motive in a memoir.

85   Clapper, *Facts and Fears*, 262, 302.

He called Obama's 2015 decision to allow gays to serve openly in the military a "courageous act."[86] He claimed that the IC had shown that it was "advantageous to employ openly transgender employees, who brought unique perspectives to mission challenges and contributed to successes."[87] Soon demographic diversity would frequently be lauded as consistent with "our values." That is, Obama's values.

Beginning in Obama's second term, IC leaders added another claim about "diversity and inclusion:" that it improved the performance of the IC. Clapper spoke often and fervently throughout the IC in support of Obama's diversity agenda, and he attended meetings of many of the agencies' newly created demographic special interest groups, which variously are known as "employee resource groups" or "affinity groups." Other senior officers followed suit. But while the rhetoric was glowing, no agency ever validated the claim with evidence.[88] It was a massive and notable omission given intelligence officers' long-time, strong emphasis on the need for evidence to support all analytic judgments in intelligence products, and its requirement per the IRTPA and ICD 203. This claim was driven by ideology, not evidence.

In 2013, Clapper initiated an annual "Intelligence Community Women's Summit." Diversity was the theme, with a special focus on the need to have more women in the IC, and more women in senior positions. The theme of the 2016 iteration of the Summit was "diversity as a core value."[89] Clapper, FBI Director James Comey, and Attorney General Loretta Lynch spoke.[90]

---

86   Ibid., 124.

87   Ibid., 301.

88   Gentry, "Demographic Diversity in U.S. Intelligence Personnel."

89   Brian Murphy, "IC Leaders Call Diversity 'Mission Critical' at Intelligence Community Women's Summit," ODNI Public Affairs, March 31, 2016, https://www.dni.gov/index.php/newsroom/item/1353-ic-leaders-call-diversity-mission-critical-at-intelligence-community-women-s-summit.

90   Ibid.

Supporting Clapper's views, Comey proclaimed, "Our credibility and effectiveness take a hit without the great diversity of this country."[91] He, too, offered no evidence to support the claim that demographic diversity enhances agencies' operational performance, although the FBI can make a good case for recruiting people who "look like America" because it deals daily with all varieties of Americans. In contrast, the foreign-focused agencies address other issues, deal with people who look like other countries' people, and correspondingly need other backgrounds and skills.

In 2014 Clapper sought to engineer politically relevant change in the organizational cultures of IC agencies by issuing a seven-part "Principles of Professional Ethics," with which he expected all IC employees to comply. One of the principles was and remains:

> DIVERSITY. We embrace the diversity of our nation, promote diversity and inclusion in our workforce, and encourage diversity in our thinking.[92]

Note that diversity of "thinking"—the operationally useful characteristic and former priority—appears after demographic diversity. The first priority is Obama's domestic political goal of making the IC "look like America." This policy entered later ODNI policy documents and remains in them.

In 2015, Clapper created the *IC Equal Employment Opportunity and Diversity Enterprise Strategy, 2015-2020*.[93] Consistent with Obama's EO 13582, this *Strategy* holds agency executives accountable for ensuring diversity and inclusion through

---

91   Ibid.

92   Director of National Intelligence, *National Intelligence Strategy, 2014*, 3.

93   ODNI website, https://www.dni.gov/files/documents/Newsroom/Press%20 Releases/2016EnterpriseStrategy.pdf.

performance objectives that include "unconscious bias training." Clapper made the course mandatory for managers throughout the IC.

Diversity became a prominent part of the quadrennial *National Intelligence Strategy* documents, which are modestly binding on IC agencies. Beginning in 2014 they included Obama's "diversity and inclusion" mantra. Clapper's intelligence code of ethics is prominently included in this *Strategy*, which also ostensibly required all intelligence officers to embrace and advance Obama's "diversity and inclusion" agenda. The 2019 version of the *Strategy*, published well after Donald Trump became president, is very similar to the 2014 edition, making clear in another of many ways that the ODNI bureaucracy had accepted and internalized Obama's agenda and that Trump's first DNI, Dan Coats, did not change IC policies on diversity. Indeed, no Trump-appointed DNI did so. Although Clapper as DNI had limited executive powers over the IC's agencies, some formal policies such as the *Strategy* documents were important prods to the reconstruction of cultures in receptive agencies, most prominently the CIA.[94]

In 2016, Clapper declared that he was not happy with the results of his diversity promotion campaign. Despite his efforts, the IC's proportions of women and minorities were below those of the rest of the federal workforce—his standard of comparison.[95] He therefore directed the ODNI's IC-oriented diversity chief, Rita Sampson, to find a way to publish the IC's diversity numbers in an unclassified format, in order to "hold us—*and more*

---

94   Woodward, *Rage*, 68-69; Brennan, *Undaunted*, 291. See also Susan M. Gordon, "CIA critics are making a false choice between diversity and excellence," *Washington Post*, May 11, 2021, Opinion | Susan Gordon: CIA critics are creating a false choice between diversity and excellence - The Washington Post.

95   Nicole Ogrysko, "Why the intelligence community declassified its demographics stats for the first time," Federal News Network, June 13, 2016, https://federalnewsnetwork.com/hiring-retention/2016/06/intelligence-community-declassified-demographics-stats-first-time/.

importantly, future leaders—accountable for our shortcomings" (emphasis added).[96] In this and many other ways, Clapper and Brennan clearly intended to make permanent changes in the IC's demography, processes, and culture that future administrations could not reverse. But despite Clapper's pessimism, the report shows gains in employment for favored groups. And as always, it contained no statement about what level or kind of diversity is appropriate or adequate.[97]

Clapper also influenced the National Intelligence Priorities Framework (NIPF), which specifies priority collection and analytic issues for the IC as a whole. Whereas for many years the individual agencies whose personnel interacted with consumers identified collection requirements and analytic priorities, President Clinton initiated the first centralized priorities identification system in his Presidential Decision Directive 35, issued in March 1995.[98] In 2003, President Bush, seeing problems with Clinton's system, introduced the NIPF, which remains in force.[99] ICD 204 explains the system, in which senior policymakers—that is, the White House—mainly determine intelligence priorities. But the IC's leaders retain some authority to influence priorities. This means that the ODNI is able to influence the issues the IC addresses. The directive orders the Deputy DNI for Intelligence Integration, who works directly for the DNI, to "oversee the development and management of the NIPF."[100] Therefore, Clapper, like any aggressive DNI, could shape both the worldviews of IC personnel

---

96   Clapper, *Facts and Fears*, 302.

97   ODNI, Diversity Report.

98   https://fas.org/irp/offdocs/pdd35.htm.

99   DNI Clapper, Intelligence Community Directive 204, "National Intelligence Priorities Framework," January 2, 2015, https://www.dni.gov/files/documents/ ICD/ICD%20204%20National%20Intelligence%20Priorities%20Framework.pdf.

100   Ibid., paragraph 5.

and the issues they addressed—potentially significant influences on the analytic priorities and biases of the IC.

These abilities were complemented by three other DNI influence mechanisms. First, as the president's senior intelligence advisor, DNIs regularly suggest issues about which presidents should be concerned. Second, the IRTPA moved the *PDB* staff from CIA to the ODNI, meaning the DNI now can review and change the wording of *PDB* articles. Third, the DNI appoints National Intelligence Managers (NIMs) and NIOs, who have overlapping responsibilities. NIMs integrate collection and analysis in key intelligence regional and functional areas. Since 2005, NIOs have directly supported senior decision-makers, especially the national security advisor, reviewed *PDB* articles, and continued to manage the national intelligence estimative process.[101] Clapper therefore was in a position to influence many aspects of the IC in politically salient ways.

In an open letter to IC leaders dated January 19, 2017, the day before he left office, Clapper reminded intelligence officers of his policies regarding diversity and inclusion, obviously intending to encourage them to continue his policies independently of the desires of his successors.[102] It was a blatant call to insubordination if needed in the Trump years, but the logic does not pertain only to Trump; its open-ended appeal applies implicitly to any president or DNI whose views differ from Clapper's.

In May 2017, Clapper joined the Center for a New American Security, a left-leaning Washington think-tank, as a Distinguished Senior Fellow for Intelligence and National Security. He also

---

101   Hutchings and Treverton, *Truth to Power.*

102   James Clapper, "DNI Letter to IC Leadership on Promoting Diversity and Inclusion within the U.S. Intelligence Community," January 19, 2017, https://www.dni.gov/index.php/newsroom/reports-publications/reports-publications-2017/item/1740-dni-letter-to-ic-leadership-on-promoting-diversity-and-inclusion-within-the-u-s-intelligence-community.

signed a contract to be a paid, on-air contributor to CNN, where he regularly criticized President Trump on a wide variety of issues, including many non-intelligence topics. In September 2018, at a forum at George Mason University, Clapper admitted that he got "blowback" from intelligence and military personnel critical of his political activism but he explained why he persevered, "I felt it was my duty, my obligation, to speak up" about Trump's alleged defects.[103]

CIA INITIATIVES

The CIA was a major, early supporter of Obama's diversity agenda. Obama's first DCIA, Leon Panetta (2009-2011), a former Democratic congressman and chief of staff for President Clinton without intelligence experience other than duty as a junior Army intelligence officer in 1964-1966[104], told the CIA workforce in an internal, unclassified memo in July 2009 that he would increase the share of minorities in CIA's staff from 22 percent then to 30 percent in 2012, a very rapid increase given the agency's lengthy hiring process.[105] This effort would help make the CIA "look like" America, Panetta averred.[106] He said nothing about how the change would affect CIA's performance. Following the smaller such effort during the Clinton years, Panetta made clear that demographic diversity, not the intellectual diversity long valued at CIA, had become a major policy focus.[107] EEO was passé, diversity quotas were in vogue.

---

103   Olivia Gazis, "Ex-NSA chief says he never discussed collusion with Trump," *CBS News*, September 12, 2018, https://www.cbsnews.com/news/nsa-admiral-mike-rogers-says-never-had-discussion-about-collusion-donald-trump/.

104   Panetta, *Worthy Fights*, 20-22.

105   Gentry, "Intelligence Learning and Adaptation," 75.

106   Ibid.

107   Jones, "The CIA Under Clinton: Continuity and Change," 504, 517-518; Obama's Executive Order 13583 of August 18, 2011.

According to Panetta, White House staffers tightly controlled the policies and activities of agency heads, including himself as DCIA, making clear that Obama drove his diversity initiative.[108] DCIAs David Petraeus (2011-2012), who did not have a close personal relationship with Obama, and John Brennan, who by many accounts was very close to Obama, followed suit.[109] Panetta thus began the Obama administration's program of Balkanizing the CIA's workforce, making identity politics a key part of personnel management of the CIA in new and controversial ways that would culminate in Brennan's years as DCIA and remain in effect through the Trump years.

A retired US Army general who was not a career intelligence officer, DCIA Petraeus made few management changes. Panetta's diversity policies remained in place. Continuing complaints that women did not have enough senior positions at the CIA led Petraeus in April 2012 to commission a study on the status of women at the CIA, which was chaired by President Clinton's last secretary of state, Madeleine Albright, who had no direct intelligence experience.[110] Albright found that while the female share of the CIA workforce was much larger than at some other IC agencies, 46 percent in 2012, up from 38 percent on 1980 and roughly the female share of the civilian labor force but higher than the share of women in the federal civilian workforce, the share of women in senior positions was lower and only 19 percent of people promoted to the senior intelligence service in 2012 were women.[111] Albright found at CIA what has been noted widely elsewhere: there are many reasons why women do not achieve senior positions

108   Panetta, *Worthy Fights*, 232.

109   John Kiriakou, "Mike Pompeo's CIA Will Not Reflect America's Diversity," *truthdig*, September 17, 2017, https://www.truthdig.com/articles/mike-pompeos-cia-will-not-reflect-america/.

110   Central Intelligence Agency, *Director's Advisory Group on Women in Leadership*.

111   Ibid., 4.

at the same rate as men, which mostly reflect personal choices, not discrimination. For example, more women than men quit before all employees normally reach senior positions, and women are more likely than men to go on leave-without-pay status for a time or take part-time jobs, impediments to promotion to senior ranks for all employees. Albright recommended ten changes in policy that effectively called for women to be treated preferentially to redress the political unattractiveness of the employment statistics.

Brennan, who had succeeded Petraeus as DCIA by the time Albright's report was completed in March 2013, accepted all of her recommendations. According to a former senior female CIA operations officer, the preferential treatment for women was controversial and divisive within CIA. While some women liked it, men felt discriminated against and senior women who had succeeded in traditional ways, such as herself, felt their accomplishments and reputations were diminished.[112] In his memoir, while he recognized that some CIA personnel did not like some of his policies, Brennan did not acknowledge this controversy.[113]

Brennan, whose close personal relationship with Obama when Brennan was a White House official in 2009-2013 has been widely noted, believed strongly in Obama's diversity agenda and moved strenuously to advance it.[114] Like Clapper, Brennan changed policies, structures, and incentives in ways designed to change CIA's organizational culture in ways that would be both politically significant and enduring. Brennan's "roadmap" plan for the agency had diversity and inclusion as one of its five goals. In December 2013 Brennan commissioned a study called *Director's Diversity in Leadership Study*, citing Obama's EO 13583 as

---

112 Discussion with a former senior CIA officer, autumn 2019.
113 Brennan, *Undaunted*, 286-287.
114 Ibid., 52, 132, 286, 289-290.

authority for his decision.[115] The *Study* was published in 2015. Prepared by a group chaired by black civil rights activist Vernon Jordan,[116] the *Study* claimed that "The Agency's workforce is not diverse."[117] This statement is flatly contradicted by figures in the report, but the study accurately reported that European-American men held a larger share of senior positions than junior ones. The study argued, again without evidence, that more demographic diversity was needed to help the agency perform better. But the study gave Brennan more material to justify his program. Said Brennan: "CIA simply must do more to develop the diverse and inclusive leadership environment that *our values require* and that our mission demands" (emphasis added).[118]

Brennan almost did not become a CIA employee. He voted for Gus Hall, leader of the Communist Party of the USA, for president of the United States in 1976.[119] He later claimed it was to protest the US system.[120] He was not a party member, which would have disqualified him from a CIA job. He also was twenty-one years old at the time. Young people often do impetuous things, but the vote was consistent with the general

---

115 John Brennan, "CIA Diversity and Inclusion Strategy (2016-2019)," 3, https://www.cia.gov/library/reports/Diversity_Inclusion_Strategy_2016_to_2019.pdf.

116 Vernon's group consisted of Michèle Flournoy, Justin Jackson, Steve Kappes, retired Admiral Mike Mullen, and Catherine Pino. Flournoy was undersecretary of defense for policy in 2009-2012. Jackson, an African-American, was a senior CIA operations officer. Kappes also was a senior CIA operations officer and deputy DCIA. Mullen, as chairman of the Joint Chiefs of Staff, supported ending the controversial "don't ask, don't tell" policy regarding gays in the military. Pino is a lesbian activist. This is not an intellectually diverse group.

117 CIA website, https://www.cia.gov/library/reports/dls-report.pdf, 13.

118 Adam B. Lerner, "CIA study: White men dominate agency's top ranks," *Politico*, June 30, 2015, https://www.politico.com/story/2015/06/cia-internal-study-white-men-dominate-agency-top-ranks-minorities-119603. See also Brennan, *Undaunted*, 289-290.

119 Tal Kopan, "Polygraph panic: CIA director fretted his vote for communist," *CNN Politics*, September 15, 2016, https://www.cnn.com/2016/09/15/politics/john-brennan-cia-communist-vote/index.html.

120 Ibid. For Brennan's account of reasons for, and implications of, his 1976 vote, see Brennan, *Undaunted*, 50-52.

political orientation Brennan demonstrated repeatedly in later life. In 1980, when he applied to CIA, his vote for Hall caused him concern. He told CIA's security people of his vote, but they did not disqualify him. The episode taught him a lesson. Said Brennan in 2016 in encouraging CIA employees to be politically active:

> "So if back in 1980, John Brennan was allowed to say, 'I voted for the Communist Party with Gus Hall' ... and still got through, rest assured that your rights and your expressions and your freedom of speech as Americans is something that's not going to be disqualifying of you as you pursue a career in government."[121]

He came close to being wrong, and may have crossed that line. The Hatch Act of 1939 specifically prohibits federal employees from participating in partisan political activities of any kind. Brennan advocated political activism repeatedly to employee groups, with evidently considerable effects.

Brennan began his CIA career as an analyst in the Near East office after the completing the agency's "career trainee" program.[122] He did a tour as a political officer at the U.S. embassy in Jeddah, Saudi Arabia in 1982-1984 and was a *PDB* briefer for President Clinton for about ten months in 1994-1995. Later, he moved into the operations world and was in 1996-1999, according to his own account, the "senior intelligence liaison" officer in Saudi Arabia.[123] Because he was a one-time operations officer, career DO people

---

121   Kopan, "Polygraph panic."

122   For a detailed account of his career path, see Brennan, *Undaunted*.

123   Brennan's biographic sketch at https://www.centeronnationalsecurity.org/john-o-brennans-undaunted-my-fight-against-americas-enemies-at-home-and-abroad. Listen also to The Lawfare Podcast: John Brennan Remains Undaunted, October 6, 2020, https://www.lawfareblog.com/lawfare-podcast-john-brennan-remains-undaunted; Brennan, *Undaunted*, 106-117.

regarded him disparagingly as an analyst, while some analysts did not regard him as top notch either.[124] But Brennan established close ties to senior intelligence and political leaders, especially with deputy DCI and then DCI George Tenet, ensuring bureaucratic success. He was chief of staff to DCI Tenet in 1999-2001 after returning from Saudi Arabia, then was deputy executive director of the CIA, and was President Bush's first (acting) director of NCTC in 2005. Soon thereafter, also in 2005, because he said he was irritated that Bush did not appoint him to be permanent director of NCTC, he retired from government service at the age of fifty after twenty-five years at CIA.

After leaving CIA, he became chief executive of a security-focused consulting group, The Analysis Corporation, which provided contract services to NCTC.[125] In 2008 he worked for Senator Obama's presidential campaign and then joined Obama's transition team. He impressed Obama.[126] Brennan was President-elect Obama's initial choice to be DCIA—a selection that quickly became controversial when some senators criticized Brennan's role in the CIA's enhanced interrogation activities, a major controversy in Washington in late 2008.[127] Brennan later said he actually opposed the interrogation techniques, but did not publicize his opposition within CIA—an unpersuasive comment.[128]

Recognizing political reality, Obama pulled Brennan's

---

124 Various personal communications. See also Smith, *Permanent Coup*, 16-20; London, *The Recruiter*, 376-382.

125 Martin Peretz, "John Brennan, Obama's (Alas) Nitwit Counterterrorism Adviser, And His Plans To Make Hezbollah Moderate. He's Also The Inventor And The Watchdog Of The Watchlist. My, My," *The New Republic*, May 20, 2010, https://newrepublic.com/article/75092/john-brennan-obamas-alas-nitwit-counterterrorism-adviser-and-his-plans-make-he.

126 For example, Hayden, *Playing to the Edge*, 168, 174-175.

127 Tom Gjelten, "Some Say Obama Team Forced Out CIA Contender," *National Public Radio*, December 8, 2008, https://www.npr.org/templates/story/story.php?storyId=97778356. For Brennan's account of this period, see Brennan, *Undaunted*, 168-188.

128 Brennan, *Undaunted*, 165-188.

nomination, instead naming him to be his homeland security advisor on the NSC staff—a position that does not require Senate confirmation. DCIA Hayden, who had discussed his job with Brennan during the presidential transition period, reported that Brennan seemed embittered by Obama's decision, a perception he confirmed in his memoir.[129] In his White House role, Brennan was by many accounts a trusted aide to Obama and a policymaker. He was, for example, a principal architect of Obama's drone-strike-based counterterrorism (CT) policy and brought CT-related policy proposals directly to Obama. Over CIA objections, he urged a greater military role in Obama's CT strategy, which prominently featured targeted killings.[130] Brennan said of his relationship with Obama in 2012:

> Ever since the first couple of months, I felt there was a real similarity of views that gave me a sense of comfort. I don't think we've had a disagreement.[131]

Brennan was a politically charged advocate of Obama's CT policies.[132] He was, in the words of Brookings Institution scholar Bruce Riedel, who knew him well at CIA, "certainly a partisan of the president."[133] Riedel compared Brennan's close political ties to his president to those of President Ronald Reagan's first DCI, William Casey, who had been Reagan's 1980 campaign manager.

---

129   Hayden, *Playing to the Edge*, 358-360; Brennan, *Undaunted*, 167.

130   Karen DeYoung, "CIA veteran John Brennan has transformed U.S. counterterrorism policy," *Washington Post*, October 24, 2012, https://www.washingtonpost.com/world/national-security/cia-veteran-john-brennan-has-transformed-us-counterterrorism-policy/2012/10/24/318b8eec-1c7c-11e2-ad90-ba5920e56eb3_story.html.

131   Ibid.

132   Sources asked for anonymity.

133   Author discussion with Bruce Riedel, September 12, 2019.

Casey also was a former intelligence officer, having served in the OSS during World War II.

Brennan slanted administration narratives in ways favorable to Obama. He inaccurately claimed that Obama had succeeded in obliterating al-Qaeda, a task the allegedly inept Bush administration was unable to do.[134] Like Obama, he initially claimed incorrectly that the "Arab Spring" was the death knell of terrorism.[135] Mimicking Obama, he did not speak of Islamic extremists, just extremists. Brennan claimed that US drone strikes in Pakistan had killed very few civilians, a view widely seen as incorrect.[136] In these and other ways, in a variety of settings, he expressed views that knowledgeable CT specialists and the press thought were either uninformed—hard to believe given his role and background—or were purposefully deceptive to try to make Obama look good.[137]

In 2010, after Obama fired DNI Blair, Brennan suggested to Obama that he name James Clapper, then Under Secretary of Defense for Intelligence, to be DNI.[138] Obama did so. As DCIA, Brennan would have what he called a close relationship with "the inimitable Jim Clapper," who was his "foxhole buddy and good friend" as well as an ideological comrade in working to re-shape the IC's demography and organizational cultures.[139]

By early 2013 the heat of the interrogation scandal had dissipated and Congressional opposition to Brennan had waned, enabling Obama to nominate Brennan to succeed Petraeus as DCIA after Petraeus was forced to resign due to a scandal. Brennan

---

134   Two sources who independently said virtually the same thing asked for anonymity.
135   Byman, "Explaining the Western Response to the Arab Spring," 300.
136   Karen DeYoung, "CIA veteran John Brennan has transformed U.S. counterterrorism policy."
137   These sources asked for anonymity.
138   Brennan, *Undaunted*, 226-227.
139   Ibid., 7, 18, 414.

won confirmation by a vote of sixty-three to thirty-four.[140] He became DCIA in March 2013 and was DCIA until Obama left office on January 20, 2017.

As DCIA, Brennan continued to display some of the behavior he had shown earlier: relatively overt embrace of domestic politics for an intelligence officer, strong loyalty to Obama, and sometimes a casual respect for facts. The latter trait, ironically, was one of Brennan's primary complaints about Donald Trump. He was loyal to the CIA and the Obama administration to the point of perhaps lying to protect their reputations. He denied that CIA people broke into a SSCI communications system in 2014.[141] Yet the CIA's inspector general concluded that CIA officers had in fact penetrated the computer network SSCI staffers used in their investigation of the agency's interrogation program, read Senate emails, and sent a referral for a criminal investigation to the Justice Department that was based on false information.[142] No CIA person was held accountable; the Justice Department declined to prosecute and Obama kept Brennan on.[143] The episode bears a passing resemblance to accusations that Brennan inappropriately encouraged the FBI's investigation of the Trump campaign's relationships with Russians in 2016, a charge whose accuracy remains contested. Brennan also denied that CIA steals secrets from other countries—a core intelligence mission that most external intelligence services do and which is a well-known CIA

---

140   Propublica, https://projects.propublica.org/represent/votes/113/senate/1/32.

141   Steve Chapman, "The intelligence community keeps lying," *Chicago Tribune*, August 7, 2014, http://www.chicagotribune.com/columns/steve-chapman/ct-cia-james-clapper-spying-steve-chapman-oped-080-20140807-column.html.

142   Mark Mazetti and Carl Hulse, "Inquiry by C.I.A. Affirms It Spied on Senate Panel," *New York Times*, July 14, 2014, https://www.nytimes.com/2014/08/01/world/senate-intelligence-commitee-cia-interrogation-report.html. For his side of this story, see Brennan, *Undaunted*, 302-330.

143   Carrie Johnson, "No Criminal Charges In Senate-CIA Spat, Justice Department Says," *NPR*, July 10, 2014, https://www.npr.org/sections/thetwo-way/2014/07/10/330465260/no-criminal-charges-in-senate-cia-spat-justice-department-says.

responsibility.[144] Some operations officers, especially, complained bitterly about the misstatement.

Brennan recounted in his book that he long had been dissatisfied with aspects of CIA culture.[145] As he progressed in rank, he took opportunities to change it. For example, in 1994, as head of a team assessing analytic tradecraft at CIA, he relished "the ability to shape the Agency's analytic culture."[146] As director, he had many more opportunities to change the culture, working closely with his good friend and fellow social engineer Jim Clapper.

Brennan had a reputation for partisanship even before he became a political appointee. Former CIA operations officer Sam Faddis wrote: "John Brennan, CIA Director under President Obama, was technically an analyst, although his real profession for most of his career was being a Democratic political hack."[147] A retired CIA analyst similarly reported that in the early 2000s Brennan had a reputation in parts of CIA for having outspokenly partisan, pro-Democratic views.[148] Later, Brennan developed a reputation among CIA analysts for politicizing intelligence by giving President Obama what he wanted to hear, not objective analysis—a cardinal analytic sin under the old normative regime.[149] Hayden made the same point, albeit aimed less pointedly at Brennan, by saying CIA politicized its products in the Brennan years by pandering to White House wishes on intelligence that partly enabled the Joint Comprehensive Plan of Action (JCPOA),

---

144   Ken Dilanian, "Former Spooks Criticize CIA Director John Brennan for Spying Comments" *NBC News*, March 2, 2016, https://www.nbcnews.com/news/us-news/brennan-joking-when-he-says-cia-spies-doesn-t-steal-n529426. For his view of this episode, see Brennan, *Undaunted*, 297.

145   Brennan, *Undaunted*, 132, 140, 283, 270, 286.

146   Ibid., 94.

147   Charles "Sam" Faddis, "We Are Late," June 25, 2019, http://andmagazine.com/talk/2019/06/25/we-are-late/.

148   Personal conversation, early 2019.

149   Private communication with a retired senior CIA analyst, September 3, 2019.

the nuclear deal with Iran concluded in July 2015, and by initially discounting signs of Russian meddling in US politics in 2015.[150] Hayden claimed incongruously that the analysts were only committing "a subtle form of self-censorship" or "self-policing," not politicization.[151] This distinction is nonsense. Retired operations officer Douglas London, who says he dealt periodically with Brennan as DCIA, went further, arguing that Brennan politicized CIA generally in support of Obama.[152] These traits of Brennan, and reactions to them at CIA, were evident long before Trump arrived on the national political scene.

Brennan actively participated in events within CIA that celebrated Obama's preferred demographic groups—minorities, LGBT persons, and women.[153] After Brennan spoke to a group of African-American intelligence personnel, the National Security Executives and Professionals Association (NSEPA) 3rd Annual National Security and Intelligence Career Development and Leadership Summit on May 21, 2016, the group's president, Reginald King, citing Brennan's substantial efforts to bring blacks into the CIA, said, "Mr. Brennan has taken the conversation about diversity and inclusion further than it has ever been taken in my 26 years with the Agency."[154] The group's conventions began during the Obama years.

Citing the *Director's Diversity in Leadership Study*, Brennan made clear that he would hold managers personally accountable for increasing "diversity." While I know of no case where Brennan explicitly punished a manager for a failure in this arena, the

---

150 Hayden, *Assault on Intelligence*, 36-37.

151 Ibid.

152 London, *The Recruiter*, 376-382.

153 Brennan. *Undaunted*, 291.

154 CIA, "Director Brennan Speaks at NSEPA Conference," CIA website, https://
www.cia.gov/news-information/featured-story-archive/2016-featured-story-
archive/director-brennan-speaks-at-nsepa-conference.html.

creation of institutional incentives—positive and negative—is often the best way to motivate desired bureaucratic behavior.[155] CIA people typically are politically savvy in the sense that they usually accurately read even modest bureaucratic pressures as de facto instructions. The incentives permeated the agency. An employee in CIA's Directorate of Support said her managers punished subordinates who did not support Brennan's diversity policies.[156] She stated explicitly that she felt intimidated. The structural, policy, and cultural changes that clearly occurred, the lack of need to punish recalcitrant managers, and ODNI figures showing "progress" on re-shaping the demographics of the CIA workforce indicate that Brennan generally got his way. Still, Brennan reported that some employees told him pointedly that they opposed his diversity policies.[157] He evidently ignored them.

Soon after Trump's election, Brennan reported in his memoir, "a significant number" of female, Muslim, black, and LGBT employees expressed to him their concerns that Trump's comments portended a possible retreat from the agency's diversity and inclusion agenda.[158] In response, he and deputy DCIA David Cohen held two meetings with employees in the agency's auditorium. He recounted his words:

> Do not let the progress be undone.... You know what is right. If you see that a colleague is not being treated fairly, speak up. If you believe that Agency leaders are not fulfilling their responsibilities to promote diversity

---

155   Gentry, "Managers of Analysts."
156   Ibid.
157   Brennan, *Undaunted*, 290.
158   Ibid., 392.

and inclusion, speak out. You have the ability to shape the Agency's future. Seize it, and never let it go.[159]

He thereby encouraged CIA employees to emulate and support his activist political agenda. Soon thereafter he told a reporter that he met with the CIA workforce several times before his departure from office to tell them that while the agency's progress on diversity and inclusion over the years had been significant, it was their responsibility to keep it moving forward. The reporter recounted that Brennan claimed he said:

> "It's up to you to make sure it's not going to be reversible," he recalled telling them. "If [you] see something that is wrong or not in keeping with the agency's commitment to diversity and inclusion ...[you] need to speak up and speak out."[160]

In other words Brennan, like Clapper at ODNI, told CIA personnel to participate overtly in political activities, internally or externally, in ways that were ideologically motivated and were designed to thwart the freedom of action of his duly appointed successors. Like Clapper, he came close to explicitly calling for insubordination against Trump. It was a radically different approach than any other DCIA or DCI before him had taken and was inappropriate given the still extant normative prohibition on overt communication of political views both inside and outside CIA by serving intelligence officers and Hatch Act prohibitions.

---

159   Ibid., 392-393.
160   Jenna McLaughlin, "More White, More Male, More Jesus: CIA Employees Fear Pompeo Is Quietly Killing the Agency's Diversity Mandate," *Foreign Policy*, September 7, 2017, https://foreignpolicy.com/2017/09/08/more-white-more-male-more-jesus-cia-employees-fear-pompeo-is-quietly-killing-the-agencys-diversity-mandate/.

But given that many employees evidently agreed with his philosophy and policies and that evolving cultural norms permitted freer expression of personal political opinions, Brennan's last words as DCIA gave an only modest additional spur to the political activism by employees that blossomed after Trump's election victory. The exhortation by a senior, sitting official presumably helped some CIA employees convince themselves that their political activism was sanctioned, legitimate, and acceptable. As discussed in chapter 5, political activism by serving intelligence officers in the form of leaks, many of them evidently by CIA personnel, spiked in late 2016 and remained high in the Trump years.

Brennan told the *Wall Street Journal* in January 2017, just before leaving office, that he hoped he would be remembered most for the "way he fought to nurture a workforce that reflected America's diversity."[161] This is a strong statement of his determination to impose a new domestic politics-oriented regime on the CIA. In contrast, soon-to-be-former intelligence leaders after nearly four years on the job usually cite major accomplishments in the operational performance of their organizations. Not Brennan.

Indeed, Brennan was successful in that he institutionalized to a considerable extent Obama's "diversity and inclusion" agenda in a major IC agency. He also left an action plan and a staff at CIA to continue his politically-oriented work after he left office.[162] As at the ODNI, "The team implementing the CIA's efforts to build a diverse workforce, which is led by a senior Agency officer dedicated to this task, is still in place and working on these

161 Shane Harris, "CIA Director John Brennan Rejects Donald Trump's Criticism," *Wall Street Journal*, January 16, 2017, https://www.wsj.com/articles/cia-director-john-brennan-rejects-donald-trumps-criticism-1484611514.

162 No byline or date, "20 Years of Pride," Central Intelligence Agency, https://www.cia.gov/news-information/featured-story-archive/2016-featured-story-archive/20-years-of-pride.html.

efforts. See our website which continues to publish that strategy," a CIA spokesperson said in September 2017.[163] Another CIA spokesperson said virtually the same thing to me personally in July 2019.[164]

In July 2019, the CIA's strategic "roadmap," promulgated by Brennan, was still Agency policy and still included "diversity and inclusion" as one of its five enabling elements.[165] When I asked a CIA Office of Public Affairs officer about the meaning of the term, he responded with two explanations. First, he said DCIA Gina Haspel (2018-2021) was committed to recruiting people with excellent area, language, and cultural expertise. This is the traditional reason for wanting diversity of experience and outlook in an intelligence service and long predates the "diversity and inclusion" agenda; it was also the view of DCIA Mike Pompeo (2017-2018), which generated opposition from CIA people. But the official also said CIA competes for young people, primarily 18- to 35-year-olds, who are steeped in this perspective, meaning the Agency needs to do so to be competitive. This comment evidently referred to the commitment to Obama's diversity agenda of many of the universities that potential recruits recently attended and by the Democratic Party. An uncharitable interpretation of this comment is that CIA may have been marketing deceptively. But the totality of CIA's activities and policies in the Haspel years suggests that she bought the Obama program to a considerable but not extreme degree while also seeking operationally useful diversity. Activist structures such as the diversity office remained in place during Haspel's tenure as DCIA and she extended their reach lower into the agency's sub-elements. These positions can

---

163   Ibid.
164   Personal communication, July 25, 2019.
165   CIA briefing for Agency annuitants and their families, July 25, 2019.

be made to look only slightly incompatible, although clearly the two goals are not identical. Bureaucracies fudge this way chronically. Haspel could get away with this balancing act far better than Pompeo could because she was female and a career CIA officer—one of their own—and not a political associate of Trump.

In sum, while many CIA personnel liked Brennan, others did not appreciate his management style or policies, independent of his opposition to Trump. A retired senior officer expressed a view of him that seems to be fairly common:

> He was not/not my favorite director. I think history will show that he did grave harm to the organization on a number of levels, but that he meant well. He was over his head as Deputy [Executive Director] back in the early 2000s. ... [When] he took the helm at [Terrorist Threat Integration Center] - which would become NCTC. Oh the battles he spawned!![166]

LESS ACTIVITY IN OTHER AGENCIES

The other IC agencies before 2017 were less enthusiastic about Obama's "diversity and inclusion" doctrine than was CIA while still seeking useful diversity and making some structural changes per Obama's directive. Although IC agencies can largely ignore most ODNI guidance if they wish, they generally obey presidential orders. For example, in June 2010, the NSA's Central Security Service, which links main NSA with the cryptologic elements of the armed services, identified nine core organizational values, none of which was close to "diversity and inclusion."[167] Later, presumably reflecting Obama's executive

---

166   Personal email communication, 2020.

167   NSA/CSS Strategy, June 2010, https://fas.org/irp/nsa/strategy.pdf.

order and pressure from Clapper, the term entered NSA's lexicon. But in contrast to ODNI and CIA, NSA in 2019 retained a more operationally-focused concept of diversity:

> NSA is committed to creating a workforce that has a diverse set of backgrounds, experiences and points of view. To provide and protect national security, we must capitalize on the rich diversity of knowledge, skills, abilities, backgrounds and perspectives of our workforce. National security and diversity go hand-in-hand as essential partners in the interest of global peace.[168]

NSA's website added:

> At NSA, diversity is about more than differences in skin color, culture, orientation, gender or gender identity. It's about cultivating an environment where talented individuals of all backgrounds can contribute to something bigger than themselves – our national security.[169]

This view evidently did not generate the opposition at NSA that occurred at CIA when DCIA Pompeo expressed a similar view. NSA did, however, divide its workforce into demographic groups consistent with Obama's identity politics. By 2019, NSA had specified and given code names to eleven demographically defined "employee resource groups:"

- AA (African-American)
- AAPI (Asian-American/Pacific Islander)
- AIAN (American Indian/Alaska Native)

---

168   NSA website, https://www.intelligence,gov/nsa/nsadiversity.html, as of August 5, 2019.
169   Ibid.

- AV (American Veteran)
- ESL (English as a Second Language)
- HLAT (Hispanic/Latino)
- IC (Islamic Culture)
- NG (Next Gen)
- PRIDE (Lesbian, Gay, Bisexual, Transgender & Allies)
- PWD (People with Disabilities)
- W (Women)[170]

Thus, the NSA workforce was Balkanized, but evidently to a considerably lesser extent than CIA's.

The DIA, like NSA, increasingly in recent years recognized identity groups. Special interest groups' dedicated months, especially Pride and Black History months, were celebrated massively. But modestly preferential treatment of women, LGBT people, and minorities seems to be generally consistent with the old affirmative action policies. One area of demographic preference DIA did push was people with physical disabilities, particularly veterans disabled in combat. DIA management did not, however, claim that blind and deaf employees contributed to the agency's performance. Indeed, it was obvious that additional associated costs were appreciable. A perceived need to advance social welfare, not politically motivated identity politics, fairly clearly was the primary motive.

RESULTS: DEMOGRAPHICS, SPECIAL INTEREST ORGANIZATIONS, CONTROVERSIES, AND POLITICAL IMPLICATIONS

The Obama/Clapper/Brennan campaign was successful in many respects. It changed the demographic composition of

---

170   Ibid.

the IC's workforce appreciably, although not as much as some wanted. The campaign helped produce and support special interest groups that pushed within the IC for even stronger commitments to "diversity," from which many of them benefited tangibly. Diversity policies also soon produced a reaction, especially in people who thought the favoritism shown to some groups meant discrimination against others in ways that damaged agencies' operational performance. This in turn generated a vigorous defense by partisans of diversity programs, who claimed that diversity in fact enhanced the IC's performance. The appreciable changes in the political outlooks of IC agencies writ large, beginning at the start of Obama's presidency, set the stage for reactions to Trump's arrival on the national political stage in 2016.

MEASURING DEMOGRAPHIC CHANGES

The results of the diversity campaign can be measured to some extent. Most tangibly, demographic statistics on many variables, including hiring, promotions, separations, and shares of pay grades demonstrated appreciable "progress" in the Clapper/Brennan years. Despite Clapper's concerns in 2016 that progress in achieving diversity goals was insufficient, the IC as a whole changed significantly on his watch. "All of the arrows are going in the right direction," said Patricia Taylor, the ODNI's chief of equal opportunity and diversity, in 2013; the agencies are "making a lot of progress in the upper pay grades and senior positions."[171] ODNI statistics indicated that intelligence agencies collectively were about 25 percent minority and 38 percent female during fiscal year 2016; minority and

---

171   Joe Davidson, "Intelligence director says budget cuts could be 'insidious' for national security," *Washington Post*, April 8, 2013, https://www.washingtonpost.com/politics/federal_government/intelligence-director-says-budget-cuts-could-be-insidious-for-national-security/2013/04/08/8795bc5e-a084-11e2-82bc-511538ae90a4_story.html?utm_term=.b056f1f26504.

female hiring rates were higher than the employment shares of the groups.[172] Women's share of the IC workforce exceeded 39 percent in 2019. The share of employees with disabilities rose from 5.3 percent in 2011 to 11.9 percent in 2019.[173]

The preferences continued with no statement of numerical goals or a definition of "enough" diversity ever being formally published, asserted, or even mused about. DCIA Panetta's goal for minority hiring by 2012 was an interim target. Instead, the de facto policy was and remains that more hiring and promotions of favored groups always is better. The Government Accountability Office (GAO) had two "benchmarks" that government agencies commonly used: (1) groups' share of the federal workforce and (2) groups' share of the civilian workforce.[174] When these did not provide adequate justification for preferences or did not seem persuasive, intelligence executives invoked others to demand or justify more preferences. Favorite other measures were: (1) distribution of groups in various agency subcomponents, specialties, and pay grades; and (2) shares of promotions and performance awards granted to each demographic group.[175] A convenient statistic could always be found. But even superficial such justifications were not needed, as DNI Blair made clear in 2009:

---

172 Office of the Director of National Intelligence, "Annual Demographic Report: Hiring and Retention of Minorities, Women, and Persons with Disabilities in the United States Intelligence Community Fiscal Year 2016," https://www.dni.gov/files/documents/Newsroom/Reports%20and%20Pubs/Annual%20Demographic%20Report%20-%202016.pdf, 43-81.

173 Ibid., 27; ODNI, "Annual Demographic Report Fiscal Year 2020," July 8, 2021, https://www.odni.gov/files/EEOD/documents/IC_Annual_Demographic_Report.pdf, p. 10.

174 U.S. Government Accountability Office, *Intelligence Community*, 3.

175 Leaders even identified various indicators at different times. For an example of DNI Clapper's thinking, see Nicole Ogrysko, "Why the intelligence community declassified its demographics stats for the first time," Federal News Network, June 13, 2016, https://federalnewsnetwork.com/hiring-retention/2016/06/intelligence-community-declassified-demographics-stats-first-time/.

> We're not where we want to be in all areas, but we are making steady progress year after year. For example, our African-American population has increased from 10.9 percent of our workforce to 11.5 percent over the last few years. That means our current representation is a percent higher than that of the Civilian Labor Force, which is the official benchmark that we use.[176]

For Blair, even meeting the standard he chose did not diminish the imperative to hire more blacks. With no declared targets for any variety of "diversity," more was better.

The IC continued to preferentially hire African-Americans. According to the ODNI's 2016 "Annual Demographic Report," blacks comprised 12.6 percent of the IC workforce in fiscal year 2016, compared with 12.7 percent of the US population, 10.4 percent of the civilian labor force, and 18.1 percent of the federal workforce.[177] That is, the black share of the IC's workforce was 21 percent greater than the black share of the civilian workforce. The black share of the federal workforce was 74 percent greater than the black share of the civilian workforce and over 42 percent greater than the black share of the population as a whole. Clapper pushed the IC to recruit and promote blacks, arguing that black persons' shares of higher pay grades and positions were not acceptable—that is, politically acceptable. The GAO's government employment benchmark was very useful for pushing hiring of blacks because blacks' share of the U.S. government workforce, being far above

---

176   DNI Dennis C. Blair, remarks to a conference, "White House Initiative on Historically Black Colleges and Universities," September 1, 2009, https://www.dni.gov/files/documents/Newsroom/Speeches%20and%20Interviews/20090901_speech.pdf.

177   Ibid., 46.

blacks' share of the population and of the civilian workforce, rationalized increasing the excess.

Justifications for the push for more women in the IC were different. While appreciable sex discrimination probably existed in the distant past, the CIA and NSA especially pushed "affirmative action" in hiring and promoting women since the 1980s, if not earlier. The share of women in the IC workforce in fiscal year 2016, at 38.5 percent, was up slightly in recent years, meaning there was already a lot of gender diversity. But preferences pushed women's share of promotions in 2016 in the IC as a whole to 44.9 percent and women's share of awards to 41.8 percent.[178] By 2013, women comprised 46 percent of CIA's workforce, up from 38 percent in 1980—virtually the same as women's share of civilian workforce.[179] In 2019, women and men were employed in approximately equal numbers at CIA, meaning women comprised a greater share of the CIA workforce than their 47 percent share of the U.S. workforce in 2019.[180] These figures exceeded both GAO benchmarks. The preferences continued nevertheless. The CIA posted in 2016:

> ... the CIA has made great strides in creating a more inclusive work environment for all officers, including its LGBT employees. While there have been successes in changing the CIA culture, like in all organizations we still have work to do.[181]

---

178 Office of the Director of National Intelligence, "Annual Demographic Report: Hiring and Retention of Minorities, Women, and Persons with Disabilities in the United States Intelligence Community Fiscal Year 2016," at https://www.dni.gov/files/documents/Newsroom/Reports%20and%20Pubs/Annual%20Demographic%20Report%20-%202016.pdf, page 18.

179 CIA, *Director's Advisory Group on Women in Leadership*, 4.

180 Catalyst, https://www.catalyst.org/research/women-in-the-workforce-united-states/.

181 No byline or date, "20 Years of Pride," Central Intelligence Agency, https://www.cia.gov/news-information/featured-story-archive/2016-featured-story-archive/20-years-of-pride.html.

NSA's efforts to increase the number of women in its workforce was more difficult given the relatively small number of women then (and now) interested in the technical aspects of many NSA jobs. Still, women's share of the NSA workforce rose from about 26 percent in 1977 to about 39 percent in 1993.[182]

The implicit and sometimes explicit assertion that women should have some "equal" share of IC jobs is inconsistent with dramatic differences in gender representations in occupations throughout the US economy, which clearly are matters of personal choice in most cases. U.S. Bureau of Labor Statistics figures illustrate that women and men self-select into various occupations at radically different rates (Table 3-1). These differences are not the result of discrimination. Employment rates in various occupations differ dramatically by sex because men and women *choose* to work in different jobs, an obvious fact the IC ignores. Only attractive (for often unspecified reasons) career fields in which women allegedly are underrepresented, such as intelligence, generate complaints. In contrast, few worry about the relative dearth of women among automotive service technicians (2.0% of the U.S. workforce in 2019), carpenters (1.9%), and plumbers, pipefitters, and steamfitters (1.4%).[183] Nor do they grouse that women comprise large shares of job categories such as nurse practitioners (87.9% of such workers in 2019), elementary and middle school teachers (80.3%), or veterinarians (64.1%).[184]

182 Johnson, *(U) American Cryptology during the Cold War, 1945-1981*, Book 4, 274, https://www.goodreads.com/book/show/45886633-american-cryptology-during-the-cold-war.

183 U.S. Department of Labor, Employment and Earnings by Occupation, 2019, https://www.dol.gov/agencies/wb/data/occupations.

184 Ibid.

TABLE 3-1

Job Categories Held by Women and Men, 2016

JOB CATEGORY	SHARE OF POSITIONS HELD BY WOMEN (%)	SHARE OF POSITIONS HELD BY MEN (%)
Secretaries and administrative assistants	94.6	5.4
Childcare workers	94.4	5.6
Registered nurses	90.0	10.0
Maids and housekeeping cleaners	89.6	10.4
Bookkeeping, accounting, and auditing clerks	88.5	11.5
Cashiers	73.2	26.8
Waiters and waitresses	70.0	30.0
Customer service representatives	65.0	35.0
Retail salespersons	48.4	51.6
US WORKFORCE AS A WHOLE	47.0	53.0
Cooks, restaurant	38.7	61.3
INTELLIGENCE EMPLOYEES	38.5	61.5
Janitors and cleaners, except maids	34.2	65.8
General and operations managers	29.8	70.2
Laborers and freight, stock, and material movers, hand	18.1	81.9
US MILITARY PERSONNEL	~ 18	~ 82
Heavy and tractor-trailer truck drivers	6.0	94.0

Sources: Bureau of Labor Statistics, "Shares of women and men employed, 2016, in occupations with the most projected annual openings, on average, 2016–26," at https://www.bls.gov/careeroutlook/2018/data-on-display/dod-women-in-labor-force.htm?view_full; Office of the Director of National Intelligence, "Annual Demographic Report: Hiring and Retention of Minorities, Women, and Persons with Disabilities in the United States Intelligence Community Fiscal Year 2016," at https://www.dni.gov/files/documents/Newsroom/Reports%20and%20Pubs/Annual%20Demographic%20Report%20-%202016.pdf, 19.

Job performance requirements and self-selection have led to very different demographic patterns in the US armed forces, including significantly different shares of minority groups in the US military, a volunteer force that reflects self-selection decisions among various ethnic groups in American society and a sharply lower rate of female employment consistent with society's (and most women's) desires to limit women's exposure to the dangers of combat.[185] Women's advocates never compare the IC's demographic patterns to those of the US military. Such a comparison does not help the drive to place more women in the IC.

While IC opponents of Trump clearly worried that he *might* reverse the "progress" of the diversity agenda, Obama's executive orders on "diversity and inclusion" remained in effect throughout Trump's presidency. While Trump rescinded or overturned some Obama-era executive orders, rules, and regulations, he did not touch these. And career operations officer Gina Haspel, whom Trump named to be the first female DCIA, promptly named women to nearly all of CIA's most senior positions, a widely noted decision that prompted much commentary. The diversity offices in the ODNI and at CIA continued to operate, and the IC's agencies continued to preferentially hire, promote, and reward minorities, women, and special interest groups. Agencies made clear that they did not intend to change Obama-era policies and practices on their own, or alter their continuing efforts to change organizational cultures. Hence, efforts to institutionalize the diversity agenda, of the sort Clapper and Brennan advocated, were largely successful.

---

185   ODNI, Annual Demographic Report, various pages; George M. Reynolds and Amanda Shendruk, "Demographics of the U.S. Military," Council on Foreign Relations, April 24, 2018, https://www.cfr.org/article/demographics-us-military.

ORGANIZATIONS

Obama's "diversity" agenda led the ODNI and the agencies to Balkanize the workforce into identity groups. They variously created and supported "employee resource groups" or "affinity groups." Each term was defined as people from distinctive identity groups other than white men. The groups reflect a social Marxian effort to generate divisions in populations other than economic/class differences and to promote "intersectionality," or identification of people belonging to multiple demographic groups that each are "oppressed" by Caucasian men. Eligible employees were pressured to join one or more groups, where employees allegedly could be "safe" from oppressive white males. My limited insight into them, from group members, is that they do indeed encourage expressions of complaints, and are effectively echo chambers in which grievances multiply. The Biden administration unsurprisingly has continued to push them, and in 2022 the FBI even asked job applicants which affinity group they planned to join or become an "ally" of—a requirement that amounts to a request for a statement of one's political views, which long has been considered inappropriate requests of federal workers and job applicants.[186]

Diversity offices organized and funded numerous events celebrating various ethnic and Pride months each year, including posters, displays, films, speeches, and meetings targeted at the agencies' interest groups and general populations. Designated celebratory months extol the contributions and virtues of the groups. Brennan showcased the contributions of LGBT people at his first Pride celebration at CIA.[187] At DIA, which conducted its first Pride celebration in 2012, these activities sometimes fill

---

186   Source: an applicant who filled out such forms.
187   Brennan, *Undaunted*, 290.

the central entry room of the headquarters building, slowing pedestrian movement in the building.[188] The IC also began to fund periodic conferences for the affinity groups, including for blacks and LGBT people, which senior officials regularly attended. Clapper described in his memoir his "pride" at meeting with LGBT employees when he was DNI.[189]

The "coming out" of employees of intelligence agencies occurred in growing numbers after gays and lesbians became more accepted in American society. President Clinton therefore decided homosexuality no longer posed a security risk, which traditionally was viewed primarily as vulnerability to blackmail. Clinton declared by executive order in 1995 that LGBT persons could receive security clearances, ending the practice of discharging employees found to be gay and enabling gays to work openly in the IC.[190] Since then, LGBT persons have been hired in apparently appreciable numbers. They quickly became politically active within the IC in ways roughly consistent with their frequently strident political activism in American society in general.

At the CIA, newly overt LGBT people quickly formed an association that still is a support group and an activist organization. The Agency Network for Gay, Lesbian, Bisexual, and Transgender Officers and Allies (ANGLE) was formed in 1996. It promotes its members' perspectives.[191] In roughly 2012, ANGLE asked CIA's history staff to write a history of gay and lesbian employees, which was denied because the staff then had a policy of not doing studies

---

188   DIA Public Affairs, "DIA Hosted 6th Annual Pride Month Event," June 21, 2017, https://www.dia.mil/News/Articles/Article/1224451/dia-hosted-6th-annual-pride-month-event/; author's personal observation.

189   Clapper, *Facts and Fears*, 301, 336.

190   President William J. Clinton, Executive Order 12968, "Access to Classified Information," August 7, 1995, section 3.1(c), https://www.dni.gov/index.php/ic-legal-reference-book/executive-order-12968.

191   No byline or date, CIA article "20 Years of Pride," at https://www.cia.gov/news-information/featured-story-archive/2016-featured-story-archive/20-years-of-pride.html.

of special interest groups (although it worked hard to document the contributions of women).[192] A history was completed about two years later but has not been released publicly.[193] DCIA Brennan expanded support for the organization. In an article posted on the CIA's website in 2016, on the twentieth anniversary of the founding of ANGLE, Brennan said, "By advancing the principles of equality and inclusion, they have helped promote fair treatment for everyone. For that, they can be truly proud."[194]

The CIA in Brennan's years condoned ANGLE's distribution of rainbow-colored lanyards, which employees wear around their necks and to which their identification documentation is attached, to enable employees to trumpet their sexual preferences or to express support for LGBT people—that is, to be an "ally."[195] The choice of a lanyard is personal; many employees traditionally have worn lanyards expressing support for favorite sports teams, for example. While employees differ good-naturedly over sports teams, lanyards previously had not referred to overtly political organizations or contentious political/social subjects. But Brennan, who is married to a female person and has three children with her, publicly said he wore a rainbow lanyard with pride.[196] He reported that he felt "especially privileged" to support LGBT employees; other senior managers dutifully followed Brennan and also wore rainbow lanyards.[197] Given the state of domestic politics in the United States, including the strong association of the LGBT community with the Democratic Party and the

---

192 Former CIA historian Nicholas Dujmović, conversation with author, June 19, 2019.

193 Nicholas Dujmović email to author, October 17, 2022.

194 Ibid.

195 Brennan, *Undaunted*, 290.

196 Elizabeth Harrington, "CIA Director Bemoans Growing Up 'A White Male from New Jersey'," *Washington Free Beacon*, January 17, 2017, https://freebeacon.com/issues/cia-director-bemoans-growing-white-male-new-jersey/.

197 Brennan, *Undaunted*, 290.

political activism of many LGBT persons, agency policy permitting rainbow lanyards enabled overt political statements that were only slightly removed from partisan politics. This policy, like others, contrasted dramatically with the CIA's former position of firmly directing employees to leave their personal views about all domestic political subjects at home. Principal Deputy DNI Stephanie O'Sullivan—the IC's second ranking official—hosted the first IC-wide event specifically designed to recruit LGBT persons in 2016.[198] According to a CIA operations officer who was offended by the practice, numerous ANGLE members and their non-LGBT supporters in 2019 still wore rainbow lanyards.[199] No senior Trump administration official sought to curb the practice as inappropriately political.

Blacks in Government (BIG), a self-described political advocacy organization as well as a support group for African-Americans, founded in 1975, was active in the IC and was especially prominent at DIA.[200] The government funded periodic BIG conferences, gave employees paid time off time to attend, and paid their travel expenses to conferences. Within the CIA, black-only groups also included the "Black Executive Board" and the "Board Room."[201] In my time at National Intelligence University (NIU), even relatively minor administrative actions recommended by committees, such as hiring decisions, had to have a minority person on the selection committee—a requirement of DIA, then NIU's executive agent.

More generally, agencies supported groups of people, perspectives, and organizations that comprised major elements of the

---

198 Mark Rosenball, "U.S. spy agencies to celebrate LGBT employees," *Reuters*, March 11, 2016, https://www.reuters.com/article/us-usa-spies-lgbt-idUSKCN0WD2EI.

199 Personal communication with author, early 2019.

200 BIG website, http://www.bignet.org/.

201 CIA, *Director's Diversity in Leadership Study*, 17, CIA website, https://www.cia.gov/library/reports/dls-report.pdf.

Democratic coalition, promoting the groups and their perceived rights in ways consistent with the Democratic Party's identity politics. Perceived rights of special interest groups sometimes conflicted, generating tensions among groups, but each got special treatment not given to Caucasian, heterosexual men. Each of the groups, moreover, consumed scarce resources as the government celebrated them, including money and senior managers' time.

Ned Price, the former CIA analyst and Obama White House staffer, said that CIA directors' support for affinity groups was a morale boost, and that there was no favoritism in hiring or promotions.[202] Merit, he said, was the sole criterion of hiring and promotion decisions. Other commentators, IC leaders in speeches, and official policy statements make clear that this was not the case. Merit-based hiring unaccompanied by a demographic "diversity" filter clearly was not Brennan's intent. Leaks in the Trump years strongly suggest it also was unacceptable to many intelligence professionals.

THE OPERATIONAL PERFORMANCE DEBATE

Obama's diversity policy was rationalized in two major ways. In his first term, the dominant rationale was that domestically defined demographic diversity is a good thing worth pursuing on its own—a philosophical or political argument consistent with Obama's politics—his "values." Clapper repeatedly claimed the IC's newly created "core values"[203] that emphasized diversity were good things.[204] "Our values" became the short-hand rationale for Obama's expansive diversity and inclusion program.

But a few years after Obama's program was operational, in

---

202 Ned Price discussion with author, July 30, 2019.

203 DNI, "Principles of Professional Ethics for the Intelligence Community," January 20, 2017, https://www.dni.gov/index.php/who-we-are/organizations/clpt/clpt-features/1789-principles-of-professional-ethics-for-the-intelligence-community.

204 Clapper, *Facts and Fears*, 337.

his second term, critics began to assert that his diversity policies had damaged the IC by hiring and promoting unqualified people and discriminating against able men, leading to damage to the quality of agencies' workforces, and thence to their operational performance. Diversity advocates vigorously contested such assertions, making in response a second claim: demographically defined diversity *improves* the performance of the IC. But no IC official ever credibly explained *how* demographic diversity improved the performance of US intelligence or even provided an example, relying on the then-common belief that diversity in workforces and on corporate boards is associated with better business performance. This controversy has continued to be a significant point of contention. Both ideology- and interest-based supporters of diversity emotionally defended the program and attacked its critics, who usually did not directly enter the intelligence/Trump fray. The performance controversy nevertheless became part of the conflict, albeit indirectly, because it called into question part of a core claim of Trump's opponents.

The new logic asserts that domestically defined minority persons and women, who allegedly have substantially different perspectives than white men, driven by race- or ethnicity-or gender-based differences alone, help the IC do its missions better. Occasionally this argument extends to gays and, bizarrely, even to persons with severe physical disabilities. The logic in essence tries to make common ground with the traditional IC reasons for recruiting intellectual diversity. Yet there are important differences between the two perspectives, leading to very different decisions about the varieties of diversity that are operationally valuable— and thence to controversy. The traditional reason for acquiring diversity was that diversity of ethnic and educational backgrounds, international experiences, as well as different personal experiences and outlooks affect operational performance by providing ethnic or regional cultural or language expertise, foreign experience, or racial "camouflage" relevant to operational environments or the targets of intelligence activities. This type of diversity was designed to make its people better able to surmount *foreign* intelligence collection and analytical challenges.

The new version, in contrast, asserts that *domestically* defined demographic diversity characteristics inherently conveys the same alleged advantages in all locations globally and on whatever subjects the "diverse" Americans work. Hence, there is a three-part, sequential argument: (1) some studies show that domestically defined employee diversity is statistically *associated* with enhanced performance of some domestic, mainly economic, tasks; (2) the correlation is assumed to be causal: diversity *causes* better domestic performance; and (3) the logic can be extended to other, foreign tasks without adjustment. All three of these claims remain controversial. Brennan described his superficial version of this argument in his book, explaining that America's status as a "melting pot" allegedly makes domestically defined diversity operationally useful.[205] This argument is inconsistent with his own policies: if there really was assimilation in the United States, the definition of "melting pot," there would be few distinctive abilities of demographic groups worth extolling, let alone fixating on alleged group differences that are the heart of identity politics.

More systematically than, and before, the IC's assertions, an appreciable effort tried to demonstrate that diversity is operationally beneficial in some domestic contexts. Commonly cited in the IC is a study by Professor Katherine Phillips of Columbia University's Business School, an African-American, and her

---

205   Brennan, *Undaunted*, 291.

colleagues.[206] Phillips et al.'s study noted that "social diversity in a group can cause discomfort, rougher interactions, a lack of trust, greater perceived interpersonal conflict, lower communication, less cohesion, more concern about disrespect, and other problems."[207] But still, the team asserted, diversity is better! Diverse groups allegedly think better than racially homogenous groups because group members feel a need to perform better against outside groups. The analysis was based on the obviously incorrect belief that "Being with similar others leads us to think we all hold the same information and share the same perspective."[208] Phillips's team, like others including the consulting firm McKinsey & Company, identified some domestic situations in which greater race and gender diversity are associated with better performance. For example, it found social diversity is *correlated* with higher profitability of American businesses; no causal mechanisms have been hypothesized.[209] The Phillips team also found that a minority person on a team of three undergraduate students in American colleges was *associated* with better ability of the teams to solve murder mysteries.[210] Why this example was chosen is unclear.[211] The study did not address problems similar to major intelligence challenges.

Diversity proponents in the IC adapted the Phillips study of domestic associations, extended her logic to other IC-favored groups, reified Phillips's hypothesis into causal logic, and extended

---

206 Phillips, "How Diversity Works."

207 Ibid., 45-46.

208 Ibid., 45.

209 Ibid., 44.

210 Ibid., 45.

211 Implicitly Phillips's group argued that minorities understand murder better, which is perhaps accurate given that black Americans commit murder, and are victims of murder, at much higher rates than all other major US demographic groups. See FBI murder statistics for 2016, crime statistics https://ucr.fbi.gov/crime-in-the-u.s/2016/crime-in-the-u.s.-2016/tables/expanded-homicide-data-table-3.xls. See also https://www.bjs.gov/content/pub/pdf/htius.pdf.

it to foreign activities—thereby making the Phillips argument ostensibly relevant to the IC. For example, former deputy chief of CIA's analysis directorate Carmen Medina, a Puerto Rican woman, borrowed extensively from Phillips's argument in claiming that an intelligence analogy is that demographic diversity in groups following the same intelligence issue makes people work harder to prepare their arguments, thereby allegedly making them perform better.[212] Medina's argument that diversity encourages analysts to think harder remains unpersuasive for several reasons in addition to the weaknesses of Phillips's argument. For example, if they are indoctrinated about anything, intelligence analysts are drilled constantly on the importance of thorough work—independent of the presence of demographic "others." The sometimes lengthy coordination and review processes of all analytic organizations, often done by many analysts and managers with appreciably different backgrounds, long have been designed to help ensure the completeness of analysis and lack of bias in analytic products; they have done so with incomplete success but have generated strong bureaucratic incentives for good work.[213] Rapid progress through the review process is well-known to be career enhancing—a far more powerful incentive to do good work than possible but not inevitable competition with demographic "others." Moreover, despite increases in team projects in recent years, analysts still generally work by themselves and are competitive with other analysts for promotion and plum assignments, meaning Medina's argument is often irrelevant.[214] Well-recognized errors caused by cognitive biases cannot be addressed by demographic diversity; only intellectual preparation, self-awareness, and diverse

212   Carmen Medina, "Want a Sharper, Stronger CIA? Hire Folks Who Look Like America," *Overt Action*, March 24, 2016, http://www.overtaction.org/2016/03/want-a-sharper-stronger-cia-hire-folks-who-look-like-america/.

213   Gentry, "Managers of Analysts," 160-163.

214   For example, Anonymous, "The DI's Organizational Culture," 21-25.

educations and experiences can help.[215] In addition, because the Office of Analytic Integrity and Standards of the ODNI (ODNI/AIS), which reviews some analytic papers' quality and reports on them to Congress, purposefully does not assess the accuracy of analyses, there is no way the IC can test Medina's assertions with any degree of methodological rigor.[216] As a former senior CIA officer, Medina presumably knew this.

Similarly, DNI Clapper wrote that increased numbers of LGBT personnel in the IC were good because they "brought unique perspectives to mission challenges and contributed to successes."[217] But Clapper, yet again, did not describe or explain *how* these different "perspectives" might help analysts, logisticians, linguists, information technology people, or persons in any other functional intelligence job category perform their work. He also undercut his argument by recognizing that a major cause of the increased hiring of LGBT people in his years as DNI was the "tremendous outside pressure from LGBT groups that were seasoned from fighting for gay, lesbian, and bisexual Americans' rights …."[218]

One former CIA analyst offered a hypothetical situation in which Clapper's argument about LGBT persons' contributions to intelligence might apply in practice. Nada Bakos asked rhetorically, "What if you have to recruit someone who's gay and that's the only reason they're talking to you?"[219] Her answer: gays would be the only people able to empathize with such a potential asset sufficiently to be able to recruit her or him. This possibility made it imperative, Bakos asserted, for CIA to hire unspecified, but

---

215   Gentry, "The 'Professionalization' of Intelligence Analysis," 658, 665-666.
216   Gentry, "Has the ODNI Improved U.S. Intelligence Analysis?" 644-645.
217   Clapper, *Facts and Fears*, 301.
218   Ibid.
219   McLaughlin, "More White, More Male, More Jesus: CIA Employees Fear Pompeo Is Quietly Killing the Agency's Diversity Mandate."

implicitly appreciable, numbers of LGBT operations officers. She offered no example, even sanitized, did not claim such a situation had ever occurred, and did not speculate about how often this situation might actually occur. To my knowledge, the literature on what leads people to commit espionage and the many thrillers about actual espionage do not contain even one such example.[220]

Such weak assertions unsurprisingly did not impress critics, who made a number of arguments in rejoinder.[221] They noted that intelligence officers long have recognized that diversity of experience, thought, and imagination are helpful in the intelligence world, but they have seen people differently able as individuals and have not seen large, allegedly homogenous demographic groups as differentially creative or competent. Because the origins of intelligence excellence at the individual and group levels have been examined at length, repeatedly, over many years, many experienced intelligence officers concluded that the new logic did not match the explanatory power of the old reasoning or of research that identified specific sources of excellent performance in the intelligence business. For example, Sherman Kent's argument that intelligence has an organizational need for the "queer bird and the eccentric with a unique talent" is one of the most commonly cited passages of his book, published in 1949.[222] Richards Heuer's widely-known book on mindsets and biases focused mainly on the biases of individual persons and tried to find ways to ameliorate them; while Heuer also observed that organizations can have dysfunctional collective mindsets, something many observers have noted, he did not claim that demographic groups are differentially

---

220   For example, Smith, *The Anatomy of a Spy*, 11-46; Taylor and Snow, "Cold War Spies."

221   Gentry and Gordon, "U.S. Strategic Warning Intelligence," 34-37.

222   Kent, *Strategic Intelligence for American World Policy*, 74.

susceptible to them.[223] In a 2011 article published in *Studies in Intelligence*, Clint Watts and John E. Brennan (not the former DCIA) noted the importance of finding insightful "outlier" ideas and searching for "demographics" of diverse people defined by their thought processes, not genes, which they, following Philip Tetlock, characterized as "groundhog" and "hedgehog" thinking.[224] Specialists in strategic warning and deception such as Uri Bar-Joseph, Cynthia Grabo, Mary McCarthy, Barton Whaley, and others have demonstrated persuasively that diversity in outlooks, curiosity, perseverance, and skepticism by individual persons are keys to insightful intelligence analysis, and that these traits are hard to find in all demographic groups.[225] A team led by University of Pennsylvania psychologists Barbara Mellers and Philip Tetlock studied for IARPA the characteristics of analysts who are particularly good predictors of future events and similarly did not identify group demographic diversity as a contributing factor.[226] Individual persons' education and distinctive personal thought processes, which occur in people across demographic groups, alone matter. Tetlock and Mellers observed that such characteristics can be taught, but only to a certain extent. And, Rose McDermott of Brown University suggested that the IC use personality tests more to identify characteristics in individuals particularly relevant to intelligence analysis in general, including open-mindedness and the absence of premature cognitive closure.[227] Such testing might

---

223 Heuer, *Psychology of Intelligence Analysis*.

224 Watts and Brennan, "Capturing the Potential of Outlier Ideas in the Intelligence Community," 6-8.

225 For example, Grabo, *Handbook of Warning Intelligence*, 102-112; Tetlock, *Superforecasting* 180-181; Whaley, *Stratagem*, 3-7. For a summary of these and other perspectives on this subject, see Gentry and Gordon, *Strategic Warning Analysis*, 178-183.

226 Mellers, et al., "Identifying and Cultivating Superforecasters as a Method of Improving Probabilistic Predictions," 268; Tetlock et al., "The Psychology of Intelligence Analysis," 1-14; Tetlock, *Expert Political Judgment*.

227 McDermott, "Experimental Intelligence," 93-95.

also be useful for finding people with the additional characteristics Grabo, Tetlock, and others identified as desirable.

In addition, some people believe that the groups the contemporary diversity advocates extol may have such monolithic interests or political perspectives on important issues that they are unusually prone to "groupthink," hindering their usefulness to intelligence agencies. For example, Yale University professor Anthony Kronman has argued, and some polling data confirm, that diversity enhancement efforts on university campuses that emphasize students' primary identities as members of discernable demographic groups, not as individuals, have led to expectations that specified identify groups should think and act in conventional, stereotypical ways—a Marxian perspective—resulting in a sharp drop in the intellectual diversity that is ostensibly at the heart of university life.[228] Kronman's argument seems applicable to the IC as well—especially to young employees who recently were on college campuses. The stereotypical beliefs expected do not include Trump's philosophy of government.

Similarly, polling data consistently indicate that African-Americans' political views are more uniform than those of any other major demographic group, and regularly show strongly Democratic attitudes among blacks.[229] Black professors Ismail K. White and Chryl N. Laird have argued that blacks associate with the Democratic Party out of "group solidarity," which is "just something you do as a black person, an expectation of behavior

---

228 Anthony Kronman, "The Downside of Diversity," *Wall Street Journal*, August 3-4, 2019, C1.

229 For example, Scott Clement, Dan Balz, and Emily Guskin, "Black Americans say racism, policing top issues for November, favor Biden by huge margin, Post-Ipsos poll finds," *Washington Post*, June 25, 2020, https://www.washingtonpost.com/politics/black-americans-say-racism-policing-top-issues-for-november-favor-biden-by-huge-margin-post-ipsos-poll-finds/2020/06/24/9143b254-b645-11ea-aca5-ebb63d27e1ff_story.html.

meant to empower the racial group."[230] This kind of orthodoxy of collective worldview may be helpful for African-Americans in general, but it is not the kind of intellectual diversity long valued in the IC, and it is not helpful for intelligence services that seek employees who understand and appreciate a broad set of *foreign* political, social, and other variables.[231] The traditional practice has been to hire African-Americans who are likely to be good intelligence officers regardless of their race. There are many such people.

In addition, some varieties of American "social diversity" may be dysfunctional in the operational environments where intelligence officers frequently work. For example, black Americans are less likely to blend into European and Asian operational environments than are Caucasians, who are common throughout the world.[232] Women are unlikely to be effective case officers in strongly Muslim countries or as good as men at paramilitary work given that intelligence agencies prefer to recruit former military special operations personnel with combat experience for these positions.[233] Reflecting American societal norms, the Defense Department still largely excludes women from *ground* combat roles—the military equivalent of CIA's paramilitary roles.[234]

---

230 White and Laird, *Why are Blacks Democrats?*

231 In the 1990s, CIA ran a three-day course for managers designed ostensibly to give managers a flavor of what it was like to be black. According to a retired CIA manager who was directed to take the course, three black instructors, two women and a man, apparently contracted to run the course, ridiculed whatever the managers, who were all white, said. The idea apparently was that blacks are always given a hard time, whatever they said or did, and this was a way of letting managers know what it was like to be black. They asserted that there were black cultural concepts that the managers needed to know and accept, including "black time," which allegedly differs from what clocks read. The manager left the course angry at the instructors' attitudes and newly prejudiced against blacks. The agency's attempt to help improve race relations clearly did not succeed in this case.

232 For example, Conboy, *Spies on the Mekong*, 150.

233 Professor Millick (pseudonym), *CIA 101*, 78.

234 Women have some combat jobs in the US armed forces, and they often go in harm's way even when not in formal combat jobs. But experience as combat air crews and ship-board duty on warships are not particularly helpful preparation for the kind of work CIA's paramilitary officers perform.

Hence, there are readily understandable reasons why women are "under" represented in some intelligence job categories that have nothing to do with gender discrimination in the IC.

Such reasoning and data help explain why the diversity and inclusion agenda has been controversial within the IC. While the agenda has many more public advocates than critics, some former intelligence officers have gone further, directly challenging the fairness of the new version of IC diversity and asserting that it hurts, not helps, the IC's performance. For example, Scott C. Uehlinger, who retired as a CIA operations officer in 2014, was a Trump delegate to the 2016 Republican National Convention, and in 2016 contributed, according to FEC data, $1,000 to a Republican organization in Pennsylvania, wrote:

> The twin serpents of politicization and political correctness—a Soviet term, by the way—walk hand in hand throughout the intelligence community, as well as every other government agency. The PC mindset that now dominates every college campus is also positioned firmly throughout our government—particularly within the intelligence community, which saw its greatest personnel influx ever in the post-9/11 environment. Today's intelligence community, the average age of which I would estimate at 32, was raised under the beleaguered Bush administration and reached professional maturity primarily under the Obama administration, immersed in a PC environment.[235]

---

235   Scott Uehlinger, "How the intel community was turned into a political weapon against President Trump," *The Hill*, April 5, 2017, http://thehill.com/blogs/pundits-blog/the-administration/327413-how-the-intel-community-was-turned-into-a-political.

Fred Fleitz, a former CIA analyst, former member of the HPSCI staff, and former staffer on Trump's NSC, argued in 2016 that Brennan's diversity strategy was misguided and destructive.[236] Noting that Brennan claimed that increasing demographic diversity improved CIA's ability to accomplish its missions, Fleitz argued that Brennan had instead created "diversity quotas" for hiring and promotion that deemphasized "competence and achievement." He wrote:

> Brennan has mandated "diversity and inclusion performance objectives for all CIA managers and supervisors and ultimately the entire workforce," so that CIA personnel must weigh diversity and gender figures in making key assignments and senior-level promotions. Brennan's plan also includes agency-wide "unconscious bias" training.[237]

By so doing, in Fleitz's view, Brennan advanced President Obama's agenda at the expense of national security. He said, "The CIA's mission is too serious to be distracted by Obama's social-engineering efforts."[238] Fleitz added:

> It is not unjust to hire a white male with a Ph.D. from Harvard and a background in nuclear science to analyze the Iranian nuclear program over someone with weaker credentials who is a member of a racial or gender minority. Altering the rules so the latter candidate will win a competition for such a job is not

---

236   Fred Fleitz, "The Obama CIA Is Putting Diversity above National Security," *National Review*, February 23, 2016, https://www.nationalreview.com/2016/02/cia-diversity-strategy-misguided-dangerous/.

237   Ibid.

238   Ibid.

in our national interest. Adding such considerations to CIA promotion rules will further complicate the agency's management, which is already suffering from politicization and political correctness. This is why in the CIA Directorate of Intelligence, where I worked for 19 years, many highly qualified officers refuse to apply for management jobs — or they last in them for only a few years before returning to analyst positions.[239]

After the December 2021 publication of my article that examined the IC's claim that demographic diversity enhances agencies' performance, finding no evidence to support the claim, a large number of people, mostly strangers, commended the article.[240] Some of them also provided as yet unpublished additional evidence that the IC's diversity policies in fact hurt agencies' performance. This issue merits much more investigation.

Other CIA people, less inclined to criticize Obama directly, nevertheless note that Brennan's policies, retained by DCIA Pompeo and to some extent extended by DCIA Haspel, make work more difficult for white men. A retired senior manager of analysts who retains close ties to many CIA people said white men at the CIA feel institutionally discriminated against and estimated that human resources offices' staffs in 2019 were about 80 percent female.[241] Others note that Haspel named women to head the operations, analysis, and science and technology directorates, as well as the diversity office, a form of sex-based preference that was clear and made some men both uncomfortable and reluctant to

---

239   Ibid.
240   Gentry, "Demographic Diversity in U.S. Intelligence Personnel."
241   Conversation with author, September 5, 2019.

speak about their own perceived reduction in career opportuni-ties.[242] The former senior official said that efforts to redress gender imbalances had "gone too far" and that "a lot of people" are quietly concerned about diversity and inclusion policies.[243]

Even government studies have found no support for the claim that demographic diversity improves the IC's performance. While the IC rarely is overseen by the Government Account-ability Office, the GAO found in a 2019-2020 study of diversity management in the IC that 12 of the then-17 IC agencies claimed that demographic diversity helped performance but, like Clapper, none of them explained to the GAO *how* demographic diversity in fact improved agencies' performance or offered examples.[244] The GAO unsurprisingly offered no anecdotal example in its report.

In 2019 the GAO also investigated one diversity-related IC program, the IC Centers for Academic Excellence (IC CAE) program, finding it deficient in important respects.[245] The program, which DIA administered from 2011 until it transitioned to the ODNI in fiscal year 2020, provided some $69 million in forty-six separate grants through fiscal year 2021 to twenty-nine colleges and universities with large minority student bodies, especially Historically Black Colleges and Universities (HBCU) and schools with large Hispanic student bodies.[246] Its stated goal is to develop intelligence-related undergraduate courses that will increase the pool of "culturally and ethnically diverse" job applicants available to the IC, and thus to recruitment of more ethnic minorities, but

---

242 Emma Newberger, "Women head the top three CIA directorates for the first time in history," CNBC, January 16, 2019, https://www.cnbc.com/2019/01/16/women-head-the-top-three-cia-directorates-for-the-first-time.html.

243 Conversation with author, September 5, 2019.

244 U.S. GAO, *Intelligence Community: Additional Actions Needed to Strengthen Workforce Diversity Planning and Oversight*, 3.

245 The program has a fairly detailed website, https://www.dia.mil/Training/IC-Centers-for-Academic-Excellence/Become-an-IC-CAE/.

246 U.S. GAO, *Intelligence Community: Actions Needed to Improve Planning and Oversight of the Centers for Academic Excellence Program*, GAO-19-529, 43-48.

its implicit purpose for doing so it to improve the performance of the IC.[247] Most IC CAE schools are not generally regarded as prestigious institutions, although the program includes some prominent universities, including Duke University, Pennsylvania State University, and Virginia Tech.

Like others, this program focuses on *domestic* demographic diversity. It is little suited to recruit the diversity of outlook, empathy, and expertise needed to address *foreign* intelligence challenges. Blacks, Hispanics, women, gays, transgender people, and persons with disabilities do not inherently speak Pashto or understand Thai culture or know North Korean politics better than do heterosexual white men. Like the others, it is instead designed primarily to appeal to domestic political constituencies.

The GAO found that DIA's management of the program was seriously deficient and that no measures of effectiveness or return on investment had been designed, let alone measured accurately.[248] The GAO reported that the CIA, after initially working with sixteen IC CAE schools, in 2014 reduced its involvement with the program, dealing with only six major universities.[249] The NSA never dealt with any IC CAE institution, preferring to recruit at universities with good cyber programs.[250]

Consistent with the GAO's fairly cryptic observation, a former CIA officer who does not want to be identified for fear of being called a racist reported that CIA's experience with IC CAE has not been favorable.[251] According to the person, CIA personnel

---

247 IC-CAE website, http://www.dia.mil/Training/IC-Centers-for-Academic-Excellence/. See also ODNI "Demographic Report: Hiring and Retention of Minorities, Women, and Persons with Disabilities in the United States Intelligence Community Fiscal Year 2016," 29-31.

248 U.S. GAO, *Intelligence Community*, 1. An academic study published in 2020 similarly did not discuss performance in any measurable way; see Landon-Murray and Coulthart, "Intelligence Studies Programs as US Public Policy."

249 U.S. GAO, *Intelligence Community*, 31-32.

250 Ibid., 32.

251 Personal communication.

who visited HBCU schools were disappointed with their visits, and recruits from these schools experienced more than average performance problems. This finding, or even perception, obviously is not politically correct. Another former intelligence officer, who had considerable experience working with IC CAE member schools, noticed that some HBCU merely added the word "intelligence" to the titles of already existing courses; in some cases, no one administering the program had a background in either education or intelligence.[252] The person reported that most IC agencies' recruits from HBCU took support, not line operational, jobs, meaning these people are not really intelligence officers. Yet another person familiar with CIA recruiting said it was hard to recruit capable blacks, who frequently had excellent professional opportunities elsewhere. The person said CIA recruiters inflated their numbers of black recruits to make themselves look good and confirmed that most CIA recruits from HBCU schools take support jobs. Agency management pressure to recruit from favored demographic groups led to hiring low quality people, or "people who shouldn't have been there," the person said. A professor at a university that caters mainly to mid-career persons similarly said many of the black graduates of his school who the CIA recruits go to support positions.[253]

On May 12-14, 2021 the IC CAE sponsored an online conference entitled "Workshop on Teaching Intelligence," which featured a number of prominent intelligence studies scholars and teachers. At the conference's conclusion, IC CAE director Michael Bennett made summary comments and asked attendees to send to him evidence that IC CAE had improved the performance of the IC. He said he was personally confident that it had, but

---

252   Ibid.
253   Personal communication, August 2022.

he needed evidence to confirm his belief and to help justify IC CAE.[254] In essence, Bennett confirmed the GAO's conclusions of two years earlier: no firm data demonstrate IC CAE's effectiveness in achieving any of its formal goals, let alone in improving the IC's performance. In October 2022, Bennett's successor reportedly said roughly the same thing at an academic conference.[255] The "our values" argument thus continues to be the primary rationale for the IC CAE's existence, buttressed strongly by the partisan Democratic imperative to change the demographics and politics of the federal workforce.

Hence, a considerable body of solid research, managerial judgment, and intelligence professionals' opinions challenged the IC's diversity logic. These views have been and are, however, generally ignored, challenged, or reformulated in ways that make them similar to the new thinking. The new conventional wisdom about the merits of demographic diversity variously remains ideologically, politically, and/or bureaucratically attractive to many intelligence people, including Brennan, Clapper, and Medina. For advocates, the challenges in the Trump years included a need to defend diversity policies against such attacks and diversity advocates were sensitive to the possibility of a more damaging attack as Trump's candidacy strengthened, giving some intelligence officers another reason to oppose him. Even the idea of investigating whether DEI policies have any dysfunctions remains politically incorrect. Unsurprisingly, the Biden administration has strengthened Obama-era diversity policies.

The stubborn commitment of diversity advocates to the idea that demographic diversity improves the IC's performance, despite a complete lack of supporting evidence, contrasts starkly with the

---

254   See conference recording.
255   Personal communication, November 2022.

perceptions of leaders of the Soviet Union that demographic diversity was America's greatest political vulnerability. Former KGB General Oleg Kalugin has reported that the KGB exploited the vulnerability for decades by placing race-focused disinformation aimed primarily at blacks and Jews in the hands of left-leaning U.S. media and other opinion makers, anticipating correctly that it would trigger outrage.[256] The KGB also ran extensive disinformation campaigns designed to convince targets to adopt positions favorable to Soviet interests without recognizing that they had been so influenced.[257] Former Soviet disinformation specialists undoubtedly are delighted with the IC's diversity policies.

POLITICAL EFFECTS OF THE NEW DIVERSITY

The push for demographic diversity had two prominent political effects on some IC institutions, primarily the ODNI and CIA. First, it became acceptable and even mandatory to support a key part of a president's domestic political agenda—in sharp contrast to previous efforts to maintain considerable independence from presidents' domestic political agendas, the Kentian perspective. Second, growing acceptance of a domestic political ideology as an integral component of organizational cultures affected operational behavior. It made activism more acceptable, even obligatory for some. These changes occurred independently of Donald Trump, but they erupted publicly when his political views appeared to be so inconsistent with those of many intelligence people.

As Nicholas Dujmović noted, "diversity and inclusion" became a mantra during the Obama years.[258] Consistent with

256   Shimer, *Rigged*, 84, 92; Kalugin, *Spymaster*, 35, 53-55, 103-104, 117, 297-298.
257   Yuri Bezmenov, *Love Letter to America*, https://ia800602.us.archive.org/11/items/love-letter-america/love-letter-america.pdf, 38-40.
258   Author discussion with Nicholas Dujmović, June 19, 2019.

Brennan's goals, there was clear internal pressure within CIA to embrace diversity policies, which Dujmović reported was widely recognized by CIA employees. For its supporters, the new doctrine variously was self-evidently intellectually right, morally good, consistent with "our values" per Brennan and Clapper, and/or personally advantageous.[259] This perspective arguably became an ideological orthodoxy—not unlike that of many university communities—that negatively affected the intellectual diversity of the CIA. It also generated tensions within the workforce, precisely what the "diversity and inclusion" agenda allegedly is supposed to end.[260]

The expectation that the new ethical principles were mandatory for all personnel was unattractive to some employees, which Brennan acknowledged.[261] It was internally called "soft totalitarianism" by analyst personnel who questioned its validity and value, a reference to the ideological orthodoxy of communist dictatorships.[262] Similarly, an administrative careerist who worked in two of the offices of the Directorate of Support in the Washington area during most of Obama's terms as president reported that starting in the Obama years—not before—it became career-damaging to question administration policies generally.[263] Employees "feared" for their careers if they did not seem to support Obama. This person, like Dujmović, thinks the intellectual censorship was Agency-wide in scope. Managers clearly bought the program. Such bureaucratic fear could not otherwise have become endemic. This suggests that the "accountability" standards

259   Adam B. Lerner, "CIA study: White men dominate agency's top ranks," *Politico*, June 30, 2015, https://www.politico.com/story/2015/06/cia-internal-study-white-men-dominate-agency-top-ranks-minorities-119603.

260   Gentry. "The Cancer of Human Rights," 95-101.

261   Brennan, *Undaunted*, 290.

262   Author discussion with Nicholas Dujmović, June 19, 2019. Author Heather Mac Donald also has used the term. See Mac Donald, *The Diversity Delusion*, 28.

263   Private conversation with author, September 5, 2019.

of Clapper and Brennan effectively established sanctions against overt protestations against their political views; they did in fact change organizational cultures.

Blacks, women, and LGBT people, the focus of Obama's program, tend to be more politically liberal than the population as a whole and the European-American men the "diversity and inclusion" program aimed to partly displace, meaning that demographic shifts altered the IC workforce's collective political orientation.[264] Most obviously, blacks' overwhelming dedication to the Democratic Party and its vision that the many problems of the black community are mainly or completely caused by discrimination by white people, help make blacks a narrowly race-focused group with relatively little collective intellectual diversity, a narrow collective worldview, and overwhelming loyalty to one political party. NBC found that 90 percent of black voters supported a Democratic candidate for the House in 2018, compared to 9 percent who voted Republican.[265] Indeed, blacks often chastise other blacks who stray from the Democratic Party and its ideals because, as many blacks argue, the Democratic Party is a core element of black identity. Some even claim that the term "black Republican" is an oxymoron.[266]

LGBT persons are only slightly less uniform in their ideological perspectives. According to an NBC News exit poll taken in 2018, 6 percent of the electorate who voted in 2018 self-identified as LGBT; of those people, 82 percent voted for the Democratic

264   Dante Chinni, "More Educated Women Favor Democrats," *Wall Street Journal*, December 27, 2017, A4.

265   Tim Fitzsimons, "Record LGBT support for Democrats in midterms, NBC News Exit Poll shows," *NBC News*, November 8, 2018, https://www.nbcnews.com/feature/nbc-out/record-lgbt-support-democrats-midterms-nbc-news-exit-poll-shows-n934211.

266   Nicole Silverio, "Sonny Hostin Says Being A "Black Republican Is An Oxymoron," *Daily Caller*, May 6, 2022, https://dailycaller.com/2022/05/06/sunny-hostin-black-republican-oxymoron/?msclkid=66192f4ed02311ec9f9dcbd7f35f91e6.

candidate for the House of Representatives in their district while 17 percent voted for the Republican candidate.[267] NBC reported that LGBT persons' support for Democrats increased from 2012, when 76 percent supported a Democrat and 22 percent voted Republican.[268] According to NBC News:

> Gary Gates, a former research director at UCLA's Williams Institute, which researches LGBTQ demographic trends, said "the LGBT community has consistently shown strong support for the Democratic Party" and characterized the 82 percent support in 2018 as a "high-water mark."

> "This isn't surprising," Gates said. "The hostility of the Trump administration to LGBT issues, including the attempted ban on transgender military service and efforts to reduce or eliminate measurement of sexual orientation and gender identity on federal surveys, may mean that LGBT voters feel particularly threatened right now by the President and his party."[269]

Moreover, according to a Pew Research Center poll taken in October 2016, lesbian, gay and bisexual persons are more liberal that the general public on a wide variety of policy issues, including issues of foreign policymaking (see Table 3-2). Some of these questions—such as perceptions of political Islam and the role of diplomacy versus the use of force in international relations—are directly relevant to the analysis of many intelligence issues.

---

267   Ibid.
268   Ibid.
269   Ibid.

TABLE 3-2

LGBT Voters' Views on Major Policy Issues, 2016

STATEMENT	ALL REGISTERED VOTERS (PERCENT IN AGREEMENT WITH STATEMENT)	LGBT REGISTERED VOTERS (PERCENT IN AGREEMENT WITH STATEMENT)
Homosexuality should be accepted by society.	68	95
The economic system unfairly favors powerful interests.	72	89
Good diplomacy is the best way to ensure peace.	61	89
Stricter environmental laws are worth the cost.	61	80
Business corporations make too much profit.	56	71
Immigrants today strengthen our country.	61	75
The Islamic religion does not encourage violence more than other religions.	42	72
Government should do more to help needy Americans.	44	70
Government regulation of business is necessary to protect public interest.	53	66
Government often does a better job than it gets credit for.	40	58
Racial discrimination is the main reason why black people can't get ahead.	33	53

Source: Pew Research Center, as quoted in Jocelyn Kiley and Shiva Maniam, "Lesbian, gay and bisexual voters remain a solidly Democratic bloc," Facttank, October 25, 2016, https://www.pewresearch.org/fact-tank/2016/10/25/lesbian-gay-and-bisexual-voters-remain-a-solidly-democratic-bloc/.

Other Obama-favored groups also lean Democratic. Hispanic voters' shares of support for Democrats and Republicans in 2018 were 69 percent and 29 percent, respectively.[270] Consistent with other polls, for young voters aged 18-29 of all races, the shares were 67 percent and 29 percent, respectively.[271] Women, while also leaning Democratic, are more diverse in their outlooks.

Asian Americans, in contrast, appear infrequently in the IC's diversity push, perhaps for several reasons. Americans of various Asian backgrounds frequently voted Republican in the Obama years, meaning they were not favored members of Obama's coalition.[272] And Asian Americans, who comprise about 4 percent of the population, frequently do well by many societal measures, meaning they do not need financial or other aid from the Democratic Party, a core tool of identity politics. And some Democratic policies directly hurt Asian Americans. For example, liberal Democrats sponsored ballot initiatives in Washington State (2019) and California (2020) to legalize racial discrimination against Asians and Caucasians in order to enable "affirmative action" designed to help their more favored black and American Indian constituencies.[273] Both measures were defeated, with substantial numbers of Asian American voters opposed. Hence, black and Asian Americans interests differ in important

---

270   Fitzsimons, "Record LGBT support for Democrats in midterms, NBC News Exit Poll shows."

271   Baker, "Why Affirmative Action Is on the Ballot in Washington State."

272   Li Zhou, "Trump could be turning Asian Americans into reliable Democratic voters," *Vox*, May 13, 2019, https://www.vox.com/policy-and-politics/2019/5/13/18308137/asian-american-voters-immigration-democrats-donald-trump.

273   Mike Baker, "Why Affirmative Action Is on the Ballot in Washington State," *New York Times*, November 4, 2019, https://www.nytimes.com/2019/11/04/us/affirmative-action-washington-ballot.html.

respects. Asian Americans' small role in contemporary IC politics is therefore unsurprising.

Hence, in total, the purposefully generated demographic changes appreciably altered the collective political perspectives—the worldviews—of parts of the IC. These shifts were enabled by societal changes and policy decisions like the post-9/11 buildup that were designed to accomplish other things. But the shift does not seem to have increased useful intellectual diversity, and probably damaged it. One of my Columbia University professor colleagues, a prominent scholar and self-described liberal, twice in conversations with me months apart in 2019 lamented that Columbia's faculty community was much more demographically than intellectually diverse. Columbia's faculty and administrators had created a leftist ideological orthodoxy that was intolerant of diverse thinking about many issues, including about the virtues of demographic diversity. Parts of the IC arguably have moved in this direction as well.

Obama's demographic agenda and many but not all of its political and bureaucratic ramifications are clear. Regardless of the intellectual merits of the argument and their applicability to the intelligence business, Obama's diversity agenda and Trump's reluctance to embrace it generated strongly emotional reactions, leading many former and currently serving intelligence officers to oppose Trump overtly in viscerally emotional, politically charged ways. The major changes Obama and his appointees made to the IC's collective politics were largely invisible to outsiders so long as Obama was president because the IC collectively was satisfied with his political outlook and policies. There was no reason to protest non-existent ideological deviance. Anger emerged publicly in mid-2016 only when the dramatically different Donald Trump became a serious contender to succeed Obama. The next chapter identifies in detail what Trump said and did that antagonized some intelligence people. These actions and attitudes in turn generated observable reactions that are discussed in chapter 5.

4

THE SHOCK OF DONALD TRUMP

DONALD TRUMP'S ELECTION SHOCKED MANY PEOPLE, perhaps including himself. The 2016 presidential campaign was bitter. Trump made many claims before his election and after becoming president that were factually incorrect. His policy positions alarmed some people and alienated others, especially those who had adopted the new norms discussed in chapter 2 and who expected another ideologically compatible president in Hillary Clinton. This chapter presents representative examples of Trump's words and actions that infuriated some current and former intelligence people, citing his language and actions as well as their context. It provides an historical base against which to evaluate intelligence persons' criticisms of Trump, which sometimes featured distortions and misrepresentations of his words and actions, some of which appear to have been purposeful.

While critics with intelligence backgrounds addressed many aspects of Trump's politics and personality, formers and current employees in 2016-2021 focused primarily on five general areas of alleged deficiencies in Trump's policies and character, which overlap to some degree: (1) his foreign policy views flouted traditional American values and were harmful to American national security and other interests, hurt friends and allies, and damaged other people; (2) his views about many domestic issues, especially social issues, were inappropriate and unacceptable; (3) his favorable views of Russia and rejection of the IC's assessment that Russia tried to help him in 2016, were unreasonable and suspicious; (4) Trump's casual respect for facts and repeated misrepresentations reflected disrespect for truth and a propensity to lie; (5) his disparaging remarks about intelligence agencies and their performance, especially the IC's findings regarding Russia and the 2016 election, and about some specific intelligence personnel, were wrong and disrespectful. Most of these concerns closely tracked the criticisms of Trump by many Democrats, but Trump's alleged "assault on intelligence" was a uniquely major complaint of intelligence people. This chapter therefore concentrates on their intelligence-related critiques, which substantively are not far from those CIA levied at President Nixon's and Carter's reform attempts.

This chapter also compares Trump's comments about intelligence to statements by previous presidents. This comparison indicates that although Trump had his own style of commentary—most prominently his propensity to tweet with abandon—and distinctively divisive political views, his attitude toward intelligence was similar to those of some past presidents, especially Nixon, Carter, and Clinton.

REVISIONIST FOREIGN POLICIES

Candidate and then President Trump alienated foreign policy elites of both major political parties, and many Americans citizens, with controversial foreign policy initiatives and perspectives, some of which overturned longstanding US positions on important issues. He also rejected prominent Obama administration policies. Among Trump's positions of considerable interest to intelligence officers were:

- *Sharp criticism of NATO allies.* While American complaints about allegedly inadequate "burden sharing"—the perceived excessive costs of the defense of Europe borne by the United States compared to activities and spending of European NATO countries—were long-standing, Trump went further by wondering aloud (and in tweets) about whether it was in America's interest to remain in NATO.[1] Such musings led to considerable consternation on both sides of the Atlantic. Trump frequently commented disparagingly about specific European countries and leaders, which normally is diplomatically inappropriate. Later, as many European NATO countries increased defense spending modestly, Trump claimed success for his pressure, again irritating Europeans.[2]

- *Complimentary comments about Putin and Russia.* Trump, who tried before he became a presidential candidate to increase his business activities in Russia, evidently communicated with but did not meet Russian President Vladimir Putin during a visit to

1   Julian E. Barnes and Helene Cooper, "Trump Discussed Pulling U.S. From NATO, Aides Say Amid New Concerns Over Russia," *New York Times*, January 14, 2019, https://www.nytimes.com/2019/01/14/us/politics/nato-president-trump.html.

2   Steve Holland and Lesley Wroughton, "Trump says NATO countries' burden-sharing improving, wants more," *Reuters*, April 2, 2019, https://www.reuters.com/article/us-usa-nato-trump/trump-says-nato-countries-burden-sharing-improving-wants-more-idUSKCN1RE23P.

Moscow in 2013. He met Putin several times as president. After talks with Putin, Trump repeatedly spoke of his trust in, and respect for, the Russian leader.[3] This commentary attracted the attention of Trump's critics, given continued Russian attacks on Ukraine, which began in 2014 and prompted international sanctions, and after Trump rejected IC assessments that Russian intelligence agencies ran an appreciable covert action program to stir dissension in the United States and to influence the 2016 presidential election.[4]

- *Trade policy.* In office, Trump continued to espouse the populist views of foreign trade that he used in the 2016 campaign, arguing that many international trade arrangements were unfair to America and its workers, and that some trade partners should not be allowed to continue to benefit from their unfair trade practices. In keeping with these views, Trump re-negotiated some trade arrangements, including the North American Free Trade Agreement with Canada and Mexico, leading to generally modest changes in terms.[5] His most prominent economic spat was with China, reflecting a long-standing concern by many countries that China did not comply with World Trade Organization rules. Trump's concerns

---

3   AFP, "Putin and Trump Hail Trust and Cooperation on WWII Anniversary," *Moscow Times*, April 25, 2020, https://www.themoscowtimes.com/2020/04/25/putin-and-trump-hail-trust-and-cooperation-on-wwii-anniversary-a70104.

4   National Intelligence Council, "Assessing Russian Activities and Intentions in Recent US Elections."

5   Jim Tankersley, "Trump Just Ripped Up Nafta. Here's What's in the New Deal." *New York Times*, October 1, 2018, https://www.nytimes.com/2018/10/01/business/trump-nafta-usmca-differences.html.

were exacerbated by the large US trade and current account deficits with China. As a candidate and as president, Trump called China "cheaters" and currency "manipulators," and he threatened punitive tariffs.[6] Critics worried that Trump risked a major trade war with China that would damage the US economy badly. Indeed, critics often used the term "trade war" to describe more modest policy differences and trade sanctions.

- *Torture of terror suspects and targeting terrorists' families.* Counterterrorism had been a major intelligence focus for fifteen years before 2016, and the CIA received much criticism for the interrogation techniques it used in the years immediately after 9/11. Candidate Trump sparked concerns when he said he wanted to resume use of waterboarding against terror suspects, claiming torture worked.[7] In March 2016, Trump said he wanted to "take out the families" of terrorists, which he later explained did not mean killing them.[8] Both positions generated significant opposition from intelligence officers who remembered the unpleasant controversy over interrogation techniques used in the George W. Bush years.[9] Opponents countered that torture does not

6   Heather Long, "How China doesn't play fair on trade," *CNN Business,* July 12, 2016, https://money.cnn.com/2016/07/12/news/economy/china-trade-donald-trump/.

7   Adam Serwer, "Can Trump Bring Back Torture?," *The Atlantic,* January 26, 2017, https://www.theatlantic.com/politics/archive/2017/01/trump-torture/514463/.

8   Andrew E. Kramer, "Russia Shows What Happens When Terrorists' Families Are Targeted," *New York Times,* March 29, 2016, https://www.nytimes.com/2016/03/30/world/europe/russia-chechnya-caucasus-terrorists-families.html.

9   Whipple, *Spy Masters,* 12.

work and was inconsistent with international law. Many said Trump's views damaged America's image in the world.

- *Immigration policy.* As candidate and as president, Trump noted that the terrorist attacks on US interests in recent decades came primarily from people who rationalized their attacks by citing the Koran. Given the established fact that Islamist "terrorist" groups often infiltrated their followers into Western countries by claiming refugee status, Trump opposed Obama's policy of granting largely open admission to migrants and refugees from several predominantly Muslim countries experiencing large-scale instability. He similarly opposed Obama's policy of admitting people from poor and troubled countries on a priority basis, telling a bipartisan panel on immigration reform in January 2018 that the United States did not need more immigrants from "shithole" countries.[10] Trump said the United States would welcome more Norwegians, but not more Haitians. Trump opposed policies that let large numbers of undocumented migrants into the country while their immigration or refugee status was adjudicated, a process that often took years. The porosity of the US border and lengthy legal proceedings led many would-be migrants to send their small children alone to enter the United States. Trump tried many legal and procedural efforts to curb this variety of

---

10   Graham Lanktree, "Trump's 'Shithole' Countries Are Worth $46.6 Billion in Trade to America," Newsweek, January 18, 2018, https://www.newsweek.com/trumps-shit-hole-countries-are-worth-466-billion-trade-america-779324.

immigration. He also asked Congress for funds to build a wall on the Mexican border. Blocked here, too, Trump reprogrammed some Defense Department funds to build portions of the wall, which generated more opposition. Such actions and rhetoric generated widespread commentary that Trump was anti-Muslim and/or a racist, not to mention undiplomatic and uncouth. These statements and policies angered many persons who agreed with Obama's immigration policies and his "diversity and inclusion" agenda.

CONTROVERSIAL DOMESTIC POLITICAL VIEWS AND POLICIES

Trump's political philosophy differed significantly from that of both President Obama and the mainstream Republican establishment.[11] His views have sometimes been called populist, but he had an unusual range of opinions on issues that he often changed, preventing easy categorization of his beliefs and giving critics from multiple perspectives opportunities to criticize him. He campaigned against many of Obama's policies but after becoming president tried to reverse only some of them.

Trump campaigned in 2016 on a pledge to "drain the swamp" in Washington.[12] While at various times he meant various aspects of political Washington, he consistently disapproved of the attitudes and performance of federal workers. As federal employees, some intelligence officers were offended. This rhetoric fueled critics' meme that Trump had launched an "assault on intelligence." As

---

11   Saldin and Teles, *Never Trump*.

12   Josh Dawsey, Rosalind S. Helderman, and David A. Fahrenthold, "How Trump abandoned his pledge to 'drain the swamp'," *Washington Post*, October 24, 2020, https://www.washingtonpost.com/politics/trump-drain-the-swamp/2020/10/24/52c7682c-0a5a-11eb-9be6-cf25fb429f1a_story.html.

recounted in chapter 2, concerns about organizational autonomy have been major concerns at some IC agencies for many years.

In July 2017 Trump announced that he would reverse Obama's 2016 decision to allow transgender persons to join the military. By 2019, some 15,000 transgender persons were uniformed military personnel.[13] Trump argued that transgender persons, who received sex-related surgeries and psychological treatment at government expense under Obama's policies, had inappropriately cost the government money and did not serve defense needs.[14] In a shift from his originally tweeted announcement of the ban, Trump's actual policy denied further surgeries to serving military personnel unless they were already receiving medical treatment, required serving military personnel to adhere to behavioral standards associated with their biological sex, and banned people who had received hormone treatments or surgery for gender transitions from joining the military.[15] Trump's opponents challenged this decision, too, in court. Ultimately, the Supreme Court backed Trump and the ban went into effect on April 12, 2019, giving him a political win but cementing the view in some quarters that Trump opposed gay rights. This position offended many LGBT people and their allies, including intelligence officers.

TRUMP AND RUSSIA

Trump had unusual personal contacts with Russia, which stemmed from business activities before he became a presidential

---

13   No Byline, "Trump Administration Announces Beginning of Transgender Military Ban on April 12," National Center for Transgender Equality, March 12, 2019, https://transequality.org/press/releases/trump-administration-announces-beginning-of-transgender-military-ban-on-april-12.

14   Abby Vesoulis, "President Trump Blamed the Transgender Military Ban on an Inaccurate Cost for Surgery," *Time*, June 5, 2019, https://time.com/5601347/trump-transgender-military-ban-costs/.

15   Elizabeth McLaughlin, "Pentagon's transgender policy for military service to take effect, nearly two years after Trump tweeted about the ban," *ABC News*, April 8, 2019, https://abcnews.go.com/Politics/pentagons-transgender-policy-military-service-effect-years-trump/story?id=62333348.

candidate. He seemed to like President Putin to a surprising degree given significant US-Russian policy differences and appeared at times to trust Putin more than his own intelligence advisers. He initially doubted the IC's judgment that Russia tried to influence the 2016 election campaign. Russian businessmen were linked to Trump's real estate businesses in New York City, leading to concern in some quarters that Trump might have ongoing business ties with Russia or that Russia had information that made Trump a blackmail target—leading to counterintelligence concerns.

In July 2016, such worries and unconfirmed reports of Russian contacts with the Trump campaign led the FBI to initiate an investigation code named "Crossfire Hurricane," which eventually became an investigation by special prosecutor Robert Mueller, a former FBI director.[16] Mueller's team found no collusion but left open the possibility that Trump had tampered with the FBI's investigation.[17] Before and after Mueller's announcement, because prominent former intelligence officers, especially DCIA John Brennan, had publicly proclaimed Trump guilty of collusion with the Russians, the president delivered many critical comments directed at the FBI and Brennan, claiming they were out to get him.[18] Trump repeatedly decried what he saw as an intelligence effort, abetted by many journalists, to use his Russia ties to first defeat him and later to drive him from office. This issue continues to irritate Trump's supporters.

While Mueller exonerated the Trump campaign of

---

16   For details, see Strzok, *Compromised*.

17   Robert S. Mueller III, "Report on the Investigation into Russian Interference in the 2016 Presidential Election," March 2019, https://www.justice.gov/storage/report.pdf.

18   Cheyenne Haslett, "Trump repeats unsubstantiated claims of 'coup' attempt after former FBI lawyer knocks them down," ABC News, May 13, 2019, https://abcnews.go.com/Politics/trump-repeats-unsubstantiated-claims-coup-attempt-fbi-lawyer/story?id=63001147.

conspiring with Russia, he and the IC concluded that Russian military intelligence, the GRU, had tried to influence the 2016 presidential election in two ways: by giving hacked emails between officials of the Democratic National Committee to WikiLeaks; and by conducting a campaign on social media designed to spur dissension generally in the United States and to damage candidate Hillary Clinton, whom Putin blamed for supporting anti-Putin demonstrations in Russia when she was secretary of state. The Clinton campaign found the subset of these activities directed against Clinton useful for explaining her unexpected and painful electoral defeat. Had Russia not aided Trump, many of her supporters claimed, Clinton would have been elected. This claim that his election victory was illegitimate seems to have irritated the competitive Trump. In contrast, most knowledgeable observers not emotionally attached to either candidate generally believe the modest Russian social media effort did not determine the election's outcome.[19]

Trump repeatedly spoke publicly and tweeted that he did not believe the Russians had done such deeds, denying Clinton supporters' assertions that only Russian aid had enabled him to win the election. Yet after initially denying the IC's finding that there had been Russian meddling, he reversed himself in July 2018. *Time* magazine reported Trump's statement:

> "While Russia's actions had no impact at all on the outcome of the election, let me be totally clear in saying

---

19 Neutral observers dismiss these accusations, saying flatly that the small Russian media effort did not influence the election result. For example, Rid, *Active Measures*, 407-408; McCombie, et al. "The US 2016 presidential election & Russia's troll farms," 96, 101-108; Shimer, *Rigged*, 223. Kathleen Hall Jamieson's *Cyberwar* cites many stories about Russian meddling with the campaign, ignores other aspects of the campaign, and does not address the key issue of whether Russian activities affected voters' choices. The book is a weak apology for Clinton's loss. She states as the first of five "presuppositions" (p. 14) that the Russians altered the electoral outcome.

– and I've said this many times – I accept our intelligence community's conclusion that Russia's meddling in the 2016 election took place," he said. "Could be other people also. A lot of people out there."[20]

Critics generally cited only Trump's initial position, not his reversal. In these ways, Russia became a major point of disagreement between Trump and intelligence officers and a source of contention about who knew truth about Russia and the 2016 election. Trump's evidently erroneous initial position on the Russian meddling issue is reminiscent of President Clinton's erroneous and politically motivated attacks on the CIA over the 1993 NIE on Haiti, discussed in chapter 2. But unlike the Haitian NIE case, in which Clinton attacked CIA over analysis of a foreign country that was domestically controversial, the eventually much bigger issue here is whether IC persons illegally persecuted a president during and beyond the Crossfire Hurricane episode. And Trump, unlike Clinton, eventually admitted his mistake in denying Russian meddling in 2016. The Justice Department, in the form of Special Counsel John Durham, continues in 2023 to investigate whether elements of the IC, especially the FBI, acted inappropriately in investigating Trump's 2016 campaign.

Apparent Dishonesty, "Fake News"

Donald Trump regularly made claims that objective observers recognized to be incorrect. He frequently changed his accounts of even public, well-known events. Newspapers and websites assigned "fact checkers" to keep tabs on his errors of fact, exaggerations, and inconsistencies, sometimes also embellishing

---

20   Alana Abramson, "President Trump Just Acknowledged Russian Meddling in the 2016 Election," *Time*, July 17, 2018, https://time.com/5341137/donald-trump-vladimir-putin-russian-meddling-correction/.

them.[21] As of May 29, 2020, the *Washington Post* had counted 19,127 allegedly false or misleading statements, or about fifteen per day in his time as president.[22] He seemed to carry political "spin," which became a commonly used term in Washington during the Clinton presidency, to new heights (or lows). His administration coined the term "alternative facts" to describe his take on things.[23]

Trump took issue with the fact checkers and comments of his political opponents, frequently criticizing the "fake news" his opponents allegedly produced. *The Hill* recounted Trump's comments in a news conference concerning the coronavirus in April 2020:

> President Trump on Thursday lashed out at reporters who questioned a report from the Department of Homeland Security that suggested the new coronavirus can be suppressed by heat and humidity.
>
> "I'm the president and you're fake news," Trump told *Washington Post* reporter Philip Rucker at a White House press briefing.
>
> "It's just a suggestion from a brilliant lab, from a very smart, perhaps brilliant man," Trump said. "He's talking about sun, he's talking about heat. And you see the

---

21   Glenn Kessler, Salvador Rizzo, and Meg Kelly, "The central feature of Trump's presidency: False claims and disinformation," *Washington Post*, June 2, 2020, https://www.washingtonpost.com/outlook/trump-fact-checker-book/2020/06/01/c6323b88-a435-11ea-b619-3f9133bbb482_story.html.

22   Ibid.

23   Eric Bradner, "Conway: Trump White House offered 'alternative facts' on crowd size," *CNN Politics*, January 23, 2017, https://www.cnn.com/2017/01/22/politics/kellyanne-conway-alternative-facts/index.html.

numbers. That's it, that's all I have. I'm just here to present talent. I'm here to present ideas."

When asked by the president, Deborah Birx, the White House coronavirus task force coordinator, said she was unaware of sunlight being an efficient tool against any virus.[24]

CRITICISMS OF INTELLIGENCE

Trump said many disparaging and incorrect things about the intelligence community, but he also praised intelligence profusely at times. He thereby was inconsistent in his comments about intelligence—as he was about many people and issues. John Helgerson, a retired senior CIA officer who studied presidential relations with intelligence, has argued that Trump was initially suspicious of intelligence, making the IC's job of establishing good relations with him more difficult than with all presidents except Nixon.[25] But his first significantly negative comments about intelligence came *after* the beginning of the partisan attacks on him by the formers, which I consider to be Michael Morell's endorsement of Hillary Clinton and scathing attack on Trump in his August 5, 2016 op-ed in the *New York Times*. Initially, Trump's critiques of intelligence were fairly mild, citing such widely recognized failures as the 9/11 attacks and the flawed NIE on Iraqi WMD programs in 2002, which virtually all intelligence officers also viewed as major failures. Nevertheless, many intelligence personnel reacted negatively to

---

24   J. Edward Moreno, "Trump hits CNN and Washington Post reporters as 'fake news' during briefing," *The Hill*, April 23, 2020, https://thehill.com/homenews/administration/494426-trump-hits-cnn-and-washington-post-reporters-as-fake-news-during.

25   Helgerson, *Getting to Know the President*, 3rd ed., 231, 236-237.

Trump's critiques of intelligence, often remembering only his negative comments while neglecting his many positive statements, intelligence history, and the formers' public criticisms of Trump, which prompted many of the president's harshest criticisms of intelligence. Hence, IC persons' perceptions of Trump in this arena often were not placed in meaningful context.

As a career businessman without political experience in Washington before 2016, candidate Trump had no significant exposure to intelligence. He said little publicly about intelligence until mid-2016. Soon after receiving the Republican nomination for president, Trump on August 17, 2016 visited an FBI office in New York City to receive his first classified briefing on foreign policy issues, prepared by the ODNI and given by CIA careerist Ted Gistaro, who then served as assistant deputy DNI for intelligence integration.[26] Such briefings have been courtesies offered to the presidential candidates of the two major political parties by most sitting presidents since 1952.[27] Sitting presidents and the IC normally want to familiarize people who may become president with intelligence on sensitive foreign policy issues that they may encounter during the campaign.[28]

Just before his briefing, a reporter asked Trump if he trusted the intelligence agencies. He replied:

> Not so much from the people that have been doing it for our country. I mean, look what's happened over the last 10 years. Look what's happened over the years. It's been catastrophic. And, in fact, I won't use some of the people

26   Ibid., 234.

27   The single exception is President Clinton's decision not to offer a briefing to Republican candidate Bob Dole in 1996. See Helgerson, *Getting to Know the President*, 2nd ed., 149, 172.

28   For a history of this process, see Helgerson, *Getting to Know the President*, 2nd ed.

that are sort of your standards, you know, just use them, use them, use them, very easy to use them, but I won't use them because they've made such bad decisions.[29]

Trump said he would bring along one of his campaign aides, retired Lieutenant General Michael Flynn, the former director of the DIA, to help him make sense of the briefing, which is a normal practice for close advisors with security clearances, which Flynn had.[30] Former DCIA Michael Hayden, who remained well-connected to the IC and had already spoken out against Trump, nevertheless reported that this briefing, and a second one on September 7, went well.[31]

Later, Trump gave the press his reactions to the briefing without revealing specific information he received. According to *Politifact*:

> When moderator Matt Lauer asked Trump about whether any information in his intelligence briefings had shocked him, Trump said yes. "What I did learn is that our leadership, Barack Obama, did not follow what our experts and our truly – when they call it intelligence, it's there for a reason – what our experts said to do," he said.
>
> Later on, Trump argued that security experts weren't happy with the current administration's strategy. "I could tell you – I have pretty good [sic] with the body

---

29 Nick Gass, "Trump: I don't trust U.S. intelligence information," *Politico*, August 17, 2016, https://www.politico.com/story/2016/08/trump-us-intelligence-briefing-227109.

30 Helgerson, *Getting to Know the President*, 2nd ed.

31 Hayden, *Assault on Intelligence*, 67-70.

language – I could tell they were not happy. Our leaders did not follow what they were recommending."[32]

This comment was unusual and almost certainly mistaken. These briefings historically have been apolitical in the partisan sense; the same briefing is given to candidates of each party.[33] Intelligence people huffed that Trump had grievously impugned the integrity of the briefers and politicized intelligence, not recalling the long history of presidential tensions with intelligence, especially at the beginning of administrations, which Helgerson had by then well documented in a book published by the CIA. Not widely commented on was Trump's assertion that presidents should always take intelligence assessments at face value—an error of historical fact, of tradition, and of judgment. It was a recommendation that he surely did not himself follow.

The anti-Trump press chronically exaggerated Trump's negative comments about intelligence. Some reporters and intelligence people claimed, for example, that Trump had "declared war" on the IC.[34] The "war" metaphor lasted, as did Trump's alleged "assault on intelligence." Both terms were used repeatedly in various forms by Trump's intelligence critics; Michael Hayden even made it the title of his second book.[35] But Trump did not in fact describe his perception of the IC, or act, in such ways. Former DNI Clapper, a harsh Trump critic who also assailed Trump's attitudes toward intelligence, wrote that Trump first attacked the IC only on December 9, 2016, long after numerous

---

32 Joseph Cariz, "What Donald Trump said about intelligence briefings, *Politifact*, September 10, 2016, https://www.politifact.com/truth-o-meter/article/2016/sep/10/what-donald-trump-said-about-intelligence-briefing/.

33 Helgerson, *Getting to Know the President*, 2ⁿᵈ ed.

34 John R. Schindler, "Trump Declares War on the Intelligence Community," *Observer*, December 12, 2016, https://observer.com/2016/12/trump-declares-war-on-the-intelligence-community/.

35 Hayden, *The Assault on Intelligence.*

former intelligence officers had publicly criticized Trump harshly, the surge in anti-Trump leaks by serving officers had begun, and Trump was feeling heat from the selective leaks of the spurious allegations of the "Steele dossier" (discussed below) that became fully public a month later.[36] Still, Trump made a point of visiting CIA headquarters on January 21, 2017, his first full day in office, to express his support for and appreciation of intelligence.

In December 2016, after he had become president-elect, Trump said he did not need "repetitive" intelligence briefings. He was happy to have senior aides, whom he identified as Vice-President-elect Mike Pence, Secretary of Defense-designate James Mattis, and Secretary of Homeland Security-designate John Kelly, receive regular briefings. They in turn could tell him what they thought he needed to know. Nevertheless, in the 10-week transition period, Trump received 14 intelligence briefings at his headquarters in the Trump Tower in New York City.[37] At his first post-election briefing, Trump told Ted Gistaro that he would like to receive the *PDB*, which is a document, every day but might only take one oral briefing a week given his busy schedule.[38] In fact, in the transition period Trump received at least one briefing per week, usually on Tuesdays for 30 to 50 minutes, but he seemed to Gistaro not to have read the *PDB* on other days. Responding to criticisms that he was not taking any daily intelligence briefings, something the press claimed incorrectly that all previous presidents had done, he told Chris Wallace of Fox News:

> You know, I'm, like, a smart person. I don't have to be told the same thing in the same words every single day

---

36   Clapper, *Facts and Fears*, 371.
37   Helgerson, *Getting to Know the President*, 3rd ed., 241.
38   Ibid., 242-243.

for the next eight years. Could be eight years — but eight years. I don't need that.

But I do say, 'If something should change, let us know.'[39]

Presidents in fact have had a wide variety of preferences for taking intelligence before and after becoming president, including wanting: written products to mainly enter formal staff channels (Eisenhower); briefings to be presented by the national security advisor (Nixon and Carter); to receive intelligence reading materials intermittently or at night (Johnson) or in the morning (most presidents); and, a wide variety of written, oral, and visual formats. These facts have been published in several reputable and widely cited books, including Helgerson's history of CIA briefings of candidates and presidents-elect and a history of the *President's Daily Brief* by David Priess, a former CIA analyst and *PDB* briefer.[40] Most critics who were career intelligence officers presumably were well aware of both books but to my knowledge never cited either, presumably because they did not help the anti-Trump campaign.

Later, Helgerson reported that in his first five weeks in office, Trump took an average of 2.5 intelligence briefings per week, which typically lasted 40 to 60 minutes and were also attended by several other senior White House officials.[41] DNI Dan Coats (March 2017-August 2019), according to Bob Woodward, joined *PDB* briefers at the White House three times per week.[42] National security advisor John Bolton (April 2018-September 2019) reported that Trump normally took two oral briefings

---

39   Louis Nelson, "Trump: I don't need daily briefings," *Politico*, December 11, 2016, https://www.politico.com/story/2016/12/trump-briefings-232479.

40   Helgerson, *Getting to Know the President*, 2nd ed.; Priess, *The President's Book of Secrets*.

41   Helgerson, *Getting to Know the President*, 3rd ed., 263.

42   Woodward, *Rage*, 29-30.

per week, one of which was attended by Coats and DCIA Gina Haspel.[43] Helgerson also reported that in the second half of his term, Trump took on average two briefings lasting on average 45 minutes from Beth Sanner, who had replaced Gistaro as briefer; other White House officials continued to attend the sessions and were active participants in the sessions.[44] Sanner reported that Trump did not read the *PDB* but raised intelligence topics with her and occasionally took specialized briefings from substantive experts.[45] In contrast, Vice President Mike Pence, who typically attended Trump's intelligence briefings, read his *PDB* six days a week—every day it was published—and asked for material that was not included in Trump's version.[46] By all accounts, intelligence flowed normally to other senior White House officials. Bolton said he tried to get Trump to receive more intelligence, without success.[47] Both Bolton and Coats reported that Trump alternatively was an eager recipient of intelligence and was resistant to some intelligence messages and/or was argumentative with his briefers.

Other presidents also were sometimes less than fully receptive to intelligence. Priess reported that President Kennedy took little interest in intelligence early in his presidency, which prompted national security advisor McGeorge Bundy to ask for creation of a new briefing format that later was renamed the *PDB*.[48] And John Brennan reported that when he was a *PDB* briefer, President Clinton took briefings in person one to three times per week—a result of his busy schedule—the same or less than Trump.[49] As

---

43   Bolton, *The Room Where It Happened*, 89, 224.

44   Helgerson, *Getting to Know the President*, 3rd ed., 266.

45   Ibid.

46   Ibid., 267. The *PDB* normally is published six days per week, Monday through Saturday.

47   Bolton, *The Room Where It Happened*, 89.

48   Priess, *The President's Book of Secrets*, 19-21.

49   Brennan, *Undaunted*, 98.

noted, DCI James Woolsey resigned because he could not get time on Clinton's calendar, which never was an IC issue with President Trump.

One of the most storied episodes of the IC-Trump conflict saga occurred in January 2017, but the story actually began months before. The IC had been monitoring Russian attempts to influence the 2016 election since early 2016, long after it began. These eventually took two major forms: (1) hacking computers of the Democratic National Committee and Democratic officials, then releasing embarrassing emails to WikiLeaks; and (2) conducting a modest social media campaign that evidently aimed, like Soviet active measures campaigns before it, to roil American society. The Soviets and then the Russians hoped such work would eventually lead to the disintegration of the United States and of NATO, their major military adversary.[50] These goals could best be accomplished by helping Trump, who they expected to lose the election. In early December 2016, President Obama asked the IC to prepare a report on the then-considerable body of evidence that Russia had tried to influence the election. Analysts from the agencies most closely involved—CIA, NSA, and FBI—worked with the NIC to prepare a highly classified report in a NIC format called an Intelligence Community Assessment (ICA). Obama asked that an unclassified version also be prepared for public release.[51] The heads of these agencies and Clapper briefed Obama on January 5, 2017 on their findings.[52]

In addition to preparing the ICA, the intelligence chiefs briefed Obama on material that was not put into either version of the report, notably information compiled by former British

50   Gentry, "Belated Success."
51   Comey, *A Higher Loyalty*, 211-215. The unclassified report is "Assessing Russian Activities and Intentions in recent US Elections, Intelligence Community Assessment, ICA 2017-01D, January 6, 2017, available at https://www.dni.gov/files/documents/ICA_2017_01.pdf.
52   Clapper, *Facts and Fears*, 373-377.

THE SHOCK OF DONALD TRUMP

intelligence officer Christopher Steele, originally as opposition research funded by the Hillary Clinton campaign. The IC had not corroborated the material in the seventeen short memos, written over a period of several months in 2016, which comprised the "Steele dossier," and so had not included it in its formal report. (In May 2022, Special Counsel John Durham revealed that the Clinton campaign authorized release of false information regarding Trump and the Russians via Steele to FBI officials, who were happy to receive it.[53])

Steele's "dossier" contained some inflammatory accusations, later proven to be incorrect, which Clapper called "salacious" and Comey called "salacious and embarrassing," including allegations that, during a 2013 trip to Moscow, Trump had engaged in what Comey called "unusual sexual activities" with Russian prostitutes. Alleged activities including urinating on a hotel bed that Obama and Mrs. Obama had slept on while on a presidential trip to Russia, which Russian officials allegedly had filmed for possible blackmail purposes—a longstanding, well-known KGB practice.[54] The three agency heads and Clapper told Obama that they had what Clapper called a "duty to warn" Trump of the accusations, which by late 2016 journalists increasingly knew due to Steele's serial leaks to them.[55] The IC's leaders decided that Comey should brief Trump, given the FBI's ongoing counterintelligence investigation of members of the Trump campaign. Obama concurred.

On January 6, 2017, Clapper and three agency heads—CIA's John Brennan, NSA's Admiral Mike Rogers, and Comey—briefed Congressional committees on the ICA, then went to New York

---

53   Brooke Singman, Jake Gibson, David Spunt, "Sussman-Durham Trial: Marc Elias says he briefed Clinton campaign on Fusion GPS oppo against Trump," Fox News, May 18, 2022, https://www.foxnews.com/politics/sussmann-durham-trial-marc-elias-briefed-clinton-campaign-officials-fusion-gps-trump.

54   Comey, *A Higher Loyalty*, 214, 216.

55   Clapper, *Facts and Fears*, 375.

City to brief the president-elect.[56] The formal briefing to Trump went "surprisingly well," according to Clapper.[57] Trump delivered what Clapper called "high praise" for his *PDB* briefer, Ted Gistaro, who was present.[58] At the session's end, as planned, Comey stayed behind to discuss one-on-one with Trump what Clapper called the "one additional matter"—the allegations of the Steele dossier. In Comey's telling, Trump protested that the charges were not true.[59] Comey said he made clear to Trump that as far as the IC was concerned, the dossier's claims were unsubstantiated. In fact, the FBI was continuing to work the case, which Comey did not tell Trump and which became part of the long-running investigation of whether the Bureau acted appropriately in its dealings with the Trump campaign and with the president himself.

Four days later, on January 10, 2017, the online publication *Buzzfeed*, which had previously been highly critical of Trump, published the 35-page Steele dossier in full.[60] It evidently had been leaked by Steele or by someone in the FBI, to which Steele had given the report, or possibly by someone from another IC agency. Although Steele, who personally was strongly anti-Trump, reportedly had been telling journalists about some of the contents of the dossier for months, neither Steele nor anyone in the IC evidently had given the report to the Trump camp, apparently eliminating the campaign staff as a source of the leak and making Trump's assumption that intelligence had leaked the dossier plausible.[61] Trump unsurprisingly was outraged. The next day, January 11, he tweeted:

---

56   Brennan, *Undaunted*, 378-390.

57   Clapper, *Facts and Fears*, 373, 377.

58   Ibid., 374. This praise suggests that Trump had had enough intelligence briefings to decide to be complimentary of them.

59   Comey, *A Higher Loyalty*, 223-225.

60   https://www.buzzfeednews.com/article/kenbensinger/these-reports-allege-trump-has-deep-ties-to-russia.

61   Strassel, *Resistance*, 36-60.

Intelligence agencies should never have allowed this fake news to "leak" into the public. One last shot at me. Are we living in Nazi Germany?[62]

Trump's retort came after a particularly damaging leak, and after multiple other leaks and overt attacks by former intelligence personnel. The now-conventional notion that Trump gratuitously called all intelligence officers "Nazis" is incorrect, but the misleading charge remains a common, bitter complaint of many intelligence personnel. As recalled, intelligence officers long have had inflated views of the quality of their insights and patriotism. Clapper claimed he was "floored" by Trump's words.[63] The Soviets, Russians, and left-leaning persons everywhere reserve the expletives "Nazi" and "fascist" for special enemies. Presumably Clapper and others would have been less riled had Trump compared the IC to Stalin's Soviet Union, which actually was far more adept at disseminating disinformation than was Hitler's Germany.

On January 21, 2017, the day after he was inaugurated, Trump visited CIA headquarters and spoke in its entryway, in front of the "Memorial Wall," into which are inscribed stars, one for each CIA employee who died in the line of duty and who was deemed worthy of the honor by the circumstances of death, particularly if the death was heroic or inspirational in nature. Trump explained why he was there:

And the reason you're my first stop is that, as you know, I have a running war with the media. They are among the most dishonest human beings on Earth. (Laughter

---

62   Reena Flores, "Donald Trump references 'Nazi Germany' in tweet about intelligence agencies," *CBS News,* January 11, 2017, https://www.cbsnews.com/news/donald-trump-references-nazi-germany-in-tweet-about-intelligence-agencies/.

63   Clapper, *Facts and Fears,* 379.

and applause.) And they sort of made it sound like I had a feud with the intelligence community. And I just want to let you know, the reason you're the number-one stop is exactly the opposite — exactly.[64]

Despite this praise, Trump spent much of his time talking about political issues, sometimes in controversial terms, such as by claiming the crowds at his inaugural events were much larger than most observers estimated. The event also prompted criticism of Trump by intelligence people because he allegedly desecrated the Memorial Wall by not being appropriately respectful to the fallen. It mattered not that Trump had already designated both DNI Coats and DCIA Pompeo as members of his cabinet and made Pompeo a member of his decision-making Principals Committee, rare honors for intelligence officers.[65] William Casey, President Reagan's long-serving DCI (1981-1987), was the only previous DCI to be a cabinet member.

Another prominent episode occurred on January 26, 2019, when DNI Coats and the major IC agency heads briefed the SSCI in open session—the IC's annual "threat assessment" session. This unclassified briefing is designed to give the American public a glimpse of how US intelligence sees the world. Among many topics addressed, Coats and DCIA Gina Haspel agreed that Iran was technically in compliance with its nuclear deal with the West and that North Korea was unlikely to agree to give up its nuclear weapons, positions at odds with President Trump's previously stated views. As the long session continued, news reports of these comments reached Trump, who reacted negatively. According to *The New Yorker*:

64   Eugene Kiely, "Trump and Intelligence Community," *FactCheck.org*, January 23, 2017, https://www.factcheck.org/2017/01/trump-and-intelligence-community/.

65   Helgerson, *Getting to Know the President*, 3rd ed., 260-261.

Trump was furious after seeing cable-television news headlines saying that the intelligence chiefs had contradicted him, according to CNN, and he attacked them in two tweets, without having seen their full testimony. "The Intelligence people seem to be extremely passive and naive when it comes to the dangers of Iran. They are wrong!" Trump tweeted. "Perhaps Intelligence should go back to school!" (On Thursday afternoon, Trump tweeted a photo of himself meeting with Coats and Haspel in the Oval Office. He suggested that people read the "*COMPLETE*" testimony from the hearing, and blamed the media for putting out a "false narrative.")[66]

Soon thereafter, Trump sat for a wide-ranging interview with CBS News, which reported:

Specifically on the threat posed by Iran, Mr. Trump still appeared to doubt the intelligence. "My intelligence people, if they said in fact that Iran is a wonderful kindergarten, I disagree with them 100 percent. It is a vicious country that kills many people," he said.

When pressed on the intelligence community's assessment that Iran was technically in compliance with the Iran nuclear deal, Trump said he doesn't "have to agree" with his intelligence chiefs.

---

66   David Rohde, "Is Trump Trying to Bully America's Intelligence Agencies Into Silence?" *The New Yorker*, January 31, 2019, https://www.newyorker.com/news/daily-comment/is-trump-trying-to-bully-americas-intelligence-agencies-into-silence.

"I have intel people, but that doesn't mean I have to agree. President Bush had intel people that said Saddam Hussein in Iraq had nuclear weapons, had all sorts of weapons of mass destruction. Guess what? Those intel people didn't know what the hell they were doing, and they got us tied up in a war that we should have never been in."

He added, "We were in many, many locations in the Middle East, in huge difficulty. Every single one of them was caused by the number one terrorist nation in the world which is Iran. So when my intelligence people tell me how wonderful Iran is — if you don't mind, I'm going to just go by my own counsel."

Mr. Trump said he wouldn't stop his intelligence chiefs from testifying again, saying, "I want them to have their own opinion and I want them to give me their opinion."[67]

Trump was right that he did not have to take the advice of intelligence. Intelligence worked for him, not the other way around. As discussed in chapter 2, presidents often ignore or pointedly reject intelligence reports they receive. While procedurally justified by tradition, the soundness of Trump's judgment in this case was debatable. As often was the case, Trump was needlessly abrasive. But he did say he wanted to keep intelligence "in the room" even when he disagreed with its assessments, something

---

67   No byline, "Trump says he doesn't 'have to agree' with intelligence chiefs on global threats," CBS News, February 3, 2019, https://www.cbsnews.com/news/donald-trump-face-the-nation-interview-margaret-brennan-today-super-bowl-2019-02-03/.

other presidents sometimes did not do. Nevertheless, intelligence people generally condemned Trump's words as another "assault on intelligence."

In March 2019, after Special Counsel Mueller reported that he did not find evidence of a Russia-Trump campaign conspiracy in 2016, Trump and his allies increasingly argued that elements in the IC, especially CIA and FBI people, conspired against him. Trump said:

> This was a coup, this was an attempted overthrow of the United States government. These are sick, sick people. ... Let's see how high it goes up because it's inconceivable when it goes to Clapper, Brennan, Comey, these people, I would imagine some other people maybe higher up also knew about it.[68]

Brennan responded by criticizing Trump's "sociopathic ramblings."[69] But the substance of this accusation remains under federal investigation and still, as I write in early 2023, is a topic of considerable debate.

In July 2019 Trump asked DNI Coats to resign. He apparently was still annoyed at Coats's testimony to Congress earlier in the year. Trump nominated as Coats's replacement Representative John Ratcliffe (R-TX), a junior congressman who had been on the HPSCI for six months and who defended Trump vigorously during Robert Mueller's testimony on the Hill. In nominating Ratcliffe, Trump argued that the IC needed new leadership

---

68   Diana Stancy Correll, "John Brennan dismisses Trump's 'sociopathic ramblings' on intelligence community trying to overthrow government," *Washington Examiner*, April 26, 2019, https://www.washingtonexaminer.com/news/john-brennan-dismisses-trumps-sociopathic-ramblings-on-intelligence-community-trying-to-overthrow-government.

69   Ibid.

because "We need somebody strong that can rein it in. Because, as I think you've all learned, the intelligence agencies have run amok. They have run amok."[70] But, as was often the case, Trump was inconsistent; he also complimented Coats, saying Coats was a "terrific person" and "a friend of mine." President Nixon explained his replacement of DCI Richard Helms with James Schlesinger similarly, but he did not effusively praise Helms although he appointed Helms to be ambassador to Iran, which padded Helms's retirement checks. Ratcliffe, unlike Schlesinger, made no serious effort to reform the IC. Also unlike Nixon, Trump did not tell Ratcliffe to "clean house."

Trump repeatedly labeled several of the former agency heads who criticized him "political hacks," often making critical comments via tweets. For example, in a series of tweets rejecting intelligence judgments about North Korea, Iran, and the Islamic State, Trump wrote in January 2019:

> The Intelligence people seem to be extremely passive and naive when it comes to the dangers of Iran. They are wrong! When I became President Iran was making trouble all over the Middle East, and beyond. Since ending the terrible Iran Nuclear Deal, they are MUCH different, but....[71]

---

70   Jonathan Landay, "In new attack, Trump says U.S. intelligence agencies 'run amok'," *Reuters*, July 31, 2019, https://news.yahoo.com/attack-trump-says-u-intelligence-222414324.html.

71   Ken Bredemeier and Jeff Seldin, "Trump Takes Aim at Intelligence Chiefs Via Tweet-Storm," *VOA News*, January 30, 2019, https://www.voanews.com/usa/trump-takes-aim-intelligence-chiefs-tweet-storm.

But he also said in late 2017, "… I'm with our intelligence agencies. As currently led by fine people, I believe very much in our intelligence agencies."[72]

In sum, President Trump was mercurial and inconsistent about intelligence, as he was about many subjects and people. Sometimes he praised intelligence officers publicly, but more often he criticized intelligence people and analyses publicly through tweets that the press and blogosphere amplified. But in private, he often was quite complimentary of intelligence. For example, in an exit interview with a retiring senior intelligence officer whom the press speculated had run afoul of him, Trump was personally very flattering.[73]

Trump and his senior advisors regularly received intelligence support in ways similar to most past administrations. Like all previous presidents, he appreciated some intelligence reporting more than others, and like other presidents he differentially paid attention to intelligence based largely on whether he found the reporting persuasive or not. However, Trump differed appreciably from many presidents in the zeal with which he publicly expressed his many strongly-felt likes and dislikes, and he was remarkably adept at annoying his adversaries, particularly those on the political Left.

---

72   No byline, "Russia at center of Asia trip," *Washington Post Express*, November 13, 2017, 13.

73   Personal communication with a person with direct access to this conversation, summer 2019.

5

INTELLIGENCE OFFICERS' REACTIONS

★

Donald Trump's polarizing rhetoric and policies generated many reactions among Americans, both favorable and unfavorable. While some observers from across the political spectrum addressed Trump's style and policies in objective, analytical ways, many reactions to Trump, especially from the Left, were highly emotional, barely rational in some cases, and overwhelmingly negative. Pundits soon began to call these extreme reactions the "Trump Derangement Syndrome."[1] Columbia University professor Richard Betts, a long-time observer of US intelligence and a self-described Democrat,[2] in commenting on an article manuscript on the general topic of this book in 2019, observed that some of his critics "hysterically exaggerate Trump's lies."[3] Most of the publicly evident reaction to Trump by intelligence officials was also negative. Some reaction was

---

1   For example, Strassel, *Resistance*, 38.
2   Betts, *Enemies of Intelligence*, xv.
3   Personal communication, referenced in Gentry, "'Truth' as a Tool of the Politicization of Intelligence," 217.

muted, analytical, and expressed criticism tinged with regret. But other intelligence personnel, like many Americans, were highly emotional and/or strongly political in partisan and ideological ways.

Negative reactions to Trump by professional intelligence officers, current and former, are the primary focus of this chapter because they were so unusual by historical standards and because they dwarfed the pro-Trump commentary. The anti-Trump activism amounted to a new and important form of overt politicization. Unlike in the 1980s when it came from the political Right, but like the CIA activists of the 1960s, the evidence is overwhelming that opposition to Trump came primarily from the Left—that is, people whose politics were associated with left-of-center ideological views and/or the Democratic Party. While as noted the CIA and INR have long collectively been liberal, intelligence officers in general previously kept their political views to themselves. The cultural changes of recent years had diminished previously strong constraints on overt activism.

Intelligence officers opposed to Trump differed sharply from the "Never Trump" Republicans of the 2016 campaign season who mostly were quiet after November 2016. An open letter by 122 Republicans who previously held senior national security positions, published in August 2016, said its signers would not vote for Trump. The letter contained only one name with significant intelligence experience: Philip Zelikow, who was executive director of the 9/11 Commission and was a political appointee in George W. Bush's State Department.[4] Former DCI Robert Gates and former DCIA Michael Hayden were cited as being members of this

---

4   One hundred twenty-two authors, "A Letter From G.O.P. National Security Officials Opposing Donald Trump," *New York Times*, August 8, 2016, https://www.nytimes.com/interactive/2016/08/08/us/politics/national-security-letter-trump.html. See also Saldin and Teles, *Never Trump*, 44-46.

group in May 2016, while the Republican primary season was still underway, but neither man signed the August 2016 letter.[5] Gates in September 2016 published an op-ed in the *Wall Street Journal* designed to assess the two major party presidential candidates' qualifications, focused narrowly on national security issues.[6] Gates wrote, "I believe Mr. Trump is beyond repair," and opined that Trump was unfit to be commander-in-chief.[7] He also criticized Hillary Clinton, albeit less harshly. Gates's comments were analytical and comparative, not partisan in terms of an endorsement or a statement of support for a candidate. Trump promptly retorted that Gates was a "clown" and a "mess" and "dopey."[8] Gates wisely let the matter drop. Neither he nor any other "Never Trumper" with significant intelligence experience except Hayden criticized Trump prominently after the 2016 election.[9]

Intelligence officers' negative reactions to Trump can be grouped in several ways. First, former intelligence officers' public commentary about Trump was limited between August 2016 and January 2017, when he was inaugurated. Second, intelligence officers' anti-Trump feelings burst forth in 2017 in comments of senior "formers," several of whom worked for Obama and had just left office. These people criticized Trump sharply and publicly, making their claims and motives clear in television interviews, op-ed writings, at academic symposia, and later in books. The

---

5   Julia Ioffe, "On the Lonely Island of 'Never Trump'," *Politico Magazine*, May 17, 2016, https://www.politico.com/magazine/story/2016/05/never-trump-hillary-clinton-foreign-policy-establishment-213898.

6   Robert M. Gates, "Sizing Up the Next Commander-in-Chief," *Wall Street Journal*, September 16, 2016, https://www.wsj.com/articles/sizing-up-the-next-commander-in-chief-1474064606.

7   Politico Staff, "Bob Gates: Trump is 'beyond repair'," *Politico*, September 17, 2016, https://www.politico.com/story/2016/09/bob-gates-donald-trump-hillary-clinton-228315.

8   Christina Coleburn, "Trump Deems Former Defense Secretary Robert Gates a 'Clown,'" NBC News, September 18, 2016, https://www.nbcnews.com/politics/2016-election/trump-deems-former-defense-secretary-robert-gates-clown-n650126.

9   Saldin and Teles, *Never Trump*.

loud formers quickly became spokespersons for an unknown, but apparently appreciable, number of serving intelligence officers who could not speak openly given policies against overt political activity by government officials. Third, serving intelligence officers acted against Trump mainly through leaks, using a variety of techniques to make their views public. The media showcased the views of the formers for their own anti-Trump purposes and created opportunities for, and publicized, leaks. Importantly but much less obviously, many intelligence people quietly disapproved of Trump's intelligence critics, wishing they had stayed silent.

THE INITIAL REACTIONS—2016

The opening salvo of overtly partisan criticisms of Trump by intelligence officers came from former Deputy CIA Director Michael Morell on August 5, 2016, when he endorsed Hillary Clinton for president and scathingly criticized Trump in an op-ed in the *New York Times*. Morell wrote:

> My training as an intelligence officer taught me to call it as I see it. This is what I did for the C.I.A. This is what I am doing now. Our nation will be much safer with Hillary Clinton as president.[10]

Morell claimed that Trump "is not only unqualified for the job, but he may well pose a threat to our national security" and alleged that "Mr. Putin had recruited Mr. Trump as an unwitting agent of the Russian Federation."[11] With these words, Morell broke a long-standing taboo by invoking his intelligence credentials

---

10   Michael J. Morell, "I Ran the C.I.A. Now I am Endorsing Hillary Clinton, *New York Times*, August 5, 2016, https://www.nytimes.com/2016/08/05/opinion/campaign-stops/i-ran-the-cia-now-im-endorsing-hillary-clinton.html.
11   Ibid.

to rationalize a domestic, partisan political action—a vote for Clinton. He also misspoke, an incongruous act given intelligence officers' legitimate complaints about Trump's lack of truthfulness but one that was consistent with misleading CIA information operations of the past: Morell incorrectly insinuated that he made *domestic* policy recommendations when he was at CIA. He did not. Intelligence officers are taught from their first day on the job that they do not recommend policy options or make policy decisions, and the record is clear that policymakers ensure that this standard is upheld. Morell advised national leaders about *foreign* events of significance to the United States. Such erroneous statements would recur frequently.

Earlier, former intelligence officials communicated publicly some general concerns about Trump that were largely analytical in nature. For example, in May 2016, when Trump was frontrunner for the Republican nomination for president but had not yet clinched it, former Deputy DCI John McLaughlin told the "progressive" magazine *Mother Jones* that "Trump's public statements don't suggest that he's someone who easily deals with things that strongly disagree with his view."[12] At about the same time, Hayden worried that Trump might blurt out classified information on the campaign trail.[13] Separately, Hayden also asserted implausibly that Trump would create a "crisis" in the military.[14]

Just before Trump's first intelligence briefing on August 17, 2016, as he was saying he distrusted intelligence, serving intelligence professionals mounted one of their first anti-Trump leak operations, reporting that some of Trump's comments led

---

12   Max J. Rosenthal, "Former CIA Deputy Director: Trump Would Be a 'Hard Brief,'" *Mother Jones*, May 6, 2016, https://www.motherjones.com/politics/2016/05/cia-official-trump-intelligence-hard-brief/.
13   Ibid.
14   Hayden, *Assault on Intelligence*, 70.

them to have significant trepidation about a Trump presidency.[15] A terrorism expert at a Washington think tank told journalists that serving intelligence people were "fearful" of Trump.[16] Leaking intelligence personnel cited several factors as causes of their concern: Trump's alleged unpredictability, his harsh rhetoric about Muslims, his support for torture as a counter-terrorism technique, and his suggestion that he would go after terrorism suspects' families.[17] As recounted in chapter 2, leaks of this sort long have reflected intelligence officers' opposition to presidents such as Johnson, Nixon, and Carter. Leaks against Trump would be much more numerous and longer-lasting than ever before.

Before Trump's August 17 briefing, Senator Harry Reid (D-NV), the minority leader of the Senate, expressed unhappiness that the IC was even giving Trump an intelligence briefing. He suggested that the IC take an overtly political step in violation of the long-standing, bipartisan tradition of presidents ordering their intelligence chiefs to brief both Democratic and Republican presidential candidates every four years. CNN reported:

> "How would the CIA and the other intelligence agencies brief this guy? How could they do that? I would suggest to the intelligence agencies, if you're forced to brief this guy, don't tell him anything, just fake it, because this man is dangerous," Reid told *The Huffington Post* last month. "Fake it, pretend you're doing a briefing, but you can't give the guy any information."[18]

15   Nahal Toosi, "Trump makes intel community queasy," *Politico*, August 17, 2016, https://www.politico.com/story/2016/08/trump-intelligence-community-unhappy-227120.
16   Ibid.
17   Ibid.
18   Shimon Prokupecz, Evan Perez, and Jeremy Diamond, "Trump received first classified intelligence briefing Wednesday," *CNN*, August 18, 2016, https://www.cnn.com/2016/08/16/politics/donald-trump-intelligence-briefing/index.html.

DNI Clapper responded appropriately by rejecting Reid's suggestion:

> "Nominees for president and vice president receive these briefings by virtue of their status as candidates and do not require separate security clearances before the briefings."... "Briefings for the candidates will be provided on an even-handed non-partisan basis."[19]

In addition to his public comments, Reid set in motion a set of events that continued to the end of Trump's presidency. Reid wrote to FBI Director Comey in late October 2016 complaining about Trump on the basis of classified briefings that he, and the other members of the "Gang of Eight" of senior Congressional leaders who frequently receive sensitive intelligence briefings, had received from DCIA Brennan.[20] Reid asserted that the FBI was meddling in the election by withholding information that Russia and the Trump campaign were colluding to defeat Hillary Clinton.[21] Reid was a highly partisan and combative politician, but his letter injected intelligence directly into the presidential campaign, which unsurprisingly leaked immediately, and was unusual even by his standards. As we know now, the Trump campaign and Russia did not collude.

Hayden said Trump's reaction to his second intelligence

---

19   Ibid.
20   Abigail Tracey, "The C.I.A. Knew About Russia's Operation to Get Trump Elected Last Summer," *Vanity Fair*, April 7, 2017, https://www.vanityfair.com/news/2017/04/john-brennan-cia-donald-trump-russia. The "Gang of Eight" is an intelligence term for the majority and minority leaders of each house of Congress, and the chair and ranking member of each of the intelligence oversight committees. These people receive sensitive intelligence information, including briefings about covert actions.
21   Aaron Blake, "Harry Reid's incendiary claim about 'coordination' between Donald Trump and Russia," *Washington Post*, October 31, 2016, https://www.washingtonpost.com/news/the-fix/wp/2016/10/31/harry-reid-just-made-a-huge-incendiary-evidence-free-claim-about-trump-and-russia/.

briefing, on September 7, 2016, which Hayden believed went well, nevertheless had troubling aspects. He reported that Trump seemed to appreciate his briefing. After the briefing, when reporters asked how it went, Trump responded, "I have great respect for the people that gave us the briefings … they were terrific people."[22] But then Trump spoke unconventionally in ways that bothered Hayden from an institutional perspective and, evidently, emotionally. In response to a question, Trump opined that President Obama and Secretaries of State Hillary Clinton and John Kerry, who allegedly was "another total disaster," did not use intelligence well. When asked how he knew that, he cited the body language of the briefers. Hayden was correct that Trump's comment about his briefers was unusual in three ways: (1) Trump did not appreciate that the briefings are a courtesy of sitting presidents, not a right of candidates; (2) he used his intelligence briefers "as political props and campaign tools," something intelligence officers do not like because they prefer to be seen as unquestionably apolitical;[23] and (3) given intelligence officers' traditionally strong efforts to stay apolitical in such settings, Trump's assertion almost certainly was mistaken.[24] But gauche and unconventional as Trump was, the history of such briefings is that intelligence officers always previously had rolled with the quirks of candidates who they know are often new to Washington and are focused on other concerns—such as their election campaigns. Intelligence people therefore traditionally have not responded to such perceived slights. Hayden's emotional reaction was abnormal.

Morell and other "high profile" former intelligence officials immediately charged that Trump's alleged attempt to politicize

---

22   Ibid., 70.
23   On the intelligence preference for these briefings to be apolitical and low-key, see Helgerson, *Getting to Know the President*, 2nd ed.
24   Hayden, *Assault on Intelligence*, 70.

the briefing had crossed a "red line."[25] It did not. Morell again was wrong. Intelligence people do not impose "red lines" on presidents and, as described in chapter 3, presidents frequently ignore or criticize intelligence as they see fit. Intelligence by long-standing custom never responds publicly to any variety of presidential behavior, however egregiously ill-considered it may be. Morell thus violated another long-standing taboo. Then-DCIA Brennan also "pushed back" against Trump's comments by publicly defending the professionalism of the CIA personnel who gave the briefing.[26] Still in office, by the standards of his later commentary Brennan's rebuke was mild.

Later in September 2016 Morell went after Trump again, as reported by the *Washington Post*:

> "He cares more about himself than anything else, including his nation," Morell said on a conference call with reporters about Trump's ties to Russia. "The definition of a patriot is someone who puts his nation above everything else in his life. In that regard, Donald Trump is not a patriot."[27]

Morell's comment reflected personal animus. Such ad hominem attacks would become a common feature of intelligence officers' critiques of Trump. Obviously, Morell's definition of patriotism was not universally held.

---

25   Sarah Wheaton, "Former intelligence officers alarmed by Trump's briefing readout," *Politico*, September 8, 2016, https://www.politico.com/story/2016/09/trump-intelligence-briefing-readout-227904.

26   Theodoric Meyer, "CIA director rebuts Trump's claim on intelligence briefing," *Politico*, September 11, 2016, https://www.politico.com/story/2016/09/trump-clinton-john-brennan-cia-228006.

27   Abby Phillip, "'Donald Trump is not a patriot,' says former acting CIA chief Michael Morell," *Washington Post*, September 22, 2016, https://www.washingtonpost.com/news/post-politics/wp/2016/09/22/donald-trump-is-not-a-patriot-says-former-acting-cia-chief-michael-morell/.

In October 2016 Morell again attacked Trump, charging incorrectly that Trump campaign officials were "working on behalf of the Russians."[28] Morell's concerns evidently reflected information currently serving intelligence officers gave him about the FBI's ongoing Crossfire Hurricane investigation of the Trump campaign. This leak was an early version of what would become another standard practice: former senior intelligence officials publicly reporting intelligence information they received from currently serving officers, some of which was evidently purpose-fully erroneous. In 2019, Morell's charge was explicitly refuted in Special Counsel Robert Mueller's final report on Russian interference with the 2016 election.[29]

A then-serving ODNI officer observed that many Clinton supporters among the ODNI staff were vocal on her behalf at work before the 2016 election and were distraught after her defeat.[30] Gregory Treverton, who was chairman of the NIC in November 2016, similarly recounted what seems to have been a common reaction at the ODNI to the election result:

> I think we, like everyone else including Trump, were surprised. I only knew the political leanings of my closest colleagues, and they were dismayed.[31]

Treverton left office in January 2017, leaving no doubt that he did not like Trump, saying that he decided to leave Washington when Trump was elected. He recounted his thoughts about Trump

---

28 Pamela Engel, "Former CIA director accuses Trump allies of 'working on behalf of the Russians'," *Business Insider*, October 14, 2016, https://www.businessinsider.com/michael-morell-trump-russia-2016-10.

29 Robert S. Mueller III, "Report on the Investigation into Russian Interference in the 2016 Presidential Election," March 2019, https://www.justice.gov/storage/report.pdf.

30 Personal communication, December 2016.

31 Treverton email to author, August 1, 2019. Other then-currently serving ODNI officials report similar reactions to the election results in private communications with the author.

in his co-edited book *Truth to Power*, and he elaborated in an email to me:

> I think I quoted my resignation letter, the one I didn't in the end use, where I praised them [his NIC colleagues] as professionals but said I wasn't one of them, for I only came to Washington to work for administrations I liked. Indeed, they were and are professionals, and I don't know of anyone who left because of Trump (other than me).[32]

Treverton did not go public in his opposition to Trump except in a modest way in *Truth to Power*, a book about the history of the National Intelligence Council that was published over two years after Trump became president. This modest commentary is not comparable to the words and actions of vocal senior formers such as Brennan, Clapper, and Hayden, who appeared regularly on television and used much stronger language.

On November 23, 2016, fifteen days after the election, the *Washington Post* reported that Trump had thus far received only two *PDB* briefings, fewer than normal at that point in a presidential transition. While some current and former intelligence officials reported that Vice President-elect Mike Pence had received briefings almost every day, the *Post* cited intelligence sources who:

> ... interpreted Trump's limited engagement with his briefing team as an additional sign of indifference from a president-elect who has no meaningful experience on national security issues and was dismissive of U.S.

---

32   Treverton email to author, August 1, 2019; Treverton, "From Afghanistan to Trump," 195-196.

intelligence agencies' capabilities and findings during the campaign.[33]

The *Post*'s story was wrong. The viscerally anti-Trump Michael Morell, who by his own later accounts retained close ties to CIA people, reported that Trump had not been offered briefings in the first days after the election. The story was another early example of the many anti-Trump "leaks" by "current and former intelligence officials" that were not true. Many of them clearly were not mistakes. They were disinformation designed to damage Trump politically. These episodes too were consistent with CIA attacks on domestic enemies in the past.

In December 2017 Morell expressed second thoughts about his political activity while also reporting the disinformation about Trump and the *PDB* noted above. In an interview with *Politico*, speaking about his activism, Morell said "there were downsides to it that I didn't think about at the time"—a surprising admission for a veteran political analyst and senior intelligence officer who had dealt regularly with politicians and the press.[34] He added:

> I was concerned about what is the impact it would have [sic] on the agency, right? Very concerned about that, thought that through. But I don't think I fully thought through the implications.
>
> So, let's put ourselves here in Donald Trump's shoes. So, what does he see? Right? He sees a former director of

---

33   Greg Miller and Adam Entous, "Trump turning away intelligence briefers since election," *Washington Post*, November 23, 2016, https://www.washingtonpost.com/world/national-security/trump-turning-away-intelligence-briefers-since-election-win/2016/11/23/5cc643c4-b1ae-11e6-be1c-8cec35b1ad25_story.html.

34   Alex Pfeiffer, "Former CIA Director Regrets How Intel Agencies Treated Trump," *The Daily Caller*, December 11, 2017, http://dailycaller.com/2017/12/11/former-cia-director-regrets-how-intel-agencies-treated-trump/.

CIA and a former director of NSA, Mike Hayden, who I have the greatest respect for, criticizing him and his policies. Right? And he could rightfully have said, 'Huh, what's going on with these intelligence guys?' Right?

And then he sees a former acting director and deputy director of CIA criticizing him and endorsing his opponent....And then he gets his first intelligence briefing, after becoming the Republican nominee, and within 24 to 48 hours, there are leaks out of that that are critical of him and his then-national security advisor, Mike Flynn.

And so, this stuff starts to build, right? And he must have said to himself, "What is it with these intelligence guys? Are they political?" The current director at the time, John Brennan, during the campaign occasionally would push back on things that Donald Trump had said.[35]

After discussing leaks, Morell continued:

Then he becomes president, and he's supposed to be getting a daily brief from the moment he becomes the president-elect. Right? And he doesn't. And within a few days, there's leaks about how he's not taking his briefing. So, he must have thought—right?—that, "Who are these guys? Are these guys out to get me? Is this a political organization? Can I think about them as a political organization when I become president?"

---

35   Ibid.

So, I think there was a significant downside to those of us who became political in that moment. So, if I could have thought of that, would I have ended up in a different place? I don't know. But it's something I didn't think about.[36]

A retired senior CIA officer who read Morell's interview, and who later himself became modestly politically active against Trump, said Morell "crossed a line" in August 2016 and added, "His ego and ambition got the better of him."[37] Errors of ego and ambition are not the same as political partisanship, but in some cases they may be related. One might wonder how many other intelligence people did not think through the short- and long-term consequences of their actions. Morell did not in fact end his attacks on Trump, but after December 2016 he toned down his public rhetoric somewhat. His continuing criticisms of Trump were more analytic and less emotional, and thereby were more effective. Other formers were not so introspective.

The Vocal Formers

With Trump's inauguration on January 20, 2017, a new group of senior formers emerged to take on Trump, including the two Obama administration officials who did so much to further Obama's political agenda within the IC—DCIA John Brennan and DNI James Clapper. Name calling soon became a favorite activity, and Trump's words and actions as president offered new opportunities for criticism. Brennan became the primary public face of CIA opposition to Trump. He was emotional and frequently made extreme accusations that annoyed Trump and

---

36   Ibid.
37   Personal communication, December 2017. Morell was rumored in 2020 to have wanted to be DCIA in Joe Biden's administration.

worried his friends and political allies. Brennan acknowledged in his memoir that he is prone to temper tantrums and that they repeatedly caused him trouble.[38] That limited awareness did not seem to restrain his anti-Trump rhetoric.

Brennan was critical of Trump in very personal terms, beginning immediately after he left office. While he had "pushed back" on Trump's comments about the first intelligence briefing for candidate Trump while he was in office, his transition to "former" status left him free to talk bluntly. When Trump traveled to CIA headquarters on January 21, 2017 to thank intelligence personnel and tell them he would back them, his speech outraged Brennan. Trump had not paid adequate homage to the then-117 stars on the Memorial Wall.[39] Brennan recounted that he was riding a stationary bicycle at his gym as Trump spoke, became angry, and sent an emotional text message to his long-time aide, Nick Shapiro, which he asked Shapiro to send to reporters. Shapiro promptly emailed about a dozen reporters.[40] Shapiro wrote:

> Former CIA Director Brennan is deeply saddened and angered at Donald Trump's despicable display of self-aggrandizement in front of CIA's Memorial Wall of Agency heroes."[41]

Shapiro also said Brennan believed Trump "should be ashamed of himself."[42] Similarly, an unnamed former senior CIA

---

38   Brennan, *Undaunted*, 89-91, 187, 376.
39   The wall has stars for CIA employees and contractors who (mainly) died in the line of duty, some to hostile action, some in accidents. One name is a suicide. For a history of the Wall, see Dujmović, "Tech Stars on the Wall."
40   Brennan, *Undaunted*, 296.
41   Andrea Mitchell and Ken Dilanian, "Ex-CIA Boss Brennan, Others Rip Trump Speech in Front of Memorial," *NBC News*, January 21, 2017, https://www.nbcnews.com/news/us-news/ex-cia-boss-brennan-others-rip-trump-speech-front-memorial-n710366.
42   Ibid.

officer told NBC News he was embarrassed watching Trump's remarks on television, saying they constituted a "free-wheeling, narcissistic diatribe."[43]

Ironically, Brennan himself cheapened the Wall, in the view of some by CIA people, by allowing a star to be placed on it for CIA targeting analyst Ranya Abdelsayed, an American of Egyptian descent, who killed herself in Afghanistan in 2013.[44] The original purpose of the Wall was to honor deaths of an inspirational or heroic character or were caused by enemy actions or hazardous conditions, not suicides. The Wall itself says the stars represent people who "gave their lives in the service of their country."[45] Despite internal opposition to adding a star for Abdelsayed, Brennan rationalized that she volunteered for the job and said, "Under those circumstances, there are a lot of stresses as well as daily challenges associated with that work."[46] Brennan elaborated:

> "Ranya was tremendously committed to the agency's mission. Her death, I felt, was a direct result of her work and her dedication in a very difficult overseas environment," he said. "It may not have been unanimous that Ranya was deserving [of a star], … but I let it be known that Ranya's death was something the agency needed to recognize as being one of those unfortunate consequences of the global challenges the CIA addresses.[47]

---

43   Ibid.
44   Ian Shapira, "A CIA suicide sparks hard questions about the agency's Memorial Wall," *Washington Post*, May 21, 2019, https://www.washingtonpost.com/local/a-cia-suicide-sparks-hard-questions-about-the-agencys-memorial-wall/2019/05/18/20c8c284-7687-11e9-bd25-c989555e7766_story.html.
45   Ibid.
46   Ibid.
47   Ibid.

One former CIA employee called Brennan's decision "a work of virtue signaling over sober reflection and respect on what the Memorial Wall is for."[48]

Uncharacteristically for the media, NBC News reported that many CIA personnel in attendance cheered Trump when he spoke in front of the Wall on January 21. NBC quoted a Trump supporter:

> "This is the part that the media doesn't get—this is not like any other president," the officer said. "The critics hate this president so much they cannot get past it. The truth of the visit was in the face to face meetings— people were happy to talk to him. That assuaged a lot of concerns and a lot of anxiety."[49]

Such press items soon became rare as the CIA rallied internally against Trump and NBC, like most of the press, became vehemently anti-Trump.

Brennan produced a steady stream of vitriol directed at Trump. For example, after Trump tweeted in January 2019 that intelligence chiefs were wrong to say Iran was not developing nuclear weapons, Brennan tweeted in return: "Your refusal to accept the unanimous assessment of U.S. Intelligence on Iran, No. Korea, ISIS, Russia, & so much more shows the extent of your intellectual bankruptcy."[50] He added: "All Americans, especially

---

48   Personal communication, July 2020.
49   Andrea Mitchell and Ken Dilanian, "Ex-CIA Boss Brennan, Others Rip Trump Speech in Front of Memorial," *NBC News*, January 21, 2017, https://www. nbcnews.com/news/us-news/ex-cia-boss-brennan-others-rip-trump-speech-front-memorial-n710366.
50   Michael Burke, "Brennan rips into Trump for criticizing intel chiefs: it shows 'your intellectual bankruptcy,'" *The Hill*, January 30, 2019, https://thehill.com/policy/national-security/427630-brennan-rips-into-trump-for-criticizing-intel-chiefs-it-shows-the.

members of Congress, need to understand the danger you pose to our national security." After Trump talked with Russian President Putin in Helsinki in July 2018, Brennan tweeted that Trump's performance was "nothing short of treasonous."[51] He added, "Not only were Trump's comments imbecilic, he is wholly in the pocket of Putin."[52] On March 17, 2018, Brennan tweeted to Trump, "When the full extent of your venality, moral turpitude, and political corruption becomes known, you will take your rightful place as a disgraced demagogue in the dustbin of history. ... America will triumph over you."[53]

Brennan asserted in an op-ed piece in the *New York Times* in 2018 that he was certain the Trump campaign colluded with Russia in 2016. Just before Special Counsel Robert Mueller released his long awaited report in March 2019, which found no such collusion, Brennan tweeted that he suspected the president was panic-stricken "over the likelihood the Special Counsel will soon further complicate your life, putting your political & financial future in jeopardy."[54] After the report's release, Brennan told MSNBC, "I don't know if I received bad information, but I think I suspected there was more than there actually was."[55] Indeed.

By late July 2018, President Trump's patience with these ad

---

51   Dylan Scott, "Former CIA director: Trump-Putin press conference 'nothing short of treasonous,'" *Vox*, July 16, 2018, https://www.vox.com/world/2018/7/16/17576804/trump-putin-meeting-john-brennan-tweet-treasonous. For his account of the emotions that led to this tweet, see Brennan, *Undaunted*, 400-401.

52   Scott, "Former CIA director: Trump-Putin press conference 'nothing short of treasonous.'"

53   Victor Davis Hanson, "Is there a dangerous 'deep state' of unelected—and untouchable—U.S. officials?" *The Mercury*, March 29, 2018, https://www.mercurynews.com/2018/03/29/hanson-is-there-a-dangerous-deep-state-of-unelected-u-s-officials-who-are-untouchable/. For his account of this event, see Brennan, *Undaunted*, 400-401.

54   Michael Burke, "Brennan on Mueller summary: 'I suspected there was more than there actually was,'" *The Hill*, March 25, 2019, https://thehill.com/policy/national-security/435653-brennan-on-mueller-report-summary-i-think-i-suspected-there-was-more.

55   Ibid.

hominem and factually erroneous attacks had worn thin. He called Brennan "a very bad person," threatened to revoke the security clearances of Brennan and other formers who used continuing access to classified information to attack him.[56] Former national security advisor John Bolton reported that Trump believed Brennan was involved in abusing surveillance laws during the federal investigation of his 2016 campaign—a charge that remains unsettled as I write—and was angered by Brennan's chronic public criticisms.[57]

In response to Trump's threat some 250 persons, whom the press characterized as intelligence and national security experts, many of them in fact Obama administration political appointees, signed a public letter that criticized Trump's threatened move.[58] Trump's opponents accused him of an unprecedented attack on free speech—a charge that reflected lack of candor about the well-known purpose of maintaining the security clearances of former senior officials, which is to tap their experiences and insights as respected, trusted advisers to current officials and has nothing whatever to do with free speech rights.[59] Brennan and many other formers plainly did not enjoy the respect and trust of the White House and may not have had credibility with then-current IC leaders. In fact, as was often the case, Trump did not follow

---

56   Max Greenwood, "Trump calls Brennan a 'very bad person' after Putin criticism," *The Hill*, July 17, 2018, http://thehill.com/homenews/administration/397437-trump-calls-brennan-a-very-bad-person-after-putin-criticism.

57   Bolton, *The Room Where It Happened*, 224-225.

58   Maegan Vasquez, "175 former US officials added to list denouncing Trump for revoking Brennan's security clearance," *CNN*, August 20, 2019, https://www.cnn.com/2018/08/20/politics/john-brennan-more-intelligence-officials-statement/index.html.

59   Jill Colvin, Trump Considers Yanking Security Clearances of His Critics, *NBC News*, July 23, 2018, https://www.nbcconnecticut.com/news/politics/Trump-Comey-Brennan-McCabe-Security-Clearance-488912161.html. See also Sean Bigley, "Trump Is Right About Clearances," *Wall Street Journal*, July 30, 2018, A17.

through on this threat. Brennan retained his clearance and access to CIA facilities and personnel.

The clearances that gave formers access to government buildings also provided serving intelligence people means of conveying their views indirectly to outside audiences via the formers in the friendly confines of government workspaces and to people nominally within government, obviating the need for the more bureaucratically (and perhaps legally) dangerous act of communicating directly with journalists.[60] As Clapper wrote, when he was DNI, former DCIA Hayden and unnamed other former intelligence officials were valuable to him on "many" occasions as an "IC surrogate" because they could "say things I couldn't say as DNI."[61] The security clearances of Trump's enemies similarly gave them access to serving officers who could provide insights about current employees' attitudes and intelligence information they could use against Trump. These conversations also enabled a degree of coordination of intelligence officers' actions against him. The usefulness of this function presumably accounts largely for the vehement condemnation of Trump's threat, which implicitly potentially endangered a valuable tool of many anti-Trump campaigners, both formers and current employees.

Contrary to the assertions of Trump's critics, possession of a security clearance is not a right—it sometimes is described as a privilege—and the government long has revoked clearances for many reasons, including statements of disloyalty to the US government. This purpose and history are well established.

The discussion point here is not whether Trump or his critics were right on the security clearance or other specific issues, but rather that a former senior intelligence officer alienated a sitting president to the point that he considered such action. The single

60   Brennan, *Undaunted*, 405-406.
61   Clapper, *Facts and Fears*, 231-232.

most critical asset that intelligence has in its relationship with senior leaders is its credibility, which generates the trust intelligence officers need to gain access to, and hold the respect of, senior decision-makers. Brennan, Clapper, Hayden, and others, including people in the IC who supported them with information, encouragement, and complementary leaks, severely damaged US intelligence in this respect.

Brennan's style and rhetoric were widely viewed as extreme, even by people who like him personally and generally agreed with his views of Trump. In my interviews with people knowledgeable about intelligence matters who mentioned Brennan, all commented on Brennan's emotional character. Of those who added a value judgment, all said Brennan's emotionalism hurt more than helped the anti-Trump cause. For example, retired senior CIA analyst Bruce Riedel judged that Brennan delivered "rhetorical flourishes that bordered on getting out of hand" and said his accusations of treason against Trump had gone too far.[62] Former senior CIA operations officer John Sipher, who repeatedly wrote critically about Trump, tweeted in response to the Brennan tweet cited above concerning Trump's meeting with Putin in Helsinki:

> Sir, I couldn't agree with you more about Trump's lack of fitness for office. However, I think your rhetoric is hurting more than it is helping. You are making the discussion too much about you. Also, you are a handy strawman for Trump to attack. It aids the deep state Bull Shit.[63]

Despite such reactions, Brennan continued his outlandish

---

62   Author discussion with Bruce Riedel, September 12, 2019.
63   Sipher tweet, July 24, 2018, https://twitter.com/johnbrennan/status/1018885971104985093?lang=da.

tweets. In September 2020, in reaction to publication of Bob Woodward's book on Trump, *Rage*, Brennan called Trump an "absolute abomination" and said Trump did not have the "conscience or a soul" to resign the presidency in response to Woodward's assertions.[64] He messaged after the first debate of the 2020 campaign season:

> I have to compliment Donald Trump on doing an excellent job at tonight's debate of demonstrating that he is a despicable ignorant fool.[65]

Yet, at virtually the same time he sent the tweet immediately above, Brennan told an interviewer he regretted his tweets even as he blamed Trump for his own immature behavior:

> I certainly wish I never felt the compulsion to go onto Twitter and to tweet, but it was because of Trump. I didn't want to cede that Twitter-sphere to him.[66]

As he did on Twitter and television, in his book Brennan levied many inflammatory charges and displayed considerable emotion but little explained his reasoning. He reported, for example, that growing up in northern New Jersey he had learned years before to dislike Trump, a New Yorker, as "a self-promoting and publicity-seeking blowhard, even by generous New York City

---

64   James Walker, "Former CIA Director Labels Trump 'Absolute Abomination' Over Woodward Book Revelations," *Newsweek*, September 10, 2020, http://www.msn.com/en-us/news/politics/former-cia-director-labels-trump-absolute-abomination-over-woodward-book-revelations/ar-BB18TtKo?li=BBnb7Kz&ocid=U453DHP.

65   John O. Brennan (@JohnBrennan), September 30, 2020.

66   Edward-Isaac Dovere, "What Else Does the CIA Know About Trump and Russia?" *The Atlantic*, October 1, 2020, https://www.theatlantic.com/politics/archive/2020/10/john-brennan-trump-russia-cia/616545/.

standards."[67] Most of Brennan's many criticisms of Trump were similarly incisive.

But as he clearly intended, Brennan influenced some former employees to speak publicly in partisan, political ways. Soon after Trump threatened to revoke Brennan's security clearance, former CIA analyst and manager Cindy Otis wrote a screed against Trump, claiming that she acted in accordance with Brennan's regular advice to CIA personnel to speak "truth to power" in defense of policies he favored. Otis wrote:

> In John Brennan's last address to employees as CIA director, he told us he planned to slip quietly into civilian life when he left. He also repeated two things that were always key points of all his talks with employees: that the work CIA employees do is critical to protecting the country, and that officers have a responsibility to speak the truth.
>
> Trump's retaliation against Brennan is sadly not unexpected given the president's almost daily insults against perceived opponents over Twitter, the war he continues to wage against our constitutional rights to a free press and free speech, and his disdain for the intelligence community. It is more important than ever before that national security professionals speak truth to power, as Brennan has long advocated.[68]

---

67   Brennan, *Undaunted*, 12.
68   Cindy Otis, "What Trump did to Brennan recalls authoritarians I studied at the CIA," *USA Today*, August 16, 2018, https://www.usatoday.com/story/opinion/2018/08/16/trump-brennan-national-security-clearance-recalls-authoritarians-studied-cia-column/1006752002/.

James Clapper was nearly as exuberant in his anti-Trump rhetoric as Brennan. Many of his accusations also were grossly exaggerated or simply false. In a June 2017 interview Clapper proclaimed that the President Nixon's Watergate scandal "pales" in comparison to Trump's involvement with Russia.[69] A common but misplaced hope of anti-Trump activists, Clapper's misunderstanding or purposeful misrepresentation on this issue is especially noteworthy because he was DNI when the issue was initially investigated. Regularly briefed on important intelligence matters, undoubtedly including the Crossfire Hurricane investigation, Clapper should have known how flimsy the Steele dossier's content was, its partisan origin as Clinton campaign-funded opposition research, and how little corroborating intelligence the FBI and other IC agencies had collected.[70] While incompetence and wishful thinking here are possibilities, a more plausible explanation is that Clapper was propagandizing against Trump. Clapper, other anti-Trump formers, congressional Democrats, and the press eventually formed a powerful disinformation machine that propagated much such erroneous information about both intelligence and Trump.

In the interview in which he invoked the Watergate metaphor, Clapper also disparaged Trump's alleged "internal assault on our institutions."[71] He complained about Trump's January 2017 tweet that purportedly called intelligence officers Nazis and said that Trump's firing of FBI Director Comey "reflected a complete disregard for the independence and autonomy" of the FBI.[72] In fact,

---

69 CNN Wire, "James Clapper: Watergate pales in comparison to Russia probe," June 7, 2017, https://www.wtvr.com/2017/06/07/james-clapper-watergate-pales-compared-to-russia-probe.

70 Dustin Volz and Alan Cullison, "Senate Panel's Russia Report Finds Fault With FBI's Handling of 2016 Election Probes," *Wall Street Journal*, August 19, 2020, https://www.wsj.com/articles/senate-panels-russia-report-finds-fault-with-fbis-handling-of-2016-election-probes-11597872094.

71 CNN Wire, "James Clapper: Watergate pales in comparison to Russia probe."

72 Ibid.

the FBI was not and never has been an independent institution. It is largely autonomous narrowly in the pursuit of criminal investigations. It always reports variously to the attorney general, the president, and the Congress. Most school children know as much. Here incompetence is far a less plausible explanation. Clapper surely knew his claim was incorrect because the FBI also reported on some counterintelligence and counterterrorism matters to him personally as DNI. But the claim was politically useful. The erroneous notion that Trump inappropriately threatened the allegedly legitimate independence of intelligence became a standard meme of anti-Trump activists. It was a logical latter-day variant of the CIA's defensive claims against the much more tangible actions of DCIs of Presidents Nixon and Carter.

Like many of the critical formers, Clapper wrote disparagingly of the "aggressive indifference of President Trump's administration to viewing Russia as a threat and its abject failure to do anything about this existential menace to our nation and our way of life."[73] Here, Clapper both exaggerated and stated a simple error. While, he correctly wrote that the Soviet Union long had conducted information operations against the United States and meddled chronically in presidential elections, he did not recognize that they evidently had no effect on electoral' outcomes.[74] None of the electoral meddling posed anything close to an existential threat to the United States, although the Soviets and Russians clearly have tried with some success to destabilize the United States via an extensive active measures campaign, which Clapper did not mention.[75]

In one of the clearest examples of hysterical exaggeration, many of the formers concluded that Trump campaign officials'

---

73   Clapper, *Facts and Fears*, 396-397.
74   Ibid., 314-315.
75   Gentry, "Belated Success."

alleged connections to Russia, and Trump's business dealing with Russian officials including President Putin, indicated that Trump was a recruited intelligence agent of the Russian government. Michael Morell claimed that Putin had recruited Trump as an unwitting agent. Michael Hayden said he preferred another term widely attributed to Lenin: Trump was a "'useful idiot,' some naif, manipulated by Moscow, secretly held in contempt, but whose blind support is happily accepted and exploited."[76] Brennan made similar points many times. Morell and Hayden apparently also were then receiving sensitive information from former colleagues still in the IC who knew the status of the investigation, which they leaked. These false assertions sprang from people who were respected, senior intelligence officers who frequently claimed that they dealt only in "truth." Former FBI officer and partisan Democrat Peter Strzok, ostensibly a counterintelligence specialist, also made such charges.

Former DCIA Hayden was a sharp critic of Trump but came from a different political background than many of the belligerent formers. A one-time self-described libertarian, he said he viewed Trump as a threat from economic, international political, and military security perspectives.[77] Even before Trump was nominated, Hayden was as harshly critical of Trump as many Democrats. His critiques soon also contained language suggesting that his views on many social issues were more consistent with common Democratic than Republican perspectives. Indeed, in his severely anti-Trump second book Hayden is dramatically more emotional, more partisan, and less persuasive than in his very credible first book, *Playing to the Edge*, which was published in 2016.[78] The change in tone between his first and second books,

---

76   Hayden, *Assault on Intelligence*, 74.
77   Saldin and Teles, *Never Trump*, 31-32.
78   Gentry, "Partisan Political Polemics."

published only two years apart, is striking. He wrote in *The Assault on Intelligence* that Trump was so bad that he deserved the same kind of "ad hominem" attacks he allegedly made on others, a logic that did not reflect thoughtful analysis and damaged his own credibility.[79]

Perceived moral obligations tied to defense of their worldviews evidently were the primary factors that led Brennan, Clapper, and Hayden to abandon professional intelligence officers' traditionally apolitical stances in criticizing Trump. Clapper and Hayden cited several motives for their entry into partisan politics, including: their opposition to Trump's views on civil rights, immigration, border security, globalization, and free trade; their "internationalist" perspectives opposed to Trump's "America First" views; and, unhappiness about how Trump treated their friends, especially Comey and McCabe.[80] Clapper was particularly outraged at Trump's firing of Comey.[81] In *Playing to the Edge*, which is a traditional, largely apolitical memoir written before he went haywire in opposition to Trump, Hayden confided that as he grew older he relied more on "basic values" than on his "professional expertise," evidently meaning he increasingly substituted his political philosophy and emotion for sound analysis.[82] This trend seemingly accelerated briskly after 2016.[83] Hayden tells readers of his 2018 book that many CIA people agreed with his "internationalist" worldview.[84] Clapper reported that more IC professionals told him they worried about Trump than Clinton before the 2016 election; after Trump was elected a young woman

---

79   Hayden, *Assault on Intelligence*, 60.
80   Clapper, *Facts and Fears*, 314, 340, 343, 393, 398; Hayden, *Assault on Intelligence*, 22, 121, 129-131, 154, 155, 243, 248.
81   Clapper, *Facts and Fears*, 392-393.
82   Hayden, *Playing to the Edge*, 253.
83   Gentry, "Partisan Political Polemics."
84   Hayden, *Assault on Intelligence*, 21, 48, 121.

supposedly asked him plaintively, "What are we supposed to do now?"[85]

Not surprisingly given the nature of their information operations, the writings of Hayden and Clapper were inconsistent with the public statements of most of the senior formers, including their own comments. Critiques of Trump's honesty, integrity, suitability for office, and dealings with Russia were more publicly presentable reasons to oppose him on television than the philosophical differences of conventional politics because they appeared to be more analytical and apolitical. More candid motives appear in their books. The discrepancy evidently was part of the effort to damage Trump as much as possible. Soviet bloc disinformation experts called this process of reputation assassination "framing."

Trump got off on the wrong foot with many other intelligence people after his address to CIA personnel in front of the agency's Memorial Wall on January 21, 2017. George Little, who was spokesman at the CIA (2010-2011) and at the Defense Department, and who was a frequent critic of Trump, wrote on his Facebook page:

> Today the president of the United States stood in front of the Memorial Wall honoring the CIA's fallen and mocked key institutions of our democracy, threatened to steal Iraq's oil, and used what is supposed to be a non-political government agency—one he recently accused of Nazi-style behavior—as a political backdrop. This will go down as the most disastrous speech ever given at CIA Headquarters.[86]

85   Clapper, *Facts and Fears*, 347, 363.
86   Taylor Link, "CIA officials have mixed reactions about President Trump's speech during his first visit," *Salon*, January 23, 2017, https://www.salon.com/2017/01/23/cia-officials-have-mixed-reactions-about-president-trumps-speech-during-his-first-visit/.

Later, after Mueller exonerated Trump and the Justice Department investigated the objectivity and political motivations of senior intelligence officials, including Brennan, in pursuing the Crossfire Hurricane "investigation" of Trump's campaign, Little defended Brennan:

> Any investigation into John Brennan by this corrupt administration must – on its face – be viewed with a minimum with maximum skepticism [sic]. The intelligence community deserves the respect of the president and his Cabinet, not politically motivated investigations.[87]

This argument reflected a basic theme of Trump's critics: intelligence is independent, always deserves unquestioning respect regardless of its performance, and therefore should not be, or even is not, subject to presidential oversight. These arguments went substantially beyond decades-old CIA and FBI claims that the agencies should be largely autonomous in their day-to-day work.

Other formers were less emotional in their attacks on Trump and used more judicious language, sometimes merely insinuating Trumpian deficiencies. Paul Pillar was a career CIA analyst who became a national intelligence officer. He was the senior analyst in CIA's Counterterrorism Center for a time and as an NIO had the misfortune to be associated with both the 9/11 and the Iraq WMD NIE failures.[88] He earlier had harshly but reasonably, in my

---

87   Natasha Bertrand and Daniel Lippman, "Trump's quest for vengeance against John Brennan," *Politico*, October 22, 2019, https://www.politico.com/news/2019/10/22/trump-vengeance-john-brennan-russia-053970.

88   Preparation of the WMD estimate reportedly was mainly overseen by another NIO. Pillar was more directly involved with a second NIE on Iraq, which gets much less attention and which reportedly was largely accurate in its assessments.

view, criticized the 9/11 Commission's report and the George W. Bush administration's use of intelligence.[89] He generally restricted his negative comments to substantive issues, including what he thought were errors in the 9/11 Commission report. For years after retiring from CIA, Pillar was associated with the Brookings Institution, a Democratic-leaning organization, strongly suggesting that he has basic philosophical differences with Trump.

Because Pillar was NIO for the Near East during 9/11 and played a major role in the Iraq WMD NIE fiasco, he implicitly was often a target when Trump periodically criticized the IC's past performance. But unlike Brennan's unsophisticated name-calling or his own criticism of the Bush administration's use of intelligence, Pillar found faults in aspects of Trump's behavior. For example, in April 2017, after Trump was accused of discussing intelligence information received from another country with Russian officials, Pillar found Trump to be a dire threat to America's intelligence liaison network, upon which US national security allegedly depended. Because of Trump, intelligence partners might find Washington an unreliable partner and cut information sharing activities, endangering Americans, Pillar opined. For that reason, he warned in an interview with National Public Radio (NPR), serving intelligence professionals were extremely worried.[90] Someone later leaked to the *New York Times* that the information came from Israel, which was more sensitive than what Trump reportedly released because it revealed a specific intelligence source; Israeli officials reportedly were understandably unhappy.[91] To put it differently, one or more serving IC officials,

---

89   For example, Pillar, "Good Literature and Bad History."
90   All Things Considered, hosted by Ari Shapiro, "Trump's Disclosure To Russian Officials Threatens To Alienate Intelligence Community," *National Public Radio*, May 16, 2017, https://www.npr.org/2017/05/16/528657240/trumps-disclosure-to-russian-officials-threatens-to-alienate-intelligence-commun.
91   Chaffetz, *The Deep State*, 158-159; Strassel, *Resistance*, 73.

intent on making Trump look bad, apparently released more damaging information than Trump (probably) inadvertently did.

While the details of the information Trump allegedly discussed with Russians properly have not been made public, Pillar's grave warning has unsurprisingly not come to pass. I know of no later information that liaison relationships were affected. This almost certainly occurred for several reasons, including: the fact that this was a one-time event, not a systemic release; liaison relationships usually involve roughly equal, or quid pro quo, sharing, and partners do not want to lose US information they value; and, the United States long has had trouble keeping secrets. Some leaks occur regularly, something partner countries have learned to live with. CIA officers, surely including Pillar, were well aware of cases in which American politicians leaked. Senior military officers have divulged very sensitive information even during the course of briefings to the press, some of these have had dire consequences for CIA assets.[92] Courts contribute to leaks by giving defendants in intelligence-related trials access to intelligence information relevant to their cases. Other countries also experience leaks, making them less critical of periodic American problems with leakers. Such accusations against Trump did not recur, suggesting that a president then still new to intelligence learned his lesson.

Pillar's venting at Trump is a good example of a sophisticated recipe for political attack that some intelligence officers used against Trump. One first identifies an event that is a potential political vulnerability of a target, then cites some closely related facts that appear to be relevant, adds dollops of innuendo divorced from context, cites hypothetical costs that are not proven to exist, and refers to unnamed and un-numbered serving intelligence officers who are allegedly appalled. Such stories lead to desired

---

92   Knowledge acquired in the 1980s when the author worked at the CIA.

insinuations: in this case that Trump was an existential threat to national intelligence capabilities who also had an obligation to keep the bureaucrats happy. Pillar's method was another example of disinformation practice the Soviets called "framing."[93] But while he was often relatively judicious in his attacks on Trump, Pillar also talked about Trump in an interview with the *Tehran Times*, an Iranian newspaper, in early 2020. Given very bad US-Iranian relations at the time, this step went well beyond participation in domestic political squabbling.[94]

Like Pillar, former senior CIA operations officer Steven Hall warned of the dangers of Trump's public comments about intelligence, in his case in a *Washington Post* op-ed. *Newsweek* reported on Hall's charges:

> "The president's comments are uniquely self-defeating, in that our best hope for monitoring and perhaps modifying the behavior of rogue states such as Iran, North Korea and Russia is working in unison with our partners. Many have already taken note of Trump's cavalier attitude toward sensitive information, as well as his apparent failure to understand the basic rules of intelligence sharing," Hall wrote.

> "I would be deeply surprised if many of our best intelligence allies were not already holding back information they would normally pass to their U.S. counterparts, for fear Trump might not be able to keep a secret. (Their concerns might even be darker when they consider the

---

93   Pacepa and Rychlak, *Disinformation*, 50.
94   Javad Heirannia, "Iranians view the killing of Soleimani as an act of war: Paul Pillar," *Tehran Times*, January 5, 2020, https://www.tehrantimes.com/news/443781/Iranians-view-the-killing-of-Soleimani-as-an-act-of-war-Paul.

possibility that our president has reportedly discussed sensitive matters with Russian President Vladimir Putin behind closed doors with no record of the conversation)," the op-ed continued.[95]

This commentary is instructive in different ways than Pillar's complaint. First, it was published in *The Washington Post*, a reliable Trump adversary that has a reputation for accepting politically charged but unconfirmed material and eagerly published anti-Trump essays by many former intelligence officers. Hall previously had strongly criticized Trump in a CNN interview, putting him firmly in the anti-Trump camp.[96] Like Pillar, Hall said there *might* be an effect on sharing, insinuating damage he could not confirm, presumably because he, like Pillar, knew that national intelligence services have established liaison relationships with each other that typically easily weather the passing political storms of national leaders' quirks and squabbles with few interruptions.[97] Hall presumably also knew well that intelligence community personnel and other US government officials are themselves chronic leakers of classified information. Over the years, independent of Trump, there have been frequent warnings about the effects of leaks on sharing, but no public evidence presented that there have been appreciable negative consequences for the IC. Quite the contrary! US intelligence liaison relationships are widely believed to have

---

95   Cristina Maza, "U.S. Allies Probably Withhold Information From Donald Trump to Stop It From Leaking to Vladimir Putin, Intelligence Expert Says," *Newsweek*, February 4, 2019, https://www.newsweek.com/us-allies-donald-trump-intelligence-putin-1316601.

96   David Chol, "Former CIA chief of Russia slams Trump's 'inappropriate public criticisms' after intel report," *CNN*, February 5, 2019, https://www.businessinsider.com/russia-cia-chief-steven-hall-trump-intelligence-report-2019-2.

97   Lefebvre, "The Difficulties and Dilemmas of International Intelligence Cooperation," 527-542.

expanded significantly since 2001, particularly in the counterterrorism arena.[98]

Trump was seen by some as an excuse for violating even laws. Said former CIA operations officer Barry Eisler, a lawyer who wrote thriller novels and contributed to left-wing blogs:

> ... if you have a secrecy obligation and the politicians you are supporting are lying to the public about the work you do, I personally think that should free you at least morally or ethically from whatever secrecy obligation is binding you.[99]

Trump's alleged badness made completely independent felony violations of the law by other people acceptable, even ethical! This bizarre logic lies considerably beyond even the weak reasoning of leakers like Snowden. It is an especially unfortunate claim for a lawyer. There are plenty of appropriate remedies for presidential misstatements of fact, most especially discrete communication of concern to the president directly or via his close advisors. In the past, in a different normative era, when presidents made erroneous statements, intelligence officers usually simply accepted them, knowing correction of presidential gaffes or coherent but erroneous views was not their job.

Two former senior FBI officials, Director James Comey, and Deputy Director Andrew McCabe, were stridently anti-Trump in ways similar to each other but appreciably different from the rhetoric of former officials of the externally-oriented intelligence agencies. Both were fired by Trump. Both were investigated by the Justice Department but found innocent of criminal activities

---

98   For example, Byman, "US counterterrorism intelligence cooperation with the developing world and its limits."
99   Quoted in O'Brien and Rodriguez, "By the Numbers," 357.

related to their conflicts with Trump. Both wrote books that are heavily autobiographical, defensive of themselves and the FBI, and bitter about Trump in very personal terms.[100] Each, like former Comey aide Josh Campbell, charged resentfully in their books that Trump demanded personal loyalty; Comey and Campbell compared Trump to Mafia bosses in this respect.[101] Both also claimed that Trump inappropriately compromised the alleged independence of the Bureau. McCabe wrote: "The FBI has to be independent and guided only by truth and the Constitution"—a claim that simply is wrong.[102] Unlike some of the formers discussed herein and many of the leakers, neither Comey nor McCabe much discussed social issues, and they little discussed differences of general political philosophy. Hence, most of their criticisms were of a different nature than those of Brennan, Clapper, Hayden, McLaughlin, Morell, Pillar, and serving CIA officers.

In February 2017, Edward "Ned" Price, a career CIA employee, resigned from the agency, writing soon thereafter in an op-ed piece in the *Washington Post*, "Despite working proudly for Republican and Democratic presidents, I reluctantly concluded that I cannot in good faith serve this administration as an intelligence professional."[103] Despite claiming to be an apolitical civil servant, Price had a long history of working for Democratic politicians and causes. Price previously served as special assistant

---

100 Comey, *A Higher Loyalty*; McCabe, *The Threat*.

101 Comey, *A Higher Loyalty*, 237-238; Campbell, *Crossfire Hurricane*, 218.

102 McCabe, *The Threat*, 137.

103 Edward Price, "I didn't think I'd ever leave the CIA. But because of Trump, I quit," *Washington Post*, February 20, 2017, https://www.washingtonpost. com/opinions/i-didnt-think-id-ever-leave-the-cia-but-because-of-trump-i- quit/2017/02/20/fd7aac3e-f456-11e6-b9c9-e83fce42fb61_story.html?utm_ term=.21e77a9e0228; Mary Louise Kelly, "Disgusted By Trump, A CIA Officer Quits. How Many More Could Follow?," *NPR*, February 23, 2017, https://www. npr.org/2017/02/23/516850237/disgusted-by-trump-a-cia-officer-quits-how- many-more-could-follow.

to President Obama and spokesperson and senior director on Obama's NSC staff while working for CIA (2015-2017). An investigator reported that Price worked: in the 2002 US Senate campaign of former Dallas Mayor Ron Kirk; in a campaign of South Dakota US Senator Tim Johnson; and in the office of former Senate Majority Leader Tom Daschle, also of South Dakota.[104] In a rare nod to journalistic integrity, the *Post* added a note to Price's op-ed, saying he had given $5,000 to Hillary Clinton's 2016 campaign. Price was then 34 years old, receiving a civil servant's salary.

Price's op-ed generated the publicity he undoubtedly desired and led to interview opportunities. When asked by an NPR reporter, "There will be people listening to this who will say you are politicizing intelligence, that the CIA broadly and you personally have an axe to grind with President Trump. Do you?" Price responded:

> The only axe I have to grind with President Trump is the way he has treated the intelligence community. Look, I will not hide the fact that I fervently disagree with many of the policies this administration has pursued. But what led me to this decision was comparing them to Nazis, accusing them of leaking, doubting their work.[105]

This critique was badly off-the-mark. Trump did not "compare" all intelligence officers to Nazis. There is plenty of evidence that

---

104   Streiff, "Why Did the Washington Post Let Democrat Operative Edward Price Lie To Their Readers?" *Red State*, February 22, 2017, https://www.redstate.com/streiff/2017/02/22/washington-post-let-democrat-operative-edward-price-lie-readers/.

105   Mary Louise Kelly, "Career CIA Analyst Ned Price Quits Rather Than Serve Trump Administration," *National Public Radio,* All Things Considered program, February 27, 2017, https://www.npr.org/2017/02/22/516695407/career-cia-analyst-ned-price-quits-rather-than-serve-trump-administration.

intelligence officers leak sensitive information, as Price surely knew, and numerous historical analytic failures are extensively documented. But Price's political philosophy surely differed sharply from Trump's. Price reported other motives for leaving in our conversation that were reasonable but not altruistic. In particular, he said he thought his duties as an aide to Obama would tar him within CIA as a partisan, limiting his career opportunities there.[106]

After leaving government, Price wrote several articles critical of Trump and Trump administration officials. Among them, he wrote an error-filled "obituary" of Mike Pompeo's tenure as DCIA, published in 2018.[107] He alleged that Pompeo had inappropriately politicized intelligence by having his own views of policy issues. In fact, this is standard practice and DCIs were, and DCIAs are, free to give presidents their own views so long as they also report the community's (or CIA's) views. He chastised Pompeo for regularly seeing the president, which in fact is a normal DCIA function that most presidents, including Obama, have required. Price reported that his CIA colleagues told him that Pompeo, in preparing for discussions on Iran, actually asked analysts hard questions, an allegedly bad thing. In fact, this is normal and analysts should expect hard questioning, as prominent CIA analyst Jack Davis and others told analysts repeatedly over many years.[108] He alleged that Pompeo played "fast and loose" with the facts in judging that Russia did not affect the 2016 election's results, saying that the CIA had not proclaimed such an influence. In fact, CIA, which only addresses foreign issues, would never assess such a clearly

---

106 Ned Price discussion with author, July 30, 2019. Price said only one topic we discussed was off-the-record. This is not it.

107 Ned Price, "Good Riddance to CIA Director Pompeo," *Foreign Policy*, March 16, 2018, https://foreignpolicy.com/2018/03/16/good-riddance-to-cia-director-pompeo/.

108 Davis, "Analytic Professionalism and the Policymaking Process."

domestic question. Moreover, as noted, independent analysts overwhelmingly agree with Pompeo that Russian meddling, while now prominent, was modest in quantity and evidently did not appreciably influence voters' choices.[109] Price, who gay, also criticized Pompeo for allegedly trying to "impose his worldview on a workforce that values diversity as a strength."[110] As evidence, Price cited Pompeo's frustration with questions about diversity at an all-hands meeting, his alteration of the 2018 Pride ceremonies and failure to attend in person, and his consultation with the Family Research Council, a Christian organization that Price called an "anti-gay hate group," regarding an initiative to expand the CIA's chaplaincy program.

Price mispresented Pompeo's position on the operational value of diversity. At the meeting at which Pompeo was criticized by the workforce on diversity issues (discussed below), Pompeo upheld the traditional view that operationally significant diversity is important while employees criticized him for not embracing the Obama-era version.[111] Price's account reversed traditional reasoning by claiming that the new version generates operational value and the old one does not—a clearly incorrect assertion. In sum, Price's piece likely appealed to persons already opposed to Trump, but it is not close to an accurate assessment of Pompeo's tenure, of the traditional roles of DCIAs, and of diversity at the CIA.

In 2019, Price was director of policy and communications at National Security Action, a liberal group whose mission statement is:

109　Rid, *Active Measures*, 407-408; McCombie, et al., "The US 2016 presidential election & Russia's troll farms," 96, 101-108.

110　Price, "Good Riddance to CIA Director Pompeo."

111　John Kiriakou, "Mike Pompeo's CIA Will Not Reflect America's Diversity," *truthdig*, September 17, 2017, https://www.truthdig.com/articles/mike-pompeos-cia-will-not-reflect-america/.

National Security Action is dedicated to advancing American global leadership and opposing the reckless policies of the Trump administration that endanger our national security and undermine U.S. strength in the world.[112]

In January 2021, Price became the spokesperson of the State Department, working for President Biden's secretary of state, Antony Blinken.

Effective July 12, 2019, State Department intelligence analyst Rod Schoonover resigned in "protest" of the Trump administration's decision to prevent him from presenting all of his views about the national security implications of global warming in testimony before the HPSCI.[113] On the face of it, this represented another principled determination to report "truth to power," and yet another claim that the Trump administration tried to quash truth.

But this story, like Price's, is more complicated. The HPSCI in mid-2019 was controlled by Democrats, who were in serious conflict with President Trump over many issues, including global warming. Some House Democrats stated publicly that they still were looking for material to justify impeaching Trump, which they found a month later. The nature of the global warming controversy was widely understood and INR, where Schoonover worked, has no institutional standing as an expert on the scientific merits of the subject but more credibility in its assessments of the global political and security implications of climate change. Trump had made publicly clear his position on the subject repeatedly in the

---

112 National Security Action website, https://nationalsecurityaction.org/.
113 No byline, "Analyst Resigns Over Testimony Curb," *Wall Street Journal*, July 11, 2019, A5; Lisa Friedman, "White House Tried to Stop Climate Science Testimony, Documents Show," *New York Times*, June 8, 2019, https://www.nytimes.com/2019/06/08/climate/rod-schoonover-testimony.html.

past. The White House permitted Schoonover to testify orally before the panel in early June 2019 but the White House legal staff and NSC officials deleted portions of his proposed written testimony when they reviewed it.

INR management, which had to have decided to send Schoonover to testify—analysts do not simply decide themselves to talk to Congressional committees—surely understood that its representative's testimony would be used for partisan political purposes. IC agencies frequently send representatives to the Hill to discuss controversial issues, knowing their testimony will be used for partisan purposes, and INR surely knew that the HPSCI recently had requested testimony from many current and former Trump administration officials for fairly obvious political reasons, and that this testimony would not be welcome at the White House. Hence, there should have been no surprise when the White House deleted part of Schoonover's written report.

At least two explanations for INR's decision are plausible. First, INR management may have decided to respond normally to a request by the HPSCI, a legitimate intelligence consumer, knowing its paper would be used for partisan purposes. This would be an example of the "politics of intelligence"—something IC agencies enable by being apolitical. Second, INR may have agreed to submit written testimony to support Congressional Democrats' view, happy that the White House would be annoyed. The former reasoning is legitimate, the latter would amount to politicization by INR. I presume INR management acted appropriately. But in either case, Schoonover's decision to publicly announce his resignation in protest constituted a political act by someone on record as a partisan Democrat. Federal Election Commission data show that he donated a total of $521 on seven occasions to Hillary Clinton's 2016 presidential campaign.[114]

114   FEC website, https://docquery.fec.gov/cgi-bin/qind/.

Schoonover's initial written testimony, and editorial changes by two White House staffers, soon were leaked to the *New York Times,* presumably by Schoonover or another INR official opposed to Trump. The paper, with White House officials' comments on it, was posted online.[115] A substantive reviewer called part of Schoonover's report "junk science" and was repeatedly critical of the quality of Schoonover's analysis. The legal reviewer told INR to stick to narrowly answering the questions the HPSCI asked.

The White House was not pleased with Schoonover's actions. Said an unnamed senior White House official:

> This appears to be a clear example of some within the behemoth of the U.S. bureaucracy running around thinking their way is the only way and desperately trying to undermine this president and the American democratic process.[116]

Representative Adam Schiff (D-CA), chairman of the HPSCI, unsurprisingly called the White House action an effort to stifle the IC's alleged responsibility to speak "truth to power."[117] He had by this time learned that the CIA's "truth to power" slogan—resurrected from its use during the Vietnam War—had developed some traction in the press as a partisan tool and used the term himself. Schiff said the HPSCI would investigate the White House's actions regarding Schoonover's testimony. But the White House "whistleblower" scandal (discussed below) erupted

---

115   Rod Schoonover, "Statement for the Record," June 5, 2019, https://int.nyt.com/data/documenthelper/1103-rod-schoonover-testimony/9ea6b07179b17035421f/optimized/full.pdf.

116   Timothy Puko and Warren P. Strobel, "State Department Analyst Resigns After White House Blocked Climate Change Testimony," *Wall Street Journal,* July 10, 2019, https://www.wsj.com/articles/state-department-analyst-resigns-after-white-house-blocks-climate-change-testimony-11562780573.

117   Ibid.

soon thereafter, giving Schiff a better weapon with which to attack Trump. The Schoonover episode quickly faded away.

Josh Campbell, a mid-level FBI special agent and one-time special assistant to Director Comey, resigned from the FBI in February 2018 after writing an anti-Trump op-ed, published by the *New York Times*. He immediately became a paid CNN contributor. In his vehemently anti-Trump book, published in September 2019, Campbell continued his assault on Trump in a highly personal way that explicitly rejected core standards of his new, ostensible profession of journalism. He made clear that he viewed Trump as a threat to the FBI and, for identical reasons, to national security, and he called on the American people to take "action."[118] "Staying out of the fray is no longer an option," he opined.[119]

Like the similarly principled Price and Schoonover, Campbell had a history of political partisanship. FEC data show that while he gave $250 to Senator Rand Paul (R-KY) in 2015, he also contributed $250 to Democrat Kamala Harris's 2015 Senate campaign in California, $250 to Representative Joaquin Castro (D-TX) in 2014, and $1,000 to Representative Karen Bass (D-CA) in 2016—all while working for the FBI.[120] Campbell coyly claimed in his book that he considered himself to be "middle-of-the-road politically" and said he had voted for both Democrats and Republicans.[121] In this way, he conformed to a politically useful but disingenuous pattern. Anti-Trump partisans, including even Brennan, frequently asserted publicly that because they worked for, and say they voted for, both Republicans and Democrats over the course of their adult lives, that their opposition to Trump was

---

118   Campbell, *Crossfire Hurricane*, 246.
119   Ibid.
120   FEC website, https://docquery.fec.gov/cgi-bin/qind/.
121   Campbell, *Crossfire Hurricane*, 246.

principled and nonpartisan.[122] In 2019, Paul remained a maverick Republican, Harris was then a leftist presidential candidate, Castro was a relatively moderate Democrat, and Bass was a member of the House progressive caucus.[123]

In response to Campbell's resignation letter, retired FBI supervisory special agent James Gagliano, who was a law enforcement analyst for CNN and wrote often on national security issues, called Campbell's charge that Trump was a threat to national security "Utter nonsense."[124] Gagliano added:

> But allow me to share another side of the debate that some, like Comey and Campbell, feel is settled. Many of us have watched the proceedings these past few years with disgust and revulsion. We are angry and disillusioned for different reasons than the ones described by Campbell, and certified by Comey.
>
> Many of us await the impending report from the Office of the Inspector General that will, hopefully, answer some questions about glaring instances of politicization within the senior ranks of FBI and [Department of Justice].[125]

The Department of Justice Inspector General, Michael Horowitz, in August 2019 released a report that did not definitively answer Gagliano's concern. The broader question of institutionalized FBI politicization in the Trump years remains open.

122   Brennan, *Undaunted*, 2.
123   https://cpc-grijalva.house.gov/caucus-members/.
124   James A. Gagliano, "An open letter to the FBI agent who resigned because of Trump," *The Hill*, February 5, 2018, https://thehill.com/opinion/whitehouse/372335-an-open-letter-to-the-fbi-agent-who-resigned-because-of-Trump.
125   Ibid.

Former Deputy DCI John McLaughlin, a career CIA analyst and manager, was sharply critical of Trump, but like Paul Pillar did so in usually more subdued and sophisticated ways than most of Trump's intelligence detractors. McLaughlin was one of the earliest intelligence critics of candidate Trump. After Trump was inaugurated, McLaughlin for a time appeared regularly on left-leaning MSNBC and on the editorial pages of anti-Trump newspapers. In September 2018, he explained why he believed so many intelligence officers had become politically active against Trump in an op-ed piece in the *Washington Post*. His words offer good insights into the reasoning of many Trump-bashers:

> People frequently ask me why so many former intelligence officers are commenting these days on matters that seem essentially political. The question usually goes "Shouldn't you stay neutral—above the fray? Isn't that the tradition for intelligence professionals, both former and still serving?"

> The short answer is yes, that is the tradition. Neutrality has certainly been our ethic on political issues, which gave us credibility when we gathered or delivered information that presidents might not want to hear. It goes against every instinct to wade into domestic politics by openly criticizing the president on personal actions or behavior. And make no mistake: Those of us who have chosen to speak out are outside our comfort zones.

> This leads people to fairly ask a second question: Do our actions mean that, in the future, intelligence officers will not be believed when they claim to be thoroughly

professional and nonpolitical? Are we raising doubts about our ability to provide balanced assessments, free of political spin?

These questions must be taken seriously. If we lose the trust of those who receive our information and analyses, the intelligence community will be seen as just another calculating player in the Washington political game—and our national security will suffer.

So what has pushed us out of our comfort zone? How can we ensure that our claims of objectivity and neutrality are believed in the future? Let's take these one at a time.

First, we are reacting to today's extraordinarily unprecedented context, one that transcends traditional party politics. (Most of us have served administrations led by both parties.) For many of us, keeping our mouths shut about what we see in our own country would be akin to not alerting our government to a threat from abroad.

Failure to warn is the ultimate sin in the intelligence world. It feels equally sinful in the world of citizenship.

A colleague from another field said to me recently: "For you and others the normal rules no longer apply, because we are all in upside-down-world today"—a world where most of the normal rules of civic discourse no longer work. Witness the unnamed Trump administration insider who just let loose in the *New York Times* about the president's dangerous behavior.

Of course, we would all love to be back in right-side-up world, where it would be unimaginable for a president to advocate jailing an election opponent, assail the Justice Department and the FBI, call a free press "the enemy of the people," insult allies, and, most important, refuse to combat a well-documented covert foreign attack on U.S. elections—in the process weakening efforts by others to do so and encouraging Russia to keep it up. And although all politicians spend time in the spin room, how wonderful it would be if our president's basic truthfulness were not automatically suspect.

All of us in intelligence have been shaped by careers assessing societies where free speech, democratic institutions and rule of law don't exist or are under attack—places such as Russia and China. We have also seen how fragile democracy can be and how it can be eroded almost imperceptibly—consider Turkey and parts of Central Europe. So our senses are finely tuned to the classic warning signs: attacks on institutions, neutralization of opponents, cowed legislatures, publics numbed by repeated falsehoods.

All those are now visible here to various degrees. While others may say our democracy can't erode that way, we know we've heard that before, somewhere else. The stakes are too high for complacency here.

Second, how can intelligence professionals come through this still meriting trust in our objectivity? Many people will just conclude we can't. But we have to hope most people will understand why we reject silence: It's because this is a threat that we cannot combat silently, as we have been able to do with foreign threats—overseas and out of the public's eye. Those who don't see a threat will of course reject that argument, and there's nothing we can do about that.

Meanwhile, we should take care, as we would in foreign intelligence assessments, to limit our comments to what the facts can reasonably support in the minds of most Americans—what we can all indisputably see, hear and document.

And if and when assaults on our institutions cease, you can expect most of us to just slip quickly back into our traditional comfort zone, stepping away from domestic politics and, with relief, returning our attention mainly to the world beyond our shores.[126]

McLaughlin expressed slightly different concerns to me in an email nearly a year after this op-ed was published. After explaining that he still believed the main points of the op-ed, he summarized why he criticized Trump:

The basic points I tried to make are: 1) Yes, we formers

---

126 John McLaughlin, "Why so many former intelligence officers are speaking out," *Washington Post*, September 7, 2018, https://www.washingtonpost.com/opinions/why-intelligence-officers-cant-stay-silent-right-now/2018/09/07/f561907a-b206-11e8-aed9-001309990777_story.html.

are uncomfortable in this role and understand that many think it is inappropriate; 2) But we think we are witnessing unique circumstances, perhaps unprecedented [in] modern times; 3) This offers some leeway to go beyond the normal restrictions we put on ourselves; 4) Many of the things we speak against mirror what we've seen in other societies that have lost democracies; 5) But we have to be careful to avoid extreme statements and stick to what we and others can see and document; 6) When things return to normal we'll step back and not be heard from much, and 7) We know this runs the risk that many people will not trust the neutrality of intelligence officers, but I hope … that this will not be so.[127]

McLaughlin added, "I wrote [the *Post* op-ed] not defensively or apologetically but because I thought it was needed. I realize that many serious people think it's inappropriate for former intelligence officers to speak out on issues involving domestic politics." He said his original draft contained a statement to the effect that his letter reflected his views only, not those of other formers, which *Post* editors cut from the published version. McLaughlin also wrote to me, "I have for the last few months cut back a lot on public commentary. I've done hardly anything on TV because I felt it was all getting to be too pat, too formulaic, too predictable."[128] Arguably so, but McLaughlin did not end his anti-Trump activities. He reduced and modified them somewhat for a time. But in autumn 2019 he exclaimed, "Thank God for the Deep State" when the revelations of a CIA "whistleblower" (discussed below) led to Trump's 2019

---

127   John McLaughlin email to author, July 30, 2019.
128   Ibid.

impeachment.[129] While one might imagine it was an ironic, off-hand exclamation, McLaughlin was a long-time Washington hand who must have known he would be quoted by Trump supporters (and book writers).

McLaughlin correctly wrote that warning is a major intelligence responsibility, but he was wrong to assert that the warning function extends to domestic politics.[130] He also was wrong to say that warning had a role long after billions of people globally knew about the alleged threat (Trump) in question. The warning function as traditionally conceived calls for alerts to key decision-makers about *emerging* events in time for decision-makers to act to deter, defend against, or otherwise prepare for the arrival of the event. Warning intelligence also backs off after policy decisions have been made—in this case the election of November 2016. Late in his tenure as DNI, Dan Coats in 2019 talked with his former colleagues in the United States Senate about Trump; they too knew his quirks well.[131] It is hard not to believe that McLaughlin and others purposefully misrepresented the warning function to publicly justify their activism.

McLaughlin alluded to two important questions of legacy, to which I return in more detail in chapter 7. First, he wondered if there will be enduring consequences regarding the extent to which intelligence is trusted, and therefore used. Were intelligence officers really the dedicated, apolitical public servants McLaughlin described, who others more loudly boasted about? He may have still thought so but others, including many of President Trump's supporters and some of his subordinate officials, clearly did and do

---

129   Ian Schwartz, Former Acting CIA Director John McLaughlin on Impeachment: "Thank God For The Deep State," *RealClear Politics*, November 1, 2019, https://www.realclearpolitics.com/video/2019/11/01/former_acting_cia_director_john_mclaughlin_on_impeachment_thank_god_for_the_deep_state.html.

130   Gentry and Gordon, *Strategic Warning Intelligence*.

131   Woodward, *Rage*, 166-167.

not. Second, would the political activism fade away when Trump left office? McLaughlin said he and the others would "step back and not be heard from much." Most activists did tone down their rhetoric after January 2021, but there is more to this story.

McLaughlin did not address another important issue. Political leaders the world over watch intelligence services closely because they, like armies, have special abilities to oppose and even to overthrow governments. It is wholly unsurprising that rhetoric like Brennan's led some observers to worry about the collective politics and the political ambitions of US intelligence. This concern led directly to the still extant assertion that a revolutionary Deep State has developed in the IC.

McLaughlin's op-ed and his email to me make important points that deserve careful consideration. He, like Michael Morell but unlike Brennan, Clapper, Hayden, Comey, and McCabe, recognized that the vocal formers were in uncharted waters and that their words and actions were controversial among intelligence officers. He implied, and I confirm from my conversations with many other formers who do not want to be quoted, that the old ethic remains strong among (mainly) older intelligence officers who stayed silent.

On October 19, 2020, on the eve of the presidential election, fifty-one former "intelligence officers," mostly from the CIA but also including Obama administration political appointees, delivered a letter to *Politico* asserting that emails discussing potentially questionable financial dealings with firms in Ukraine and China by then-presidential candidate Joe Biden's son Hunter, found on Hunter's discarded computer in Delaware in 2019 and provided to the FBI, had "all the classic earmarks of a Russian information operation."[132] The original story was published in the *New York Post*.[133] The signing formers included the serially outspoken Brennan, Clapper, Hayden, McLaughlin, and Morell. Many other signers had records of giving to Democrats, according to the FEC.[134] The formers had no evidence of Russian involvement, they admitted, but wanted the American people to know their allegedly expertise-informed suspicions. Immediate problems for these formers included facts that the ODNI and FBI had already concluded that the emails really were Hunter's, and both Bidens confirmed their authenticity.[135] The formers' partisanship was more obvious than usual. It was a transparent effort to derail a potentially serious corruption scandal for candidate Biden at a critical time just before the election. *Politico* and other media highlighted the letter while the anti-Trump media ignored or suppressed the story. Especially egregiously, Twitter barred the *New York Post*'s feed until the election was safely passed. HPSCI chairman Schiff predictably again joined the formers, this time alleging a joint Russian-Trump smear campaign against Biden without a shred of supporting evidence.[136] It was another, very obvious, joint intelligence-press-HPSCI effort to derail Trump's presidency.

The *New York Post*'s story was ultimately vindicated, prompting

---

132   Natasha Bertrand, "Hunter Biden story is Russian disinfo, dozens of former intel officials say," *Politico*, October 19, 2020, https://www.politico.com/news/2020/10/19/hunter-biden-story-russian-disinfo-430276.

133   Peter Schweizer and Seamus Bruner, "Long-standing claims of Biden corruption all but confirmed with Hunter's emails." *New York Post*, October 24, 2020, https://nypost.com/2020/10/24/biden-corruption-claims-all-but-confirmed-with-hunter-emails/.

134   Ibid.

135   Olivia Beavers and Joe Concha, "Ratcliffe, Schiff battle over Biden emails, politicized intelligence," *The Hill*, https://thehill.com/policy/national-security/521712-ratcliffe-schiff-battle-over-biden-emails-politicized-intelligence.

136   Ibid.

the *Wall Street Journal*'s editors to criticize the press and the formers, saying:

> Their letter will now join the FBI's collusion with the Clinton campaign in 2016 as cause for even more Americans to assume that the U.S. intelligence community is a partisan interest group that can't be trusted. This is damaging to those institutions and the country.[137]

Only in early 2022, long after the original *New York Post* story was fully confirmed and as the Justice Department continued to investigate Hunter Biden, did the *Washington Post* and a few other anti-Trump media admit that they had erred in suppressing the story, far too late to undo the effects of their potentially significant interference in the 2020 presidential election campaign.

The vocal formers operated originally as individuals who collaborated episodically. In 2017, however, an institutional home for intelligence-related criticism of Trump was established, which eventually assumed an appreciable role in the anti-Trump campaign and continues to be politically active. Former DCIA Hayden was a principal in the Chertoff Group, a security consulting firm run by former Secretary of Homeland Security Michael Chertoff, and he served on several corporate boards, which are lucrative positions. After teaching courses at George Mason University for several years, Hayden evidently donated to Mason and convinced the university to establish the Michael V. Hayden Center for Intelligence, Policy, and International Security

---

137   No byline, "Vindication Over Hunter's Emails, *Wall Street Journal*, September 25-26, 2021, A14.

as a part of its Schar School of Policy and Government, located in Arlington, Virginia. The Hayden Center quickly specialized on the intelligence part of its title and soon was staffed with former IC officials with strongly anti-Trump views: Center director Laurence (Larry) Pfeiffer, who was Hayden's chief of staff at CIA; Hayden Center Senior Fellows Michael Morell and David Priess; and Schar Distinguished Visiting Professor Andrew McCabe.

After Hayden suffered a stroke in late 2018, the Center under Larry Pfeiffer continued his work. It ran a series of seminars and then podcasts during the Covid-19 pandemic, often moderated by Pfeiffer and usually involving Morell, which frequently featured guests with anti-Trump and left-of-center political views. While some of the Center's activities were close to scholarly in focus and tone, many were blatantly partisan—such as an unsuccessful effort in September 2018 by Hayden and Clapper, aided by an actively participating "moderator," to browbeat former NSA director Admiral Mike Rogers into attacking Trump.[138] Rogers resisted the onslaught. The Hayden Center apparently did not again invite anyone opposed to IC political activism to one of its events. Extending its activities to social media, Pfeiffer used the Hayden Center hashtag to continue his partisan activity long after Trump was defeated for reelection. For example, the "Hayden Center" tweeted in February 2021 that General Hayden had joined other former security officials in urging the Senate to convict Trump in his second impeachment trial. Pfeiffer regularly mixed intelligence and domestic politics in his own tweets. Given its status as part of a reputable university, the Hayden Center's partisanship surely has influenced appreciable numbers of students and participants in its events.

---

138 https://www.c-span.org/video/?451323-1/intel-chiefs-discuss-intelligence-community-presidency-relationship.

ATTITUDES AND ACTIONS OF SERVING INTELLIGENCE OFFICERS

Currently serving intelligence officers cannot go on television or write op-eds the way formers do, meaning government employees had to use other means to get their messages of unhappiness with Trump to the public. Although as noted the "leak" is a long-established political tool of intelligence officers, in recent years the purpose of leaks changed and the volume of leaks rose sharply. Serving intelligence officers who wanted to make their views publicly known did so in one or more of three general ways. They: (1) conveyed their views in government work spaces to former senior officials such as Brennan and Hayden who retained security clearances, thereby speaking with "insiders" and avoiding the charge that they had unauthorized contacts with journalists, letting the formers speak publicly for them; (2) communicated their views informally to friends who were former officials, such as Morell, who then talked with the press; and (3) leaked directly to sympathetic journalists, reporting factual and sensitive material as well as disinformation.

While CIA officers repeatedly over the decades selectively attacked DCIs they did not like, they generally did not directly attack presidents. But one of the best-known CIA leak cases had a strongly partisan angle. During the 2004 presidential campaign, senior CIA officer Mary O. McCarthy, then on rotation to the NSC staff, allegedly leaked classified material about CIA's controversial interrogation program, which was damaging to the Bush administration, to *Washington Post* reporter Dana Priest, who used the information in stories that won Priest a Pulitzer Prize.[139] After

---

139   R. Jeffrey Smith, "Fired Officer Believed CIA Lied to Congress, *Washington Post*, May 14, 2006, http://www.washingtonpost.com/wp-dyn/content/article/2006/05/13/AR2006051301311.html.

an investigation, the CIA fired McCarthy in 2006, although she was not criminally charged.[140] FEC data show that McCarthy gave $2,000 to Democratic presidential candidate John Kerry's campaign on March 14, 2004. In addition, retired senior CIA operations officer Joseph W. Wippl reported that CIA sources told him that CIA personnel, evidently in addition to McCarthy, tried to sabotage Bush's 2004 reelection bid.[141] As noted above, some NIC personnel opposed Bush's Iraq policies. Similarly, *New York Times* correspondent Mark Mazzetti, who had long communicated with US intelligence officials who speak without authorization, reported that Vice President Dick Cheney was convinced that CIA analysts personally opposed to the US war in Iraq leaked negative intelligence assessments about the war to members of Congress and the press.[142] Mazzetti did not specify why Cheney reached this judgment, but the belief evidently damaged Bush White House relations with the CIA for a time. Hence, there were recent precedents for CIA officers to use leaks to attack a Republican president. CIA people clearly retained their leaking skills in 2016.

The motives of older formers and young, serving officers seem to have differed. The older formers mostly espoused traditional Democratic, liberal views consistent with CIA's long-time culture. John McLaughlin, for example, retired from the CIA in 2004. Paul Pillar retired in 2005. General Hayden was DCIA for only a few months in 2009 before Obama replaced him with Leon Panetta. The concerns of serving officers, younger formers, and retirees who recently became formers such as Brennan, were more ideological in nature. While some clearly reflected some of the senior formers' perspectives, others more directly reflected

---

140 Ibid.
141 Wippl, "HUMINT With Spiritual Awareness," 6.
142 Mazzetti, *The Way of the Knife*, 128.

Obama's politically motivated "diversity and inclusion" agenda. This was not surprising given that younger people had recently come from universities where "diversity and inclusion" had, especially following Obama's lead, blossomed as a popular left-wing ideology. Indeed, it was an obsession for some. Many of the younger officers had benefited materially from Obama's policies in the form of demography-based preferences for jobs, promotions, and performance awards. Many of them also seem to have bought the dire warnings of zealots who extravagantly exaggerated the possible effects of Trump's proposed programs on the IC and them personally. Hence, their leaks both defended Obama and his agents—especially Brennan—and attacked perceived threats to existing IC policies in the persons of Trump and DCIA Pompeo. They thereby defended the sanctity of the cultural changes recently made, which they did in part by asserting the alleged right of intelligence agencies to "independence"—especially to independent, internally-focused policymaking on social issues.

The volume of leaks in 2016 and later was large and probably unprecedented, although identifying the sources and number of leaks is difficult at best. Still, reputable people made estimates that all point in the same direction. For example, then-Attorney General Jeff Sessions announced in August 2017 that the Justice Department received more criminal referrals from government agencies requesting investigations into unauthorized disclosures of classified information in the first half of 2017 (President Trump's first months in office) than in the previous three years combined.[143] Sessions provided few details but said the FBI had created a new counterintelligence unit to manage the cases. The Federation of American Scientists, which has closely followed US intelligence for many years, counted 120 leak referrals to the FBI

---

143   Del Quentin Wilber, "Sessions Promises Crackdown on Leaks," *Wall Street Journal*, August 5-6, 2017, A4.

in 2017 and 88 in 2018, compared to 18 in 2015 and 37 in 2016, Obama's last two years in office.[144] Senator Ron Johnson (R-WI), chair of the Senate Homeland Security and Governmental Affairs Committee, became concerned about leaks and had his staff look into the matter. Staffers found that in Trump's first 126 days in office—January 20 to May 25, 2017—125 leaks of national security information, as defined by Obama in an executive order issued in 2009, targeted the new administration.[145] This rate of about one per day was seven times the rate of targeted leaks, similarly defined, that Obama faced in his first 126 days in office.[146]

Anecdotal evidence similarly points to a much higher volume of leaks. Hayden's "journalist friends" told him in 2017 that "a lot of [intelligence] folks are certainly more willing to talk to them."[147] John McLaughlin told a television audience "so many people are coming out of the woodwork."[148] He incongruously added that he doubted many of them were intelligence people. Clapper in 2017 denied, wholly without credibility, that *any* intelligence people leak classified material.[149] Yet he admitted in his book that he himself had leaked.[150] The HPSCI in 2018, then under Republican leadership, issued a report suggesting that Clapper leaked to CNN reporter Jake Tapper intelligence about the IC's Russia investigation and its connection to the Steele dossier.[151]

144   Strassel, *Resistance*, 74.
145   Ibid., 73.
146   Ibid.
147   Hayden, *Assault on Intelligence;* 86.
148   MSNBC, 2017, https://video.search.yahoo.com/search/video;_ ylt=AwrBT9fVeiRZDtUAMklXNyoA;_ylu=X3oDMTEyNHY5aGhmBGNvbG 8DYmYxBHBvcwMxBHZ0aWQDQjM1MTFfMQRzZWMDc2M-?p=%22Jo hn+McLaughlin%22+and+MSNBC&fr=fp-comodo#id=24&vid=66440ec7e7adc 0bf342d10e3656d0fb6&action=view.
149   Gabrielle Levy, "Clapper Denies Intelligence Agencies Leaked Dirt on Trump," *U.S. News and World Report*, January 12, 2017, https://www.usnews.com/news/ national-news/articles/2017-01-12/dni-clapper-intelligence-community-did-not- leak-damaging-dossier-on-donald-trump.
150   Clapper, *Facts and Fears*, 231-232.
151   Jonathan Turley, "Clapper's actions sure do look like political manipulations," *The Hill*, April 28, 2018, https://thehill.com/opinion/white-house/385351-clappers- actions-sure-look-like-political-manipulations.

Clapper soon thereafter became a paid consultant to CNN. Representative Jim Jordan (R-OH) later more pointedly accused Clapper of leaking.[152]

Eric Ciaramella, in detailing his background to the Federal Election Commission when contributing $10 to a political action committee on November 13, 2019, said his employer was the CIA and his occupation was "LEAKER."[153] As if leaking was a joke. Leaks in recent years overwhelmingly reflected anti-Trump sentiments; they were not about mundane policy or intelligence issues.

Hayden reported that many serving CIA officers approached him in 2016-2017 to pass information and encouraged him to continue to publicly criticize Trump. CIA people told him "thank you" and "keep it up" in reference to his Trump-bashing.[154] He added that CIA personnel regularly talked partisan politics in the office, something that once was anathema to the organizational culture of CIA, which other knowledgeable persons also have reported.[155] Hayden said Trump's election seemed to some in the IC to be a "hostile corporate takeover" and that Trump's initial NSC senior director for intelligence issues, Ezra Cohen-Watnick, and CIA people had a "fully reciprocated hate-hate relationship."[156] Other anti-Trump formers who variously claimed publicly to represent the views of serving officers include Nada Bakos, Michael Morell, Paul Pillar, Marc Polymeropoulos, and Ned Price.

The FBI's Andrew McCabe wrote that in 2016 the "problem of leaks in the White House, the FBI, and elsewhere had been growing ...."[157] McCabe recounted several cases of leaks and

---

152 Tim Graham, "Clapper News Network? CNN Pays Source for Leaking With Paid On-Air Gig," *MRCNewsBusters*, March 19, 2018, https://www.newsbusters.org/blogs/nb/tim-graham/2018/03/17/clapper-news-network-cnn-pays-source-leaking-paid-air-gig.
153 FEC database.
154 Hayden, *Assault on Intelligence*, 248.
155 Ibid., 148-149.
156 Ibid., 84, 153.
157 McCabe, *The Threat*, 205.

implied that leaking by FBI personnel had increased in recent years.[158] For example, he cited an allegedly erroneous *Wall Street Journal* article published in October 2016 that seemed to be based on information coming from the Bureau.[159] He also accused Representative Devin Nunes (R-CA), a former chairman of the HPSCI, of leaking intelligence information about the ongoing Russia investigation to the press.[160] Ironically, the FBI fired McCabe in March 2018 for lying under oath about his own role in leaking information about the FBI inquiry into the Clinton Foundation to the *Wall Street Journal*.[161]

NSA contractor and former US Air Force linguist Reality Winner, who on social media expressed outrage at Trump's election, in May 2017 smuggled classified documents about Russian meddling in the 2016 presidential election out of the NSA facility in Georgia where she worked and mailed them to a reporter of a left-leaning website, *The Intercept*.[162] The documents had marks that identified the photocopier on which they were made. *The Intercept* asked government officials if the documents were authentic. Soon thereafter Winner, then aged twenty-five, was arrested, answering the question. According to the *New York Times*, on Twitter Winner earlier had "denounced Mr. Trump as 'the orange fascist we let into the white house' [sic] and mocked Attorney General Jeff Sessions as a 'Confederate.' She expressed concern about climate change, support for the Black Lives Matter

---

158 Ibid., 205.
159 Ibid., 196.
160 Ibid., 244-245.
161 Philip Ewing, "Justice Department Details Case Against Fired Deputy FBI Director McCabe," *NPR*, April 13, 2018, https://www.npr.org/2018/04/13/602331134/justice-department-details-case-against-fired-deputy-fbi-director-mccabe.
162 Charlie Savage, Scott Shane, and Alan Blinder, "Reality Winner, N.S.A. Contractor Accused of Leak, Was Undone by Trail of Clues," *New York Times*, June 6, 2017, https://www.nytimes.com/2017/06/06/us/politics/reality-leigh-winner-leak-nsa.html.

movement and other liberal views."[163] Winner later explained why she acted:

> I felt really hopeless and seeing that information that had been contested back and forth, back and forth in the public domain for so long, trying to figure out with everything else that keeps getting released and keeps getting leaked, why isn't this getting out there? Why can't this be public?[164]

Winner evidently shared the common, soothing view of Clinton's supporters that she lost the 2016 election only because Russia helped Trump. Said the occasionally perceptive Winner after her arrest, "I screwed up."[165] In August 2018 Winner was sentenced to five years and three months in federal prison for violating the Espionage Act.

Winner's explanation for her actions is consistent with the increasingly common rationale of younger people that aggressive self-expression is a good thing when perceived principles are involved.[166] Most leakers are considerably more discrete than Winner was, however.

The anti-Trump media encouraged leaks in many ways, including by providing what CIA psychologist Ursula Wilder called "leak bait"—websites designed to enable intelligence officers to leak anonymously.[167] When DCIA Brennan encouraged

163 Ibid.
164 David Choi, 'I felt really hopeless': NSA leak suspect Reality Winner explains why she smuggled a classified report," *Business Insider*, September 28, 2017, http://www.businessinsider.com/reality-winner-nsa-leaker-fox-news-al-jazeera-pantyhose-2017-9.
165 Alan Blinder, "N.S.A. Contractor May Have Mishandled Secrets Before, Prosecutor Says," *New York Times*, June 8, 2017, https://www.nytimes.com/2017/06/08/us/reality-leigh-winner-nsa-secrets-plea.html.
166 Marangione, "Millennials: Truthtellers or Threats?"
167 Wilder, "The Psychology of Espionage and Leaking in the Digital Age," 1.

CIA officers to fight for diversity and inclusion, as he did often, in opposition to established leaders' perspectives if necessary, he implicitly encouraged use of such sites.

Intelligence people evidently leaked to the *Washington Post* and other media the routine and tone of Trump's *PDB* briefings—information only intelligence officials or senior White House officials could know, given the tight security the *PDB* always has.[168] After alleging that Trump little understood the nuances of sophisticated intelligence, the *Post* reported that Trump got briefings almost every day that often lasted longer than scheduled—30 to 45 minutes, similar to the time many presidents have devoted to daily intelligence briefings.[169] In May 2017, the *Post* reported that Trump's standing with intelligence professionals remained "strained" because he disparaged their "motives and work," implying that Trump should not evaluate the performance of people who work for him—consistent with the claims of formers such as Clapper, McLaughlin, and Price but inconsistent with longstanding CIA norms.[170] The *Post* also claimed incorrectly that Trump was wrong to say he could declassify material as he wished—an act many presidents have done for foreign policy purposes—and then charged that Trump's actions showed he thought IC people were his adversaries.[171]

By 2020, leaks attributed to *PDB* briefers, once among the most tight-lipped of intelligence officers, mounted. Former CIA operations officer Marc Polymeropoulos said, "No one's going to

---

168   Philip Rucker and Ashley Parker, "Serving intelligence to Trump in small bites," *Washington Post*, May 30, 2017, A1.

169   Priess, *The President's Book of Secrets*.

170   Rucker and Parker, "Serving intelligence to Trump in small bites."

171   Examples of presidential release of intelligence information for foreign policy and domestic political reasons include President Kennedy's release of photos of Soviet bases in Cuba to pressure Moscow and rationalize the US "blockade" of Cuba, and President Reagan's release of phone conversations of Libyan officials with terrorists allegedly involved in bombing a disco in Berlin in 1986.

brief anything on Russia to the president."[172] He added, "They're terrified of doing that. I know that from the briefers. Because he'll explode and the whole thing will get derailed, because he has this weird affinity for Putin."[173] Polymeropoulos in October 2020 joined the group of formers who signed the open letter discussed above that suggested that press reporting that Joe and Hunter Biden had dealt corruptly with Ukraine *might* have been a Russian fabrication—the obvious effort to help Biden win the 2020 election.[174]

CIA leakers prominently targeted Mike Pompeo, Trump's first DCIA, who did not share Brennan's penchant for social activism. After his first address to the CIA workforce, employees repeatedly asked Pompeo about his commitment to Obama's diversity agenda. After the third question, he said he was committed to finding the best people for jobs—the traditional standard—which was plainly unacceptable to some people in attendance.[175] Said one employee who heard Pompeo speak, "He didn't seem to understand the need for a workforce that reflects America."[176] Ned Price similarly said in mid-2019 that he still saw a need for the CIA to "resemble the country we protect"—a domestic political imperative that was not an operational motive or a desire to ensure equal opportunities for all, a view that became popular in the IC in Obama years.[177]

172   Sara Boboltz, "Intel Officers 'Terrified' of Briefing Trump on Russia Because He Would 'Explode': Report," *Huffpost*, October 20, 2020, https://www.yahoo.com/huffpost/trump-russia-intelligence-explode-220746995.html.
173   Ibid.
174   Lauren Frias, "More than 50 former intel officials signed a public letter saying they believe the Hunter Biden story has 'all the classic earmarks of a Russian information operation'," *Business Insider*, October 20, 2020, https://www.businessinsider.com/ex-intel-officials-suspect-russian-involvement-in-hunter-biden-stories-2020-10.
175   John Kiriakou, "Mike Pompeo's CIA Will Not Reflect America's Diversity," *truthdig*, September, 17, 2017, https://www.truthdig.com/articles/mike-pompeos-cia-will-not-reflect-america/.
176   Ibid.
177   Ned Price discussion with author, July 30, 2019.

Pompeo did not participate in the CIA's celebrations of gays as Brennan had. He did not attend the 2017 Pride festivities, generating resentful leaks and then press reports critical of his non-action in this arena.[178] Pompeo reportedly canceled at least one Pride month event.[179] Gays were angered that the CIA disinvited the parents of Matthew Shepard, a young gay man murdered in 1998, whom ANGLE had unilaterally invited, prompting leaks critical of CIA management in general.[180] LGBT people claimed in their leaks that this decision amounted to a reversal of the progress Brennan had made.[181] Former CIA analyst Nada Bakos reported that many CIA employees believed Pompeo's alleged "backtracking" on diversity and inclusion was a threat to the workforce and to national security, evidently linking the concepts.[182] Media reported incorrectly that Pompeo reversed Brennan's demographic diversity policies, reports akin to the self-serving but erroneous CIA leaks about firings of operations officers in the 1970s.[183] Serving officers complained in leaks that Pompeo was a practicing Christian, which also was a complaint of Ned Price.[184] The CIA responded that it invited U.S. Senator Tammy Baldwin (D-WI), a lesbian, to speak at Pride festivities, and that there was no backsliding in the agency's commitment to diversity—that is, Brennan's version thereof. Pompeo repeatedly said he wanted to

---

178 McLaughlin, "More White, More Male, More Jesus."
179 Curtis M. Wong, "Activists Blast Trump's Secretary of State Pick for Anti-LGBTQ Record," *Queer Voices*, March 13, 2018, https://www.huffpost.com/entry/mike-pompeo-lgbtq-rights-record_n_5aa80654e4b0a09afeae88cd.
180 McLaughlin, "More White, More Male, More Jesus."
181 John Kiriakou, "Mike Pompeo's CIA Will Not Reflect America's Diversity," *truthdig*, September 17, 2017, https://www.truthdig.com/articles/mike-pompeos-cia-will-not-reflect-america/.
182 Ibid.
183 Ursulafaw, "Mike Pompeo Killing CIA Diversity Mandate; Recruiting For Bible Studies," *Daily Kos*, September 11, 2017, https://www.dailykos.com/stories/2017/9/11/1697777/-Mike-Pompeo-Killing-CIA-Diversity-Mandate-Recruiting-For-Bible-Studies.
184 Kiriakou, "Mike Pompeo's CIA Will Not Reflect America's Diversity."

hire the very best people for all agency jobs—the traditional "equal opportunity" position that was not what activists wanted to hear and was not in fact what CIA did. According to the CIA in 2017, "Pompeo and his senior leaders" had their own view of diversity: "They demonstrate their commitment to the diversity required to achieve that mission in the most important way possible: by living the creed of crushing our adversaries by hiring and training the best spies the world will ever know."[185] Diversity advocates at the CIA could rationalize keeping Brennan-era preferences because they believed, or wanted to believe, their own rhetoric that demographic diversity enhanced the agency's performance.

In March 2018, after Trump had nominated Pompeo to be secretary of state, a new round of leaks included criticism of Mrs. Susan Pompeo's role as honorary chair of the CIA's Family Advisory Board, a group that addresses employee quality-of-life issues. Ryan Trapani, a CIA spokesman, responded:

> These false and disgusting rumors being peddled about Director Pompeo, his wife, and their family are nothing more than a disgraceful attempt to politicize his nomination for Secretary of State without regard for the truth.[186]

The focus of many leaks thus was consistent with Nicholas Dujmović's observation that political discussions within the CIA during his later years there focused on social issues. Gina Haspel, who replaced Pompeo as DCIA in April 2018, was a

---

185   Ibid.
186   Shane Harris, "Susan Pompeo's role as 'first lady of the CIA' draws critics and defenders," *Washington Post*, March 19, 2018, https://www.washingtonpost.com/world/national-security/susan-pompeos-role-as-first-lady-of-the-cia-draws-critics-and-defenders/2018/03/19/d6e55646-2baf-11e8-911f-ca7f68bff0fc_story.html.

CIA careerist and so was less threatening to CIA personnel, contributing to the lower volume of leaks after 2018 directed at the DCIA personally. Her obvious acceptance of Brennan's diversity program, and formal re-confirmation of it in 2020, undoubtedly also contributed appreciably to the reduction in leaks.

On October 2, 2018, Saudi Arabian dissident Jamal Khashoggi, a *Washington Post* stringer, was murdered in the Saudi consulate in Istanbul, Turkey. Early reports were somewhat contradictory but implicated Saudi Crown Prince Mohammed bin Salman. The *Post*, which had editorially criticized the prince before, launched a strong "news" and editorial campaign against him. President Trump, who had a good relationship with the prince and with the Saudi government, expressed skepticism about the initial reports. Soon thereafter, the *Post* and other media reported leaked intelligence information, including alleged communications intercepts, which supposedly confirmed the prince's responsibility for the murder—thereby damaging a foreign leader Trump valued.[187] Their magnitude, detail, and timing suggested to many observers another case of policy-motivated anti-Trump leaks by intelligence officers. Former CIA analyst Bruce Riedel told *Vanity Fair*:

> "Somebody wanted this information to come out, obviously. I think there is, inside the American national security bureaucracy, a fair number of people who have been warning for some time that Mohammed bin Salman is a dangerous, reckless, impulsive person and they weren't getting any attention. And now they have proof positive of how dangerous and reckless he is." ...

---

187 For example, see Shane Harris, Greg Miller, and Josh Dawsey, "CIA concludes Saudi crown prince ordered Jamal Khashoggi's assassination," *Washington Post*, November 16, 2018, https://www.washingtonpost.com/world/national-security/cia-concludes-saudi-crown-prince-ordered-jamal-khashoggis-assassination/2018/11/16/98c89fe6-e9b2-11e8-a939-9469f1166f9d_story.html.

"In Washington, the way you say, 'I told you so,' is to leak something."[188]

Peter Strzok, the FBI official whom Special Counsel Robert Mueller fired from his team after discovering that Strzok emailed derogatory comments about Trump to his girlfriend, FBI lawyer Lisa Page, evidently believed CIA people were leaking to the press. Republican Senators Ron Johnson and Chuck Grassley quoted Strzok as saying in a December 15, 2016 email to Page, apparently about CIA personnel, "Our sisters have begun leaking like mad... They're kicking it into overdrive."[189] In another email to colleagues, Strzok reportedly wrote:

> "I'm beginning to think the agency got information a lot earlier than we thought and hasn't shared it completely with us." ... "Might explain all these weird / seemingly incorrect leads all these media folks have. Would also highlight agency as source of some of these leaks."[190]

Former FBI Director Comey admitted that he leaked memos he wrote about his conversations with President Trump, using a friend at Columbia University's law school to deliver the memos

---

188 Abigal Tracy, "In Washington, the Way You Say, 'I Told You So,' Is to Leak Something": With a Calculated Leak, the War Between Trump and the Intelligence Community Escalates," *Vanity Fair*, December 4, 2018, https://www.vanityfair.com/news/2018/12/donald-trump-mohammed-bin-salman-jamal-khashoggi-murder.

189 Jerry Dunleavy, "Peter Strzok thought CIA was leaking to media in Trump-Russia investigation," *The Washington Examiner*, May 6, 2019, https://www.washingtonexaminer.com/news/peter-strzok-thought-cia-was-leaking-to-media-in-trump-russia-investigation. See also Chuck Ross, "Peter Strzok Suspected CIA Was Behind Inaccurate Media Leaks," *The Daily Caller*, May 6, 2019, https://dailycaller.com/2019/05/06/peter-strzok-cia-leaks-email/.

190 Dunleavy, "Peter Strzok thought CIA was leaking to media in Trump-Russia investigation."

to the *New York Times*.[191] Comey later said he hoped the leaks would advance the cause of naming a special counsel to investigate the president, which soon thereafter occurred with the naming of Robert Mueller to the position. Mueller's investigation was a major part of Trump's presidency, making Comey one of the most consequential leakers in American history. Some of Comey's leaked memos contained small amounts of low-level classified information.[192] After an investigation, the Justice Department decided not to prosecute him for revealing classified information.

Hayden reported that many people in the IC despised retired General Flynn, the former director of DIA, who was Trump's first national security advisor but immediately got into political trouble over his inflammatory public statements and his accounts to administration officials of his authorized conversation with Russian ambassador to Washington Sergey Kislyak before Trump was inaugurated. Trump fired him in February 2017. About Flynn's troubles Hayden wrote, "... there was probably intelligence community leaking that poured oil on this fire."[193]

John Bolton reported that Trump was "very unhappy" about a story in *Time* in February 2019 that said, citing his intelligence briefers, that Trump little paid attention to, or understood, his intelligence briefings.[194] Bolton said the episode "nearly severed an already tense [Trump] relationship with the intelligence

---

191   John Solomon, "Comey's private memos on Trump conversations contained classified material," *The Hill*, July 9, 2017, https://thehill.com/policy/national-security/341225-comeys-private-memos-on-trump-conversations-contained-classified.

192   Barr, *One Damn Thing After Another*, 291.

193   Hayden, *Assault on Intelligence*, 150. John Bolton wrote that he thought holdover Obama NSC staffers may also have leaked unfavorable information about Flynn. See Bolton, *The Room Where It Happened*, 12.

194   Bolton, *The Room Where It Happened*, 323-324; John Walcott, "'Willful Ignorance.' Inside President Trump's Troubled Intelligence Briefings," *Time*, February 5, 2019, https://time.com/5518947/donald-trump-intelligence-briefings-national-security/.

community;" Trump called DNI Dan Coats an "idiot" and wondered aloud in aides' presence if his choice of DCIA Gina Haspel had been a mistake.[195] Soon thereafter, in March 2019, chronic intelligence leaks about Trump finally led Coats and Haspel to issue an unusual joint statement, saying that unnamed media had published leaked information about President Trump's intelligence briefings that was "false, unproductive and harmful to our nation's security."[196] They added:

> Speculation, including that from former and unnamed intelligence officers, about what occurs in our Oval Office briefings is wrong.... Simply put, these anonymous sources are not there as we deliver timely, unbiased intelligence and work alongside an engaged and knowledgeable President on the most complex national security issues.[197]

In April 2020, at least four leakers confirmed this Coats-Haspel assessment yet again. The *Washington Post* and then ABC News and other media reported what Trump's press critics immediately called a "bombshell" story that in November 2019 US intelligence allegedly warned President Trump about the implications of the Corona virus pandemic then spreading in China, but Trump ignored the warnings.[198] In the press spin, the president had blood on his hands given the many Covid-19 deaths in the United States to that point and the numerous accusations

---

195   Bolton, *The Room Where It Happened*, 324.
196   Lee Ferran, "Intel chiefs push back on reports about Trump's intelligence briefings," *ABC News*, March 5, 2019, https://abcnews.go.com/Politics/intel-chiefs-push-back-reports-trumps-intelligence-briefings/story?id=61492729.
197   Ibid.
198   Josh Margolin and James Gordon Meek, "Intelligence report warned of coronavirus crisis as early as November: Sources," *ABC News*, April 8, 2020, https://abcnews.go.com/Politics/intelligence-report-warned-coronavirus-crisis-early-november-sources/story?id=70031273.

that the US government's response to the pandemic had been slow and ineffective.

The report was untrue, however. A few days after the initial, breathless media stories, the commander of the National Center for Medical Intelligence (NCMI), a DIA unit based at Fort Detrick, Maryland whose primary job is to monitor epidemiological and other medical threats to deployed US military forces, flatly denied the press reports. Colonel R. Shane Day, in a rare public comment, said NCMI had not published such finished intelligence analyses.[199] Senior military officers at the Pentagon corroborated Dr. Day's statement. In fact, while some NCMI analysts were monitoring events earlier, no IC element included the virus story in any published intelligence report until early January 2020, by which time many American medical professionals, and much of the world, were well aware of the pandemic.[200] According to Bob Woodward's sources, Trump's *PDB* briefer, Beth Sanner, told the president on January 24, 2020 that the IC had a benign view of the virus and predicted that it would not be a pandemic.[201] "Just like the flu," she reportedly said, referring to its severity. "We don't think it's as deadly as [Severe Acute Respiratory Syndrome]."[202] The leakers not only criticized Trump inaccurately and unfairly, they claimed far better intelligence performance than was warranted.

In addition, serving intelligence officers continue to tell me that intelligence professionals frequently talk politics at work, mainly about social issues, extending practices Nicholas Dujmović and David Muller observed at the CIA and the ODNI, respectively, years earlier. In the Trump years it took forms as

---

199   Tobias Hoonhout, "Pentagon Bashes Bombshell ABC Report, Denies U.S. Intel Identified Coronavirus Threat in November," *National Review*, April 9, 2020, https://www.nationalreview.com/news/pentagon-bashes-bombshell-abc-report-denies-u-s-intel-identified-coronavirus-threat-in-november/.

200   Woodward, *Rage*, 211-220.

201   Ibid., 230.

202   Ibid.

"water cooler banter" and, reflecting new technologies, social media such as Facebook postings.[203] A 30-something analyst at NGA said there was no need to talk politics at work; Facebook provided ample opportunities for political banter with friends and workmates outside government spaces.[204] A serving CIA officer reported in mid-2020 that highly partisan anti-Trump talk at work was much more pronounced among CIA analysts than among the staff of CIA's Directorate of Science and Technology.[205] Michael Morell said in January 2021 that his CIA sources told him that in the office "American politics is the thing that gets talked about the most."[206] It is "… probably not a good thing. Let's hope it recedes," Morell opined.[207] Hope? Implicitly, he suggested that management had no role to play. This comment came from a former senior executive who helped select many of the managers then running the CIA, some of whom, by his own accounts, he still communicated with regularly. Elsewhere, in 2019, according to a Defense Department intelligence official, a black employee of the USD(I) prominently displayed a photograph of former President Obama in her work space, an inappropriate display of partisanship given that Obama had left office.[208] According to my source, no one in authority asked her to remove the photo. It remained in place. And in early 2022, an employee of CIA's Directorate of Operations said that partisan talk at work was still

---

203 For example, Gentry, "An INS Special Forum," 5-6.
204 Author communication with the analyst, 2018.
205 Personal communication.
206 George Mason University, Hayden Center, podcast, January 26, 2021, https://youtu.be/d_jgMYBGRkI, minute 1:05.
207 Ibid.
208 Personal communication, mid-2019. Government offices often have a row of photographs of officials in the organization's chain of command, including the president, which frequently is near the director's office. These official photos are of standard size and are not campaign or otherwise promotional materials. Agencies often police their offices for displays of inappropriate material, such as sexually provocative pictures and displays of political partisanship.

common and was intimidating for people who disagreed with the dominant, prevailing anti-Trump opinions.[209]

A knowledgeable official told me that serving CIA officers since 2016 used classified and unclassified government communications systems to share anti-Trump messages among themselves and with outsiders. This activity, which evidently continued to the end of Trump's term of office, is especially noteworthy because government information technology systems are closely monitored for unethical behavior (such as gambling) and for counterintelligence purposes. Large-scale group discussions of Trump reportedly included persons in the private sector. This activity suggests that IT and security personnel as well as managers were complicit by not stopping the practice. A source of author Lee Smith, who Smith described as a former senior intelligence official, said:

> It is highly fashionable to promote an anti-Trump atmosphere everywhere, including the CIA.... The rules have been bent dramatically to make room for Trump bashing. People who are pro-Trump or neutral about Trump have to keep their mouths shut. Overall, CIA is a very liberal institution, a reflection of the East Coast establishment, a reflection of society.[210]

BLOWING WHISTLES AT TRUMP

A new form of leak—intelligence "whistleblowing" aimed at the president—emerged in 2019.[211] While it had a near-precedent in the Mary McCarthy leaks of 2004, the new one was different in that stronger whistleblower protection laws and

---

209   Personal communication.
210   Smith, *Permanent Coup*, 96.
211   Rogg, "The U.S. Intelligence Community's 'MacArthur Moment'," 13-14.

shifting definitions of appropriate government employee behavior gave leakers a new avenue for attacking political opponents in ways that also gave them legal protection—if done in procedurally proper ways. Essential complements to this form of leak are allies on at least one Congressional intelligence oversight committee and a sympathetic press, both of which were present in 2019. This leak led directly to the first impeachment of President Trump.

Events unfolded as follows. In September 2019, the press reported that an unnamed CIA official filed a "whistleblower" complaint against President Trump, claiming that in a telephone conversation in July 2019 Trump had inappropriately pressured the president of Ukraine, Volodymyr Zelensky, to investigate potential corruption by Hunter Biden, son of former Vice President Joe Biden, who then was a contender for the Democrats' 2020 presidential nomination.[212] Hunter had received a lucrative (roughly $50,000 per month) contract with a Ukrainian energy company, for which he was not obviously qualified, when Vice President Biden supervised US policy regarding Ukraine. (Readers will recall that plausible charges that Hunter Biden benefited financially from his father's position became prominent in 2020 and remain under Justice Department investigation.) The CIA person filed a complaint with the ODNI's inspector general (IG), Michael K. Atkinson, who found it to be credible.

News of the filing predictably soon leaked, leading HPSCI chairman Schiff to publicly demand to receive the full complaint, which Atkinson initially said he refused to do but soon thereafter did release to Schiff. Reporting on the case to this point immediately led some observers to think that Trump opponents

212 Greg Miller, Ellen Nakashima, and Shane Harris, "Trump is subject of intelligence complaint," *Washington Post*, September 19, 2019, A1; Schmidt, *Donald Trump v. the United States*, 381-389; Smith, *Permanent Coup*, 143-151.

in the IC, perhaps abetted by Atkinson and Schiff, had used a procedure designed mainly to report relatively minor cases of criminality and mismanagement in an imaginative new way to attack Trump. Soon it was reported that Atkinson changed IG procedures to allow a whistleblowing complaint from a source with only second-hand knowledge of an event and backdated the whistleblower's complaint.[213] Schiff and Atkinson apparently coordinated their public statements. Trump later fired Atkinson.

Michael McFaul, a member of President Obama's NSC staff and the US ambassador to Russia in 2012-2014, promptly tweeted:

> I cannot remember a whistleblower trying to blow a whistle on a president. & this cant just be about Trump's handling of classified materials. Like it or not, the president can declassify whatever he wants when he wants. Something bigger seems to be going on [sic][214]

At about the same time, Fred Fleitz, one of the few former CIA officers who publicly backed Trump, also found initial reports of the complaint suspiciously legalistic and political. Fleitz wrote:

> I am troubled by the complaint and wonder how an intelligence officer could file it over something a president said to a foreign leader. How could this be an intelligence matter?

> It appears likely to me that this so-called whistleblower was pursuing a political agenda.

---

213 Smith, *Permanent Coup*, 148.
214 McFaul tweet, @McFaul and https://www.yahoo.com/huffpost/donald-trump-world-leader-reported-promise-reaction-071248019.html.

I am very familiar with transcripts of presidential phone calls since I edited and processed dozens of them when I worked for the NSC. I also know a lot about intelligence whistleblowers from my time with the CIA.

My suspicions grew this morning when I saw the declassified whistleblowing complaint. It appears to be written by a law professor and includes legal references and detailed footnotes. It also has an unusual legalistic reference on how this complaint should be classified.

From my experience, such an extremely polished whistleblowing complaint is unheard of. This document looks as if this leaker had outside help, possibly from congressional members or staff.

Moreover, it looks like more than a coincidence that this complaint surfaced and was directed to the House Intelligence Committee just after Adam Schiff (D-Calif.), an outspoken opponent of President Trump, expressed numerous complaints in August 2019 accusing President Trump of abusing aid to Ukraine to hurt Joe Biden. This includes an August 28 tweet that closely resembled the whistleblowing complaint.

House Republicans need to ask the whistleblower under oath whether he spoke to the press or Congress about his complaint.

Also very concerning to me is how the complaint indicates intelligence officers and possibly other federal employees are violating the rules governing presidential phone calls with foreign leaders.

The content and transcripts of these calls are highly restricted. The whistleblower makes clear in his complaint that he did not listen to a call in question, nor did he read the transcript—he was told about the call by others. If true, intelligence officers have grossly violated the rules as well as the trust placed on them to protect this sensitive information.

I refuse to believe that the leaking, timing and presentation of this complaint is coincidence. I don't think the American people will buy this either.

I'm more worried, however, that this latest instance of blatant politicization of intelligence by Trump haters will do long term damage to the relationship between the intelligence community and US presidents for many years to come (emphasis added).[215]

Later, it was reported that the CIA whistleblower was an analyst who had been assigned to the NSC staff during the Obama years, repeatedly demonstrated personal animus toward Trump after he was elected, and had been sent back to Langley before his end of tour because of his partisanship. The person heard about the conversation from a then-serving NSC staffer he knew from his time at the White House, Army Lieutenant Colonel Alexander

---

215 Fred Fleitz, "Former CIA official on whistleblower: 'How could this be an intelligence matter?'" *New York Post*, September 26, 2019, https://nypost.com/2019/09/26/former-cia-official-on-whistleblower-how-could-this-be-an-intelligence-matter/.

Vindman, and so did not actually hear the conversation or read the official transcript of the conversation. The White House promptly declassified the transcript and released it to the public.[216] As Fleitz suspected, the CIA whistleblower contacted a member of Schiff's staff before filing his complaint. The staffer recommended that the analyst approach the ODNI's inspector general rather than the CIA's general counsel, Courtney Elwood, whom the staffer believed was likely to be less receptive to the complaint than Atkinson.[217] The whistleblower evidently contacted a CIA lawyer anyway and Elwood in turn told White House lawyers, who unsurprisingly were not interested in pursuing the matter.[218] Schiff initially denied any contact with the whistleblower. However, it soon became clear that Schiff had lied about his relationship, via his staffer, with the analyst.[219] This part of the story predictably was not much covered by anti-Trump media.

Congressional Democrats immediately seized upon Trump's phone conversation as a rationale for reshaping and accelerating their ongoing efforts to find an excuse to impeach him. Some Democrats had called for Trump's impeachment the day after his 2016 election triumph—not normally considered an impeachable offense—while others had been looking for more plausible excuses, or even a good reason, ever since. They were disappointed that Robert Mueller's investigation found little of use to them. Interest in INR analyst Rod Schoonover plummeted as Democrats saw a

---

216 White House, Memorandum of Telephone Conversation, July 25, 2019, https://www.whitehouse.gov/wp-content/uploads/2019/09/Unclassified09.2019.pdf. See also Smith, *Permanent Coup*, 94-95, 143-151.

217 Julian E. Barnes, Michael S. Schmidt, and Matthew Rosenberg, "Schiff Got Early Account of Accusations as Whistle-Blower's Concerns Grew," *New York Times*, October 2, 2019, https://www.nytimes.com/2019/10/02/us/politics/adam-schiff-whistleblower.html.

218 Schmidt, *Donald Trump v. the United States*, 383-384.

219 Lee Smith, "Adam Schiff lied about the Trump investigation—and the media let him," *New York Post*, May 2, 2020, https://nypost.com/2020/05/08/adam-schiff-lied-about-the-trump-probe-and-the-media-let-him/.

better opportunity to get Trump via the "whistleblower." Trump was impeached on December 18, 2019, mainly on the basis of the whistleblower's story, and was acquitted by the Senate on February 5, 2020, both on nearly party-line votes. Polls indicated that the general public overwhelmingly was unimpressed by the substance of the impeachment case, and it was largely ignored in the 2020 presidential campaign—a sure sign of its weakness.[220] Schiff was one of the House prosecutors at Trump's trial, making the HPSCI, whose members once had tried to do their work largely on a bipartisan basis, even more divided. Knowledgeable observers McFaul and Fleitz got the core of the story about right very early in the saga.

The publicity surrounding this episode suggests that detailees to the White House may use this technique again. An obvious defense by a president suspicious of intelligence personnel would be to deny intelligence people jobs at the White House.

In a less prominent case, in early 2017 a letter written in US diplomats' "dissent channel"[221] that opposed President Trump's temporary ban on immigration from seven predominantly Muslim countries attracted about 1,000 signatures from State Department employees, more than any other such message in the department's history.[222] It then went to the IC's inspector general, an unusual move. According to *Vanity Fair*:

> One Justice Department employee told the [*Washington*] *Post*, "You're going to see the bureaucrats using time to

---

220   Bade and Demirjian, *Unchecked*.
221   Since 1971 State has had a nominally confidential mechanism, the "dissent channel," to enable State and Agency for International Development employees to express constructive criticism of US foreign policies directly to senior department officials. The channel reportedly is used infrequently.
222   Abigail Tracy, "Anti-Trump Resistance Movement Growing Within the U.S. Government," *Vanity Fair*, February 1, 2017, https://www.vanityfair.com/news/2017/02/donald-trump-federal-government-workers.

their advantage," and added that "people here will resist and push back against orders they find unconscionable," by whistle-blowing, leaking to the press, and lodging internal complaints. Others are staying in contact with officials appointed by President Obama to learn more about how they can undermine Trump's agenda and attending workshops on how to effectively engage in civil disobedience, the *Post* reports.[223]

The IC Inspector General's (ICIG) office, which viewed credibly the August 2019 whistleblower letter that helped trigger Democrats' impeachment movement of 2019, under different leadership in this case noted political bias in the complaint:

> [T]he ICIG's preliminary review identified some indicia of an arguable political bias on the part of the Complainant in favor of a rival political candidate.[224]

TRUTH IN THE ANTI-TRUMP CAMPAIGN

In intelligence officers' battle against Trump, there were two versions of truth. I refer to "truth" as reality as best it can be determined by methodologically sound data gathering and objective analysis. In contrast, "Truth" is a facsimile or part of reality that is misleading, misrepresented, or untrue and which is generated subconsciously or purposefully by a worldview, overt political partisanship, or an ideology in service of parochial material or ideational interests. It is a form of disinformation.

---

223   Ibid.
224   William A. Jacobson, "The 'Whistleblower Complaint' is the real 2020 election interference," *Legal Insurrection*, September 28, 2019 at https://legalinsurrection.com/2019/09/the-whistleblower-complaint-is-the-real-2020-election-interferenc e/?eType=EmailBlastContent&eId=52bffd92-bf7a-4f0c-879f-d3672faa85bc.

By these definitions, Truth included selective use of Trump's words, "hysterical exaggerations" of Trump's language and behavior, misrepresentations, and outright lies.

The "truth to power" slogan, while generally recognized to be an inaccurate characterization of the role of intelligence, was resurrected to be a rallying cry of anti-Trump intelligence activists in 2016. As its attractiveness and apparent usefulness became clearer, press critics and Congressional Democrats such as Representative Schiff also came to use it commonly. While the claim was useful for both bashing Trump on integrity and character grounds and assisting the IC independence argument, former C/NIC Greg Treverton provided another insightful explanation for the term's popularity.[225] He observed that while sound, objective analysis that sometimes approximates truth by generating the best possible understanding of events in a complicated, uncertain world can be a major help in policy formulation, it also is a constraint on poorly conceived policies, especially if it encourages or supports opposing views. Anti-Trump activists were clearly determined to stop both Trump and many of his policies and programs; they used claims of possession of truth and Truth as tools for both purposes. Both versions were delivered overtly and via leaks. Trump's alleged racism, which quickly became a Truth based on his views about nearly unfettered immigration and some ill-chosen remarks, was especially useful in defense of Obama's diversity regime, the special concern of some serving intelligence personnel.

Both truth and Truth played prominent roles in the context of allegations that Russia aided Trump's 2016 campaign. In the truth-based narrative, Trump lied chronically in general, massively exceeding the misstatements that virtually all politicians often make—a point containing both elements of truth and

---

225   Treverton, "Conclusion," 207.

exaggeration or "spin" (think of Bill Clinton!). Critics noted accurately that Trump initially denied Russian activities that seemed to be confirmed as fact but most of them ignored that Trump eventually recognized Russian meddling in 2016. Hence a Truth: Trump uniquely and chronically denied the truth of insightful IC analyses. Then the charges often went much further, employing partisan and ideology-based arguments and substantial exaggeration to advance alternative Truths, such as Brennan's assertion that Trump acted in a "treasonous" manner in his dealings with Putin[226] and Hayden's allegation that Trump was a "useful idiot" in service of the Russians.[227]

This meme held that Russia not only tried to influence the election but decisively affected its outcome, costing Clinton the triumph she so obviously deserved. The latter claim is debatable because it is virtually impossible to identify determinants of the electoral decisions of large numbers of individual voters. No matter. As Clapper contended, it was inconceivable (to him) that Americans could elect Trump unless they had been misled by the Russians.[228] Therefore, the Truth was that Russia made Trump president. Reputable observers continue to generally reject Clapper's assertion.[229]

Brennan played the Truth card repeatedly after going overtly political upon leaving office in January 2017. Neglecting history and context, Brennan repeatedly invoked truth and Truth, both mainly of hysterical exaggeration sorts, frequently in Twitter messages and on television. For example, in a tweet addressed to

---

226 Dylan Scott, "Former CIA director: Trump-Putin press conference "nothing short of treasonous," *Vox*, July 16, 2018, https://www.vox.com/world/2018/7/16/17576804/trump-putin-meeting-john-brennan-tweet-treasonous.

227 Hayden, *Assault on Intelligence*, 74.

228 Clapper, *Facts and Fears*, 395-396.

229 Rid, *Active Measures*, 407-408; McCombie, et al., "The US 2016 presidential election & Russia's troll farms," 96, 101-108.

the president personally, Brennan compared Trump to financier Bernie Madoff, who was convicted of running a Ponzi scheme. Brennan depicted him as a liar:

> You are to governance & politics what Bernie Madoff was to the stock market & investment advice. The two of you share a remarkably unethical ability to deceive & manipulate others, building Ponzi schemes to aggrandize yourselves. Truth & justice ultimately caught up with Bernie.[230]

In a *Washington Post* op-ed piece, Brennan invoked his CIA career to compare Trump to despotic, dishonest, lying tyrants:

> For more than three decades, I observed and analyzed the traits and tactics of corrupt, incompetent and narcissistic foreign officials who did whatever they thought was necessary to retain power. Exploiting the fears and concerns of their citizenry, these demagogues routinely relied on lies, deceit and suppression of political opposition to cast themselves as populist heroes and to mask self-serving priorities. By gaining control of intelligence and security services, stifling the independence of the judiciary and discrediting a free press, these authoritarian rulers followed a time-tested recipe for how to inhibit democracy's development, retard individual freedoms and liberties, and reserve the spoils of corrupt governance for themselves and their

---

230   Emily Birnbaum, "Ex-CIA chief Brennan compares Trump to Bernie Madoff," *The Hill*, July 5, 2018, http://thehill.com/homenews/administration/395744-ex-cia-chief-brennan-compares-trump-to-bernie-madoff.

ilk. It never dawned on me that we could face such a development in the United States.[231]

Former Deputy DCI John McLaughlin criticized Trump using truth-based arguments more frequently than most critics of Trump, but he also resorted to claims of Truth, sometimes in unusual ways. For example, he wrote in early 2017 that the IC's assessment about Russian meddling in the 2016 election deserved to be "taken seriously" because it was issued with "high confidence."[232] The IC's well-publicized and internally recognized errors of the past, which Trump and other politicians and many intelligence officers have said damaged the IC's credibility, did not matter, according to McLaughlin, because the IC effectively learned from earlier mistakes—a useful Truth.[233] Hence the IC, despite its many past lapses and its continuing denigration of expertise and emphasis on pithy current intelligence, now could be counted upon to consistently know truth.[234] This logic evidently sounded reasonable to some intelligence neophytes and appealed to anti-Trump newspaper editors looking for allies. It surely was consistent with the demands of many intelligence officers for "respect" as a right, not a reward for sound performance.[235] In contrast to McLaughlin, former DCI Robert Gates's observation that intelligence analysts err periodically by being biased and

---

231   John Brennan, "I will speak out until integrity returns to the White House," *Washington Post*, June 1, 2018, https://www.washingtonpost.com/opinions/john-brennan-i-will-speak-out-until-integrity-returns-to-the-white-house/2018/05/31/afbccafa-64e8-11e8-a69c-b944de66d9e7_story.html?utm_term=.132ce7ddc703.
232   John McLaughlin, "The CIA's Trump Challenge," January 11, 2017, https://www.realclearworld.com/articles/2017/01/11/the_cia_trump_challenge.html.
233   For a glimpse of how CIA addressed its Iraq WMD failures, see Jervis, *Why Intelligence Fails*, chapter 3.
234   Gentry, "The 'Professionalization' of Intelligence Analysis."
235   For example, Petersen, "What I Learned," 15.

overconfident in their judgments was not a useful truth and was consequently ignored.[236]

Clapper, Hayden, and Brennan repeatedly made clear in their memoirs that perceived moral obligations associated with their worldviews—a variety of Truth—were the primary factors that led them to abandon professional intelligence officers' traditionally apolitical stances and to attack Trump. Hayden criticized Trump extensively on issues of truth, pointedly claiming the IC had it and Trump did not.[237] Indeed, the subtitle of his 2018 book is *American National Security in an Age of Lies*. Trump's lies. Like Clapper, Hayden claimed he and the IC know a variety of Truth consistent with his internationalist worldview—an ideological argument—and portrayed Trump as a uniquely despicable purveyor of lies, a true fact-based assertion amplified by often near-hysterical exaggeration.[238] Comey focused extensively on truth in his memoir, the subtitle of which is *Truth, Lies, and Leadership*.[239] Like Clapper and Hayden, Comey emphasized Trump's alleged errors, misrepresentations, and lies.

Given the critics' extensive focus on honesty, it is especially noteworthy that several of the senior formers were themselves accused convincingly of dishonesty. Brennan was caught lying when he denied that the CIA had penetrated computers of the Senate intelligence committee in 2014; the CIA's inspector general later confirmed the incident.[240] Clapper was accused of lying to Congress in 2013 about NSA surveillance operations; he claimed

---

236   Gates, *Exercise of Power*, 71-72. Jack Davis also believed analysts tend to be over confident. See Davis, "Intelligence Analysts and Policymakers," 1001. Richards Heuer identified conditions under which analysts are likely to be overconfident. See Heuer, *Psychology of Intelligence Analysis*, 122, 123, 151.
237   Hayden, *Assault on Intelligence*, 239, 243, 257.
238   Ibid., 121, 239, 243, 257.
239   Comey, *A Higher Loyalty*.
240   Mark Mazzetti and Carl Hulse, "Inquiry by C.I.A. Affirms It Spied on Senate Panel," *New York Times*, July 31, 2014, https://www.nytimes.com/2014/08/01/world/senate-intelligence-commitee-cia-interrogation-report.html.

in response that he misspoke because he "made a big mistake" in interpreting a question; some in Congress were not convinced.[241] As noted, Clapper once claimed no intelligence person ever leaks, then was caught leaking himself. And, McCabe was fired for lying to FBI investigators. As reported throughout this book, many others also have exaggerated, spoken deceptively, and outright lied.

Historian Victor Davis Hanson wrote accurately of this group:

> A common strategy of the deep state careerist is the psychological tactic known as "projection." To square their own circles of lying, our so-called best and brightest loudly accuse others of precisely the sins that they themselves commit as a matter of habit.[242]

Hayden recounted that people at a CIA location in the United States at one time wore T-shirts emblazoned with the words "Deny Everything, Admit Nothing, Make Counter-Accusations."[243] Hayden claimed the shirts were a "joke," but in fact, as Hanson noted, projection is a standard technique of practitioners of disinformation.[244]

ROLES OF THE PRESS

Many media facilitated anti-Trump activism by intelligence officers, becoming the third element of a de facto intelligence

---

241 Andrew Blake, "James Clapper denies lying to Congress about NSA surveillance program, *Washington Times*, March 6, 2019, https://apnews.com/33a88feb083ea35515de3c73e3d854ad.
242 Victor Davis Hanson, "Is there a dangerous 'deep state' of unelected—and untouchable—U.S. officials?" *The Mercury*, March 29, 2018, https://www.mercurynews.com/2018/03/29/hanson-is-there-a-dangerous-deep-state-of-unelected-u-s-officials-who-are-untouchable/.
243 Hayden, *Assault on Intelligence*, 45.
244 Rid, *Active Measures*.

officer-HPSCI-press alliance against Trump. Media published leaked anti-Trump material, including disinformation, offered space for anti-Trump op-eds by intelligence persons, paid formers as "consultants" to speak regularly against Trump on television, and repeatedly interviewed still others. This activity was overwhelmingly done by media with strongly left-leaning editorial policies, which in recent years commonly also infected "news" reporting. More mainstream and conservative media, including the *Wall Street Journal* and Fox, respectively, acted very differently than did the anti-Trump organizations.

In 2001, then-CBS television reporter Bernard Goldberg alienated many of his colleagues by explaining liberal bias in the media.[245] He argued that the bias was less a conscious effort to present left-of-center views than one of groupthink, that there was no conscious collective political agenda among journalists. There were no secret meetings or cabals to plot against Republicans, just a powerful collective worldview that slanted news appreciably. Goldberg made clear that journalists ostracized—that is, punished—people like him who had the temerity to point out their biases. As Goldberg summarized later:

> Liberal journalists, I said, live in a comfortable liberal bubble and don't even necessarily believe their views are liberal. Instead, they believe they are moderate, mainstream and mainly reasonable views—unlike, of course, conservative views which, to them, are none of those things.[246]

---

245 Goldberg, *Bias*.
246 Bernard Goldberg, "In the age of Trump, media bias comes into the spotlight," *The Hill*, May 6, 2020, https://thehill.com/opinion/white-house/495927-in-the-age-of-trump-media-bias-comes-into-the-spotlight.

Nearly two decades after his book was published, Goldberg updated his argument in an opinion piece. In 2020, he thought a liberal conspiracy against Trump had by then developed.[247] He argued that the conspiracy influenced what was covered and what was ignored or suppressed. For example, Goldberg wrote, critical allegations such as variants of "Trump is a racist" were stated as facts without supporting evidence. A good example of suppression was the liberal press's unwillingness to report the Hunter Biden corruption story in October 2020 and long thereafter. Goldberg asserted that mainstream journalists had joined "The Resistance," the anti-Trump movement declared by Democrats immediately after Hillary Clinton's defeat in 2016.[248] Disinformation specialists operate similarly in their "framing" operations; they misrepresent history, dissemble, selectively use favorable facts, and fabricate stories to either build up organizations and personalities they like or tear down enemies. The obvious purpose of information operations by anti-Trump activists and their press allies was to damage him.[249]

In 2019, *Wall Street Journal* editorial board member Kimberley Strassel made similar points.[250] The bias of reporters is due primarily to their insularity, she argued. Journalists interact mainly with each other, see themselves as normal, and view people with different perspectives as weird outliers. They do not know they are biased. In 2018 former *Washington Post* columnist Howard Kurtz similarly assessed the media's antagonism to Trump while also emphasizing Trump's determination to discredit the press.[251] Scholars have confirmed these impressions.[252]

---

247 Ibid.
248 Strassel, *Resistance,* 206-207, 212.
249 Pacepa and Rychlak, *Disinformation,* 50.
250 Strassel, *Resistance,* 206-207.
251 Kurtz, *Media Madness.*
252 For example, Groseclose, *Left Turn.*

Steve Coll, then-dean of Columbia University's journalism school, a prominent writer and former managing editor of the *Washington Post*, told me that none of the electronic media makes any effort to adhere to traditional journalistic standards.[253] The cable television networks, including the left-leaning anti-Trump networks, had adopted what Coll called an innovation of Fox—a business model based on feeding a narrow slice of the television market what they want to hear, making no claim of objectivity or balance.

These assessments of knowledgeable observers are powerful statements of the influence of journalists' worldviews on what news is covered, how it is covered, and what statements of both fact and baseless accusation are regarded as, or touted as, "truth" by journalists and their audiences. Politically significant worldviews of journalists thereby influence popular definitions of truth, which some intelligence officers adopt. Hence, the media do indeed generate "fake news," sometimes purposefully, at other times unconsciously via the influence of their worldview-generated biases.

These insights help explain anti-Trump formers' choices of words to use against Trump and the selections by serving personnel of reporters and press institutions to which to leak. Careful readers will have noted that many of the quotations cited herein of the anti-Trump formers, leakers, and congressional opponents of Trump make similar points about Trump's character and policies. They often used the same words to characterize Trump. They shared what Strassel called "insularity," not to mention similar partisan political preferences.[254] They therefore used similar terminology, such as the "truth to power" slogan.

---

253   Author discussion with Steve Coll, October 9, 2019.
254   Strassel, *Resistance*, 247-248.

Another reason is the longstanding practice of hard leftists to monitor the "party line" as established by communist party leaders. As demonstrated over the years by the Communist Party of the United States of America and many other communist parties globally, keen attention to established party lines is key to bureaucratic success within the parties and, in some cases, literal survival. The CPUSA is alive and well. In 2000, after the death of long-time leader Gus Hall, party leaders told members to go underground as communists, to join the Democratic Party, and be politically active as nominal Democrats.[255] CPUSA leaders reportedly were delighted by the election of Barack Obama as president of the United States in 2008, and the party supported Joe Biden in 2020.[256] Sensitivity to the imperative of identifying and repeating "lines" of designated opinion leaders, including the press, seems to have spread to non-communist leftists as well. The CPUSA's newspaper, *People's World*, frequently publishes stories that read a lot like those of the *Washington Post*.

Anti-Trump media encouraged and used the convictions of many intelligence officers, past and current, that they had special access to truth and a moral obligation to share it. The press exploited this belief by showcasing intelligence activists, conveying to audiences that intelligence credentials qualified anti-Trump people to talk on virtually any subject, including domestic political issues on which none of them worked when they were in government. It was a clever manipulation of intelligence personnel by politically motivated journalists. This relationship and campaign were intended, and they achieved results. In April 2021 CNN network technical director Charles Chester reportedly admitted to an undercover journalist that CNN actively worked

---

255 Rosenberg, "From Crisis to Split," 54.
256 Ibid.

to defeat Trump in 2020, called its coverage of him "propaganda," and claimed CNN might have been the difference between a Trump win and his defeat.[257]

But intelligence officers used the press, too. Media enabled anti-Trump intelligence officers to conduct an unprecedentedly large, enduring, and effective public campaign against Trump. The apparently growing employment of disinformation in many forms exploited the obvious anti-Trump biases of major media, which were happy for yet more ammunition to fire at enemy number one. At a forum on intelligence and the press at Catholic University in October 2019, I asked two prominent journalists who write regularly on intelligence-related subjects if they ever worried that intelligence people used them. Neither expressed a concern. Good news for leakers and talking heads!!

Not coincidentally, Thomas Rid argued in a study of active measures, the intelligence activity that includes creation and dissemination of disinformation, that during the Cold War the Soviet KGB and its East European allied intelligence services chronically targeted the *Washington Post* and *New York Times*; they were left-leaning, easy to fool, ostensibly credible, and had big audiences, which all were advantageous characteristics from the perspective of Soviet purveyors of disinformation.[258] These characteristics also appealed to anti-Trump US intelligence officers.

Indeed, a large majority of the anti-Trump leaks appeared in left-leaning media that strongly opposed Trump. The *Washington Post* and *New York Times*, among print media, and the CNN, MSNBC, and NPR networks were especially important outlets for activist intelligence officers. Specialty media *The Hill* and *Politico* were favorite outlets for politically motivated "open letters."

---

257 Joseph A. Wulfsohn and Brian Flood, "CNN staffer admits network's focus was to 'get Trump out of office,' calls its coverage 'propaganda," Fox News, April 14, 2021.
258 Rid, *Active Measures*, 247, 285-286.

The Wall Street Journal, which is not generally considered a left-leaning newspaper, also sometimes reported information sourced to "current and former" intelligence officials not authorized to speak publicly. The preponderance of anti-Trump leaks going to prominently anti-Trump media surely was not coincidental.

While it frequently breaks intelligence-related stories, the *New York Times* has a long history of slanting leaks and its intelligence stories in general to criticize administrations, especially Republican administrations. For example, in late 1990 as Congress debated the wisdom of launching a war to rescue Kuwait from Iraqi occupation, alone among major media the *Times* spun congressional testimony of DCI William Webster to suggest that the CIA opposed Bush administration policies and implicitly supported those in Congress, mainly Democrats, who wanted to wait for sanctions to work.[259] When CIA confirmed that its analyses were consistent with administration views, proponents of a "wait-and-see" policy accused the CIA of "cooking the books" in support of administration policy.

Never missing an opportunity, during the extended national demonstrations against the death of George Floyd while in police custody in May 2020, the *Washington Post* used anti-Trump former CIA analysts to compare Trump to an authoritarian ruler trying to quell opposition with force. Reporter Greg Miller wrote:

> "I've seen this kind of violence," said Gail Helt, a former CIA analyst responsible for tracking developments in China and Southeast Asia. "This is what autocrats do. This is what happens in countries before a collapse. It really does unnerve me."

---

259 Leadbetter and Bury, "Prelude to Desert Storm: The Politicization of Intelligence," 48.

Marc Polymeropoulos, who formerly ran CIA operations in Europe and Asia, was among several former agency officials who recoiled at images of Trump hoisting a Bible in front of St. John's Episcopal Church in Washington after authorities fired rubber bullets and tear gas to clear the president's path of protesters.

> "It reminded me of what I reported on for years in the third world," Polymeropoulos said on Twitter. Referring to the despotic leaders of Iraq, Syria and Libya, he said: "Saddam. Bashar. Qaddafi. They all did this."[260]

Beginning in 2016, as intelligence formers began to attack Trump, the press embraced the IC in unprecedented other ways, reflecting mutual intelligence-press interests in collaborating against Trump. This de facto alliance dramatically reversed the traditional hostility of the press toward American intelligence services, especially the CIA, and operated in new ways.[261] For example, in December 2017 a group of reporters started asking people to contribute money to the FBI Agents Association, a union-like organization representing current and former agents. Benjamin Wittes, editor-in-chief of the *Lawfare* blog, tweeted that he donated $1,000 to the group, saying it was in response to Trump's attacks on several agents and adding, "I urge others to give as well and tweet that you did so to #thanksFBI."[262] Others contributing included Joe Scarborough, a co-host of MSNBC's

---

260   Greg Miller, "CIA veterans who monitored crackdowns abroad see troubling parallels in Trump's handling of protests," *Washington Post*, June 3, 2020, http://www.msn.com/en-us/news/us/cia-veterans-who-monitored-crackdowns-abroad-see-troubling-parallels-in-trumps-handling-of-protests/ar-BB14Wcoi?li=BBnb7Kz&ocid=U453DHP.
261   James Bamford, "Anti-Intelligence: What happens when a president goes to war against his own spies?" *The New Republic*, March 18, 2018, https://newrepublic.com/article/147366/anti-intelligence.
262   Ibid.

Morning Joe program. The association later said it had raised more than $140,000 from 2,000 donors in the course of a month.[263]

Television "news" networks provided paid consulting positions to at least eighteen anti-Trump formers (Table 5-1). Of them, CNN and MSNBC hired fifteen former intelligence officers, all from ODNI, CIA, or FBI.[264] John Brennan became a paid commentator for NBC and MSNBC in early 2018 and used his television access to attack Trump unrelentingly.[265] CNN signed Clapper and Hayden.

In August 2019, CNN hired Andrew McCabe as an on-air contributor.[266] This event was particularly noteworthy because McCabe was fired in March 2018 for lying under oath about his role in leaking information about the FBI inquiry into the Clinton Foundation to the *Wall Street Journal,* and he was still under criminal investigation by the Justice Department for allegedly lying to FBI personnel when CNN hired him.[267] The move seemed to many observers to be a perfect example of press bias against Trump. Senator Josh Hawley (R-MO) tweeted in reaction:

> The guy who DOJ inspector general found committed federal crimes & is a serial liar? Good work, CNN. Love to see that commitment to serious journalism.[268]

263 Ibid.

264 Chuck Ross, "15 Former Spooks Who Work At CNN And MSNBC Now," *Daily Caller,* August 23, 2019, https://dailycaller.com/2019/08/23/cnn-msnbc-15-spooks-mccabe/?utm_source=&utm_medium=email&utm_campaign=9814.

265 Jon Levine, "Ex-CIA Chief John Brennan Signs as MSNBC/NBC Contributor," *The Wrap,* February 2, 2018, https://www.thewrap.com/ex-cia-chief-john-brennan-signs-as-msnbc-nbc-as-contributor/.

266 Jack Crowe, "CNN Hires Fired FBI Deputy Director Andrew McCabe as Contributor," *National Review,* August 23, 2019, https://news.yahoo.com/cnn-hires-fired-fbi-deputy-165743304.html.

267 Philip Ewing, "Justice Department Details Case Against Fired Deputy FBI Director McCabe," *NPR,* April 13, 2018, https://www.npr.org/2018/04/13/602331134/justice-department-details-case-against-fired-deputy-fbi-director-mccabe.

268 Crowe, "CNN Hires Fired FBI Deputy Director Andrew McCabe as Contributor."

TABLE 5-1

Former Intelligence Officers Who Worked for, or Appreciably Contributed to, Media

	FORMER IC AGENCY	CBS	CNN	FOX	MSNBC	NBC	NEW YORK TIMES	WASH POST	COMMENT
JAMES BAKER	FBI		X						Lawyer. Former general counsel of FBI. Attacked Trump for criticizing the Bureau.
JEREMY BASH	CIA				X				Lawyer. CIA chief of staff, 2009-2011. Anti-Trump.
JOHN BRENNAN	CIA				X	X			DCIA 2013-2017. Obama confidant. Signed with NBC February 2018. Virulently anti-Trump.
JOSH CAMPBELL	FBI		X						Former aide to FBI Director Comey.
JAMES CLAPPER	ODNI		X						DNI, 2010-2017. Strongly anti-Trump.
FRANK FIGLIUZZI	FBI				X	X			Career FBI agent. Was chief of counterintelligence, 2011-2012. Worked for General Electric, 2012-2017. Linked Trump to Nazi ideology, August 2019.

	FORMER IC AGENCY	CBS	CNN	FOX	MSNBC	NBC	NEW YORK TIMES	WASH POST	COMMENT
JAMES GAGLIANO	FBI		X						Former FBI special agent. Critic of Comey and McCabe. Generally discussed actual news stories.
STEVEN HALL	CIA		X						Former station chief in Moscow. Fierce Trump critic.
MICHAEL HAYDEN	CIA, NSA		X						Was television regular until he suffered a stroke in late 2018. Harsh Trump critic.
SUSAN HENNESSY	NSA		X						Former NSA attorney. Works at Lawfare blog, Brookings Institution. Born in 1985. No operational intelligence experience. Trump critic.
DANIEL HOFFMAN	CIA			X					Former station chief. Became a Fox contributor in May 2018. Was critical of Trump's critics.
MICHAEL LEITER	ODNI, NCTC					X			Formerly was a national security, counterterrorism, and cyber analyst. Headed NCTC. Trained as a lawyer. Wrote anti-Trump op-eds, contributor to Democrats, per FEC database.

	FORMER IC AGENCY	CBS	CNN	FOX	MSNBC	NBC	NEW YORK TIMES	WASH POST	COMMENT
ANDREW MCCABE	FBI		X						Former deputy FBI director. Under criminal investigation for lying under oath. Has sued President Trump.
JOHN MCLAUGHLIN	CIA				C			C	Former Deputy DCI, chief of analysis directorate.
MICHAEL MORELL	CIA	X					C	C	Joined CBS in January 2014. Regularly contributes newspaper columns. Often commented on real national security issues, not just anti-Trump diatribes. Runs *Intelligence Matters* podcast on CBS, relatively subtle in criticism of Trump.
PHILIP MUDD	CIA, FBI		X						Generally critical of Trump.
MALCOLM NANCE	Navy				X				Former US Navy enlisted man. Pushed anti-Trump conspiracy theories.
ASHA RANGAPPA	FBI		X						Strongly anti-Trump. Was FBI counterintelligence special agent, 2002-2005. Now at Yale University. Evidently no recent experience in IC.

FORMER IC AGENCY	CBS	CNN	FOX	MSNBC	NBC	NEW YORK TIMES	WASH POST	COMMENT
CHUCK ROSENBERG	FBI				X			Former aide to director Comey. Strongly anti-Trump.

LEGEND:
X – paid contributor
C – unpaid, regular contributor
Source: *Author assembly of data from numerous sources.*

Some journalists were unhappy with the way anti-Trump networks collaborated with anti-Trump formers and believed they should not be trusted to speak truthfully about intelligence. Jack Shafer, *Politico*'s senior media writer, assessed the press's relationships with former intelligence officers:

> Like the armchair TV generals who served as network co-anchors during the Iraq War, the spooks occupy a slippery taxonomical journalistic position. They're news sources who go on TV, where they're asked questions by official journalists. But because they draw pay from the networks, they can't really be called sources—the standard U.S. journalistic code prohibits paying sources. Instead, they're called contributors. But that's not a perfect title, either. Standard journalistic contributors—reporters, anchors, editors, producers—pursue the news wherever it goes without fear or favor, as the famous motto puts it. But almost to a one, the TV spooks still identify with their former employers at the CIA, FBI,

DEA, DHS, or other security agencies and remain protective of their institutions. This makes nearly every word that comes out of their mouths suspect. Are they telling God's truth or are they shilling for their former bosses? Or worse yet, do they have other employers (some of the TV generals were also working for defense contractors), causing them to pull punches in yet another direction?[269]

REACTIONS TO THE REACTIONS

While it is clear that most of the overtly anti-Trump formers had partisan associations of varying sorts, and most of the leakers opposed Trump, many former and undoubtedly current intelligence officers were appalled at the politicization, believing it was both incompatible with long-standing norms and broadly damaging. A retired very senior and well-known operations officer said that his continued adherence to the old operations officers' ethic of secrecy precluded even a public statement of his strong disapproval of the commentators, whom he called "talking heads;" even former intelligence officers who run for political office violate the ethic, in his view.[270] One retired CIA analyst who opposed the politicization asked me not to mention her name for fear, she said, evidently only partly in jest, that the Agency would "take away my pension."[271] The few formers who criticized Trump's critics, such as Sam Faddis, Fred Fleitz, and Scott Uehlinger, generally focused on the critical formers'

---

269   Jack Shafer, "The Spies Who Came in to the TV Studio," *Politico*, February 6, 2018, https://www.politico.com/magazine/story/2018/02/06/john-brennan-james-claper-michael-hayden-former-cia-media-216943.
270   Personal communication, September 2019.
271   Personal communication, May 2019.

words and policies while they were in office—especially Brennan—not on defending Trump.

While it is impossible to know the attitudes of all intelligence officers, past and present, on this matter, the large number of current and former intelligence personnel who have described their quiet opposition to me personally, senior formers' occasional references to evidently numerous former colleagues who opposed their actions in communications with them, and the large number of prominent senior former officers who have not spoken publicly on this issue suggest that a "silent majority" of intelligence officers disapproved of political activism by all intelligence officers, independently of their views of Donald Trump as a man and as president. The absence of this group from public discussion skewed the external image of the feelings of intelligence personnel about Trump. Their silence amounted to acquiescence to allowing the critical formers to dominate the discussion. This well-intentioned but ultimately dysfunctional view enabled a relatively small number of vocal formers and leakers to damage the IC by making suspect the objectivity of US intelligence as a whole.

6

Is There an Intelligence "Deep State?"

★

THE EVIDENT ANIMOSITY OF MANY GOVERNMENT officials to him prompted Trump and some of his supporters to assert that a "Deep State" of US government employees was trying to subvert or even to overthrow his administration.[1] The most prominent examples of overt political activism against Trump were in departments and agencies not in the IC, such as the Environmental Protection Agency (EPA). But former intelligence officers and, only a little less obviously, serving personnel acted in ways that generated credible charges that there was an intelligence Deep State opposed to Trump. Some argued that senior FBI officials, including Director Comey and personnel of its counterintelligence division such as Peter Strzok, and DCIA Brennan worked to prevent Trump's election, then tried to engineer his impeachment after his unexpected electoral

1   Alana Abramson, "President Trump's Allies Keep Talking About the 'Deep State.' What's That?," *Time*, March 8, 2017, http://time.com/4692178/donald-trump-deep-state-breitbart-barack-obama/.

success.[2] In different ways, former intelligence officers' public claims of "independence" from the White House and leaks that disparaged Trump, his appointees, and his policies prompted and sustained such beliefs. But other people strongly disagreed, saying conspiracy theorists unfairly misrepresented bureaucrats' apolitical professionalism and that unwarranted criticism of intelligence professionals undermined their performance of vital duties. The issue quickly assumed starkly partisan characteristics. This chapter examines the accuracy of the various claims, first defining "Deep State" and then assessing the competing arguments.

WHAT IS A "DEEP STATE?"

The term "Deep State" has at least two prominent meanings, as well as some variants. First, the term long has referred to elements of governments in countries such as Egypt, Pakistan, Thailand, and Turkey that exert substantial power in opposition to formally empowered government leaders, including democratically elected leaders.[3] Key characteristics of this variety of "Deep State" are: (1) independence, agencies of the Deep State operate arrogantly independently of elected or appointed officials; (2) substantial power accompanied by a willingness to use it to thwart the policies and programs of political leaders they dislike, sometimes including violent attacks on leaders; (3) motives driven primarily by organizational interests but sometimes also the political goals of elements of the bureaucracy; and (4) structure, in the form of an internal organization with leaders, followers, culture, programmatic cohesion, and

---

2   For example, McCarthy, *Ball of Collusion.* Jarrett, *Witch Hunt.*
3   Mérieau, "Thailand's Deep State, Royal Power and the Constitutional Court (1997–2015);" Söyler, "Informal institutions, forms of state and democracy: the Turkish deep state;" Gkotzaridis, "'Who Really Rules this Country?'"

permanence. This form of Deep State usually resides in military and internal security services. Specific characteristics vary across national cases.

Second, aggressive forms of what traditionally has been called the "permanent government" in the United States feature public servants focused mainly on their assigned missions in support of national leaders who also protect and promote organizational interests, often through lobbying for responsibilities and funding and fighting other bureaucratic units over turf and kudos. As discussed in chapter 2, the FBI's J. Edgar Hoover was a long-time master practitioner of this variety of government. He kept files on political leaders and was accused of blackmail in his pursuit of the Bureau's organizational interests—a practice the Bureau now publicly repudiates. Within non-intelligence entities such as the Department of Defense that legitimately enter some public policy debates, bureaucrats act to protect their organizations (and themselves) by questioning the appropriateness of missions assigned, sizes and allocations of budgets, and attribution of kudos for jobs well done. Intelligence agencies generally stay away from publicly entering policy frays, but they quietly fight each other over budgets, turf, and kudos by lobbying Congress and administration officials, and by leaking to the press.

A large literature over the years has documented the existence and roles of the permanent government, including works by Graham Allison and Philip Zelikow,[4] Michael Glennon,[5] and Leslie Gelb and Richard Betts.[6] Samuel Huntington famously argued that "objective control" of the military should give generals and admirals significant control over the day-to-day operations of their organizations, but only under the firm guidance of civilians

---

4   Allison and Zelikow, *Essence of Decision.*
5   Glennon, *National Security and Double Government.*
6   Gelb and Betts, *The Irony of Vietnam.*

concerning major policy issues, including determination of military missions.[7] Considerable day-to-day operational autonomy is not the same as organizational independence.

Other observers, less favorably disposed toward the bureaucracy, see the "permanent government" as more aggressive in defending and advancing bureaucratic and political interests at the expense of taxpayers' monies and the interests of the country in general. For example, former US Representative Jason Chaffetz (R-UT), who once was chairman of the House Committee on Oversight and Government Reform, has argued that the bureaucracy long has been politically active, although not violent or revolutionary in conduct. Chaffetz and others believe it was further empowered and emboldened by President Obama, who relied extensively on executive orders to expand government regulatory powers when Congress thwarted elements of his political agenda. This Deep State, they argue, liked Obama because he gave it welcome new powers and shared its collective ideological leanings. Trump, in contrast, sought to reduce agencies' powers by deregulating the country to some degree, disparaged allegedly dysfunctional aspects of the bureaucracy, and threatened to "drain the swamp" in Washington, meaning he had sharply different views than Obama about the proper role and value of government. A threatened and thereby energized Deep State, they allege, reacted with unusual ferocity to oppose Trump and his policies. Hence, Chaffetz and others differ from the standard "permanent government" school by asserting that the bureaucracy has a stronger ideological agenda that is firmly left-of-center in political orientation and is organized, often through unions that represent federal workers. It willingly, even eagerly, attacks presidential appointees whose policies federal employees do not like. Given their public

---

7   Huntington, *The Soldier and the State.*

commentary, some of the anti-Trump intelligence formers, notably Brennan, Clapper, Comey, and McCabe, appear in some of these narratives.[8] So, too, do the large number of anti-Trump leaks by intelligence personnel.

An even stronger and as yet unproven assertion is that in 2016 a group of Democratic partisans at the FBI and the CIA latched onto inflammatory accusations against Trump prepared for the Hillary Clinton campaign by former British MI-6 officer Christopher Steele to try to help ensure Clinton's election by inaccurately tarring Trump as a compromised tool of the Kremlin and a sexual deviant, among other things. Steele, who as a former employee of a closely allied foreign intelligence service had ties to the CIA and was on the FBI's payroll, reportedly received $168,000 from the Clinton camp for his dossier on issues related to Trump.[9] FBI Director Comey evidently used Steele's allegations to justify opening the Crossfire Hurricane investigation in July 2016 against persons who were tangentially associated with the Trump campaign.[10] Brennan allegedly passed flimsy information from foreign sources to the FBI, and in 2020 DCIA Haspel was accused of collaborating with Brennan's anti-Trump activities while she was chief of station in London and later of preventing declassification of relevant CIA documents.[11] Anti-Trump activists claimed that because minor Trump campaign staffers allegedly were in cahoots with Moscow, these connections showed that Trump personally was deeply involved with the Russians. Leaks and formally released government information insinuating such

---

8 Chaffetz, *The Deep State*, 157 158, 167; Strassel, *Resistance*, 56-57, 64, 87.

9 Jarrett, *Witch Hunt*, 41.

10 Page, *Abuse and Power*.

11 Sean Davis, "Intel Sources: CIA Director Gina Haspel Banking on Trump Loss to Keep Russia Gate Documents Hidden," *The Federalist*, October 5, 2020, https://thefederalist.com/2020/10/05/intel-sources-cia-director-gina-haspel-banking-on-trump-loss-to-keep-russiagate-documents-hidden/.

a connection would, they purportedly hoped, sink the Trump campaign.

When no such connections were found and Trump was elected despite their efforts, the plot allegedly shifted to trying to engineer his removal through a 25th Amendment incapacity finding or discovering or asserting impeachable offenses, including obstruction of justice by opposing their operation within the Justice Department. Comey and McCabe worked via leaks and insinuation to convince Deputy Attorney General Rod Rosenstein to name a special prosecutor to investigate the Trump campaign and Trump himself, with the goal of generating allegations that would lead to Trump's impeachment, conviction, and removal from office. These accusations increasingly come from reputable sources, not just firm Trump supporters with histories of entertaining conspiracy theories.[12]

If anything close to the allegations above are true, the actions would constitute an ambitious, albeit physically non-violent, form of political action against a national leader generally consistent with traditional international variants of Deep State. If even some of the charges are true, Trump's intelligence critics' claims that they were civic-minded patriots trying to alert the public to the dangers of a problematic president would be substantially undercut. But those so accused and anti-Trumpers generally unsurprisingly reject the charges vehemently.[13]

An alternative perception, closely associated with anti-Trump intelligence activists and their supporters but not by most knowledgeable observers of the US government, is that there was no Deep State or even a "permanent government," only dedicated public servants doing their duty in service to the citizenry and the

---

12   Ron Johnson, "An American Coup Attempt," *Wall Street Journal*, October 9, 2020, A15.
13   For example, Strzok, *Compromised*.

Constitution. Government employees who opposed Trump were patriots responding appropriately and bravely to a dire national emergency—the existence of Donald Trump's presidency.

Hence some questions: Do any of these concepts of Deep State, or the absence of one, accurately describe the IC's anti-Trump activities in 2016-2021? Is a Deep State a continuing feature of the IC? Why or why not? If so, where, when, and how was it constructed and what are its key characteristics and implications? Or, was something less traditional in place or under construction? Independent of the still bitterly debated coup plot allegations, I argue that a new form of Deep State developed in parts of the IC before 2016, albeit one that shares some traits with Chaffetz's version of the permanent government. Built to support left-of-center American presidents, it was quiet during the Obama presidency and activated quickly in a publicly obvious way only when a Trump presidency became a serious possibility.

THE CASE FOR AN INTELLIGENCE DEEP STATE

The case for the existence of an intelligence Deep State rests on observable activities and expressions of politically relevant attitudes of current and former intelligence personnel, including arguments by people who try to debunk the Deep State notion. The issue first gained prominence early in the Trump administration when large numbers of State Department and EPA personnel, most prominently, publicly opposed Trump and vowed "Resistance" to him and his policies in terms closely aligned with those of many Democratic Party officials in the immediate wake of Clinton's defeat in November 2016.[14] Some

---

14   Juliet Eilperin, Lisa Rein, and Marc Fisher, "Resistance from within: Federal workers push back against Trump," *Washington Post*, January 31, 2017, https://www.washingtonpost.com/politics/resistance-from-within-federal-workers-push-back-against-trump/2017/01/31/c65b110e-e7cb-11e6-b82f-687d6e6a3e7c_story.html; Strassel, *Resistance*, 132-146.

career civil servants discussed with former Obama administration political appointees what they could do to "push back" against unattractive Trump administration policies. According to the *Washington Post*, some bureaucrats established social media accounts where they could anonymously leak information damaging to the Trump administration.[15] In January 2017 the *Post* reported the views of a serving Justice Department official who opposed Trump:

> "You're going to see the bureaucrats using time to their advantage," said the employee, who spoke on the condition of anonymity for fear of retaliation. Through leaks to news organizations and internal complaints, he said, "people here will resist and push back against orders they find unconscionable."[16]

Consistent with this warning, resistance to the Trump agenda soon appeared in several parts of the executive branch, including the Departments of Justice and Energy. Even the courts seemed to become activist, with district judges issuing unprecedented numbers of injunctions against Trump administration policies.[17] Government employees' widespread opposition to Trump was so significant and vocal that White House press secretary Sean Spicer said the bureaucrats "should either get with the program, or they can go."[18] Such partisan activities were far stronger than those cited in the standard "permanent government" theory of the civil service. The overt political activity of federal workers soon led to a sharp increase in accusations by Trump supporters that an

---

15   Eilperin, Rein, and Fisher, "Resistance from within."
16   Ibid.
17   Strassel, *Resistance*, 147-161.
18   Ibid.

alleged Deep State, belligerently opposed to Trump, had sought to and continued to try to undermine his presidency or to depose him.[19] Trump himself began to use the word "coup" in this context.

While by many accounts the bureaucracy as a whole has long leaned Democratic, there was evidence before the election of things to come.[20] In October 2016, *The Hill* examined presidential election campaign giving of $200 or more by employees of fourteen government agencies, as reported to the Federal Election Commission. Federal employees, who by law may contribute financially to political candidates but cannot work in their campaigns or otherwise engage in partisan political activities, had given nearly $2 million to the major candidates, of which $1,852,881, or 94.2 percent, went to Clinton; $106,586 was donated to the Trump campaign.[21] Agencies commonly cited as hotbeds of anti-Trump feeling unsurprisingly gave larger percentages to Clinton. For example, employees of the Department of State gave 97 percent of their contributions to Clinton. Department of Justice employees gave $286,797 (also 97 percent) to Clinton and $8,756 to Trump.[22] Even Defense Department employees gave Clinton about 84 percent of their contributions.[23] Trump's share of all contributions was considerably smaller than Republican Mitt Romney's share in 2012, which was much less than Obama's take.

Although massive by traditional intelligence standards, initially observable political activism by intelligence officers

---

19   For example, Jody Hice, "The Unraveling of the Deep State's Coup Against President Trump," *Newsweek*, June 10, 2020, https://www.newsweek.com/unraveling-deep-states-coup-against-president-trump-opinion-1503187.

20   While beyond the scope of this discussion, there is much other evidence that the federal workforce as a whole does indeed lean Democratic, including many anecdotes and the strongly and increasingly Democratic voting patterns displayed by jurisdictions in and surrounding Washington, where many federal workers live.

21   Jonathan Swan, "Government workers shun Trump, give big money to Clinton," *The Hill*, October 26, 2016, https://thehill.com/homenews/campaign/302817-government-workers-shun-trump-give-big-money-to-clinton-campaign.

22   Ibid.

23   Ibid.

against Trump was modest compared to employees of some agencies in the sense that no intelligence people staged public anti-Trump rallies or established anti-Trump social media sites. But few senior formers of other agencies assumed prominently critical roles, whereas senior intelligence formers opposing Trump soon became vocal and obvious and the volume and ferocity of anti-Trump commentary and leaks by intelligence people grew markedly in 2017 when new formers Brennan, Clapper, Comey, and McCabe joined the ranks of vociferous critics who the press warmly embraced.

Some of the loud formers, most notably Brennan and Comey, made clear that they did indeed want to wreck the Trump presidency, consistent with strong definitions of "Deep State." Comey admitted that his leaks to the *New York Times* were designed to pressure the Justice Department into naming a special persecutor, whom he hoped would generate an inquiry that would lead to Trump's impeachment and removal from office. Other anti-Trump formers accepted the term "Deep State" and seemed at times to revel in it. Even former Deputy DCI McLaughlin, who previously was relatively restrained linguistically in his criticism of Trump, in November 2019 praised the CIA "whistleblower" who fueled House Democrats' first impeachment of Trump, quipping "Thank God for the Deep State."[24] McLaughlin elaborated:

> "Everyone here has seen this progression of diplomats and intelligence officers and White House people trooping up to Capitol Hill right now and saying they are doing their duty and responding to a higher call,"

24   Ian Schwartz, "Former Acting CIA Director John McLaughlin on Impeachment: 'Thank God For The Deep State,'" *RealClear Politics*, November 1, 2019, https://www.realclearpolitics.com/video/2019/11/01/former_acting_cia_director_john_mclaughlin_on_impeachment_thank_god_for_the_deep_state.html.

McLaughlin said. "It doesn't surprise me — with all of the people who knew what was going on here, it took an intelligence officer to step forward and say something about it, which was the trigger that then unleashed everything else."

"Now why does that happen?" he explained. "I'll tell the American people why that happens. This is the institution in the U.S. government, that with all of its flaws and it makes mistakes, it is institutionally committed to objectivity and telling the truth. It is one of the few institutions in Washington that is not in a chain of command that makes or implements policy. Its whole job is to speak the truth, it's engraved in marble in the lobby."[25]

McLaughlin made clear that he was talking about CIA, not the IC in general. His former agency alone had such independence of spirit and ostensible knowledge of the truth, which made the CIA an especially valuable institution, he asserted, because it marshals truth against bad elected leaders. The biblical verse about truth that is engraved in CIA's foyer reflected its mission and ethos! Looked at differently, McLaughlin implicitly acknowledged that the CIA was a center of anti-Trump activism—a perspective much evidence supports.

McLaughlin's comments and related claims are worth examining in detail. The first and general point he asserted is that CIA is a special, independent organization with a self-perceived obligation to convey, and act in accordance with, the truth it uniquely knows. McLaughlin must have known that many prominent CIA

---

25   Ibid.

people historically have publicly called this view both factually incorrect and arrogant.[26] His comment misrepresented the reason DCI Allen Dulles directed that biblical words be engraved in the wall of the entrance of CIA's headquarters building, then under construction, "And Ye Shall Know the Truth and the Truth Will Make You Free."[27] According to Ray Cline, who headed CIA's analysis directorate at the time (late 1950s) and who interacted regularly with Dulles, the words reflected Dulles's personal, and therefore the CIA's organizational, commitment to battle Soviet disinformation operations globally; it was *not* a reference to domestic US intelligence consumers or a claim that CIA's analyses were especially insightful, let alone always "true."[28]

While the agencies of the IC, like the military services, long have had considerable autonomy in the conduct of most day-to-day operations, their freedom is distinctly limited in many ways, especially concerning domestic operational activities. Historically, the most autonomous agencies have been the CIA and the FBI, which like other agencies report to the president and to Congress in its oversight role, but have considerable freedom to conduct espionage activities and analysis (the CIA), and to conduct counterintelligence and law enforcement activities (the FBI) with minimal oversight. This limited autonomy is designed to protect the objectivity of intelligence analyses and criminal investigations from interference by political leaders or others who might compromise the usefulness of FBI information in court; close oversight of activities in general is designed to ensure that these agencies to do exceed or misuse their authorities. Until recently, the still-extant 1947 National Security Act that requires the CIA to support the NSC, and therefore the president, was

---

26   For example, Davis, "Analytic Professionalism and the Policymaking Process."
27   Cited from John 8:31-32.
28   Cline, *The CIA Under Reagan Bush & Casey*, 175.

not a debatable issue. The DCI was a statutory advisor to the NSC. Period. The FBI under Director Hoover also operated fairly autonomously, and had political goals, but Hoover's political objectives were not overtly partisan and focused on protecting and fostering the FBI's bureaucratic interests. Nor did he claim formal organizational independence or battle presidents personally. Bureaucratic combat centered on rivalries within the bureaucracy and efforts to advance the FBI's parochial interests.

The IC's activities in 2016-2021 were different in several important respects and varied in strength and nature among the agencies. First, some IC agencies' leaders and their advocates claimed that the agencies have, or should have, complete independence from the president. This attitude was especially strong among FBI people. Comey and McCabe asserted repeatedly that the FBI did not have to report to the attorney general or the president, that the Bureau's ability to do its valuable work—protecting the Constitution and the American people—depended on complete independence from the White House.[29] Clapper supported this claim.[30] McCabe asserted repeatedly that the Bureau's altruism made it indispensable and immune from any criticism by responsible people, despite his recognition of repeatedly slow learning, analytical errors, and bias against individuals and other government agencies. Josh Campbell, went further by claiming that:

> [F]ederal law enforcement—charged with enforcing criminal statutes and holding accountable those who violate the law—is not an arm of the executive branch.[31]

---

29   Comey, *A Higher Loyalty*, McCabe, *The Threat*, 137, 204, 261.
30   CNN Wire, "James Clapper: Watergate pales in comparison to Russia probe."
31   Campbell, *Crossfire Hurricane*, 230.

These stunningly inaccurate claims of institutional independence are symptomatic of a Deep State perspective. Peter Strzok also claimed inaccurately that FBI personnel only seek to uphold the Constitution and the rule of law and that Trump acted inappropriately when he fired Comey, McCabe, and indirectly, himself.

The criticisms of Trump, and their rationalizations, coming from the externally-focused intelligence agencies were different. While CIA people, especially, castigated Trump over many issues related to judgments of political philosophy, they typically did not claim organizational independence; they knew they worked for the president. Rather, their demands were indirect appeals for greater operational autonomy from a bad president and unchallenged respect for their work, for their ways of doing things, and for themselves as civil servants; CIA people remained eager to work for "good" presidents—people who agreed with them politically and who permitted them to operate as they wished. As recounted in chapter 2, these are long-standing CIA ambitions that previously were less pronounced. But McLaughlin and others also made a new and strong demand: the IC's judgments and intelligence officers generally must be accepted without criticism or qualification, reflecting the claimed ability of intelligence to consistently divine truth—an ability they asserted Trump obviously did not have. This line of reasoning was prominent over the issue of Russian meddling in the 2016 election but was occasionally evident on other controversial intelligence issues, such as the state of North Korea's nuclear program and the alleged role of Saudi Crown Prince Mohammed bin Salman in the murder of dissident Saudi journalist Jamal Khashoggi.

The claim of truth regarding Russia was especially inappropriate given that the IC was slow to recognize the nature and extent of Russian information operations concerning the

2016 election, which began in 2015 if not before—a widely recognized failing. The IC's overall performance on the election issue amounted to an "intelligence failure," in Michael Morell's reasonable view.[32] Others saying similar things included deputy DCIA David Cohen (2015-2017), former DCIA Leon Panetta, former senior CIA operations officer and then deputy director of the DIA Douglas Wise, then-chief of the DO division following Russia Steven Hall, Clapper, and Hayden.[33] Strzok admitted that he personally, the FBI generally, unnamed IC agencies, and the Obama White House missed the Russian effort for too long.[34] Even Brennan, on whose watch the CIA missed early signs of meddling despite his recognition that Russia had done similar things around the 2008 and 2012 elections, agreed.[35] The IC's ability to discern much (but not all) of the truth of the matter occurred late, and looks good only in comparison to Trump's initial refusal to accept the fact of Russian meddling.

Brennan institutionalized Obama's domestic policies and politics at CIA to a considerable degree when he was DCIA, creating philosophical, organizational cultural, and interest-based reasons for many CIA personnel to operate as de facto staffers of an ideologically motivated Deep State—one that backed like-minded Democrats and opposed differently-minded Republicans. Brennan called on employees to speak out to protect the diversity policies he implemented, to verbally attack even very senior officials with other perspectives if necessary—an intolerant, anti-fa-like attitude.[36] They did so by criticizing Trump and Pompeo for failing to understand CIA's allegedly self-evident need to "look like America," for example. And as a former, Brennan

---

32   Shimer, *Rigged*, 206.
33   Ibid., 146, 155, 167, 206-207. See also McMaster, *Battlegrounds*, 52-53.
34   Strzok, *Compromised*, 136, 176-177.
35   Brennan, *Undaunted*, 359, 363-366, 408.
36   McLaughlin, "More White, More Male, More Jesus;" Ngo, *Unmasked*.

called on serving government employees to refuse presidential orders if Trump acted in ways inconsistent with his views, telling an MSNBC audience that FBI employees should "not follow" presidential orders related to a 2019 Justice Department investigation into whether the FBI, and other IC personnel including himself, acted improperly in prompting or supporting the Mueller probe of Russian connections to the 2016 Trump campaign.[37] Other formers also advocated rebellious, even extra-legal steps in opposition to Trump, including Josh Campbell's call to "action" against Trump. Leakers by definition think they know better than the government what classified material should be released to the public. These attitudes are consistent with traditional definitions of Deep State and Chaffetz's view but differ sharply from the standard "permanent government" notions of Glennon and others. Even Glennon's "Trumanite" leaders do not assert such authority; they seek only to influence government policy-making. The rhetoric used by rebellious formers was consistent with the Democratic Party's formal "Resistance" to Trump and his administration, which explicitly was designed to hobble or, better, overthrow them.

Numerous current and former officials asserted that the main role of the leaders of the intelligence agencies should be to protect their agencies from Trump, a weak variant of the claim of independence. The worry was not over turf or kudos, but instead focused on protection of internal policies, especially at CIA the diversity agenda. This emphasis differed dramatically from the longstanding competition among agencies for the budget largesse of presidents and Congress—a characteristic of the permanent government—and even their historical willingness to attack appointed agency heads they do not like.

---

37   No byline, "Brennan: FBI Officials 'Have an Obligation' to 'Not Follow' Trump's Declassification Order," *Grabien News*, September 18, 2018, https://grabien.com/story.php?id=194013.

Former NIO Paul Pillar said of Haspel at the time of her DCIA confirmation hearings, "Her main priority should be protecting the institution of the CIA."[38] Later, the *Washington Post* quoted a "former senior intelligence official" as similarly saying of Haspel's responsibilities:

> Your first responsibility as director is to protect your organization. With a normal president, there is tremendous upside for the director to be out publicly, talking about what the agency is doing and being transparent with the American people. But this is not a normal president.[39]

Hayden reported that he urged an IC person concerned about Trump to "Protect yourself. Take notes and save them. And, above all, protect the institution."[40] Protecting themselves in these cases meant defending themselves against the president—the person they ostensibly worked hard to support. And Ted Gistaro, Trump's *PDB* briefer in 2016-2019, after Trump criticized him sharply one day, said "I am not working for this president," .... "I'm working for the integrity of the intelligence community."[41] These perspectives go well beyond the bureaucratic self-interest long displayed by the "permanent government" in intramural games against other agencies.

One of the core characteristics of the stereotypical Deep State is its capacity and willingness to fight opponents—literally in ways that sometimes involve lethal violence but also in non-violent political ways. No IC agency had yet engaged in physical

---

38   No byline, "Who is Gina Haspel, Trump's pick to lead the CIA?," *PBS NewsHour*, May 9, 2018, https://www.pbs.org/newshour/politics/who-is-gina-haspel-trumps-pick-to-lead-the-cia.

39   Shane Harris, "How to avoid Trump's ire: CIA chief keeps a low profile," *Washington Post*, July 31, 2019, A1.

40   Hayden, *Assault on Intelligence*, 248.

41   Woodward, *Rage*, 121.

violence against domestic political opponents, but as noted in chapter 2 CIA careerists developed over the years many ways of fighting bureaucratic rivals and political enemies via information operations that were designed to destroy reputations and careers. They developed a reputation for using leaks to damage enemies, sometimes in ways designed to "get even" in political/bureaucratic terms. These sometimes effectively damaged targets' reputations. Conflict between Trump and intelligence officers increased the magnitude and importance of these fights and broadened their scope. Trump was a tougher and more important target than Porter Goss. In addition to his harsh tweets, Brennan in particular developed a reputation for partisan political combativeness, something no previous DCI or DCIA except Hayden has shown. Former UN Ambassador Samantha Power, who worked for Obama when Brennan was DCIA, tweeted crudely but succinctly that it was: "Not a good idea to piss off John Brennan."[42] Brennan clearly had political motives to fight Trump and knowledge about how to do so, although his frequently extreme language and temper tantrums damaged his credibility, and thereby his effectiveness.

Others in the Trump years also recognized CIA persons' occasional propensity for belligerence—reputations that developed long before Trump became a national political figure. For example, Senator Chuck Schumer (D-NY) said in late 2016 that Trump was being "really dumb" for criticizing the IC.[43] He added, "Let me tell you, you take on the intelligence community, they have six ways from Sunday at getting back at you." And Daniel Benjamin,

---

42   Victor Davis Hanson, "Is there a dangerous 'deep state' of unelected—and untouchable—U.S. officials?" *The Mercury*, March 29, 2018, https://www.mercurynews.com/2018/03/29/hanson-is-there-a-dangerous-deep-state-of-unelected-u-s-officials-who-are-untouchable/.

43   Mallory Shelbourne, "Schumer: Trump 'really dumb' for attacking intelligence agencies," *The Hill*, January 3, 2017, https://thehill.com/homenews/administration/312605-schumer-trump-being-really-dumb-by-going-after-intelligence-community.

counterterrorism advisor to Secretary of State Hillary Clinton, similarly said before Trump became president that intelligence officers sometimes take revenge on politicians:

> What [former Deputy CIA Director Michael] Morell and other intelligence veterans are too decorous to mention is that Trump's treatment of his spies will also come back to bite him in the form of leaking and whistleblowing. The intelligence community doesn't leak as much as the Pentagon or Congress, but when its reputation is at stake, it can do so to devastating effect.[44]

And the FBI, which for years in the Hoover era harassed perceived enemies and blackmailed political leaders in pursuit of organizational interests, evidently misused requests for warrants from the Foreign Intelligence Surveillance Court in its ultimately fruitless effort to demonstrate that the Trump campaign colluded with Russia in 2016 and may have gone much further. It surely went to great lengths to pursue, even harass, minor Trump campaign volunteers George Papoudopolis and Carter Page, who previously had business dealings with Russians.[45] Both ultimately were completely cleared of wrongdoing.

COUNTER-ARGUMENTS

Critics of Trump and defenders of the IC against Trump's alleged "assault on intelligence" primarily used elements of four arguments to deny the existence of an intelligence-related Deep State and to make the IC appear to be the victim, not

---

44 Daniel Benjamin, "How Trump's Attacks on U.S. Intelligence Will Come Back to Haunt Him," *Politico*, January 11, 2017, https://www.politico.com/magazine/story/2017/01/how-trumps-attacks-on-us-intelligence-will-come-back-to-haunt-him-214622.

45 For Carter Page's account of his ordeal, see Page, *Abuse and Power*.

the aggressor, in the intelligence-Trump conflict. The easiest claim was that the Deep State charge was a baseless slur, easily dismissed simply because it came from Trump; no elaboration or serious defense was necessary. For example, McCabe defined "Deep State" as "the pejorative term [President Trump] uses to refer to professional public servants who conduct the nation's business without regard to politics."[46] This was an effort to reframe the issue, consistent with the well-known disinformation technique.

Second, they claimed that the characterization was substantively inaccurate because IC agencies' employees were in fact selfless public servants who protected the country by doing their duty, including speaking truth to power. Hayden wrote, "There is no 'deep state' .... There is merely 'the state' [and] career professionals doing their best within the rule of law."[47] They highlighted the accuracy of their belated finding that Russia meddled in the 2016 election, which Trump initially derided as "fake news." These arguments all featured clearly inaccurate assertions that intelligence people consistently perform only superlatively.

Third, critics claimed that the rhetoric against the uniquely troublesome Trump would end promptly when he left office, meaning that it was Trump-specific and hence did not display a core characteristic of Deep States elsewhere—institutional permanence. It implicitly was a spontaneous reaction to Trump; it had no origins other than the Trump candidacy for president, a claim refuted in chapter 3. The argument about the emergence of overt anti-Trump activism came in two varieties. The stronger version, asserted by people such as Ned Price, was that the core norm of apolitical public service remained intact, but the extreme nature of the Trump's evil made action necessary. Because the

---

46   McCabe, *The Threat*, 21.
47   Hayden, *Assault on Intelligence*, 85.

activism was unique to Trump, it *will* disappear promptly and completely when Trump leaves the political scene, he asserted. The second version, usually stated by supporters of Trump's critics but also by John McLaughlin, was that they *hoped* the activism would fade away after Trump left office. The latter view suggested recognition of the possibility of a Deep State—or at minimum a legacy of enduring animosity. No advocate of any variant of this view traced the activism to the policies, statements, or actions of Clapper or Obama. Brennan was mentioned occasionally, as by Cindy Otis.[48]

Fourth, the alleged Deep State was nothing more than a new name for the long-recognized "permanent government." It was normal, nothing to worry about. In some arguments, the IC's activist role was minimized while others recognized that bureaucrats had been modestly political actors in the past.

Some of Trump's critics discussed aspects of the "Deep State" controversy. Of them, Michael Hayden addressed the issue most completely—erroneously but revealingly at the same time. He seemed not to know the standard definition of the term, leading him to reveal that he himself was a member of a Deep State in substance if not in name. After denying there was a Deep State in the IC, he provided much evidence that one, defined traditionally, did exist. Hayden's anecdotes confirmed the existence of a Deep State in terms of both attitudes and behavior, and he made clear that he shared the perspectives and served the interests of a semi-organized community of intelligence officers who opposed Trump.

While recognizing the existence of different perspectives in the IC, Hayden focused on several characteristics common to the CIA, in particular, including a dominant collective worldview,

---

48   Otis, "What Trump did to Brennan recalls authoritarians I studied at the CIA."

an organizational culture, and parochial institutional interests. He wrote, "A lot of the noises in Washington these days are (thankfully) the sounds of American institutions pushing back against a president who routinely sounds authoritarian."[49] Hayden added that the Deep State term "... is not a particularly useful description, frankly one that enhanced rather than dampened internal opposition ..."[50] This is a classic Deep State perspective. An elected leader had failed by not appreciating the concerns and fostering the interests of bureaucrats.

Hayden observed that he and other former senior intelligence officers, including Brennan, Clapper, and McLaughlin for a time appeared so regularly on television criticizing Trump in such similar ways that some people thought they were spokesmen of a unified intelligence Deep State. But he pooh-poohed the idea, saying tangentially that because the talking-heads did not coordinate their comments, it would be an "inefficient" Deep State operation.[51] He then explained why there was no need to coordinate comments; these people had a "common worldview and shared life experiences."[52] Hayden added that the talkative formers and others were worried because Steve Bannon, an early Trump advisor, had called for "deconstruction of the administrative state"—that is, the permanent government and, implicitly, its more politicized elements.[53] Bannon's comment was plainly consistent with Trump's "drain the swamp" rhetoric. Hence, Hayden and the others were protecting both the traditional organizational and the newer ideological interests of the IC's still-developing Deep State. Yet after denying the applicability of the term, Hayden added:

---

49   Hayden, *Assault on Intelligence.*
50   Ibid., 86.
51   Ibid., 247-248.
52   Ibid.
53   Ibid., 84.

> There is no doubt that large bureaucracies are set in
> their ways, and I can aver from personal experience that
> it is hard to get them to change course. But the "deep
> state" calumny is neither accurate nor useful. All it did
> was to harden the lines that presidential transitions are
> designed to soften and eventually merge.[54]

This characterization of the relationship—that it was Trump's
responsibility to make the IC like him—became a common
assertion of Trump's critics. But it is radically different from
the way CIA has long seen its dealings with presidents, as documented by John Helgerson and David Priess. In CIA-centric
discussions that are mild by Hayden's standard, Helgerson's
history of the CIA's relationships with presidents-elect and
Priess's history of the *PDB* make clear that the CIA's leaders
long believed that it was CIA's responsibility—and only CIA's
responsibility—to find ways make its intelligence useful to all
presidents, whatever their quirks may be.[55]

Brennan yet again in May 2019 attacked President Trump
after he gave Attorney General William Barr authority to declassify intelligence information in the context of his investigation into
whether IC agencies acted properly in their 2016 investigation of
possible collusion between Trump's campaign and Russia, which
the Mueller investigation did not find. Said Brennan on MSNBC,
"I see it as a very, very serious and outrageous move on the part
of Mr. Trump, once again, trampling on the statutory authorities
of the Director of National Intelligence and the heads of the
independent intelligence agencies (emphasis added)."[56] Contrary

---

54   Ibid., 88.
55   Helgerson, *Getting to Know the President*. Priess, *The President's Book of Secrets*.
56   Joseph A. Wulfsohn, "Brennan, Clapper lash out at Trump for declassifying 2016
      election intel," *Fox News*, May 25, 2019, https://www.foxnews.com/politics/
      brennan-clapper-trump-declassifying-surveillance.

to Brennan's claim, presidents indisputably have declassification authority and use it periodically when needed for foreign policy or political reasons, sometimes over the objections of intelligence officers legitimately worried about protecting sources and methods.[57]

Brennan's reaction was unsurprising because Barr evidently planned to investigate him, among others, and his words can be seen as a pre-emptive defense against what could have become serious legal proceedings against him. But his use of the term "independent" to describe the intelligence agencies is relevant to the issue of the existence of a Deep State. As he surely knew, the traditions and cultures of all IC agencies are clear that they are *not* independent; they work for the president and they report to Congress as required by law. Nevertheless, as noted, he repeatedly told his employees to sabotage the policies of presidents whose policies differed from those of Obama and himself.

Brennan once claimed that he would stop his attacks on Trump when "integrity" returned to the White House.[58] Perhaps Brennan will reach such a decision one day. But there is not a chance that his definition of integrity matches those of many, probably the great majority of, other people. Brennan gave himself authority to determine when the White House is running properly. This, too, is a Deep State perspective.

---

57 For example, President Kennedy declassified aerial photographs of Soviet facilities in Cuba in 1962, which Ambassador to the United Nations Adlai Stephenson presented to the UN to discredit Moscow's claims that Soviet troops were not in Cuba. In 1986, President Reagan declassified communications intercepts to prove Libyan involvement in the La Belle disco bombing in West Berlin, which killed two American servicemen and precipitated US air strikes on Libya. And President Biden authorized the release of much intelligence information in 2022 to combat Russian disinformation associated with the Russian war against Ukraine.

58 John Brennan, "I will speak out until integrity returns to the White House," *Washington Post*, June 1, 2018, https://www.washingtonpost.com/opinions/john-brennan-i-will-speak-out-until-integrity-returns-to-the-white-house/2018/05/31/afbccafa-64e8-11e8-a69c-b944de66d9e7_story.html?utm_term=.132ce7ddc703.

Critics inevitably asserted, when discussing Trump's appointees to the relatively few formal political positions in the IC, that they were unqualified, were threats to national security, and were "political hacks." Intelligence scholar Loch Johnson, for example, called Mike Pompeo "a highly partisan Tea Party stalwart," clearly a disqualifying description in Johnson's view.[59] And, they went ballistic when officials they liked were relieved. For example, when Trump asked Principal Deputy DNI (PDDNI) Sue Gordon to resign so that he could name retired Navy Vice Admiral Joseph Maguire, then head of NCTC, to be acting DNI, Trump critics were apoplectic, misrepresenting the role and significance of individual intelligence officers. For example, Greg Brower, a former senior FBI official, said Gordon's departure could make the US less safe:

> Her departure is extremely unfortunate for the IC and would suggest a continuing effort on the part of the White House to fill extremely important positions that are supposed to be completely a-political and nonpartisan with people who are simply loyal to the president. ...And that would obviously be a very bad thing for U.S. intelligence operations generally and, more broadly, for the national security of our country.[60]

In fact, such positions are never apolitical or nonpartisan. They are political for a reason: subject to Senate approval, presidents get to pick people they want for senior administration positions including intelligence jobs, not excluding personal friends and

---

59   Gentry, "An INS Special Forum," 11.
60   Betsy Woodruff, "Deputy Intel Chief Sue Gordon Is Out After Trump Snub," *The Daily Beast*, August 8, 2019, https://www.thedailybeast.com/sue-gordon-out-as-deputy-intelligence-director.

political allies, with or without relevant experience. Obama's choice of former Congressman Leon Panetta, an intelligence neophyte, to be DCIA elicited no such negative reactions. And Obama's clear intent to restructure the IC for political reasons met minimal resistance, internally or externally. Once again, the meme: good intelligence is independent of Republicans and Trump was wrong to try to control the IC.

Given the structure of the IC, the ODNI is always in the business of herding agency cats. In the Trump years, as before and since, the agencies from the ODNI perspective were largely autonomous members of the intelligence confederation. Hence, Gordon's departure little affected the day-to-day activities or performance of any individual agency or the IC as a whole.

Another concern cited by one of my contacts, a former intelligence officer, was that the episode indicated that personal loyalty to Trump allegedly mattered more than competence in the job and that the implications of that message for the IC at large were negative.[61] Implicitly, again, intelligence people asserted that they should properly determine who is competent and where loyalties should lie, not the president. But this argument, too, is inconsistent with long-standard American practice.

A better explanation for the outrage, one not publicly presentable, was that Gordon as a loyal Brennanite had protected the politically-oriented personnel policies of the Clapper-Brennan era, still in place, from the externally focused DNI Dan Coats. A new PDDNI and/or DNI, more responsive to White House wishes, *might* have sought to change them.

While their charges and defenses generally are unpersuasive, the IC's defenders were largely correct in one sense. Overt, externally observable criticism of Trump by senior formers and

---

61   Personal communication, August 2020.

leakers diminished considerably soon after he left office and was largely gone by 2022. The obvious explanation is that politically active intelligence officers found a new kindred spirit in President Biden. Obama's vice president was arguably an even stronger proponent of the DEI agenda that so many intelligence people liked than even Obama had been. No longer in need of overt and possibly dangerous activism to protect its institutional and ideological interests, the Deep State returned to its quiescent, pre-2016 posture.

These "defenses" are inconsistent with the notion that the Trump-intelligence conflict was just another of the minor intramural squabbles of the permanent government. Bureaucrats repeatedly over an extended period of time attacked a sitting president for political reasons—a new phenomenon that damaged Trump appreciably. They did not struggle among themselves for influence with senior leaders over kudos, turf, and resources within the boundaries of traditional governmental intercourse. Leaders of the CIA and FBI collaborated in opposing Trump in ways uncommon in the past. Historically, bureaucrats have not challenged presidents on policy issues, committed to anything close to a partisan "Resistance" movement, challenged the legal authorities of any president generally, claimed that they always deserve respect, or claimed independence from the office of the president. Hence, a new self-conception of the roles, duties, and privileges of federal bureaucracy emerged for the first time publicly in the Trump years. Clearly not all intelligence officers have abandoned traditional IC norms, but the number and positions of people who did so created a uniquely American intelligence Deep State that was obvious and important for the first time in US history.

A New Variety of Deep State

The Deep State theories discussed so far, while helpful in some ways, are incorrect in the American context in important respects. There is no Deep State of the sort identified in countries such as Egypt, Pakistan, Thailand, and Turkey, in which well organized groups sometimes employ violence against their political opponents, including national leaders.[62] While Obama, Clapper, and Brennan enhanced left-leaning organizational cultures at the ODNI and CIA, they did not form a dedicated structure that has any degree of permanence. There are no unions or armed militias at the intelligence agencies and organizations like BIG and ANGLE are too narrowly focused on the special interests of small groups to perform a centralizing role. The closest thing to a Deep State structure is the diversity offices, now resident in all IC agencies, which are coordinated by the ODNI's diversity office, promulgate politically salient personnel policies, and enforce them within agencies by punishing managers (and their subordinates) who fail to comply. Like the massive structures at most American universities that advance and defend the special interests of minorities, women, and LGBT persons, they are the custodians and, importantly, enforcers of the now dominant, left-wing DEI orthodoxy, which focuses on personnel management.[63] Hence while, as described in chapter 3, several factors led to the current state of affairs, the primary institutional foundation of the modern intelligence Deep State is Obama's Executive Order 13548 of 2011, which created the diversity offices. Because they were creations of executive orders, the offices' ideological agendas

---

62   Mérieau, "Thailand's Deep State, Royal Power and the Constitutional Court (1997-2015)," 445-466; Park, "Turkey's Deep State," 54-59; Söyler, "Informal institutions, forms of state and democracy: the Turkish deep state," 310-334.
63   Mac Donald, *The Diversity Delusion*; Bloom, *The Closing of the American Mind*.

were in 2017 still susceptible to relatively simple administrative reform—no legislation was needed to revise executive orders and bureaucrats know that presidents frequently change or rescind their predecessors' EOs. As Brennan accurately told his supporters repeatedly in 2016, the "progress" achieved in his years as DCIA through his "diversity and inclusion" policies was reversible—hence the worries about what Trump, his DNIs, and DCIA Pompeo *might* do to them.

Combined with ongoing cultural changes, executives' policies and the diversity and personnel offices helped shape an IC workforce that contains an appreciable but probably unknowable number of people willing as individuals to oppose in various ways perceived threats to their ideological beliefs, parochial interests, and personal concepts of moral obligation, including potential threats from the White House. Activists' beliefs, decreasingly constrained by organizational cultural norms, increasingly permit or encourage federal workers to engage in political activities. Yet even with the diminished norms against politicization and modest American legal sanctions against leaks of classified information, most leakers still, unlike Snowden, prefer anonymity. Hence, there is no organized, recognizable Deep State as traditionally defined, or as defined by antagonists such as Chaffetz, who got the some-time-belligerence of the federal bureaucracy right but focused generally on the federal workforce as a whole and so missed the several IC-specific factors discussed in chapter 3. Moreover, because to an appreciable extent the modern intelligence Deep State was created and maintained by legitimate government leaders—notably Obama, Clapper, and Brennan—for their own political purposes, it differs sharply from those of other countries, which originate within bureaucracies. It also is distinctive in its support for a particularly American brand of left-wing national government that it sees as consistent with its interests.

The activism at the CIA varied by component within the agency. While Brennan's policies were applicable throughout CIA, they evidently took especially strong root in the analysis directorate—people especially attuned to political issues. In contrast, according to some sources, operations officers were less affected for several reasons, including their focus on tactical level, field activities, and their more military-like culture of obeying orders from presidents. The support and science & technology directorates appear to have been even less politically active. While many CIA personnel presumably disliked Trump, they recognized presidential authorities and acted in ways they considered to be important for the national interest—by helping the elected president make better decisions.

Hence, what might be called proto-Deep States exist in parts of the IC—ones that Clapper and Brennan helped create and then supervised. It is limited but is already considerable and deeply entrenched at the CIA, especially. Structures in the form of diversity-advocating personnel offices and senior professional managers, such as Sue Gordon, were committed to their goals and remained in important positions at the ODNI and CIA in the Trump years. Haspel less enthusiastically emphasized Brennan's diversity and inclusion agenda than he did but she packed senior executive suites with women to such an extent that she was said to have formed a "sisterhood" of senior executives.[64] Diversity advocate Carmen Medina incongruously proclaimed her "brave"

---

64   Tom Embury-Dennis, "Women now run top three CIA departments for first time in history," *Independent*, January 6, 2019, https://www.independent.co.uk/news/world/americas/cia-women-gina-haspel-didi-rapp-elizabeth-kimber-dana-meyerriecks-a8714176.html.

for having done so.[65] Others more plausibly suggest chauvinist self-interest was at work. Biden's policies clearly have further advanced Obama's diversity agenda, meaning institutionalization is continuing to occur. Some IC personnel now claim that legislation mandates the activism of the diversity offices.

It is already an unusual "Deep State." Motivated largely by liberal, even left-wing, ideals, it institutionalizes the bureaucratic ascendance at CIA and the ODNI of the constellation of special demographic interests important to the Democratic Party's identity politics. The era of keeping partisan politics out of the IC is over. Politically active components of the IC and support staffs motivated by this agenda—especially the human resources and diversity offices—are able to set and enforce incentives for managers, making support for the agenda personally rewarding and opposition costly. But other agencies seem to be less affected, and FBI activism is evidently driven by a different mix of motives that much more strongly features personal grievances and efforts to ensure organizational interests. Hence, at most, there is a weak IC-wide Deep State, with stronger but smaller agency-specific versions at the CIA and ODNI. Its diffuse nature reduces its strength but also has a major institutional advantage: its rank-and-file members are hard to identify and therefore are also hard to root out.

Because the Deep State's activism is ideologically motivated, it emerges visibly only when presidents or senior IC managers espouse policy positions or political philosophies at odds with those of "progressive" employees whose perceived rights to express their views and to oppose allegedly retrograde senior

---

65   Samantha Mitchell, "More women take top posts at CIA under director Gina Haspel," CBS News, January 7, 2019, https://www.wtsp.com/article/news/politics/more-women-take-top-posts-at-cia-under-director-gina-haspel/67-ec6ce2a6-a658-46d8-9885-31671fb6fa6d.

administration officials now seem to them to be clear. This means the politically-motivated activism that fought Trump recedes when a sympathetic Democrat like Biden occupies the White House. But under Biden the Deep State remains alive and is consolidating although it is quiet and therefore harder to spot from outside the insular intelligence agencies.

As some CIA people note, the culture of apolitical service to presidents and objective analysis is not completely gone, especially among older and more conservative employees. But the evolving IC cultures, variously either little challenged or actively encouraged by agency leaders, make political activism increasingly acceptable and opposition to the new ideology increasingly dangerous. Each passing day without remedial action makes the intelligence Deep State harder to excise. Should a new president or senior IC leader try to do so, the activists virtually certainly will again quickly energize, and treat interloper(s) much like they treated Trump and Pompeo. Its fundamental nature virtually ensures that it will reemerge if/when even a much more conventional Republican than Trump again is president. Leakers will "warn" the world promptly when such a "threat" becomes even a remote possibility. The major politicization of intelligence it fosters has many ramifications, the subject of chapter 7.

1

Implications of the Activism

---★---

EARLIER CHAPTERS ARGUED that a new form of politicization emerged publicly in the US intelligence community
in 2016 and identified some of its causes and forms. This
chapter turns to implications of these changes for national
level decision-making, the IC, and indirectly for the country
as a whole. The activists little discussed this subject, except to
complain about the largely imaginary damage Trump allegedly
inflicted on intelligence. Trump's intelligence critics, and people
sympathetic to them, also tended to believe the activism was a
Trump-era phenomenon, created by him, that would quickly
fade away when he left the White House, leaving little or no
significant, long-lasting impact on intelligence and none on
national-level decision-making.

In contrast, many knowledgeable observers of US intelligence
during the Trump years, critics of the critics, and more politically
conservative people believed and still believe the consequences
of the politicization are serious, negative, and enduring. Earlier
chapters documented the pre-Trump origins of the IC's opposition

to him. Hence, in this view, the Trump-IC conflict is part of a much larger, enduring situation. Intelligence officers who told me they considered even public statements about the activism to be inappropriate political activity, given historical intelligence norms, usually also worried that the activism damaged their agencies bureaucratically. A retired senior CIA manager of analysts put the widely held view well:

> I am one of those who believe that there is no place for the IC or its people in the public arena. I am especially unconvinced that success as an intelligence officer/ analyst can serve to validate an individual's thoughts and preferences on debated societal issues.[1]

I outline here the two general perspectives in more detail, note variations in each, and assess them. In sum, the skeptical case is far stronger on both logical and evidentiary grounds. As I write in early 2023 two years have passed since Trump left office; we can test many but still not all prognostications for intelligence life after Trump.

THE MINIMALIST POSITION

If there was one central belief of the anti-Trump activists, it was that Trump was such a uniquely bad person that all good people were authorized, even morally obliged, to oppose him. Intelligence officers, as self-evidently good people, appropriately responded to the challenge. When Trump leaves the political scene, this reasoning went, the IC will return to its traditional apolitical stance, providing "truth" to appreciative presidents who do not damage the IC by unfairly criticizing

---

1   Personal communication, August 2020.

it, or criticizing it at all. The activists will not have caused any damage, although Trump's nefarious "assault on intelligence" generally, and on some activists such as Brennan by name, may have caused some lasting damage to IC persons' morale and agency reputations. Variants of this argument featured differences about the speed of the IC's return to normal activities—immediately or a little longer—and whether there would be enduring consequences—none or maybe some. Many of the activist formers who discussed this issue held this view even though they recognized that substantial numbers of their former colleagues retained the apolitical ethics of old and wished the activists had not spoken out. Some, including Clapper, Hayden, and Josh Campbell, pointedly rejected such concerns, usually acknowledging respect for their former co-workers but asserting a moral obligation to speak out, to call for action against the undeniably obvious evils of Trump. Brennan ignored this issue in his memoir while reminding readers that he remained determined to attack Trump in the future as he alone would determine.[2]

Ned Price, a strong and sometimes inaccurate critic of Trump who thought about the implications of the actions of people he called "rogue formers," meaning people such as Brennan who linked their intelligence credentials to their criticisms of Trump, thought the Trump era of political activism by intelligence officers was unique. It was, he said in 2019, the "singular result of a singular president."[3] No one, he asserted, suppressed the IC like Trump. Had the Republican nominee in 2016 been Marco Rubio or Jeb Bush, there would have been no outburst. Asked in a different way later in our conversation, Price said he "might be Pollyannaish," but if the Republican candidate had been Mitt

2   Brennan, *Undaunted*, 410.
3   Author discussion with Ned Price, July 30, 2019.

Romney, there would not have been any of this activism. When a mainstream Republican or a Democrat assumes the presidency, the stridency of recent years will disappear, Price asserted. He hoped the practice of formers using their intelligence backgrounds to legitimize criticisms of politicians also would disappear. He saw what he called the "nexus to intelligence" of the critics of Trump throughout society as "a problem." But he offered no explanation of this "nexus" or a solution. He did not assess implications of the problem.

Retired senior CIA analyst Bruce Riedel in September 2019 said he thought the IC-presidential relationship would return to normal when, as he expected, a Democrat became president in 2021.[4] The IC would appreciate a return to a normal NSC-led decision-making process that used intelligence in structured ways. The "us against them" mentality of intelligence officers then would disappear, he asserted. A President Joe Biden, experienced in the Obama White House, would do things normally. Riedel said he thought the only possible exception to this scenario might be a President Bernie Sanders because many intelligence officers knew that Sanders remained a big fan of the Soviet Union, which would concern intelligence officers who knew the USSR's dismal history. Of course, Sanders did not win the Democrats' 2020 presidential nomination. The generally well-informed Riedel did not seem to recognize that Trump's NSC staff processes operated largely as other recent presidents' have, his sometimes mercurial decision-making notwithstanding.[5] Obama's interagency processes were widely seen in Washington as unusually longwinded and inefficient.

---

4   Author discussion with Bruce Riedel, September 12, 2019.
5   See books by two of Trump's national security advisors: McMaster, *Battlegrounds* and Bolton, *The Room Where It Happened.*

A prominent academic student of intelligence wrote to me, expressing somewhat different thoughts:

> The politicization that has occurred with respect to White House/intel relations really is appalling and thank goodness that some insiders have been willing to complain about this publicly. I think this will end with a new administration, that is, I think it is Trump-centric. After all, the intel agencies are fiercely defensive against politicization (most of the time), plus they have friends on the Hill ... who can be supportive of their integrity. The damage will not be long-term; the agencies are resilient and will shoulder their way through this storm. When the White House bends the facts, there remain many fact-defenders in the IC, on the Hill, in academe, and in the media—the glory of the American system.[6]

This prognosis extolled as glorious the very elements of American society—Congress, the academy, and the press—that became most politicized in opposition to Trump in alliance with activist formers. Universities and the press, especially, were prominently politicized well before Trump arrived on the national political stage. This assessment is hard to take seriously.

Others less confidently *hoped* normalcy would return without appreciable, enduring effects, but were less certain this would happen. John McLaughlin wrote to me, talking about the senior activist formers:

> When things return to normal we'll step back and not be heard from much. We know this runs the risk that

---

6   Personal email, August 12, 2019.

many people will not trust the neutrality of intelligence officers, but I hope ... that this will not be so.[7]

A prominent academic, a former CIA officer who is an avowed but low-key Democrat strongly opposed to Trump and who sometimes writes on intelligence topics, similarly said in 2019 he "hoped" the effects of the Trump-era conflict would quickly fade, but was not sure they would.[8] He did not speculate about implications if the episode did not recede completely, but his facial expressions during our conversation led me to believe he had appreciable worries.

Another former CIA analyst who also is now a prominent scholar (and an avowed Democrat) in 2019 assessed the long-term implications of the activism.[9] He said its future depends on the future of the Republican Party. If it remains the party of Trump, IC activism will remain, he forecast. If a mainstream Republican becomes president, even a conservative who many intelligence officers do not personally like, the activism will recede. He cited Senator Ted Cruz as an example, and backed his assessment with reporting that DCIA Mike Pompeo was respected at CIA even though he too was a conservative Republican, because he studied intelligence and worked hard. Hayden and Bruce Riedel also praised Pompeo for working hard to learn about intelligence—a view many younger, serving CIA officers who focused primarily on Pompeo's views on social issues clearly did not share.[10] But mainstream Republicans will remember the Trump era and may not trust intelligence, the professor suspected. He saw little danger that analysis would be biased during the next Democratic

---

7   John McLaughlin email to author, July 30, 2019.
8   Discussion with author, July 17, 2019.
9   Personal discussion, July 2019.
10   Hayden, *Assault on Intelligence*, 92.

administration. He thought the norm of analytic objectivity would remain strong and analysts would be objective in providing intelligence support even to Democrats they like, thereby rejecting Sherman Kent's worry about biases that spring from intelligence getting "too close" to policymaking.

A retired senior CIA analyst who retains close ties to many CIA people also said he hoped the IC-Trump situation would pass, based on his belief that Trump was the cause of the problem.[11] He asserted that CIA personnel still largely retained the agency's traditional apolitical ethos—a more reasonable judgment at the time he retired (before 2016) than after Trump's arrival in Washington.

Other anti-Trump people saw negative consequences restricted to fairly narrow arenas—mainly caused by Trump alone. For example, asked when and how this would end and whether the IC-White House rift could be healed, former C/NIC Greg Treverton wrote in 2019:

> The current administration will end, though after how much damage to constitutional order remains in question. In the normal course of American politics, it will be followed by a swing to the left, and a foul-mouthed narcissist will be replaced by a more decent person, one who realizes that those 80,000 professionals in the U.S. Intelligence Community work for the nation, not for an administration or political view. Politics will seem more normal, and those patriots will feel less urgency in breaking a lifetime of silence on "political" issues. There will be less risk that young people will shun careers in intelligence, asking themselves why they

---

11   Personal conversation, September 5, 2019.

should pay the costs—in money and lifestyle—only to be dissed by their commander-in-chief.

Yet damage will endure. Our political dialogue has been debased, and that will not go away. It is driven by the polarized anger of our politics, which Trump dramatically exacerbated but did not cause. The great irony of the information technology revolution is that all those wonderful devices intended to connect people have so far sorted them into echo chambers where their views are only reinforced. That seems likely to get worse as, for instance, end-to-end encryption makes it easier for people to hide in those like-minded echo chambers. Perhaps "civil political discourse" is an oxymoron. It will, in any case, be so for us as far as the eye can see.

The still greater damage is the assault on truth. The National Intelligence Council, which I had the honor to chair in the Obama administration, takes bed and board from the CIA. Whenever a car took me downtown for a meeting, I would ask to meet it outside the front door of the old CIA headquarters building, with the grand marble lobby and big CIA seal in the floor. It was light and airy but also reminded me of the business I was in. I always smiled, though, at the quote from John 8:32 etched into the wall: "Ye shall know the truth, and the truth shall set you free." Perhaps divine truth is absolute but intelligence truth is not. It is the best we mortals can do, often under intense time pressure. And sometimes it is, as they say, "good enough for government work." In my experience, moreover, intelligence truth was more likely to constrain—identifying all the reasons a policy-maker's favorite idea wouldn't work—than to set free.[12]

Treverton elaborated in an email:

> With a more normal administration and a president who isn't a terminal narcissist, I think the rift can be healed. So far as I can tell, this administration has no process, and so restoring the vitality of the NSC policy committees would help. My concern is long-term recruitment: intelligence officers pay a price in money and life style for serving their country. It's one thing to do that if your work is appreciated and making a difference, but quite another when the commander in chief is constantly dissing you, saying you are running amok or need to go back to school. Who would serve in those conditions?[13]

Treverton's worries about recruiting were misplaced. In fact, according to a CIA public affairs officer in July 2019, the number of applications the agency then was processing remained high.[14] And, different CIA recruiters told me in March 2019 and February 2020 that the CIA continued to receive large numbers applications from high-quality applicants.

Also apparently misplaced were worries about morale and attrition. A common complaint of critics was that Trump so damaged IC morale that the workforce was leaving in volumes sufficient to degrade the quality of the workforce. Hayden wrote of his concerns in this area and Morell repeatedly cited in his

---

12 Gentry, "An INS Special Forum," 14-15.
13 Treverton email to author, August 1, 2019.
14 CIA briefing to annuitants and their families, July 25, 2019.

public statements the concerns of employees with whom he was in contact.[15] The CIA, however, debunked this notion, too. In its annual briefing to annuitants and their families in 2019 at CIA headquarters, a public affairs spokesperson reported that "morale here is very good," and cited attrition figures as evidence. She reported that while annual attrition rates for most government agencies were in the 15- to 20-percent range, at CIA it then was 4 percent, with three of those percentage points reflecting retirements.[16] Hence, she argued, there was no loss of mission focus during the Trump years.

The senior formers (and their backers) frequently defended their actions by appealing to the constitutional right of citizens to speak their minds, implicitly arguing that the right obviates the possibility of, and responsibility for, damage to the IC or the country.[17] Former senior ODNI official Mark Lowenthal put the case more strongly than most:

> But having never given up any of our Constitutional rights, and as citizens of the Republic, do we not have a right—once retired—to speak out?
>
> Some of my colleagues, as well as some outside critics, would say, "No." Some have argued that we owe the president "loyalty." Here I disagree. I am loyal to the Constitution. I carry a copy of the Constitution with me, along with a quote from Representative Barbara Jordan, which she stated at the outset of the Watergate

---

15   Hayden, *Assault on Intelligence*, 143. See also Michael Morell comments, George Mason University, Hayden Center, podcast, January 26, 2021, https://youtu.be/d_jgMYBGRkI, minute 25.

16   Unclassified briefing at CIA headquarters, July 25, 2019.

17   Gentry, "An INS Special Forum," 3, 11.

hearings: "My faith in the Constitution is whole, it is complete, it is total. I am not going to sit here and be an idle spectator to the diminution, the subversion, the destruction of the Constitution."

As intelligence officers have made public statements and signed letters (I signed the letter protesting the decision to lift John Brennan's clearances), I have seen something of a cleavage between civil and military intelligence officers. The cleavage is not absolute but, on the whole, retired senior military intelligence officers appear to have been more reticent about criticizing President Trump. The military oath differs from the civil oath. Military personnel also swear to obey the orders of the president and officers appointed by him.

But neither group takes an oath of loyalty to the president. The very concept reminds me of the Fuhrer oath taken by the German military, pledging "unconditional obedience" to Adolf Hitler. I assume this is not what my colleagues mean when they talk of loyalty to the president. In US usage, such a concept simply does not exist.[18]

Lowenthal added:

Speaking out entails risks. It can look self-serving and may be so to a degree. Several historical figures have asked the same question: "If not us, then who?" There has already been discernible damage to US intelligence

---

18   Ibid., 11-12.

since 2017. If veteran intelligence officers do not speak up and alert Congress and the public, what can we expect at the end? We are being true to our oath, to our duty and to our professional responsibility—to warn. But we must do so in a way that builds support without sinking to the level of our harsh and often uninformed critics.[19]

But Trump critics' rhetoric often sank to levels akin to Trump's. Most prominent among Trump's harsh, impetuous, and sometimes uninformed critics, but not alone, was John Brennan. Literally all of the anti-Trump people with whom I conversed who mentioned Brennan said he had damaged their cause. And none of Trump's intelligence critics addressed the question of whether it was *appropriate* for senior formers to engage in partisan politics even if it was constitutionally permitted.[20]

In sum, Trump critics typically argued that the costs were manageable, surely were justifiable, were likely to be temporary in nature, and were disproportionately and inappropriately borne by intelligence agencies and personnel as a result of unreasonable presidential attacks. Intelligence therefore needed protection. Intelligence scholar Loch Johnson made the latter point more strongly than most:

It will be important, too, for lawmakers, the courts, scholars, and the American people to stand guard against the unfair castigation of the nation's security agencies and the dangerous dismissal of their thoughtful reports.[21]

---

19   Ibid., 12.
20   Gentry, "Trump-Era Politicization,"
21   Gentry, "An INS Special Forum," 11.

While some of these arguments were insightful, many others were questionable on grounds of logic, the well-established histories of intelligence-presidential relations, and the increasingly evident decay of the IC's once deeply-held norms of apolitical behavior by intelligence officers. In general, Trump's critics did not accurately identify the causes or implications of their activism.

THE "COSTS WILL BE GREATER" ARGUMENTS

In sharp contrast, many observers, including long-time students of intelligence and current and former intelligence officers, were (and remain) concerned about negative implications of the Trump-IC conflict for the usefulness of intelligence to decision-makers. Even some Democrats saw long-term damage of several sorts that was caused mainly by the activists, not Trump. These prominently featured worry that intelligence analyses would become, or will be perceived to have become, tainted with ideological or partisan biases and that intelligence would become less trusted by consumers as a result. Intelligence therefore will be used less, policy decisions will be less well informed, avoidable policy errors will increase in number and significance, and national security therefore might be endangered. This concern reflected the view that despite its occasional failings, intelligence usually helps improve senior-level decision-making, a widely-held and uncontroversial belief.

This worry clearly also reflected concern that the controversies damaged the parochial interests of the intelligence agencies. There is little reason to fund an intelligence service that leaders do not trust or use. In this view, the activist formers who ostensibly defended the agencies actually harmed them. There have been no politicization-related cuts in intelligence budgets yet, however.

Trump asked for large sums in each of his budget submissions to Congress and President Biden's fiscal year 2023 request for the National Intelligence Program was $67.1 billion, up $4.8 billion from what Congress allocated for fiscal year 2022.[22]

Philip Zelikow of the University of Virginia, who knows intelligence well, was a policymaker and a Republican Never Trumper, in late 2019 thought the impact would be modest if the issue of the possible politicization of analysis is perceived to be one of "atmospherics."[23] He noted that "experienced policymakers often know a fair amount about how the [intelligence] sausage is made," and focus instead on the "authors and content of specific product."[24] I suspect Zelikow would be right if in fact intelligence consumers focus on the intelligence analyses and the persons who wrote them. But many intelligence products no longer have authors' names on them, and all go through agency review processes, which often change analysts' original drafts considerably. Moreover, it is always hard to tell whether intelligence analyses that focus on the future will eventually be seen as insightful or weak because of analysts' unfortunate choices of data, biases, bad judgment, or genuinely unforeseeable circumstances. Hence, agency reputations matter. The politics of senior formers (such as Brennan) who chose the leaders now reviewing products also may make many intelligence consumers suspicious. There is no easy way to check objectivity, and a questionable reputation in intelligence, as broadly in life, once made is likely to be enduring.

Robert Jervis, a keen observer of intelligence, in 2019 asked rhetorically if the then-current situation was "reversible."[25] He

---

22   ODNI, "U.S. Intelligence Community Budget, https://www.dni.gov/index.php/what-we-do/ic-budget#:~:text=U.S.%20INTELLIGENCE%20COMMUNITY%20BUDGET%20%20%20%20Fis.
23   Zelikow email to author, September 17, 2019.
24   Ibid.
25   Gentry, "An INS Special Forum," 9.

wrote that he expected the situation to "return to something closer to the previous normal" when Trump left office, arguing that the personalities of successors in the White House and in leadership positions of the IC would be major factors.[26] But he anticipated some long-term negative implications of the activism:

> Although we cannot measure the size of the effects, they are surely malign. The American public and perhaps interested audiences abroad who give some credit to Trump's opinions will come to doubt not only the competence but also the integrity of the IC; the attacks by former IC leaders will reinforce the impression that intelligence cannot be separated from politics.[27]

A long-time student of the effects of worldviews on the objectivity of analysis, Jervis worried most about the impact on analysis and its reception by consumers:

> Perhaps more important is the question of how the current controversies have affected IC analysis. Here the problem in answering is not that the question is speculative, but that we lack access to relevant evidence, which is the intelligence that is being produced. My sense from talking to an admittedly small number of analysts is that the impact is slight. Politicization is always a danger, but the physical isolation of CIA and the strong sense of professionalization provide at least some degree of insulation. Furthermore, to the extent that analysts' liberal biases and reinforcing opposition to the rhetoric and policies of the president are operating,

26   Ibid.
27   Ibid.

they would be met with counter-pressure against producing papers that fly in the face of administration policies.[28]

We have few examples of the causes, nature, and effects of Obama-era politicization, but David Muller, the retired Navy intelligence officer who worked at NCTC in 2009-2014, provided a useful case study of how President Obama's views of Islam altered the way the IC in general viewed, and may continue to view, Islamist terrorism and demographic diversity in the IC in the pre-Trump era. Appreciable American attention to the connection between Islam and terrorism directed against the United States began soon after the 9/11 attacks. President George W. Bush appeared to link Islam in general to terrorism, a view that quickly offended people who saw most Muslims as peaceable people. Recognizing his misstep, Bush thereafter sharply distinguished Islam from Islamist terrorism. According to Muller, NCTC analysts generally viewed this perspective as reasonable and Bush was popular at NCTC.[29]

The IC's perspectives on terrorism changed appreciably, however, when Obama took office. Obama was much less concerned than Bush about terrorism, and he called Islam-motivated terrorism "violent extremism," effectively denying that Islam motivated groups such as al-Qaeda. Even DNI Clapper, who bought Obama's diversity and inclusion agenda wholeheartedly, wrote that Obama refused to use the term "radical Islam."[30] Muller recounted an episode in which several CIA analysts talked to a

---

28   Ibid.
29   Author discussion with David Muller, July 11, 2019. Former CIA officials generally agree that Bush was well regarded at Langley. One former senior official told me that Bush was much more impressive in personal dealing with intelligence issues than in his public appearances.
30   Clapper, *Facts and Fears*, 336-337.

group of about 100 people at an NCTC location, mainly NCTC analysts, using words that closely mimicked Obama White House language on terrorism.[31] (Later DCIA John Brennan was Obama's counterterrorism advisor at this time.) Muller believed the NCTC group was overwhelmingly unimpressed by the CIA presentation. Several people in the audience asked pointed questions and expressed disagreement with the presenters.

Muller said that at about the same time as the CIA briefing, M. Javed A. was appointed to manage the NCTC office charged with overseeing and coordinating the counterterrorism intelligence programs of all federal agencies. A practicing Muslim, Javed expressed pleasure about how he had excised Islam from training courses at the FBI, where he previously worked, and he said he planned to do the same in the ODNI and in the IC generally.[32] Javed went to Obama's NSC staff after he left ODNI.

Muller noted the incongruity of Obama's and Javed's views of the Islamic world. The overwhelming majority of terrorism in the world was then (and remains) motivated and/or justified by interpretations of the Koran. There would not have been an NCTC if not for Islamist terrorism. In our discussion, Muller argued that banning Islam as an analytic variable in terrorism analyses was akin to discussing World War II and the Holocaust without assessing the impact of Nazi Party ideology and Hitler's *Mein Kampf* on Germany's foreign policies in 1933-1945. The IC might have accepted that the connection between Islam and terrorism is politically sensitive and been careful in wording its analyses, as Bush belatedly tried to be, but it did not have to accept a near-ban on considering Islam when analyzing terrorism. Former FBI official William Gawthrop has made similar points,

---

31   Author discussion with David Muller, July 11, 2019.
32   Ibid.

observing that U.S. government officials have many vulnerabilities to misrepresentations of Islam.[33]

Muller concluded that what he called Obama's Islamophilia was largely accepted in the IC, creating a worldview-driven bias in analysis of an issue of national and global importance. In his last years in office, Obama proposed that the Census Bureau create a new minority group called MENA—for Middle East and North Africa—that would include people from the mainly Muslim countries from Morocco to Iran.[34] This move, not completed before he left office and then stopped by the Trump administration, would have specified another demographic group meriting the special preferences of identity politics by the government as a whole. It presumably would have created another "employee resource group" that the IC would have had to cater to, further Balkanizing the workforce.

Hence, Obama's views about Islam may have affected organizational cultures as well as analysis. Obama's view of Islam evidently contributed the associated idea that "diversity is a good thing," which played a major role in the IC outbursts of 2016 in opposition to Trump's proposal to restrict immigration from several predominantly Muslim countries. This occurred even though the countries were hotbeds of terrorist activity and Islamist radical groups were then well known to use refugee flows to infiltrate fighters into target countries.[35] DCIA Brennan agreed with Obama in this arena, too. He told a reporter in 2017:

> Over the last couple years, we really tried to make a real effort to have the Muslims within the CIA workforce feel that they were as special and as valued and important as everyone else. Too often, there has been

---

33   Gawthrop, *The Criminal Investigator-Intelligence Analysts Handbook of Islam*, especially 92-104.

34   Gonzales, *The Plot to Change America*, 77-94.

35   For example, Wege, "The Changing Islamic State Intelligence Apparatus," 278.

unfortunate rhetoric that has been the equivalent of Muslim-bashing. A lot of employees took that rather personally.[36]

One impact of the sort Jervis worried about that almost certainly occurred was that CIA analysts' "liberal biases" pushed publication on subjects President Trump was sensitive about, especially Russian meddling in American elections."[37] Trump like all presidents had his biases and blind spots, but intelligence exacerbated the problem by persistently pushing its variety of Truth regarding Russian meddling in the 2016 election at him. The issue boiled into the public again in mid-2020 in a different way when US intelligence learned that Russian military intelligence, the GRU, may have paid bounties to Afghan Taliban fighters for killing American soldiers. But NSA and CIA disagreed about the evidence, and there is no (public) evidence that American soldiers were harmed as a result of this "program." The White House vehemently denied that the story had appeared in the *PDB*.[38] Trump, yet again displaying distrust of the IC, called the story a "hoax."[39] Undeterred, the *New York Times* printed an op-ed by Douglas London, the retired CIA operations officer who was a Middle Eastern specialist, claiming that Trump knew about Russian activities in Afghanistan but shockingly did nothing about them.[40] Yet this issue was a tempest in a teapot. Of course Russia helped the Taliban kill American soldiers in Afghanistan

---

36   Jenna McLaughlin, "More White, More Male, More Jesus: CIA Employees Fear Pompeo Is Quietly Killing the Agency's Diversity Mandate," *Foreign Policy*, September 7, 2017, https://foreignpolicy.com/2017/09/08/more-white-more-male-more-jesus-cia-employees-fear-pompeo-is-quietly-killing-the-agencys-diversity-mandate/.

37   Dustin Volz and Warren P. Stroubal, "Clash Quiets Spies," *Wall Street Journal*, July 6, 2020, A4.

38   Gordon Lubold and Warren P. Stroubal, "NSA Differed From CIA on Russia Bounty Intelligence," *Wall Street Journal*, July 1, 2020, A3.

39   Volz and Stroubal, "Clash Quiets Spies."

40   Douglas London, "I Was a Counterterrorism Chief. Trump Knew What Russia Was Doing.," *New York Times*, July 12, 2020, https://www.nytimes.com/2020/07/12/opinion/trump-russia-bounties.html.

in recent years, as the Soviets did in Vietnam. The United States reciprocated in Afghanistan in the 1980s and in Ukraine in 2022.

Self-censorship, or "politicization by omission," also has a long history. For example, NIC chairs have reported that they avoided doing NIEs on sensitive subjects because they or the White House worried that the NIEs would leak. Former C/NIC Joseph Nye (1993-1994) restricted distribution of sensitive NIEs for this reason.[41] And former C/NIC Thomas Fingar (2005-2008) believed there was a danger that analysts would pull punches on controversial issues if they believed analyses would be either declassified or leaked.[42]

This kind of politicization by omission may have occurred in the Trump years for three reasons. First, for traditional reasons, some intelligence officers may not have wanted to needlessly or excessively irritate Trump about issues on which he had formed firm judgments even as others pushed Russia stories, Jervis's "counter-pressure" reason. *PDB* briefers reportedly told *Time* that they had been directed to avoid issues about which Trump had publicly expressed opinions.[43] Douglas London complained about such "counter-pressure" while ignoring Jervis's other concerns.[44] Second, the White House may have told the agencies not to address some issues because officials believed that intelligence officers or the HPSCI would leak analyses seen as damaging to the White House, C/NIC Nye's reason. Third, intelligence officers may have chosen to skip writing on subjects they believed might support administration policies they did not like—a variant of Vietnam-era politicization.[45]

---

41   Nye, "Estimative Intelligence after the Cold War, 1993-1994," 37.
42   Fingar, "New Missions, New Challenges, 2005-2008," 144-145.
43   John Walcott, "'Willful Ignorance.' Inside President Trump's Troubled Intelligence Briefings," *Time*, February 5, 2019, https://time.com/5518947/donald-trump-intelligence-briefings-national-security/.
44   London, *The Recruiter*, 396.
45   Gentry, *Lost Promise*, 33.

Jervis was also right that the impact on analysis of changing organizational worldviews is not yet clear, although Muller's example gives us some hints and polling data about the impact of universities' use of "critical" theories to indoctrinate young minds suggest that effects may be significant. If, as seems evident, the collective worldviews of some parts of the IC have moved appreciably further leftward in traditional political terms, then the literature on the impact of worldview on intelligence biases—and intelligence failures—may become more salient. Jervis, other academics, practitioners such as C/NIC John Gannon, Hayden, and even Brennan repeatedly have observed that analytic units tend to get stuck on positions that lead them to analytic errors, including warning failures. It takes little imagination to suspect that increasingly politicized organizational cultures, engineered by Obama's appointees and left largely untouched by Trump's, are likely to have generated biased analyses. This probably will continue to be a problem because the Biden administration has made no evident effort to address politicization issues anywhere in the IC, and Biden enthusiastically resumed the social engineering efforts of the Obama years on the federal workforce. The risk of politicized analysis seems likely to have grown exponentially, not linearly, because institutional biases become more pronounced as the number of people willing or able to provide reasonable alternative views during drafting and review processes diminishes and views that run counter to increasingly doctrinaire notions of truth are less likely to prevail or even to be offered for consideration.

As Jervis noted, these biases surely exist. A small social science literature has documented the intellectual costs to research in scholarly fields whose practitioners lack *intellectual* diversity— something very different than the demographic diversity that so concerned Obama, Clapper, and Brennan, and later Biden.

The lessons of this literature apply to the IC. For example, in 1994 Philip Tetlock identified ways in which the moral-political values of researchers led to unjustified conclusions about nuclear deterrence—a major intelligence issue during the Cold War.[46] Later, Tetlock and several colleagues argued that the dominance of political liberals in their discipline, social psychology, and the lack of political conservatives therein, had damaged their discipline in ways that also can damage intelligence analysis. They made three important points:

1. "Liberal values and assumptions can become embedded into theory and method."[47] That is, political values misidentified as objective observations can become part of research questions and acceptable analytic methods, and objective truth as traditionally defined that deviates from ideological values can be regarded as error.

2. "Researchers may concentrate on topics that validate the liberal progress narrative and avoid topics that contest the narrative."[48] Although the NIPF identifies general topics of concern to policymakers, intelligence agencies retain considerable latitude to pick aspects of the topics for analysis, to shape how they frame intelligence questions, to decide how they reach conclusions, and to decide levels of confidence in their judgments. Gaps caused by focus on topics that primarily interest political liberals may mislead intelligence consumers about the actual state of the

---

46 Tetlock, "Political psychology or politicized psychology," 510-512.
47 Duarte, et al., "Political diversity will improve social psychology," 4.
48 Ibid., 5.

world and contribute to warning failures. The IC's current, controversial faith that demographic diversity improves its operational performance is likely to continue to inhibit investigation of assertions that the faith is unwarranted.[49]

3. "Negative attitudes towards conservatives can produce a psychological science that mischaracterizes their traits and attributes."[50] This seems to apply directly to Trump bashers' often extreme perceptions of the alleged deficiencies Trump and Republicans generally, and the selective use of truth in their attacks on both.

Some journalists and critical observers of the media make similar points about liberal bias in journalism that are directly comparable to ways the worldviews of intelligence analytic organizations affect "reporting" in politically significant ways. As recalled, former CBS television reporter Bernard Goldberg observed that mainstream media personnel in the United States are decidedly liberal in political outlook but typically do not realize that they are politically left-of-center. They are insular, interacting mainly among themselves, seeing each other as mainstream and normal while people who do not agree with them are, mostly, right-wing nuts.[51] This kind of organizational culture establishes priority topics to report and defines the truth and value of the stories, sometimes unconsciously. *Wall Street Journal* columnist Kimberley Strassel made the same points in only slightly different

---

49   Gentry, "Demographic Diversity."
50   Duarte, et al., "Political diversity will improve social psychology," 6.
51   Goldberg, *Bias.*

terms.[52] As *Washington Post* reporter Deborah Howell said, "Journalism naturally draws liberals; we like to change the world."[53] Such people cannot be politically neutral observers, their standard claims to the contrary notwithstanding. These observations are especially relevant to US intelligence because survey research in the IC indicates that analysts in recent years have seen themselves doing work closer to that of journalists than of scholars or other professionals and young people increasingly see political activism as attractive.[54]

Many government people, too, like to "change the world." As Nicholas Dujmović noted, Brennan created at the CIA a form of ideology-driven "soft totalitarianism," enforced by the diversity offices, which focused on advancing "progress" in the social arenas he embraced. Brennan and Clapper talked often about their determination to make politically salient changes in the IC's organizational cultures that would institutionalize the "progress." Biden's DCIA, William Burns, has followed suit. He touted CIA's adherence to President Biden's "diversity, equity, and inclusion" policies in a speech at Georgia Tech on April 14, 2022.[55] And in an email message to all CIA retirees on June 22, 2022, Burns wrote:

> Nothing is higher on my list of priorities than shaping a strong, healthy, diverse workforce. … I'm also pleased with the progress we're making on building a more diverse and inclusive CIA, although we still have a ways to go. So far in FY22, we're on pace to match or exceed the CIA's highest ever percentage of minority

---

52   Strassel, *Resistance*, 206-207, 212.
53   As quoted in Groseclose, *Left Turn*, 115.
54   Johnston, *Analytic Culture in the U.S. Intelligence Community*, Marrin, "Evaluating the Quality of Intelligence Analysis."
55   CIA, "Director Burns' Remarks at Georgia Tech," April 14, 2022, https://www.cia.gov/stories/story/director-burns-georgia-tech-remarks-2022/.

hires. Just as importantly, we're making clear that there's a pathway to the top for officers who merit it, whatever their background. During the annual SIS promotion ceremony a few weeks ago, I inducted the most diverse class in the Agency's seventy-five year history into our senior ranks. It was a profound reminder of how far we have come, and also a reminder of all the hard work ahead of us.[56]

Burns re-confirmed his woke credentials in late-July 2022 by sending a stern warning to *all* CIA employees globally that racism and racist symbols would not be tolerated at the agency after what *might* have been a noose was found *near* a small clandestine CIA facility in Virginia shared with businesses and other, unidentified organizations that presumably do not know of the CIA's presence.[57] A CIA connection to the putative "noose" was never established. It therefore is unsurprising that Biden's leaders of the IC, convinced that personnel policies consistent with Democratic "values" are indisputably good, evidently have not tried to assess the magnitude and significance of any systematic changes in worldview-influenced biases of recent years on intelligence analyses.

UCLA political science professor Tim Groseclose has identified ways that worldview-driven biases affect journalists' choices of topics to report and the treatment of the topics.[58] Groseclose argued that worldviews affect media stories in several related ways, which he described in his "distortion theory," which measures political bias defined as divergence from mainstream

56   https://mail.google.com/mail/u/0/#inbox/
       FMfcgzGpGdftvRMszZFmXTVsdNRGdzst.
57   Julian E. Barnes and Adam Goldman, "C.I.A. Director Issues Warning After
       Possible Noose Is Found Near Facility," *New York Times*, July 18, 2022, https://
       www.nytimes.com/2022/07/18/us/politics/cia-noose-racism.html.
58   Groseclose, *Left Turn*.

coverage of issues.[59] These biases lead readers to see the world in different, politically significant, and measurable ways. While he discussed these biases in the context of newspaper and television reporting, his points apply to the intelligence analytical process of identifying issues of importance for US policymakers and crafting current intelligence, especially. Ways of influencing the slant of stories that contain only accurate facts include:

- *Choice of topic* to cover. There are lots of "news" items in the world. Choices about topics to cover reflect political judgments about what is important.
- *Choice of facts* to report. Selectivity in choices of "true" facts to report can significantly alter the meaning of an analysis. Not all facts can be reported. Decisions about which facts are important can radically alter the analytic slant and meaning of a story.
- *Choice of sources* to cite. There often are many sources applicable to intelligence "stories," too. Choices of sources to reference may skew the direction and credibility of analyses and change relative emphases.
- *Choice of words* to use. Events and meanings of them can be conveyed in many ways. Political and ideological perspectives often determine word choices. Words that slant meanings can be blatant or subtle. Chinese communist use of the pejorative term "capitalist running dogs" arguably is of the former category. In slightly more subtle contemporary American usage, people who came to the United States in unconventional ways are frequently known as either "illegal aliens" or "undocumented persons."

---

59   Ibid., 63-77.

The choice of terms conveys approval or not of the people and their status.

Groseclose offered a useful metaphor in the context of the "truth to power" sloganeering of anti-Trump activists. Journalists, he observed, ostensibly shine light on the topics they cover, but political biases put the light generated through ideology-based prisms, coloring reporting and analysis, and implicitly variants of "truth."[60]

All of these points are relevant to the basic issue of trust between intelligence professionals and senior consumers, especially presidents. While mutual trust is highly desirable, the importance of the halves of mutual trust are not close to equal. Intelligence needs presidents, while presidents can and sometimes do ignore intelligence. As noted, a large literature makes clear that presidents will not use intelligence if they do not trust intelligence officers individually or the institutions for which they work.[61] Former national security advisor John Bolton, in his memoir, argued that when Brennan was DCIA the CIA became more politicized than at any previous time in its history; he received intelligence from the agency Brennan had left two years before.[62] According to Bolton, Trump became unhappy with intelligence in general after multiple published leaks unfavorable to him were attributed to intelligence personnel, including to his personal briefers.[63] Bob Woodward reported, evidently based on interviews with former DNI Dan Coats, that the Trump-Coats relationship frayed badly after Coats reacted negatively to the White House announcement in July 2018 that Trump would

---

60   Groseclose, *Left Turn*, 68.
61   Gentry, "An INS Special Forum," 15.
62   Bolton, *The Room Where It Happened*, 224.
63   Ibid.

host a visit by Putin, and then deteriorated further over several issues, including the FBI's investigation of Trump's connections to Russia.[64] It thus is no wonder Trump took fewer briefings than *some* of his predecessors, and that none of them except perhaps Nixon had as enduringly negative a relationship with the IC as Trump did. Trump reportedly fired acting DNI Joseph Maguire in February 2020 because he believed intelligence officers had given Democrats political ammunition to fire at him concerning Russia during the 2020 presidential campaign, a plausible suspicion given the extent of anti-Trump activism.[65] As noted, similar presidential thoughts reportedly occurred in 1960 and 2004 but they were not, apparently, historically common.

More generally, if intelligence becomes chronically distrusted, it has no reason to exist. Rightly or not, it is beyond doubt that many people, presumably mainly Republicans, now distrust US intelligence. It matters not that the activists who generated the distrust may be, and I presume are, a small share of the intelligence workforce. Consumers cannot know as they read each intelligence report whether they are getting objective analyses or are being misled in an important way, perhaps unintentionally due to a culture-driven worldview among intelligence analysts and their managers. To apply a metaphor, it takes only a small amount of oil to make much larger volumes of water undrinkable.

But contrary to the "assault on intelligence" meme of some critics, Trump continued to receive intelligence briefings regularly (if relatively infrequently compared to Obama and George W. Bush) and evidently judged most of their content to be helpful. That is, to the end he seemed to trust intelligence to at least some degree. He did not wholly reject intelligence and intelligence personnel, a real possibility if he had come to fully distrust his

---

64   Woodward, *Rage*, 115-122.
65   Shane Harris, Ellen Nakashima, and Josh Dawsey, "DNI's ouster has intelligence community lying low," *Washington Post*, February 23, 2020, A4.

senior intelligence advisors, something that would not have been a surprise given some intelligence officers' behavior. It also would not have been surprising if Trump sent all intelligence people on rotational assignments to the White House and the NSC staff back to their home agencies as a legacy of the CIA "whistleblower" episode of 2019 or excluded them from discussion of sensitive issues they once would have joined. But he did not. He could have done both easily, without Congressional interference, thereby limiting the ability of intelligence to support national decision-making.

Politicization of intelligence, however generated, damages the credibility, the perceived trustworthiness, and thereby the value of US intelligence. Widespread belief that worldview-influenced errors may be increasing will do the same. Former NSA officer Dan Gressang summarized the impact of the intelligence-Trump conflict on trust, putting blame on both parties:

> I think that trust relationship has suffered, and I suspect it will take considerable time, regardless of the party in the White House and in control of Congress, to reestablish it. President Trump continues to undermine confidence in Intelligence Community production, and that has a negative impact on how other senior level consumers perceive intelligence. At the same time, the activism of IC formers has contributed to that level of distrust and lost confidence.[66]

Michael Rubin of the American Enterprise Institute made a similar point, but laid more blame on the formers:

> While I share Brennan's concerns about many of

---

66   Gressang email to author, July 28, 2019.

Trump's policies, and the manner in which Trump treats the institution of the presidency, Brennan's partisan broadsides do more damage to the intelligence community than Trump. They reinforce all of Trump's suspicions about the partisan nature of the CIA and the inability of its employees to separate personal political leanings and policy preferences from analysis.[67]

Consistent with Rubin's perspective, a former CIA analyst wrote to me after reading one of my articles: "Trump exposed the latent tendencies in the IC leadership, which, selectively, speaks truth to power. I don't think they realize how much credibility has been lost with the public."[68]

Many others, including most conservatives interviewed for this book, see the trust-related implications as dire, widespread, and enduring. One observer whose personal politics I do not know wrote: "The hyper-politicization of the IC should have a devastating effect on public trust in government."[69] In other words, the negative effects will spread to confidence in the government as a whole. This is a credible hypothesis that may yet turn out to be accurate, but sparse polling data indicate that public confidence in the IC remains fairly strong.[70]

The hypothesis already has been supported by the ignominious demise of President Biden's U.S. Disinformation Governance Board, which collapsed in May 2022, soon after it was launched. The Board ostensibly was designed to advise the Department of Homeland Security about misinformation- and

---

67 Michael Rubin, "John Brennan and his defenders do more damage to the intelligence community than Trump," *Washington Examiner*, August 22, 2018, http://www.aei.org/publication/john-brennan-and-his-defenders-do-more-damage-to-the-intelligence-community-than-trump/.
68 Personal communication, September 2021.
69 Personal communication, August 1, 2019.
70 Gentry, "An INS Special Forum," 16.

disinformation-related security threats to the homeland originating both at home and abroad. But its appointed head, Nina Jankowicz was herself accused of political bias in favor of the Democratic Party. Initial reactions, especially but not exclusively from Republicans, about the trustworthiness of the Board were therefore severely negative. Some compared the Board to the "Ministry of Truth," the disinformation and history-rewriting element of the totalitarian state in George Orwell's novel *1984*, which reflected his aversion to Stalin's Soviet Union.[71] In my conversations with astute people, there was widespread agreement from both the political Left and Right that the U.S. government in 2022 could not be trusted to adjudicate competing claims of truth. Not completely irrelevant to the performance of the modern America press, Orwell wrote that a slogan of the ruling party was: "Who controls the past controls the future; who controls the present controls the past."[72] Many people clearly also do not want the likes of Jankowicz to be controlling popular perceptions of the present.

Some anti-Trump formers have the trust issue exactly backward. For example, former CIA chief counsel Jeffrey Smith (1995-1996), a regular Trump critic and serial contributor to Democratic candidates, per FEC data, in January 2017 claimed explicitly that it was Trump's duty to earn the trust of intelligence officers.[73] Others have claimed as much less pointedly. It is hard to believe that Smith and other Trump bashers really believe such claims, which are more useful for misleading the public, most of

---

71   Aaron Blake, "The tempest over DHS's Disinformation Governance Board," *Washington Post*, April 28, 2022, https://www.msn.com/en-us/news/politics/the-tempest-over-dhs-s-disinformation-governance-board/ar-AAWKIqX.

72   Orwell, *1984*, 33.

73   Judy Woodruff, "Why trust is essential between the president and the intelligence community," *PBS News Hour*, January 4, 2017, https://www.pbs.org/newshour/show/trust-essential-president-intelligence-community.

whom have modest knowledge of the actual workings and history of intelligence.

The effects of the controversy go beyond those directly affecting White House-intelligence interactions. Retired senior CIA operations officer Daniel Hoffman, who worked Russian issues for many years, asserted that Brennan's incendiary attacks on Trump played into the hands of Russian President Putin.[74] Hoffman argued that Putin, like his Soviet predecessors, worked to sow dissension in the United States, and Putin's intelligence officers purposefully left a traceable trail of Russian connections to the Trump campaign, which they hoped would generate politically important, partisan attacks on Trump.[75] He argued that Brennan, who should have known better, fell into the trap, embroiling US intelligence in domestic American politics, thereby damaging a major operational adversary of Russian intelligence as well as the American body politic—and producing a Russian intelligence success.[76] Hoffman and others noted that it was senior former Russian intelligence officers who gave Christopher Steele the "salacious," never-verified information about Trump that Steele included in his 2016 dossier.[77] The SSCI also speculated in 2020 that the Steele dossier that seemed so attractive to anti-Trump intelligence officers may have contained Russian disinformation.[78] Former national security advisor H.R. McMaster in 2020 stated

---

74   Daniel Hoffman, "Ex-CIA Chief Brennan's Broadsides Against Trump Only Help Putin," *The Cipher Brief*, April 5, 2018, https://www.thecipherbrief.com/column_article/ex-cia-chief-brennans-broadsides-trump-help-putin.

75   For the same point in detail, see McMaster, *Battlegrounds*, 48-53.

76   Daniel Hoffman, "What was Brennan thinking by running with 'bad information' on collusion?" *Fox News*, April 5, 2019, https://www.foxnews.com/opinion/daniel-hoffman-what-was-brennan-thinking-by-running-with-bad-information-on-collusion.

77   McCarthy, *Ball of Collusion*, 168-169.

78   Dustin Volz and Alan Cullison, "Senate Panel's Russia Report Finds Fault With FBI's Handling of 2016 Election Probes," *Wall Street Journal*, August 19, 2020, https://www.wsj.com/articles/senate-panels-russia-report-finds-fault-with-fbis-handling-of-2016-election-probes-11597872094.

as much explicitly.[79] The idea that the Russians were trying mainly to generate discord in America is consistent with Thomas Rid's argument that Russian and even Soviet active measures still are influential in the United States and with James Simon's similar view that Soviet and Russian active measures affected political aspects of US intelligence agencies' cultures.[80] Former senior Romanian intelligence officer Ion Mihai Pacepa has made similar points.[81] Hoffman's hypothesis is ironic given that Brennan and many other critics of the president claimed repeatedly that they were smart enough to have identified the Truth that Trump was a Russian agent of influence.[82] They, it now seems probable, were the actual but still-oblivious Russian dupes.

Others also see the politicization as a symptom of bigger issues, meaning that the legacy of the IC-Trump conflict, even with Trump's tenure lasting only four years, will be enduring. For example, Columbia University professor Richard Betts predicted that if societal polarization continues, so will politicization in the IC.[83] Hence, conflict with another Republican president, or with Trump if he is again even a serious contender for the Republican nomination, will recur. But it will not with Democratic presidents whose political views more closely match those of most intelligence personnel and who give intelligence officers the autonomy they crave. In these cases, the Kentian worry will return to the fore—concerns about intelligence politicizing by getting "too close" to policy-making, as Hayden and David Muller believe it did in the Obama years. And, as Nicholas Dujmović has argued,

79   McMaster, *Battlegrounds*, 52.
80   Thomas Rid's history of Soviet and Russian active measures provides considerable support for this hypothesis. See Rid, *Active Measures*; Gentry, "Belated Success."
81   Pacepa and Rychlak, *Disinformation*, 309, 315, 333, 352.
82   Dylan Scott, "Former CIA director: Trump-Putin press conference 'nothing short of treasonous,'" *Vox*, July 16, 2018, https://www.vox.com/world/2018/7/16/17576804/trump-putin-meeting-john-brennan-tweet-treasonous.
83   Ibid., 4.

Deep State conspiracy theories will remain popular if objectivity is not perceived to have returned to the IC—which is likely to be a lengthy process under the best of circumstances.[84] The relative silence of Trump's vocal critics since early 2021, and strong Biden administration DEI policies that clearly are politically motivated and continue to squelch internal introspection, suggest that these arguments have much merit.

Robert Jervis saw an enduring legacy of the CIA "whistleblower" incident of 2019. This event will surely be remembered for a very long time because it led directly to the rare impeachment of a president. Contrary to the view of John McLaughlin, who praised the whistleblowers, Jervis had a distinctly negative view:

> The future of relations between the IC and not only this administration but subsequent ones is likely to be affected by the fallout from the charges by the whistleblower about Trump's policy toward Ukraine and the handling of the relevant documents. At minimum, it will complicate the lives of analysts working on Ukraine and Russia. Writing papers on how leaders of both countries see the United States and how they are likely to react to various events will be challenging, to say the least. The other side of this coin is that this administration, if not later ones, may be even more hesitant to share with intelligence the information that is needed for sensible analysis, especially when it deals with American policy toward that country and what American leaders have conveyed to their opposite numbers.[85]

The task for current policy-makers and IC leaders is to

---

84 Ibid., 6.
85 Ibid., 9.

limit the further deterioration of relations. Continuing on the current trajectory would mean that policy would be even less informed by intelligence than is usually the case. A new administration will have a new start but it will inherit the legacies of heightened political conflict. One danger is that the IC will take any critical scrutiny as an attempt at censorship; another is that policy-makers will be quick to take intelligence indicating that their preferred policies will not work as political sabotage. These thoughts can never be banished (and indeed may have some validity), and dealing with them will take mutual attention, patience, and understanding if the country is not to suffer.[86]

There may be partisan "payback." Retired CIA operations officer Sam Faddis, a rare Trump backer among intelligence officers who was twice an unsuccessful Republican candidate for public office in Maryland, made the point bluntly: "No way in hell is it going to go away."[87] Contrary to the assertions and hopes of Trump's intelligence critics, he said, Trump's supporters will not forget or forgive the actions of the anti-Trump intelligence activists. The techniques intelligence personnel used against Trump are likely to be used against Democratic presidents, Faddis said. The type and magnitude of any such activity remain to be seen.

As Mark Lowenthal observed especially clearly, the senior formers' frequent assertion that their constitutional rights as citizens to speak their minds were paramount implicitly amounted to a claim that their civic activism was cost-free.[88] The claim also appealed to an irrelevancy. The right of free speech in this context was never in question. What was and remains at issue is whether

---

86 Ibid.
87 Author telephone conversation with Sam Faddis, September 18, 2019.
88 Gentry, "An INS Special Forum," 3, 11.

professional norms condone such behavior and whether the polit-icization of intelligence is good for presidential decision-making, the bureaucratic interests of the agencies, and the country as a whole. As noted in chapter 2, for many years the strongly held CIA norm was for senior formers to avoid commentary about all domestic political issues, let alone engage in partisan advocacy. The large literature on civil-military relations similarly strongly disapproves of such activities by former military officers, as most of the formers surely knew, meaning they had a strong vested interest in distinguishing intelligence officers from military personnel, thereby minimizing the relevance of the civil-military relations literature for their activism.[89] This claim helped the activist formers rationalize their actions to themselves, but it is not convincing.

Contrary to Lowenthal's assertion, the rights and roles of former senior military and intelligence officers are similar, and the consequences of their political activism are also similar, a point made by historian of intelligence Michael Warner.[90] Intelligence officers, like soldiers, obey lawful presidential orders, sometimes use violence, work to further foreign policy goals, go in harm's way, operate in secretive ways, and usually enhance national security. Failures of the operations of each may embarrass presidents. Hence, military personnel long have recognized that discussing issues that may be seen as critical of their commander-in-chief is not good for themselves as individuals, the military services, or the country.

Peter Usowski, the director of CIA's Center for the Study of Intelligence, made a similar point delicately in an article that addressed the issue of former intelligence officers writing in the public domain:

---

89 For example, Feaver, *Armed Servants.*
90 Warner, "The Use and Abuse of Intelligence in the Public Square," 16.

The more controversial writings of the formers were those that crossed over into the political arena. Those who wrote these pieces emphasized that they were not speaking as government officials but as private citizens, who do not live in isolation from national and international developments, and that they were merely exercising the freedoms allowed by having transitioned from government service into life as private citizens.

Readers, however, may not always be able easily to distinguish between the former senior government intelligence official and the private citizen. It is, after all, because of their previous service that their writings are published and receive attention. Thus, there are political consequences when formers publicly enter political debates. As noted earlier, the objectivity of senior CIA leaders and the agency itself can come under scrutiny.[91]

Because the surge in political activism by intelligence officers in 2016 led some observers to compare it, and standards for judging it, to the generally accepted roles of current and former US military personnel, it is worth reviewing the norms of conduct for military personnel related to political activities. This is a very different discussion than the well-established norms of appropriate conduct of intelligence "producer-consumer relations," which developed in an era when there was no doubt that intelligence served presidents in clearly subordinate, supporting roles. While there are some differences in the situations of military personnel and intelligence officers, similarities are much more compelling. Yet, no anti-Trump former mentioned the large, closely related, and well-known civil-military relations literature, I presume because they knew there was no way such a comparison could be

---

91   Usowski, "Former CIA Officers Writings," 11-12.

favorable to them. When I debated US Army veteran and former NIO Paul Pillar about the politicization of the IC at a Council on Foreign Relations session in February 2020, he rejected my application of lessons of the civil-military literature to the IC.

By longstanding tradition, serving US military personnel do not take public political stances and they do not challenge presidential decisions, directly or via leaks. General George Marshall famously did not vote—an extreme and unnecessary way to maintain one's distance from partisan politics. Military people, like all American citizens in good standing, are encouraged to vote. But in American history presidents periodically have relieved military officers for challenging significant foreign and security policies or criticizing political leaders. For example, in 1951 President Truman fired General Douglas MacArthur over what he considered to be MacArthur's insubordination concerning Korean War policy.[92] President Carter relieved General John Singlaub in 1977 for publicly challenging Carter's decision to reduce US troop strength in South Korea. And in 2011 President Obama relieved General Stanley McChrystal from his command in Afghanistan for his ostensibly private, negative comments about administration personalities and policies that later were published in a magazine.[93] The fact that soldiers indisputably work for presidents and the prominent firings of officers who challenged this hierarchy lead most serving military officers to rely on retirees, who are beyond most administrative sanctions, to publicize their political views or to lobby for budget increases or increased benefits, for example. Retired officers also sometimes address defense and

---

92   Rogg, "The U.S. Intelligence Community's 'MacArthur Moment.'"
93   Michael Hastings, "The Runaway General: The Profile That Brought Down McChrystal," *Rolling Stone*, June 22, 2010, https://www.rollingstone.com/politics/news/the-runaway-general-2010622.

foreign policy issues as expert commentators—generally without becoming politically partisan. Occasionally senior officers endorse a political candidate, which raises-eyebrows, but they typically do not chronically criticize candidates or sitting presidents, or use their military careers to rationalize their partisanship, as some former intelligence officers have done since 2016.

Jeff Rogg has argued that the IC in the Trump era had an extended "MacArthur Moment"—a reference to General MacArthur's public challenge to President Truman's policies in his farewell speech to Congress in 1951, an affront to the constitutional status of the president as commander-in-chief.[94] The original "Moment" stimulated development of a clear understanding within the US military that such behavior is inappropriate. The IC had not in 2016 learned the lessons the military knew because, as Rogg argued, there had not, until 2016, been such a massive, extended "moment" of evident insubordination.

Retired intelligence officers perform functions and engage in activities similar to those of retired military officers. Formers discuss international affairs analytically. They complain about budget cuts and lobby for intelligence officers to receive more respect. Former intelligence officers also are conduits for leakers, not normally a military concern. They perform these functions during interviews with the press and by writing memoirs.

Former intelligence people also enter politics as candidates for elective office, necessarily in most cases becoming associated with a political party. In recent years there has been an increase in such activity by former CIA officers, especially, who won three congressional seats in 2018: Will Hurd (R-TX); Elissa Slotkin (D-MI), and Abigail Spanberger (D-VA). Slotkin and Spanberger

---

94   Rogg, "The U.S. Intelligence Community's 'MacArthur Moment.'"

ran for Congress for the first time in 2018. All three naturally discussed national politics, including President Trump, but as candidates they represented themselves, communicating their own positions and running against opponents who were not named Trump. Hurd did not run for re-election in 2020. Slotkin and Spanberger were reelected in 2020 and 2022. Former CIA operations officer Valerie Plame ran unsuccessfully for Congress in New Mexico in 2020; she was defeated in the Democratic primary.

Anti-Trump political activity by intelligence officers was distinctive in that formers and the media that sponsored them made clear that the formers' association with intelligence legitimized their attacks on Trump's personal characteristics and political philosophy. Recall Michael Morell's claim of August 2016, which was repeated by other formers in various forms and was the rationale the press used to pay the formers to criticize Trump on a wide range of issues:

> My training as an intelligence officer taught me to call it as I see it. This is what I did for the C.I.A. This is what I am doing now. Our nation will be much safer with Hillary Clinton as president.[95]

This claim is similar to arguments that senior military officers occasionally make—that their professional credentials qualify them to make national-level political-military decisions—a claim universally rejected in Western democratic states.[96] This is the attitude that got General MacArthur fired.

The credentials issue is more important than usually noted in one respect: very senior former intelligence officers who retain security clearances have access to serving intelligence officers,

95   Michael J. Morell, "I Ran the C.I.A. Now I am Endorsing Hillary Clinton, *New York Times*, August 5, 2016, https://www.nytimes.com/2016/08/05/opinion/campaign-stops/i-ran-the-cia-now-im-endorsing-hillary-clinton.html.
96   See, for example, Cohen, *Supreme Command*.

receive periodic intelligence briefings, and sometimes consult with current agency leaders, meaning they are not really "former" intelligence officers at all. As advisors, they retain limited roles as occasionally active participants in the intelligence business. This makes the "first amendment rights" of "private citizen" argument that senior formers can speak politically at will without consequences both inapplicable and wrong. The claim that Trump's threat to revoke Brennan's clearance was an inappropriate effort to "stifle free speech" was also incorrect.[97] Some senior formers were in essence part-time government employees who criticized a president in partisan terms—a very different activity that arguably was a Hatch Act violation. The US government explicitly treats government employees and government contractors differently than fully former officers—people whose connections to the government consist at maximum of receiving pension checks and paying taxes. According to a senior official with knowledge of such matters, agency directors and some deputy directors retain clearances for varying periods of time, depending on current leaders' policies.[98] If this information is correct, prominent Trump critics who retained clearances, access to sensitive information, and access to serving officers in secure spaces in the Trump years may have included Brennan, Clapper, Hayden, McLaughlin, and Morell.

Brennan reported in his memoir that as a former he had a CIA badge and went to CIA "facilities" whenever he wanted, "more than a dozen times" by the April 2020 completion of his book draft.[99] He attended retirement ceremonies and unspecified

---

97   Dan Balz, "Former intelligence officers bite back after Trump goes after Brennan's clearance," *Washington Post*, August 18, 2018, https://www.washingtonpost.com/politics/former-intelligence-officials-bite-back-after-trump-goes-after-brennans-clearance/2018/08/18/91efe7a0-a255-11e8-8e87-c869fe70a721_story.html?utm_term=.1b7ddf1586a7.

98   Personal communication, July 2020. CIA's Public Affairs Office did not answer my request for clarification of this issue, made in July 2020.

99   Brennan, *Undaunted*, 406-407.

"nonsubstantive" meetings to which he was invited. Such access gave Brennan opportunities to listen to, and talk at, CIA people who could speak freely to him without security concerns. Morell has made clear in his podcasts that he, too, as a former retained access to inside information. For example, he noted that he knew who President Biden's primary *PDB* briefer would be several days before the ODNI announced the appointment of Morgan Muir, a decision soon thereafter changed.[100] Hayden commented similarly. People who are wholly "private citizens" cannot do such things or have such knowledge.

An intriguing comparison between military and intelligence people concerns the extent of their comments about President Trump and reactions to them. In general, former senior military officers avoided commenting about Trump's character—a marked contrast to the comments of critical intelligence formers. And, while intelligence formers received considerable support for their rights to speak even from formers who disagreed with their views, retired Navy Admiral William McRaven, a career SEAL, was not so fortunate. In 2017, McRaven began to criticize Trump for his negative comments about government institutions. In May 2019, he called Trump, not terrorism, the greatest threat to US national security.[101] A few days later, McRaven acknowledged that friends in the military had criticized his actions, but he said he had

---

100 For example, George Mason University, Hayden Center, podcast, January 26, 2021, https://youtu.be/d_jgMYBGRkI. For the announcement of Muir's appointment, see Julian E. Barnes and Adam Goldman, "Veteran C.I.A. Officer, Who Previously Briefed George W. Bush, to Lead Biden Intelligence Sessions, *New York Times*, January 29, 2021, https://www-nytimes-com.cdn.ampproject. org/c/s/www.nytimes.com/2021/01/29/us/politics/biden-intelligence-briefings-morgan-muir.amp.html.
101 Susan Page, "What threatens democracy? Navy SEAL warns of Trump's attacks on US institutions," *USA Today*, May 17, 2019, https://www.usatoday.com/ story/news/politics/2019/05/17/navy-seal-mcraven-trump-threatens-national-security/1183799001/.

no regrets.[102] "That is fair criticism. You've got to be prepared to listen to your critics because historically retired military officers, particularly senior officers, don't make a point of speaking up against the commander-in-chief," McRaven said.[103] He added that "in general" he agreed that military officers should refrain from blasting the president but, like some intelligence formers, said he felt duty-bound in this situation. McRaven remains the only former senior military officer who was not an intelligence officer to attack Trump in the personal ways that retired Generals Clapper and Hayden did.

Brennan showed far less introspection than McRaven about this issue in his memoir—or even an awareness that his whining about Trump had broader implications. He too claimed he had both a right to his CIA badge and "First Amendment rights" as a "private citizen" to speak as he saw fit.[104] He asserted a responsibility to speak out—an authority he gave himself.[105] He did not address the longstanding norm against such partisanship. He rejected a call in mid-2017 by then-DCIA Pompeo to cut back on his public criticism of President Trump—Pompeo argued it was unhelpful—and he casually dismissed worries by intelligence professionals that his outspokenness was counterproductive.[106] Brennan's disregard of a major part of CIA's institutional history and culture and his lack of self-awareness about the implications of his actions are striking, but are consistent with his longstanding tendencies toward strongly partisan political views, stubbornness,

---

102   Daniel Trotta, "Retired Admiral McRaven has no regrets over criticizing Trump," Reuters, May 22, 2019, https://www.reuters.com/article/us-usa-security-mcraven/retired-admiral-mcraven-has-no-regrets-over-criticizing-trump-idUSKCN1ST02F.
103   Ibid.
104   Brennan, *Undaunted*, 398.
105   Ibid., 392-393.
106   Ibid., 398.

and temper tantrums. Occasional glimpses in his book of cognition about the consequences of his actions fade quickly.

In sharp contrast, Admiral Mike Rogers, then recently retired from the Navy and as director of the NSA, during a panel discussion at George Mason University in September 2018 rejected repeated efforts by fellow panelists Clapper and Hayden to get him to attack Trump.[107] Rogers responded, "Guys, this is not helping," and added, "Pouring gasoline on the fire is not going to reduce the flame."[108] Rogers said he worried about how the controversy was affecting the continuing work of intelligence professionals and, recounting a long-held core belief of intelligence officers, reminded his colleagues that intelligence is the most effective when customers—in this case President Trump—understand they are receiving honest assessments that are not tinged with politics. He said, "We must ensure that nothing we do calls in question the objective nature of intelligence."[109] It is now clear that Trump and senior advisors such as John Bolton, as well as many outside observers, asked this question frequently.

The apparently cooler reception to anti-Trump critics among military personnel, compared with intelligence professionals, contrasts with a period of American history in which civil-military relations were unusually stressed—the early 1990s when President Clinton angered many military personnel over his emphasis on peacekeeping operations they considered unattractive and permitting gays to serve in the military under Clinton's "don't ask, don't tell" policy. They also disapproved of Clinton's character, especially his alleged draft dodging during the Vietnam War and then

---

107   https://www.c-span.org/video/?451323-1/intel-chiefs-discuss-intelligence-community-presidency-relationship.
108   Lee Ferran, "Ex-NSA chief says former intel officials taking on Trump 'not helping'," ABC News, September 12, 2018, https://abcnews.go.com/Politics/nsa-chief-intel-officials-taking-trump-helping/story?id=57771478.
109   Ibid.

lying about it. In this case, the long-recognized "gap"[110] between military and civilian perspectives led some people to worry that a military coup against Clinton might be in the making.[111] The tensions lessened after senior serving officers publicly reminded their personnel that criticizing the commander-in-chief was inappropriate and told them pointedly to stop it. Tensions eased further after Clinton left office and the more military-supportive George W. Bush became president. Bush soon conducted real wars in Afghanistan and Iraq that initially, at least, had strong public support and which military personnel saw as legitimate uses of military force.

The issue of senior military officers' endorsement of presidential candidates has grown in the last several election cycles. As noted, former General Michael Flynn spoke disparagingly about Hillary Clinton in 2016, while retired Marine General John Allen endorsed Clinton at the Democratic National Convention.[112] Allen went further than Flynn in one respect: he called on active duty military personnel to be politically active.[113] But senior serving and retired officers such as former chairmen of the Joint Chiefs General Martin Dempsey and Admiral Mike Mullen publicly chastised both Allen and Flynn, arguing that such political activity was inappropriate. Prominent student of civil-military relations Peter Feaver of Duke University explained the dangers:

> Retired senior military officers should not let political
> parties trade on their service in uniform by becoming

---

110   Feaver and Kohn, *Soldiers and Civilians.*
111   Kohn, "Out of Control."
112   Heidi Urben, "Generals Shouldn't be Welcome at These Parties: Stopping Retired Flag Officer Endorsements," *War on the Rocks,* July 27, 2020, https://warontherocks.com/2020/07/generals-shouldnt-be-welcome-at-these-parties-stopping-retired-flag-officer-endorsements/.
113   Peter Feaver, "We Don't Need Generals to Become Cheerleaders at Political Conventions," *Foreign Policy,* July 29, 2016, https://foreignpolicy.com/2016/07/29/we-dont-need-generals-to-become-cheerleaders-at-political-conventions/.

high-profile partisan endorsers of presidential candidates.

For the past several decades, my tribe of specialists in civil-military relations has been debating this norm— whether it really should be a norm, why it is being challenged, and what can be done to strengthen it.

The argument is quite simple. Of course, retired senior military figures enjoy the rights of any citizen. They have a right to run for office, a right to vote, a right to be politically active, a right to hold views and to opine on policy. But they also have special responsibilities that derive from the fact that they enjoy the special privileges that come with their rank while on active duty—privileges, and thus responsibilities, that extend even into retirement. It is telling that we have a strong custom in our country of referring to retired generals and admirals by their rank, even long after they have left uniformed service—their first name, even in retirement, continues to be general or admiral.

As such, when they speak as "retired General So-and-So" they appear to be speaking for the military. They are cloaking themselves in the extraordinarily high degree of respect that the American public accords to the uniformed military. However, a crucial pillar of that respect is the belief that the military self-consciously and purposefully stands outside of partisan politics. The military pledges to uphold the Constitution and obey the constitutional chain of command, to follow legal orders regardless of who is at the top of that chain. The public holds in low esteem those public institutions that are unavoidably in the middle of partisan fights—such as Congress—or those that are supposed to stand above partisanship but in fact appear not to—such as the media, or in recent years, the Supreme Court. The very act of wading into partisan politics while also pretending to be above partisan politics politicizes the military and risks undermining public confidence in this vital institution.

What is corrosive is claiming the authority that comes from nonpartisan military service but then deploying that authority in pursuit of a quintessentially partisan mission—electing one candidate over another. Every time a senior retired military officer makes a high-profile political endorsement, it has an impact on junior officers still serving in uniform, and it chips away at the outside-partisan-politics norm. Such political endorsements contribute to toxic civil-military relations. They encourage political leaders to view the military as an interest group to be mobilized and professional military advice as one more partisan voice to be spun.[114]

The analogy between senior military and intelligence officers is close but inexact in several ways. Unlike military personnel, civilian intelligence officers are not bound by the Uniform Code of Military Justice (UCMJ) to obey lawful orders. Article 88 of the UCMJ says:

Any commissioned officer who uses contemptuous

---

114 Ibid.

words against the President, the Vice President, Congress, the Secretary of Defense, the Secretary of a military department, the Secretary of Transportation, or the Governor or legislature of any State, Territory, Commonwealth, or possession in which he is on duty or present shall be punished as a court martial may direct.[115]

But civilian intelligence officers know they must obey lawful presidential directives or risk ruining their careers. They know that they have reporting requirements to the Congress, that strict laws govern key aspects of their collection activities and covert actions, and that Congress people sometimes change policies in midstream, threatening operations personnel, especially, with criminal prosecution for doing the jobs they were lawfully directed to do. Unlike during period of military unhappiness with Clinton in the 1990s, no senior serving career intelligence officer ever publicly, pointedly told serving intelligence officers to stop criticizing Trump in the office or told them to stop leaking information damaging to the president. DCIA Haspel would have had some credibility in doing so, but she did not.

These similarities and differences suggest a need for a national debate about "civil-intelligence relations." Although the conduct of anti-Trump formers and their refusal to accept that civil-military traditions generally apply to them indicates that more than talk is needed, establishment of a new cultural norm of appropriate civil-intelligence relations is overdue.[116] Sherman Kent and others debated how intelligence could best support

115   Uniform Code of Military Justice, 2021 edition, https://ucmj.us/888-article-88-contempt-toward-officials/.
116   Rogg, "The U.S. Intelligence Community's 'MacArthur Moment;'" Gentry, "Trump-Era Politicization."

policy-makers. Kent also made the point that professions must have a professional literature—and started one. But the intelligence literature until recently had no need to discuss widespread opposition by intelligence officers to a president, or to address claims that intelligence should have institutional autonomy from presidents, which were previously unthinkable. There thus were, until recently, no writings in intelligence studies equivalent to the classic writings on civil-military relations by Samuel Huntington and Morris Janowitz, for example.[117]

Indirectly, the activism has further damaged congressional oversight of intelligence. While partisanship on the HPSCI and SSCI had grown in recent years, partisanship worsened considerably when the Democrats took control of the House of Representatives after the 2018 elections.[118] Under new Chairman Adam Schiff, the HPSCI promptly developed a de facto alliance with anti-Trump intelligence activists and the anti-Trump press—an unprecedentedly partisan coalition of strange bedfellows. Schiff was outspokenly critical of Trump, who returned the favor. Speaker Nancy Pelosi made Schiff one of her managers of the impeachment trial of Trump in 2019, unwisely injecting the HPSCI further into a bitter partisan fight.[119] Even before Trump's first impeachment, in 2018 staffers had divided the HPSCI's secure workspace into separate Republican and Democratic sections.[120] Schiff's close cooperation with the CIA "whistleblower" and his dishonesty about his involvement in the case further damaged intra-committee cooperation and the credibility of oversight generally. The SSCI was less blatantly politicized but tensions appeared there, too. Chairman Mark Warner (D-VA),

---

117 Huntington, *The Soldier and the State*; Janowitz, *The Professional Soldier*.
118 Kibbe, "Congressional Oversight of Intelligence;" Ott, "Partisanship and the Decline of Intelligence Oversight."
119 Bade and Demirjian, *Unchecked*, 492-493, 498-500.
120 Sources: two congressional staffers, late 2018 and 2020.

like Schiff, added the "truth to power" slogan to his vernacular.[121] This much-heightened partisanship of congressional oversight of intelligence is a legacy that will surely endure.[122]

Other implications are also likely to be long-term in nature. Although Trump evidently cared little about the Obama-Clapper-Brennan program to advance "diversity and inclusion," fear of the emergence of opposition to it played a major role in stoking serving intelligence officers' concerns about him. DCIA Mike Pompeo made the traditional case for *intellectual* diversity in intelligence agencies and was criticized heavily internally for not focusing instead on domestically defined demographic diversity. According to Bob Woodward, DNI Coats initially was overwhelmed by the workload and chose to focus on dealing with the president and external matters as a "Mr. Outside," leaving day-to-day management of the internal workings of the IC to "Mrs. Inside," Principal Deputy DNI Sue Gordon, who thrived bureaucratically as a CIA officer in the Clapper-Brennan years and who evidently shared their demographic ambitions; she certainly indicated as much after leaving office. Neither Pompeo nor Coats tried to reform the diversity offices that had become de facto homes of senior-level advocates for diversity and inclusion policies. Nor did acting DNI Richard Grenell, DNI John Ratcliffe, or DCIA Haspel do anything to roll back Obama-era diversity policies.

Indeed, Haspel issued a multi-year extension of CIA's diversity and inclusion policy in March 2020.[123] While her introductory statement is traditional, emphasizing the operational advantages of diversity in perspectives, the body of the document is Brennan-like,

---

121   For example, Mark R. Warner, "SSCI Vice Chair Mark R. Warner on Sue Gordon," Warner web site, https://www.warner.senate.gov/public/index. cfm/2019/8/statement-ssci-vice-chair-mark-r-warner-on-sue-gordon.

122   Karoun Demirjian, "With Trump, Russia probes behind it, polarized House panel looks to heal partisan rifts," *Washington Post*, November 22, 2020, https://www. msn.com/en-us/news/politics/with-trump-russia-probes-behind-it-polarized-house-panel-looks-to-heal-partisan-rifts/ar-BB1bfDHw?ocid=hplocalnews.

123   CIA, "Diversity and Inclusion Strategy, 2020-2023," March 2020, https://www. cia.gov/library/reports/DI_Strategy_2020.pdf.

re-emphasizing the importance of diversity defined in terms of the domestic demographic groups. Strategic goal 2.2 adds yet another domestic constituency to the list of politically favored groups at the CIA: people "identifying as neurodiverse."[124] That is, people who have brain disorders such as dyslexia. There was no immediate assertion that hiring more people with such handicaps would improve the agency's performance; that came after Biden's team took over in 2021. Also in 2020, Haspel mandated creation of a "diversity coordinator" position in each office of the agency's directorates—the next bureaucratic layer down—to more closely monitor adherence to the agency's diversity policies.[125]

President Biden in June 2021 issued EO 14035, "Diversity, Equity, Inclusion, and Accessibility in the Federal Workforce," which effectively reestablished Obama's EO 13548 of 2011 on diversity in a stronger form, also with an implementing organizational structure."[126] DCIA Burns made clear his support for the program in April 2022. And Biden's Secretary of State, Antony Blinken, imposed a DEI-motivated system at State, including INR, that awards "points" for adherence to DEI orthodoxy, including points for adding pronouns to one's email signature block, a favorite of LGBTQ+ advocates.[127] High point earners are periodically celebrated at special awards ceremonies. The practice looks a lot like the Chinese Communist Party's Social Credit System, which rewards adherence to ideological orthodoxy and punishes deviance. Hence, from 2011 to the end of Biden's term in 2025, over 13 years will have passed before meaningful reform

---

124   Ibid., 5.
125   Personal communication with a CIA officer, mid-2020.
126   EO 14035, https://www.whitehouse.gov/briefing-room/presidential-actions/2021/06/25/executive-order-on-diversity-equity-inclusion-and-accessibility-in-the-federal-workforce/.
127   Personal communication, late 2022.

will begin to be possible—plenty of time for Obama's program to continue to evolve and to become deeply institutionalized.

Therefore, the IC's embrace of identity politics-motivated personnel policies remains strong. This policy continues to generate significant divisions among employees at the CIA, which also is likely to have lasting, negative effects on the cohesion of the CIA's workforce as a whole. Other IC agencies evidently made lesser changes in this arena and so were not as badly damaged.

The larger question of the impact of recent events on the overall performance of US intelligence—its ability consistently to accurately collect and insightfully analyze—remains open due to a lack of information, as Robert Jervis noted. Concerns seem to be growing in some quarters, however. While the charge that the IC has hurt itself by favoring members of some demographic groups over more qualified heterosexual, healthy, Caucasian men is long-standing—and still is vigorously disputed by DEI advocates—new concerns are emerging that cover aspects of intelligence life other than hiring. For example, a retired CIA officer, working as a contractor, said in mid-2021 that at CIA there was "much more emphasis on diversity and inclusion than before" during the course of normal workdays.[128] In December 2021 I published an article on the operational effects of diversity in the IC that generated much positive commentary from current and former intelligence officers as well as some opposition and an only slightly veiled threat to my teaching job at Georgetown University.[129] A former senior CIA manager wrote in reaction to the article:

> The growth of the workforce since 9/11 in CIA has been tremendous, including the DI (now the DA), but so has been the bureaucratic support structure. As the

---

128 Personal communication, July 2021.
129 Gentry, "Demographic Diversity in U.S. Intelligence Personnel."

workforce has gotten larger, so has diversity. Political correctness rules. With the increased political divide, it is hard to be outspoken. We choose our close colleagues carefully.

This suggests damage to a core CIA asset: its people's willingness to work together constructively. Another CIA employee reported in April 2022 that political correctness reigned in the person's directorate. Minority and women employees regularly complained to diversity offices about even mild critiques of their work by managers who performed what once were standard activities of managers—correcting and offering suggestions for improving their subordinates' performance.[130] Diversity offices normally backed complainers, the person said, leading to inappropriate punishment of sound managers and incentives for others to avoid legitimate critiques of sub-standard work for reasons of self-preservation.[131] As a result, the person said, shoddy work was not only frequently accepted, it sometimes was rewarded. In this way, the diversity offices seem to be assuming roles once held by communist party commissars in the Soviet Union—people who overrode nominal commanders and chains of command when ideological doctrine was threatened. My repository of such anecdotes is still only moderately sized, but these problems are consistent with the worries of Jervis and Betts, noted above. While these and other problems reportedly are internally obvious to many CIA personnel, they are not evaluated because, given Biden's views, they are too politically hot to handle.

SUMMARY

---

130   Personal communication, April 2022.
131   For the very different practice of only a few years before, see Gentry, "Managers of Analysts."

While activists tried hard to keep observers' focus on Trump and his exceptionalism, the preponderance of evidence points strongly to the continued existence of a politicized IC that will cause problems for years to come—long after Trump has left the political scene. Regardless of Trump's character flaws, intelligence officers alone chose to abandon longstanding, highly functional norms of apolitical public service, primarily to defend ideology-based beliefs and the self-interests of advantaged groups. Intelligence officers therefore bear primary responsibility for the Trump-intelligence conflict. They damaged the credibility and perceived trustworthiness of US intelligence. Even if the CIA is not as politicized as I argue, many people surely believe it is more politicized, and these people will act on their beliefs. Their perceptions have strong factual bases, which will remain powerful even if observers are mistaken in matters of small detail. While there are many aspects to the issue, key points are these:

- The IC has squandered much of the trust that it earned in years past. Like perceptions of honesty in other walks of life, trust is earned through long, painstaking work but can be destroyed in a single episode of bad judgment. The IC cannot claim that it knows truth simply because Trump rejected the fairly clear Russian meddling role in 2016 and other intelligence findings later. Clear Trump errors do not establish the IC's commitment to, or consistent capacity to generate, anything close to "truth."
- Because trust (or lack thereof) is generated mainly by the analytic components of the IC—they interact most directly with senior decision-makers—the

reported or feared biases in analytic components and the leaks mean that analyses generally are now suspect. There is less reason to distrust raw collection reports.

- The negative consequences of institutional engineering by Clapper, Brennan, Haspel, and Burns at CIA have not been addressed. Hence, careful observers will reasonably assume that the capacity for politicization of intelligence products and of destructive leaks remain intact—and that politicization of intelligence is still occurring. Ignorance of the actual numbers of such activists and size and magnitude of the politicization of analyses does not diminish a need to worry about them. Because such concerns clearly exist, as Peter Usowski observed, the agencies' leaders and the agencies themselves are now understandably suspect. Only the IC's leaders can credibly assess the size and importance of these phenomena, and they refuse to do so.

- The fact that the Trump administration did not try to reform intelligence is striking, especially given Trump's more than occasional rhetorical slings at intelligence agencies and personalities, suggesting that Nicholas Dujmović is right: Trump was not really as anti-intelligence as his tweets let on. Biden may be more dangerous than even Obama as an instigator of politicization, but a successor someday may try to redress what many observers regard, understandably even if not completely accurately, as an unacceptable rebellion at the CIA, especially.

Given the tendency of the U.S. government to critically examine intelligence only after major intelligence failures, DEI policies likely will be, and should be, examined as a possible contributing factor to another big failure. This examination would be long overdue.

- The highly polarized American domestic scene means there may be some "payback" when Democrats occupy the Oval Office. Presumably these acts will include misleading innuendo by critical formers and inaccurate leaks by serving officers, two of the mainstays of the anti-Trump campaign. But the much smaller number of hard-core Trump supporters in the IC and the residual ethic of apolitical public service seem likely to keep payback much smaller than the politicization that will have triggered it. "Payback" against Biden does not yet seem to have occurred.

This is a sad assessment, but a successor to Biden can do some things to help remedy the situation. Plausibly effective remedial action is the subject of chapter 8.

8

CAN RECENT TRENDS
BE REVERSED?

PRECEDING CHAPTERS IDENTIFIED PROBLEMS in the intelligence-presidential relationship that arose or grew worse in 2016 and assessed some implications. While I have no illusions about Mr. Trump's unusual character traits and am sure he was at times needlessly abrasive, I hold a traditional view that decisions about the fitness of persons to be president are best left to voters, not bureaucrats or former bureaucrats who justify their actions by extolling their intelligence credentials. Intelligence officers' attempts to discredit, thwart, and perhaps overthrow President Trump were inappropriate and should be addressed institutionally at the direction of presidents. While the partisan nature of the IC-Trump conflict undoubtedly makes Democrats less eager to tackle this issue—and chastise friends—as Sam Faddis and others forecast, payback may be occurring. And, as many people worry, politicization-related dysfunctions are evident and probably are growing. Hence people who want sound government—from all parties and political persuasions—have good reasons to want to reverse the politicization of intelligence that has become obvious in recent years. While the abrasive commentary of belligerent formers such as Brennan is unfortunate, the country can live with it because Brennan and others badly damaged their own credibility. The real challenges are within the agencies—dealing with the political activities and worldview-generated biases of serving intelligence officers and reforming the policies, structures, and cultures that fostered and now sustain them.

In one of his many inconsistencies, despite his criticism of intelligence Trump made no effort to reform the IC, the fears and allegations of many intelligence personnel notwithstanding. Even more surprisingly, he did not reduce the number of intelligence people on the NSC staff and in other positions at the White House even after the CIA "whistleblower" incident of 2019.[1] Aside from the whistleblower, there are no reports that White House staffers returned intelligence officers to Langley before the scheduled ends of their tours. Army Lieutenant Colonel Alexander Vindman evidently was sent back to the Pentagon before the end of his anticipated tour for testifying against Trump at his impeachment hearings, not for his role in passing information to the "whistleblower." There were no complaining leaks or blasts by formers or the HPSCI that Trump reduced the intelligence presence at the White House or took any serious action to change policies and practices within the IC. Given intelligence officers' propensity to leak about even modest political concerns, the lack of complaining leaks is strong evidence that Trump's appointees did not act in any meaningful way to strengthen apolitical public service as a core norm of US intelligence.

---

1   Rogg, "The U.S. Intelligence Community's 'MacArthur Moment'," 13-14.

The 2020 presidential election altered the history of politicization by intelligence personnel by making sure it would not soon be addressed. President Joe Biden did not criticize the IC as Trump did, and senior formers came directly to his aid at a potentially critical time in the campaign by debunking the legitimate, incriminating emails on Hunter Biden's laptop computer. The Democrats among anti-Trump IC activists—evidently almost all of them—evidently have been pleased by Biden's politics, which have surprised many observers by being even more left-leaning than Obama's. Indeed, discussions of many of Biden's domestic policies are often accompanied by the adjective "woke." Hence, most of the vocal formers quickly toned down their rhetoric and leaks diminished over the course of 2021. Intelligence activists undoubtedly think, for good reason, that they helped beat Trump. Biden's people know that intelligence officers helped them, and they know it makes little sense to alienate ideological comrades who can be vindictive over even minor perceived slights and who might again be useful allies.

Biden named Avril Haines to be his DNI on November 23, 2020.[2] She was the first Biden administration official confirmed by the Senate—on January 20, 2021. Haines was deputy DCIA from August 2013 to January 2015, working for Brennan. A lawyer, Haines had no previous intelligence experience. After her stint at CIA, she became Obama's deputy national security advisor. While she talked a lot about restoring trust in the IC and exorcizing politicization in her opening statement to the SSCI at her confirmation hearings, it was not then clear whether she was concerned about career intelligence officers or the alleged politicization of

2   Paul D. Shinkman, "Biden to Nominate Avril Haines for DNI," *U.S. News*, November 23, 2020, https://www.usnews.com/news/elections/articles/2020-11-23/joe-biden-to-nominate-avril-haines-for-dni.

Trump's appointees.[3] Two years later, it is evident that she has taken no action against internal politicization. She presumably will continue to adhere closely to the Obama-Clapper-Brennan ways of managing the IC that Biden has embraced.

Biden named retired Foreign Service officer William J. Burns to be DCIA on January 11, 2021. He was confirmed in March 2021. Burns had a good reputation as a successful senior diplomat who worked well with both Republican and Democratic administrations.[4] Biden's appointment announcement said Burns "shares my profound belief that intelligence must be apolitical and that the dedicated intelligence professionals serving our nation deserve our gratitude and respect."[5] The first part of Biden's comment is good, the latter part comes straight from Trump critics' verbal repertoire—a demand for respect regardless of the performance of intelligence. Biden' announcement did not specify Burns' marching orders, if any, but there remains no evidence that Biden wants to depoliticize the CIA. As a senior policymaker Burns surely learned a lot about intelligence but he was not a CIA insider, meaning he undoubtedly knew he faced the standard challenge of gaining CIA employees' acceptance. He soon ingratiated himself with fawning public commentary about how wonderful CIA people are, and he accepted established CIA ways of doings things—the formula for bureaucratic success used earlier by outsiders such as DCI George Tenet and DCIA Leon Panetta. Looked at another way, the CIA successfully coopted another outside director.

Hence, Biden administration officials have implemented policies similar to those that helped build and sustain the

---

3   Haines statement, https://mail.google.com/mail/u/1/#inbox/
     FMfcgxwKkbkTbdmNZGdkFRbnfXxTVkDq?projector=1.
4   Burns, *The Back Channel*.
5   Pranshu Verma, "William Burns, a career diplomat, is Biden's choice to head the
     C.I.A.," *New York Times*, January 11, 2021, http://www.msn.com/en-us/news/
     politics/william-burns-a-career-diplomat-is-bidens-choice-to-head-the-cia/ar-
     BB1cEhej?ocid=U453DHP&li=BBnb7Kz.

politicization of intelligence in recent years. Sheronda Dorsey, CIA's deputy associate director for talent, said in late January 2021, before Burns arrived as DCIA, that the agency wanted to continue to work to attract people of more diverse backgrounds, including racial, cultural, disability, sexual orientation, and gender diversity so that the workforce is "reflective of America."[6] Then, in June 2021, Biden's EO 14035 made clear his desire to continue to re-engineer the demographic composition of the federal workforce for political reasons.[7] Examining whether a presidential directive has had unintended (or intended) negative consequences is not attractive to most bureaucrats and political appointees. Unsurprisingly, neither Burns nor Haines have done so.

Strikingly, elements of the IC seem to recognize that it has a public relations problem but is in denial about the nature of the problem. For example, the National Intelligence University in 2021 created a "Center for Truth, Trust, and Transparency" ("Tr3") that ostensibly is focused on identifying better ways to inform the public about what the IC does. But an article by the center's directors explaining this need ignores the politicization issue.[8] And the title perpetuates the arrogant myth that the IC is about truth. A year later, Tr3 still focused on redressing the allegedly nefarious influences of "Hollywood, Tom Clancy, or Fox News."[9] Apparently separately, the Intelligence and National Security Foundation on July 12, 2022 hosted an online discussion by retired senior DIA and ODNI officer Neil Wiley and Kelli Arena, NSA's chief of strategic communications, entitled "Trusting the IC,"

---

6   Krithika Varagur, "The CIA Fine-Tunes Its Hiring Pitch," *Wall Street Journal*, February 1, 2021, A11.

7   EO 14035, https://www.opm.gov/policy-data-oversight/diversity-and-inclusion/reference-materials/diversity-equity-inclusion-accessibility-in-the-federal-workforce.pdf?msclkid=26691032d13211ec95e6cb4ba03ea8bc.

8   Deborah Pfaff and Bowman Miller, "From a Whisper to a Shout: The IC Should Use Its Outside Voice," June 23, 2021, at https://ni-u.edu/wp/wp-content/uploads/2021/09/NIUShort_06232021_21C193.pdf.

9   Personal communication, July 2022.

which also did not mention the politicization issue.[10] It is hard to know whether these people are clueless or delusional or are again practicing what they hope is IC-enhancing propaganda.

Appreciable reforms therefore remain to be implemented because the IC's serious politicization problems remain untouched. Some fairly obvious reform options could help ameliorate politicization but almost certainly cannot not eliminate it. Research by insiders is needed to better identify the nature and extent of the problems within IC agencies that bloomed during the Trump years, and thereby to develop more targeted reforms. If leadership efforts within agencies remain insufficient, it may eventually be necessary for outsiders—the White House or Congress—to make structural changes within and among IC agencies to minimize the negative consequences of enduring biases in parts of the IC and to create organizations in which presidents have more confidence—and trust. This chapter offers potential remedies for these ailments.

UNKNOWNS TO BE RESEARCHED

Details of several important variables are as yet only partially known, even to IC agencies' leaders. They can be investigated initially only by government personnel, who are the only people with access to relevant, now classified, data. Later, outsiders can evaluate documents as they are declassified and assess personal accounts of events as they become public. But the general nature of politicization within IC agencies during the Trump era is clear enough that it is certain that effective remedial actions will be time-consuming at best. Clarification of unknowns can help refine the emphases placed on various

---

10   Link to presentation, https://register.gotowebinar.com/recording/
      viewRecording/7296014338746369295/3172282785515088129/jag411@
      georgetown.edu?registrantKey=7574492047200525070&type=
      ATTENDEEEMAILRECORDINGLINK.

remedial measures. Research might also identify other problems not discussed herein.

The first and arguably most important issue to investigate is the state of political activism within the individual agencies of the IC. The CIA and ODNI certainly are significantly infected, other agencies seem less so. Questions include: How many people are involved? At what agencies and in what sub-components thereof? What are the activists' specific concerns? Are there any beyond the social issues embedded in the "diversity, equity, and inclusion" agenda overseen by the diversity offices? What are details of ongoing politically-oriented activities within agencies? How committed are employees to political activism? What arguments or incentives or orders, if any, could persuade them to desist? Are activists associated with any outside organizations? Is there evidence that political activism is being encouraged directly by foreign actors, including intelligence services? Is there correspondingly cause for counterintelligence concerns? Answers to these questions can be gathered in town hall meetings, junior leaders' daily interactions with their subordinates, and through surveys. "Anonymous" computer questionnaires will be viewed skeptically because employees know there is no such thing as anonymity on a government computer, and so are likely to be less than candid in their answers. But personal contacts with trustworthy persons and anonymous paper surveys may be less threatening, thereby generating useful information. A model adaptable for this use might be the large-scale ethnographic study of analysis in the IC conducted by CIA anthropologist Rob Johnston, which was published in 2005.[11]

A second important issue is the extent to which analytic products are being politicized, with what slant. As Robert Jervis

---

11   Johnston, *Analytic Culture in the U.S. Intelligence Community.*

observed, this issue is a major unknown for outside observers, especially. It needs to be understood better if it is to be addressed effectively. This will require a comprehensive internal assessment, then appreciable action. While the current situation is a not clear, as the insightful Jervis worried, there are reasons to suspect that bias problems may be significant.

Once problems are better identified, a major remedial program is needed. While employees should be the main focus, this effort should also have a public component. Because current and future intelligence consumers' trust is at stake, an outreach program explaining in general terms the nature and extent of identified problems, planned reforms, and anticipated improvements is required. Current and future decision-makers, and the citizenry, need to know that politicization has been effectively addressed if confidence in the IC is to be restored.

Changed leadership emphases and revised incentives informed by research are unlikely to remedy all problems. A new president therefore should also consider structural changes designed to marginalize or eliminate intelligence units that cannot be effectively reformed and to create new organizations that can assume functions now performed by politicized elements. Limited such purges, focused on organizational structures and cultures, would be a first for the United States given that President Nixon aborted his when he moved DCI Schlesinger to the Pentagon, but many other countries have conducted them and the IC may need one.[12]

NEEDED REFORMS

The venerable norm of apolitical support for the office of the president, whomever the incumbent may be, clearly has eroded

---

12   Gentry, "Purges of Intelligence Services."

and needs to be restored. The unprecedented volume of partisan talk by formers is obvious, and reports of growing numbers of politically-motivated leaks are too numerous to doubt. Currently serving intelligence officers similarly report that in-office political banter has increased in recent years, especially in the CIA's analysis directorate. American political and intelligence traditions, which severe critics of Trump did not challenge even as they said the norms needed to be temporarily suspended, are that if intelligence is to be trusted, and thence used, it must be seen to be objective and apolitical. Hence, leadership efforts to restore this normative tradition are imperative.

This effort will entail revising policy directives and adjusting leaders' command emphases, radically scaling back and reforming the diversity offices and their programs, giving speeches, and talking with employees as leaders make their rounds to line units. It will mean sending regular reminders to subordinate managers about the importance of political neutrality when reviewing written and other intelligence products and a renewed emphasis on objectivity in training programs for analysts, especially. And it will require close monitoring of analytic products and removal of persons who intentionally or consistently but even inadvertently violate the objectivity norm. Despite their discard of some exemptions from normal civil service rules in recent years, intelligence agencies still have greater leeway than most federal agencies to terminate employees, which they should use judiciously.

More specifically, CIA management in the Trump years was grossly irresponsible in permitting the chronic use of information technology (IT) systems for partisan political messaging, which in recent years had a distinctly anti-Trump tone. It matters not who targets are or what views are promoted, this practice must stop. Just as officers caught watching pornography on government systems are terminated, persons talking politics on government time and on government IT systems should be "walked out"—that is, promptly fired. Activities on IT systems are recorded and routinely monitored for inappropriate behavior and security matters. Management therefore should institute formal reviews of the use of IT systems since 2016, looking for inappropriately partisan communications. Managers who failed to stop the partisan chatter also should be relieved or fired.

The IC needs to do a much better job of combatting leaks. Increased use of polygraphs on suspected leakers would be a good start. Offering employees rewards for turning in leakers may help. While some employees surely will rebel at this, lamely claiming that management is trying to "divide" employees or squelch "free speech," the main goal of the policy would be to convince employees that management disapproves of leaks, intends to police leaking more effectively, and wants to discourage organized leaks by groups of people, thereby creating additional disincentives for leaking. The limited number of people caught leaking each year offers no serious threat to a leaker who employs minimally competent "tradecraft"—something Reality Winner did not do.

If legally possible, "leak bait" websites of news media should be monitored closely, and the Department of Justice should close them down if possible. If not, legislation to do so can be proposed. The point is not to infringe on journalists' First Amendment rights, but rather to deter leaks of classified information by intelligence officers, which clearly are criminal acts. If they cannot be closed or watched legally, the IC might target intelligence officers who are considering leaking by spreading rumors that a non-existent monitoring capacity actually does exist, the law and official denials notwithstanding, and reminding employees that some counterintelligence officers really are belligerently paranoid. Encouraging intelligence officers to worry more about the dangers of leaking should help reduce the number of leaks.

The practice of giving life-long security clearances to appreciable numbers of senior formers should end. As recalled, Trump's unfulfilled threat to revoke Brennan's clearance in 2018 stoked negative reactions among Brennan's defenders and some controversy even among more neutral observers. The purpose of maintaining these clearances is to enable current IC leaders to tap the experiences and wisdom of their predecessors to help tackle difficult contemporary issues. This need is occasional and depends upon current leaders' trust in the formers. There is no need for a large number of such advisors, whose expertise overlaps, whose memories fade with time, and whose relevant experiences diminish as world affairs evolve. A better policy would be to "read out" all intelligence personnel when they leave government but conduct periodic security re-investigations of a few well-respected formers to enable quick restoration of clearances if necessary or desirable. That means the default policy should be that all senior officers lose their clearances and thus badges when they leave government. This would maintain access to trusted expertise but eliminate a favored mechanism of leaking: passage of information to formers with clearances in government workspaces—not a leak from employees' perspectives—who then pass the information to journalists.

The IC, and if necessary Congress or the president, should ensure that formers who are active political partisans do not have continuing roles in supervising or advising intelligence elements. For example, in mid-2020 Robert Cardillo, who had recently retired after being director of the NGA for five years, co-authored an anti-Trump op-ed in the *Washington Post* with two other anti-Trump formers.[13] In the first half of 2020 alone, Cardillo gave money on fifteen occasions to Joe Biden's presidential campaign, sometimes directly, other times through ActBlue, the Democrats' fundraising organization.[14] The contributions are legal under federal law and the article alone was fine if properly reviewed. The contributions and his partisan rhetoric are concerning because he and fellow anti-Trump activist Carmen Medina were, and remain at this writing, members of the Board of Visitors, or oversight body, of National Intelligence University, a unit of the ODNI.[15] The board makes policy recommendations to NIU leaders and the DNI about a broad range of the activities of the IC's only educational, as opposed to training, organization. Because partisan political activity is incompatible with even part-time government service, Cardillo and Medina should be replaced, and the DNI should make clear that overt partisanship is incompatible with this role.

Restoring the objectivity of intelligence means revising the IC's "diversity and inclusion" policies and substantially reforming or eliminating the offices that implement them. These offices are centers of ideology-driven political activism. Identity politics in IC personnel management has become divisive and controversial in the IC, as it has in the country at large.[16] As they are diminished in size and reshaped as less doctrinaire EEO offices, demographic diversity in these offices should also include appointment of more than token numbers of Caucasian men. The old practice of seeking

---

13   Michael Leiter, Michael Hayden, and Robert Cardillo, "We've briefed many presidents. Uncertainty comes with the job." *Washington Post*, July 7, 2020, https://www.washingtonpost.com/opinions/2020/07/06/weve-briefed-many-presidents-uncertainty-comes-with-job/.

14   Federal Election Commission website, accessed July 9, 2020.

15   For a list of the members of the Board of Visitors, see https://ni-u.edu/wp/about-niu/leadership-2/board-of-visitors/.

16   Gonzales, *The Plot to Change America*. For a similar view, see McMaster, *Battlegrounds*, 19.

diversity of perspectives and ethnic backgrounds for operational purposes remains appropriate. Just a vague, implicit threat to the new orthodoxy was a major trigger for the outburst of partisan activism in 2016, suggesting that a serious reform effort in this arena will be very challenging. No small number of intelligence officers evidently have become as convinced as employees of some Silicon Valley firms and Disney that they have a right to demand DEI and other IC personnel policies consistent with their personal political beliefs. Young officers, especially, know that radical students often intimidate even leftist university administrators in their quest for various forms of imagined "social justice." They need to be convinced definitively that intelligence agencies work differently.

A critically important task is to identify systemic biases in analysis and to address any problems in this core intelligence function—Robert Jervis's primary concern. This work must be done by introspective, independent thinkers. Holders of world-views that contribute to biased analyses, including those pushed by Obama and Biden, may not be able to identify their own biases, let alone assess their manifestations in intelligence products or the implications for intelligence consumers. Outsiders eventually may be able to assess bias in analyses as intelligence documents are declassified, but they too will have worldview-generated blinders to overcome. The need for objectivity in such studies means the diversity offices should not play significant roles. This may not be a problem if, as seems possible, studies of the impact of DEI policies on the IC's performance come only after a major new intelligence failure that is examined by an independent commission.

To search for and root out biases, the IC needs to review its published products much more carefully and comprehensively, looking explicitly for political bias derived from slowly evolving organizational cultures. As required by the IRTPA, the ODNI/ AIS conducts annual reviews of published products, but they long have been few in number and shift evaluations of topics covered and product formats reviewed from year to year, purposefully making time series assessments of product types and agency comparisons impossible.[17] Per requirements of the IRTPA, ICD 203, "Analytic Standards," has five "analytic standards," two of which are that intelligence analytic products should be "objective," and "[i]ndependent of political consideration."[18] It also has "tradecraft standards." The ODNI has never assessed Tradecraft Standard 8, "Makes accurate judgments and assessments."[19] Biases that affect the accuracy of judgments and assessments may take years to fully appreciate. Each of these standards needs much greater emphasis.

This work could also be done by a version of CIA's old Product Evaluation Staff, which gave products thorough examinations, often to analysts' discomfort. The staff's acronym therefore morphed from its original PES to PEST in the hallway usage of analysts—a high compliment. The CIA's Center for the Study of

---

17   Gentry, "Has the ODNI Improved U.S. Intelligence Analysis?" 644-645; author
      discussion with ODNI/AIS personnel, January 2015; email communication in
      October, 2020.
18   DNI, "ICD 203," 2.
19   This decision reflected simple facts of the intelligence business such as the
      difficulty in obtaining reliable information about the accuracy of judgments and
      forecasts and the varying times into the future—if ever—that enough relevant
      data might become available to make a confident determination of analytic
      accuracy. It also reflected mundane bureaucratic motives; the agencies did not
      want to look bad absolutely or in comparison to their bureaucratic rivals when
      their analyses were found to be faulty, which they knew would occur. A senior
      executive of a major analytic agency said that his organization opposed any
      attempt at "measurement" of analytic accuracy because his leadership believed that
      such efforts would lead other agencies to publish elementary facts and watered-
      down judgments in order to get good "grades" from the ODNI/AIS for accuracy
      at the expense of writing analyses useful for decision-makers. Intelligence typically
      is most useful to decision-makers when uncertainties abound but intelligence
      clarifies situations somewhat and reduces uncertainties, improving but not
      perfecting decision-making. Put another way, this individual believed his fellow
      agencies' leaders were willing to, and likely to, try to do well bureaucratically at the
      expense of service to national leaders by providing "truth" that was so obvious it
      would not help decision-making processes.

Intelligence, which has a solid record of objective assessments of past intelligence operations and analyses and has a good reputation, is another possibility. So is the inspector general's office. Efforts to overcome the effects of such organizational worldviews should include restoration of the position of NIO for Warning, which DNI Clapper unwisely abolished in 2011, damaging the IC's warning capabilities. The restored office of the NIO/W should be tasked formally with watching for worldview-related biases in analytical products in addition to its other duties. Enhanced use of "red teams" and "devil's advocates" also would help.

There are hints that a small version of this process may have operated for a short time at the CIA in the Trump years. In a September 2020 leak, nine current and former CIA analysts complained to *Politico* that DCIA Haspel had cracked down on the volume of intelligence products on Russia going to the White House.[20] Although it is not uncommon for CIA and NIC managers to shape the flow of intelligence products to the White House and NSC staff based on stated consumer preferences, and President Trump had made clear that he was sensitive about, and angered by, repetitive intelligence on Russian interference with American electoral processes, CIA analysts and evidently the *PDB* staff kept trying to hit him with Russia stories. The leak suggested that the nine analysts believed they had a right to override agency management decisions and repeatedly thrust their version of Truth at a power they did not like, thereby further annoying Trump and undercutting DCIA Haspel's position with the president. Haspel reportedly had asked CIA general counsel Courtney Elwood in 2019 to review the work of "Russia House," a unit that works Russia-related issues, suggesting that she distrusted the objectivity of

---

20   Natasha Bertrand and Daniel Lippman, "CIA clamps down on flow of Russia intelligence to White House," *Politico*, September 23, 2020, https://www.politico.com/news/2020/09/23/cia-russia-intelligence-white-house-420351.

personnel of the unit, its products, and at least some normal agency product review processes.[21] Reportedly, Haspel accused Russia House analysts of repeatedly lying to her and replaced the unit's head for undisclosed reasons earlier in 2020.[22] These actions in sum were unprecedented. Leakers unsurprisingly accused Haspel of suppressing intelligence to appease Trump—charges similar to those anti-Vietnam war "zealots" at CIA leveled against DCI Helms during the order-of-battle controversy with the Pentagon in 1967, discussed in chapter 2. The absence of complaining leaks indicates that DCIA Burns has done nothing similar.

Perhaps relatedly, in early January 2021 just before Trump left office, the IC's analytic ombudsman, Barry Zulauf, wrote an unclassified report to the SSCI, in response to its questions, concerning IC views of Russian and Chinese efforts to influence the 2020 US national elections.[23] Noting differences in views among unnamed IC analysts and ODNI officials on the issue, Zulauf said some China analysts "appeared reluctant to have their analyses on China brought forward because they tended to disagree with the Administration's policies, saying in effect, I don't want our intelligence to support those policies."[24] This too constituted a violation of IRTPA section 1019, which bans analyses slanted by political considerations, ICD 203, and long-standing cultural norms. In contrast, Russia analysts evidently politicized by excessively trumpeting Russian election meddling in order to annoy Trump.

---

21   Ibid.

22   Ibid.

23   Ellen Nakashima, "Political appointees, career analysts clashed over assessments of Russian, Chinese interference in 2020 election," *Washington Post*, January 8, 2021, https://www.washingtonpost.com/national-security/russia-china-election-interference-intelligence-assessment/2021/01/08/7dc844ce-5172-11eb-83e3-322644d82356_story.html.

24   Julian E. Barnes, Charlie Savage, and Adam Goldman, "Trump Administration Politicized Some Intelligence on Foreign Election Influence, Report Finds," *New York Times*, January 8, 2021, https://www.nytimes.com/2021/01/08/us/politics/trump-administration-politicized-election-intelligence.html. Zulauf's letter to SSCI acting chairman and ranking member, January 6, 2021, page 3, is embedded.

Zulauf also said senior ODNI officials including DNI John Ratcliffe did not adhere to established tradecraft standards in reporting Russian election interference in several reports in 2020. Perceptions of politicization threaten the "legitimacy" of the IC's work, Zulauf wrote. Trump's critics unsurprisingly trumpeted only Zulauf's comments about Ratcliffe. Zulauf soon thereafter went into de facto exile as the intelligence representative at a prominent university.

There is also at least one potential change that would be counterproductive and should be avoided: consideration of persons' political views during "security" processing or reviews of employment applications. Such activities would be virtually impossible to administer with any degree of accuracy or fairness and would be open to abuses of the sort that Franklin Roosevelt administration officials committed in the 1930s, which led to enactment of the Hatch Act of 1939. Efforts to restore political neutrality in the workplace, even if less than fully successful, are a far better option.

INSTITUTIONAL REMEDIES

If revised policy, stronger leadership, active product monitoring, heightened leak detection, and re-focused training do not reverse recent trends, more drastic structural changes may be needed. I am skeptical of all but one option, however. Changing most laws will make no difference because many are vague and bureaucrats can evade or ignore them easily—or interpret them in favorable ways unintended by their authors. Besides, Democrats in Congress and the White House, for the moment at least, seem to like an "independent" IC that is an ideological ally. Some of President Biden's advisors and some Congress people are more likely to wish to thank intelligence activists for helping them win a tough election fight than to punish partisan allies who may be politically helpful again, limiting legislative possibilities. Some have suggested splitting CIA in two, separating the analysis and collection directorates. This is probably a bad idea from the perspective of operational performance, and it would have no obvious impact on the politicization of the analysis directorate; indeed, making the analytic element more insular might make the politicization problem worse. Modest purges of agencies also make little sense; politicized leaders would ensure that their favored people remain employed, perpetuating the problem.[25]

One option that may work is creation of a small, National Intelligence Council-like body within the NSC staff that would focus mainly on current intelligence support for senior policymakers, especially the president, by preparing the *PDB* or an alternative product with input from the agencies. This unit would manage White House inputs to the NIPF, thereby focusing the activities of the agencies. It also would recommend to the president revisions in Executive Order 12333, which assigns missions and establishes bureaucratic "lanes" for each agency, expanding authorities of capable, helpful, and unbiased agencies and reducing those of problematic ones. Active use of these powers would generate strong incentives for the agencies to provide useful, analytically objective and politically neutral information and analyses to the White House. Agencies that do not perform well would have their responsibilities reduced, thereby diminishing prestige and eventually budgets, which are powerful incentives for all bureaucracies. All of these actions can be accomplished administratively. That is, they would not require legislation.

The idea of setting up a new analytic body in the White

---

25   Gentry, "Purges of Intelligence Services."

House that reduces the analytic role of the CIA and assumes the duties of the *PDB* staff has precedents in past US government practice and in the proposals of former CIA analysts, especially. For example, President Nixon proposed in the early 1970s a NIC-like intelligence entity in the White House, which was to be known as the National Intelligence Committee and headed by national security advisor Henry Kissinger.[26] Nixon did not carry through with the idea, however, although for a time he gave Kissinger major responsibilities for monitoring the intelligence that flowed to him and the White House staff assumed a greater role in providing intelligence to him.[27] In 2014 James Steinberg, a senior policymaker in Democratic administrations, similarly suggested unification of policy and intelligence functions at the NSC staff level.[28]

Then-recently former DCI Robert Gates argued in 1994 that the analytic part of the CIA should be "much smaller."[29] Surprisingly, given that he was a career CIA analyst and had just been director, Gates argued that the CIA addressed too many issues, such as health and economic affairs, which were better covered by other government agencies. If I am right that the CIA is a relative hotbed of political activity and that it will strenuously resist outside reform efforts, this fix is easy: use one or more revisions of EO 12333 or a new executive order to reduce the scope of permitted CIA activities by shifting functions to other government agencies that can handle them better—not eliminating them as government efforts. This would entail a de facto re-shaping of the IC—such as adding the Centers for Disease Control to the IC or tasking the Treasury Department to do more economic analyses, for

---

26   Moran, "Nixon's Axe Man," 105-106.
27   Ford, "The US government's experience with intelligence analysis," 40.
28   Steinberg, "The Policymaker's Perspective," 88-89. See also Marrin, "Why strategic intelligence has limited influence on American foreign policy," 736-738.
29   Hedley, "The Intelligence Community," 16.

example. This would amount to movement toward what has been called in other countries a "whole-of-government" intelligence philosophy.[30] This process could be employed repeatedly as needed, making incremental changes that would be individually minor and modestly controversial but have appreciable cumulative effects. If CIA does not respond to these changes in missions, budget cuts could come administratively at first by the DNI, then by reductions in presidential budget requests and by Congressional appropriations. Tangible incentives motivate bureaucrats, and few things focus attention faster than threats to their budgets.

Former senior CIA analyst Harold Ford in the early 1990s suggested creation of an independent, national-level "think tank" to do national estimates, which would be modeled on the Research and Analysis arm of the OSS during World War II, which Ford considered to be the best intelligence analytic outfit the United States has ever had.[31] Ford said the think tank should dive deeply into important issues and reach useful conclusions, which the current intelligence-focused IC of his day did not do as well as he thought desirable.[32] He suggested that the head of the organization be a person of national stature. It should be staffed by the IC's best analysts and excellent outsiders—a small group of "elite" intelligence officers who would have direct access to senior decision-makers; the purpose of this institution would be to ensure that excellent insights and advice reach decision-makers without interference by the normal processes of the intelligence bureaucracy.[33] The warning element of this organization should similarly be composed of talented and well-connected people. Such an organization could remedy most of the recurrent institutional

---

30   Gentry and Gordon, *Strategic Warning Intelligence*, 62-64.
31   Ford, *Estimative Intelligence*, 210-211.
32   Ibid., 201.
33   Ibid., 204, 208.

problems of strategic warning as well as perform current and estimative intelligence duties.

Former senior CIA analyst and NIO Roger George, in an article published in 2015, lamented what he called the sorry state of CIA analysis, arguing that the CIA had hobbled itself by excessively emphasizing the *PDB* (the "First Customer" doctrine discussed in chapter 3) and by enacting security rules that sharply restricted analysts' dealings with outside experts, who he believed to be important sources of insights and valuable alternative views, which also was a complaint of C/NIC Greg Treverton.[34] George suggested several reforms including, as a last resort if CIA management failed to address the problems, moving CIA's analysis directorate to either the NIC or to a new, independent analytic organization created by the DNI.

There are some potential downsides to a White House-based intelligence unit, but they are modest compared to the potential advantages. The most important danger is that it could itself become a source of politicization if a culture emerges that differs from the one Ford and other prominent CIA analysts favored. This is not inevitable, however, and excellent models of how intelligence units can work well in direct support of national political leaders include the United Kingdom's Joint Intelligence Committee, created in 1936,[35] and Australia's Office of National Intelligence,[36] which was created in 2018 to enhance national-level coordination functions and subsumed the previous Office of National Assessments. Both perform US NIC-like functions in the offices of their respective prime ministers. Both are small by US standards, work directly for prime ministers, feature intelligence officers working closely with personnel from policy-making departments, and have good reputations for competence and objectivity. Indeed, these structures

---

34 George, "Reflections on CIA Analysis," 80-81.
35 Goodman, "Learning to Walk."
36 Jones, "Intelligence and the management of national security."

work so well that the intelligence literature features few significant concerns about the politicization of intelligence in either country.[37] British and Australian intelligence personnel do not use the term "truth to power" as code for opposition to their prime ministers, and staffers do not leak in opposition to their chief executives as CIA personnel periodically have done for decades.

Finding and keeping high-quality, apolitical personnel would be a constant challenge, but this is not unusual. This body probably should have a relatively large share of its people on short-term assignments, including academics on leave from their universities and think tank professionals, as well as a career White House staff. The new NIC therefore might look a lot like an expanded version of the Office of National Estimates of the 1950s, a small but intellectually powerful body that by all accounts analyzed apolitically and well.[38]

---

37   Marrin, "At Arm's Length or at the Elbow?" 411. For a discussion mainly about historical politicization "from above"'—by policymakers—in Australia, see McPhee, *Spinning the Secrets of State.*
38   Ford, *Estimative Intelligence.*

9

A SORRY STATE OF AFFAIRS

IT IS NOW POSSIBLE TO TENTATIVELY ANSWER the three questions outlined in the preface of this book: (1) What political activities and attitudes are new, at which IC agencies? (2) Why and how did the changes occur? And (3), what are the immediate and long-term implications of the politicization of intelligence for senior national policy-makers including the president, for specific intelligence agencies, for the IC, and for the country as a whole? While some gaps in public knowledge about the political activities of serving intelligence officers remain, credible aggregate answers are discernible.

A new, dramatically stronger and damaging form of politicization—partisan, political activism willing to damage or destroy politically a sitting American president—has taken root in parts of the US intelligence community. It dwarfs the politicization episodes of the past in magnitude and importance, and it promises to have lasting, negative consequences. The root causes of the activism are ideological, the products of ongoing societal evolution and purposeful institutional engineering of IC agencies, primarily by appointees of President Obama who implemented his Executive Order 13583 of 2011. Given the insularity of the agencies and their relatively low attrition rates, prospects for restoring the organizational cultures of affected agencies to the largely apolitical stances of the 1980s soon, if ever, are not good. But some remedial action is possible, if presidents and leaders of the IC so desire. For the good of the country, it is important that they do so soon.

The activism is concentrated in the CIA, the ODNI, and the FBI. The substantial evidence supporting this conclusion is of several sorts. Most obviously, the largest share of the outspoken, anti-Trump formers were CIA people. They frequently cited unnamed former CIA colleagues who backed their activism and sometimes gave them material to leak. My sources in the IC recurrently point to CIA's analysis directorate as a center of partisan political activity, although the CIA's other directorates also are affected. Journalists often identified unnamed CIA people as their information sources. And the topics of leaks in recent years have been issues CIA generally covers, suggesting CIA leakers. Some of these leaks may also come from the ODNI, especially the NIC. DNI Clapper and DCIA Brennan, prominent critics of Trump, aimed to institutionally re-engineer the IC but could most directly influence the CIA and ODNI. The activism of CIA officers is especially worrisome because in many respects the CIA is the primary US externally-focused intelligence service and its analyses directly support presidential foreign policy decision-making.

The FBI's activists were of a different sort. Concentrated in Washington, they were of two varieties: complainers such as Comey and McCabe who had personal grievances against Trump; and political partisans such as Peter Strzok, who had some characteristics of CIA's ideological warriors. But the field offices outside

Washington were quiet. Many agents undoubtedly were unhappy with the negative publicity the Bureau received, and some surely resented Trump's broad blasts at the FBI. But few could deny that the FBI earned a prominent place in this politicization story due to the actions and inflammatory public commentary of Comey and McCabe and the Crossfire Hurricane "investigation," a story that is still unfolding as I write.

In contrast, few activists came from other agencies. DIA and NSA personnel were very quiet. The military leaders of these agencies seemed determined to conduct business as usual, to the extent they could, given aggressive presidential directives to change agency personnel policies.

NGA's former director Robert Cardillo's emergence as an activist in mid-2020 leads to questions about his impact on NGA's organizational culture during the five years he was director and whether he politicized his choices of second-tier and more junior leaders who now are making assignment and promotion choices that will affect the agency for years to come. Perhaps an impact of Cardillo's political views on NGA analyses will emerge over time, but it seems unlikely to come close to that of Brennan, whose political activism was blatant and who ran a more influential agency. NGA's technical analyses usually have only modest political content and frequently support all-source analyses done by other agencies, including CIA, limiting NGA's ability to politicize intelligence analyses.

INR has a distinctly liberal reputation for good reasons but its only apparent recent display of pointed political activism was the Rod Schoonover testimony flap, which quickly faded. The reasons why liberals at INR and prominent INR formers such as Tom Fingar have held their tongues while many CIA people were vociferous are not clear, but merit some thought. My tentative hypothesis is that INR's unwillingness to chase the hot topics of the day, the significant expertise of its older and more mature workforce, a continuing commitment to research excellence, and the close relationship INR has with State Department decision-makers helped keep the old norms stronger at INR than at the CIA. And, INR people seem to mainly be liberals, not hard leftists of the sort who now work in agencies' diversity offices. This demographic and personnel management pattern may offer a model for reformers who try to both depoliticize intelligence and improve its performance.

The activists had different views and different ways of expressing their opinions, but most shared three characteristics. First, Trump's critics justified their political activism by citing their intelligence credentials as authority for their views. Because they were intelligence people, they saw themselves as specially qualified to talk about virtually any subject, including domestic political topics. This propensity was encouraged by the media, which used it in their coverage of both anti-Trump formers' opinions and leaks. The critics implicitly denied that they politicized intelligence; they allegedly served the nation in a new way. Because none of them acknowledged that they politicized intelligence, they did not directly defend themselves against charges that they did so. Instead, they asserted that critiques of their actions reflected the blatant biases of others. Partly, I suspect, this reflected the immaturity and a lack of understanding of, and disrespect for, traditional intelligence norms by young intelligence officers. But for senior formers, it was another strategic use of the long-known propaganda tactic of "projection"—assertion that one's own motives and activities are actually those of opponents.

Second, most activists spoke in self-righteous terms, claiming they knew "truth" that others did not, the inherent uncertainties of intelligence work and the checkered history of accuracy of intelligence analyses notwithstanding. They often claimed to feel a moral obligation to share their versions of truth, primarily about social issues of importance to the younger workforce. They ignored Jack Davis's warning that analysts often suffer from a "conceit" that their analyses are objective and unbiased.[1] The conceit grew to become a widespread, belligerently arrogant claim that intelligence people knew better than other people absolute truths that transcended intelligence work. The practice seems to have two primary causes, which often intersected: (1) Trump's casual respect for facts gave them an opening—an easy way to make themselves seem virtuous in an arena in which Trump obviously was not; and (2) the historical practice of occasionally thrusting "truth to power" at presidents they do not like was resurrected by deep, ideology-driven antipathy toward Trump, a gross perversion of the original goal of providing objective analyses to presidents regardless of their domestic political implications.

Third, the critics defended themselves and their agencies vigorously in ways earlier intelligence officers did not. The latter recognized that they sometimes made mistakes and that one of their roles was to take blame for presidential policy failures. The critics' focus on protecting their organizations from Trump's often alleged, sometimes threatened, but actually non-existent "assault on intelligence" reflected new political thinking, traits character-istic of a Deep State. It also reflected hypersensitivity to disrespect of themselves and their personal political views, especially on the social issues embedded in Obama's diversity and inclusion agenda. The claim of organizational independence implicitly was also a demand for agency-established ideological orthodoxies, independent of presidential wishes, and a defense of policies that

---

1   Davis, "Intelligence Analysts and Policymakers," 1001.

materially benefited many intelligence officers personally. It is ironic that so many erstwhile defenders of the IC instead damaged its credibility, thereby also damaging the agencies' perceived value and their agencies' bureaucratic interests.

Several factors contributed to the rise of this activism. Some reflected societal evolution of attitudes, especially by young people. The development of technologies of social media and agency training programs played roles. So too did the decision to hire many young people who had just come from the indoctrination mills of American universities to fight President's Bush's "global war on terrorism." I doubt that there was a conscious effort in the Bush years to alter the demographics of agencies in politically important ways; that happened as an unintended side effect. The social engineering effort of Obama and his key IC subordinates, especially Clapper and Brennan, was a very different matter. Obama's policies and associated institutional changes were specifically designed to produce long-lasting, politically important changes in the personnel makeup and organizational cultures of IC agencies. They succeeded to a considerable degree. To reiterate, Obama and his agents in the IC are primarily responsible for the institutional politicization of US intelligence. After Trump administration officials effectively ignored politicization as a systemic issue, Biden resumed the effort to change the demographics and politics of the federal workforce in ways favorable to the Democratic Party and the ideological hard Left.

The activism reflected the political polarization of the country as a whole, which also was caused appreciably by Obama. Perhaps most obviously, race relations, once thought to be an area an African-American president was unusually qualified to help improve, instead worsened markedly after 2009. The "diversity and inclusion" agenda, and then its stronger DEI version, were major claimants on management's attention in the Obama years. The interests and emotions of young people recently indoctrinated in critical race theory and related doctrines in public schools and universities drove the justifications for, and perceived worth of, the political activism of serving intelligence officers. For Trump's ideologically motivated critics, his evil in repudiating or ignoring Obama's ethical priorities made political activism a moral duty. It was completely understandable that the self-evidently noble, anti-racist, truth-seeking civil servants of the IC would rise to the challenge. Warning the country of Trump's ethical evils persistently for years was incorrectly but usefully alleged to be consistent with the long-established duty of intelligence to warn of threats to the nation.[2] Why experienced intelligence people who really should have known better believed they had a special, continuing responsibility to "warn" about Trump chronically when millions of people criticized him daily is not close to understandable except as a tactically useful tool to defend strongly held ideological beliefs. The coddling of prominent formers by the anti-Trump press surely was also a factor.

As in society generally, adherence to "diversity and inclusion," once focused legitimately on real issues of discrimination, had degenerated in the IC as well as in much of American society, into an ideological orthodoxy that is intolerant of intellectual diversity and seeks to destroy, not include, diverse thought in public discourse. Trump represented an ideological threat that the "cancel culture" warriors of the IC felt a need to excise.

There is little doubt any longer that domestic politics drove the intelligence revolt against Trump. References to DEI as well as issues of race, gender, and sexual orientation dominated serving intelligence persons' criticisms of Trump. Nicholas Dujmović

---

2   Gentry and Gordon, *Strategic Warning Intelligence.*

was right: beliefs about controversial domestic social issues drove politicization of intelligence in the Trump years, and beyond. There were no consistent critiques of Trump in legitimate arenas of national security in general. Critics' many references to Russia virtually all had a personal Trump angle; Russia was a way to get at Trump.

Like most elements of the activism, its effects remain debated. Almost all anti-Trump activists blame him alone. They argue that intelligence people had a moral responsibility to act, resurrecting as justification the traditional "truth to power" slogan and invoking constitutional rights of free speech.

The critics of Trump's critics, including essentially all who do so quietly, more insightfully see much greater damage and place most of the blame on the activists. They were and are well aware that presidents always have quirks and failings and that Trump's arguably were more severe than those of most others. They also knew that intelligence officers had never before gone political in public in the volumes and intensity evident in 2016-2021. The fundamental contemporary damage therefore was and is to the perceived credibility and trustworthiness of the IC. The longer-range threat is that overt political activism may burst forth again, further politicizing intelligence and further damaging its usefulness. Many observers, mainly Republicans but many others as well, already question the objectivity of intelligence analyses. Should Biden's successors decide to use intelligence less than Trump did, much of the value of intelligence would vanish and there correspondingly would be less reason for the United States to maintain a large intelligence establishment. Presidential decision-making would be negatively affected, and the intelligence agencies themselves surely also would be damaged.

The number of radical activists in the IC, even at CIA,

undoubtedly is fairly small. But there are more than enough of them, supported by much larger numbers of sympathetic colleagues, to lead reasonable observers of US intelligence to question the intellectual integrity of the IC as a whole. Intelligence consumers and the general public cannot know who or where they are, what intelligence products may be tainted, or how reports may be slanted. Biden administration officers prolong this dysfunctional uncertainty by refusing to acknowledge a problem.

The Deep State charge remains viable. Critics of Trump made a new and dangerous assertion: bureaucrats are justified in attacking a president they do not like and who does not give them, their organizations, and their ideals the respect and autonomy they want. Some variants of this view combined such assertions with a claim of total bureaucratic independence—another defense mechanism that rationalized their proto-Deep State—while also saying their behavior was temporary and dependent only on Trump's behavior. The last claim, especially, strains credulity, given Obama's publicly stated political/demographic goals in restructuring the federal workforce and his determination to achieve them. The Deep State was built by Obama and his appointees for domestic political reasons. It sprang into overt action for the first time when Trump became a viable presidential contender, thereby potentially threatening their ideals bureaucratically and displaying an ideological heresy that deserved to be punished. Now established, the perceived right to oppose any president the bureaucracy dislikes remains to be activated as desired, with bureaucrats assigning to themselves alone the authority to decide when overt opposition to a president is warranted. These attitudes are not consistent with those of "Trumanite" bureaucrats of the "permanent government," per Michael Glennon, but are close to the attitudes and actions decried by Jason Chaffetz.

This conflict occurred in the context of an extended period of polarization of political life of the United States and is widely seen by Trump supporters as part of the attack by the political Left on Trump and those who supported him. The polarization seems to be deepening, not healing, as Richard Betts argued. There is no reason to think that Trump supporters will forget what the critics have said about, and done to, him. Nor will Republicans generally and many other observant citizens accept the basic premise of Trump's critics: political activism is an acceptable, morally justifiable bureaucratic reaction to a president whom activists decide is "abnormal"—a view that is fundamentally undemocratic. They are more likely to continue to see the attacks on Trump, and ones that arise against another Republican presidential candidate, as evidence of extreme, unprecedented, even subversive behavior by the political Left. And they may see reciprocal attacks as both legitimate payback and a different form of Resistance to President Biden or another Democratic president, especially if the person comes from the large "progressive" wing of the party.

It is striking that so many anti-Trump formers, people who know the history of US intelligence and of political conflict in general, have been so cavalierly optimistic that this conflict would end well when they want it to end, with no lingering effects. This reflects truly bad analysis and denial of the lessons of US intelligence and political history. As soldiers say, "the enemy gets a vote." So do historians and consumers of US intelligence, whose memories are well-established as being long. The best explanation may be that people who know the history of politicization and of civil-military relations consciously misrepresented the nature of their opposition to Trump to rationalize to the general public, and to themselves, that their actions were altruistic in motive and unique to a bizarre era, not an example of a new type of intelligence dysfunction, hoping the disinformation would stick. If so, this would amount to a form of systematic disinformation by the senior formers that younger employees, indoctrinated to believe that the ideology of DEI is unquestionably good, also bought.

The young activists against Trump will also have long memories. They will recall slogans that appealed to the media and the public and tactics used against Trump that seemed to work. And like earlier zealots, they will be ready to spring into action the next time an unattractive president or even credible presidential candidate appears.

The loud formers continued their anti-Trump tirades for a time after Trump left office. Initially they were silent about their electoral success, but Brennan was back in action two weeks after Biden's election in November 2020, charging that Trump, who had not accepted defeat and had recently fired a cyber security official, knew "nothing" about cyber security and was trying to "steal the election" from Biden.[3] Unable to contain his undisciplined, immature comments to and about Trump, Brennan also exchanged barbed tweets with Republican Senator Ted Cruz over the assassination of an Iranian nuclear scientist in late November 2020, saying "Your lawless attitude & simple-minded approach to serious national security matters demonstrate that you are unworthy to represent the good people of Texas."[4]

After the January 6, 2021 riot at the Capitol Building by

---

3   Thomas Colson, "Former CIA Director John Brennan ripped into Trump for firing Chris Krebs, saying he 'knows nothing about cybersecurity' and is trying to 'steal the election' from Biden," *Business Insider*, November 18, 2020, http://www.msn.com/en-us/news/politics/former-cia-director-john-brennan-ripped-into-trump-for-firing-chris-krebs-saying-he-knows-nothing-about-cybersecurity-and-is-trying-to-steal-the-election-from-biden/ar-BB1b8elw?li=BB141NW3&ocid=U453DHP.

4   Brendan Cole, "Ex-CIA Head John Brennan Calls Ted Cruz 'Simple-Minded' in Twitter Row Over Iran Killing," *Newsweek*, November 28, 2020, https://www.newsweek.com/ex-cia-head-john-brennan-calls-ted-cruz-simple-minded-twitter-row-over-iran-killing-1550905.

Trump supporters, Brennan and others turned to domestic political action, suggesting that Biden use his intelligence services to
attack domestic political opponents. Said Brennan to MSNBC,

> I know looking forward that the members of the
> Biden team who have been nominated or have been
> appointed, are now moving in laser-like fashion to
> try to uncover as much as they can about what looks
> very similar to insurgency movements that we've seen
> overseas, where they germinate in different parts of a
> country, and they gain strength, and it brings together
> an unholy alliance, frequently, of religious extremists,
> authoritarians, fascists, bigots, racists, nativists, even
> libertarians.[5]

Even libertarians!! It was vintage Brennan.

In late February 2021 a Brennan tweet chided President
Biden for not sanctioning Saudi Arabia more strongly after
DNI Haines released a superficial report concluding that Saudi
Crown Prince Mohammad bin Salman was behind the 2018
killing of Jamal Khashoggi because he then was in charge of
Saudi Arabian security affairs.[6] The "undaunted" Brennan seems
most unlikely among the vocal senior intelligence formers to
return to the responsible obscurity of past decades, serving as an
enduring reminder of the politicization of US intelligence in the
Trump years. Also unable to soon forget, former CIA officers

---

5   Tyler Stone, "John Brennan: Biden Admin Has 'Laser-Like' Focus On 'Insurgency
     Movements' Of Bigots, Racists, Libertarians," *RealClearPolitics*, January 21, 2021,
     https://www.realclearpolitics.com/video/2021/01/21/john_brennan_biden_
     admin_has_laser-like_focus_on_insurgency_movements_of_bigots_racists_
     libertarians.html.
6   Gordon Lubold and Stephen Kalin, "Biden Administration Urged to Penalize
     Saudi Crown Prince Over Khashoggi Killing," *Wall Street Journal*, February 28,
     2021, https://www.wsj.com/articles/biden-administration-urged-to-penalize-
     saudi-crown-prince-over-khashoggi-killing-11614546231.

Nada Bakos, Alex Finley, Cindy Otis, John Sipher, and Tracy Walder, and former FBI employee Asha Rangappa, continued to denounce Trump frequently on Twitter in 2021, long after he left office. The Hayden Center at George Mason University and intelligence programs at other universities seem likely to continue to give activists opportunities to vent—and to prepare for new ideological battles.

The full effects of recent events may only become apparent years from this writing. Long memories in the intelligence world will combine with newly available information and new insights to change perspectives over time. Failures much smaller in magnitude and importance than the current troubles, such as the Vietnam politicization controversies of the 1960s, continue to generate discussion in the context of biased analyses and politicization.

Hayden claimed it would be "disastrous" for the IC if it is seen by the administration after Trump's to have been too accommodating to Trump, but he did not assess the effects of the largest IC opposition to a presidency in US history and the IC's increased collective partisanship.[7] He did not address the concerns of many current and former intelligence officers that the real damage to intelligence instead is likely to be sharply diminished public confidence in the IC's objectivity and directly consequent long-term damage to its ability to earn the trust of political leaders—the single most important determinant of whether leaders use intelligence.

While the story of the politicization of recent years is clarifying, much remains to be learned. Chief among the unknowns is Robert Jervis's concern—the extent and nature of the politicization of intelligence analysis. This is critical because it is intelligence analyses that most directly inform decision-makers.

---

7   Hayden, *Assault on Intelligence*, 248.

The government itself needs to know much more about what has happened and is happening in this area and to take appropriate steps to remedy any problems discovered.

Biden may initially be happy with a politicized intelligence bureaucracy that defines truth largely as he does and that only morphs into an overtly active Deep State when a Republican occupies the White House. But he may not always do as CIA's latter-day "zealots" wish, risking renewed intelligence activism against him this time, especially if he follows the well-established presidential precedent of blaming intelligence for a major policy failure. His advisors likely appreciate how ideology drove intelligence to fight "enemies at home and abroad," as Brennan subtitled his book, and will try to ensure that Biden keeps US intelligence mainly focused abroad. Despite risks to the future of the country, Biden seems unlikely to push Burns to make a major effort to reform the political culture at the CIA that Obama and Brennan helped make, and which helped elect him in 2020. It would confound his political base.

The activists quieted down by late 2021, but they have gone nowhere. Now further institutionalizing the cultural orthodoxies that led to the outburst of 2016, they remain ready to reactivate as, and when, they alone determine. When they do so, their motives will again be primarily ideological. The major task of reforming US intelligence remains undone.

BIBLIOGRAPHY

Adams, Sam. *War of Numbers: An Intelligence Memoir.* South Royalton, VT: Steerforth, 1994.

Ahern, Jr., Thomas L. *Good Questions, Wrong Answers: CIA's Estimates of Arms Traffic Through Sihanoukville, Cambodia, During the Vietnam War.* Washington: CIA Center for the Study of Intelligence, 2004.

Allison, Graham, and Philip Zelikow, *Essence of Decision: Explaining the Cuban Missile Crisis.* 2nd ed. New York: Pearson, 1999.

Andrew, Christopher. "American presidents and their intelligence communities." *Intelligence and National Security* 10:4 (1995): 95-112.

Andrew, Christopher. *For the President's Eyes Only: Secret Intelligence and the American Presidency from Washington to Bush.* New York: HarperPerennial, 1996.

Anonymous, "The DI's Organizational Culture." *Studies in Intelligence* 34 (Summer 1990): 21-25.

Anonymous (Michael Scheuer). *Imperial Hubris: Why the West Is Losing the War on Terror.* Washington DC: Brassey's, 2004.

Bade, Rachael, and Karoun Demirjian, *Unchecked: The Untold Story Behind Congress's Botched Impeachments of Donald Trump.* New York: HarperCollins, 2022.

Baer, Robert. *The Fourth Man: The Hunt for a KGB Spy at the Top of the CIA and the Rise of Putin's Russia.* New York: Hachette, 2022.

Bakos, Nada. *The Targeter: My Life in the CIA, Hunting Terrorists and Challenging the White House.* New York: Little, Brown, 2019.

Bar-Joseph, Uri. "The Politicization of Intelligence: A Comparative Study." *International Journal of Intelligence and CounterIntelligence* 26:2 (2013): 347-369.

Barr, William P. *One Damn Thing After Another: Memoirs of an Attorney General.* New York: William Morrow, 2022.

Bean, Hamilton. "Rhetorical and Critical/Cultural Intelligence Studies." *Intelligence and National Security* 28:4 (2013): 495-519.

Betts, Richard K. "Analysis, War, and Decision: Why Intelligence Failures Are Inevitable." *World Politics* 31:1 (1978): 61-89.

Betts, Richard K. *Enemies of Intelligence: Knowledge & Power in American National Security.* New York: Columbia University Press, 2007.

Bolton, John. *The Room Where It Happened: A White House Memoir.* New York: Simon & Schuster, 2020.

Bradley, Mark A. *A Very Principled Boy: The Life of Duncan Lee, Red Spy and Cold Warrior.* New York: Basic, 2014.

Brand, Melanie. "Mind games: cognitive bias, US intelligence and the 1968 Soviet invasion of Czechoslovakia." *Intelligence and National Security* 34:5 (2019): 743-757.

Brennan, John O. *Undaunted: My Fight Against America's Enemies, At Home and Abroad.* New York: Celadon, 2020.

Burns, William J. *The Back Channel: A Memoir of American Diplomacy and the Case for Its Renewal.* New York: Random House, 2020.

Byman, Daniel. "Explaining the Western Response to the Arab Spring." *Journal of Strategic Studies* 36:2 (2013): 289-320.

Byman, Daniel. "US counterterrorism intelligence cooperation with the developing world and its limits." *Intelligence and National Security* 32:2 (2017): 145-160.

Callum, Robert. "The Case for Cultural Diversity in the Intelligence Community." *International Journal of Intelligence and CounterIntelligence* 14:1 (2001): 25-48.

Campbell. Josh. *Crossfire Hurricane: Inside Donald Trump's War on the FBI.* Chapel Hill, NC: Algonquin, 2019.

Carle, Glenn L. *The Interrogator: An Education.* New York: National Books, 2011.

Central Intelligence Agency, *Director's Advisory Group on Women in Leadership,* 2013, https://www.cia.gov/library/reports/CIA_Women_In_Leadership_March2013.pdf.

Chaffetz, Jason. *The Deep State: How an Army of Bureaucrats Protected Barack Obama and is Working to Destroy the Trump Agenda.* New York: Broadside, 2018.

Chang, Welton, Elissabeth Berdini, David R. Mandel, and Philip E. Tetlock. "Restructuring structured analytic techniques in intelligence." *Intelligence and National Security* 33:3 (2018): 337-356.

Chin, William Y. "Diversity in the Age of Terror: How Racial and Ethnic Diversity in the U.S. Intelligence Community Enhances National Security." *Florida A&M University Law Review* 6:1 (2010): 49-88.

Clapper, James R., with Trey Brown. *Facts and Fears: Hard Truths from a Life in Intelligence.* New York: Viking, 2018.

Cline, Ray S. *The CIA Under Reagan, Bush & Casey.* Washington: Acropolis, 1981.

Cohen, Eliot A. *Supreme Command: Soldiers, Statesmen and Leadership in Wartime.* New York: Free Press, 2002.

Cogan, Charles G. "The in-culture of the DO." *Intelligence and National Security* 8:1 (1993): 78-86.

Colby, William, and Peter Forbach. *Honorable Men: My Life in the CIA.* New York: Simon & Schuster 1978.

Comey, James. *A Higher Loyalty: Truth, Lies, and Leadership.* New York: Flatiron, 2018.

Conboy, Ken. *Spies on the Mekong: CIA Clandestine Operations in Laos.* Philadelphia: Casemate, 2021.

Cooper, Richard N. "Controlling Controversy: 1995-1997." In Hutchings and Treverton, *Truth to Power,* 42-56.

Crosston, Matthew. "Petticoat Promise: Gender and the CIA in the #MeToo Era." *International Journal of Intelligence and CounterIntelligence* 33:4 (2020): 731-746.

Darder Antonia, et al., eds. *The Critical Pedagogy Reader,* 3rd ed. Milton Park, UK: Routledge, 2017.

Davis, Jack. "Analytic Professionalism and the Policymaking Process: Q&A on a Challenging Relationship." Washington: The Sherman Kent Center for Intelligence Analysis Occasional Papers: Vol. 2, No. 4 (2003): 2-8.

Davis, Jack. "Intelligence Analysts and Policymakers: Benefits and Dangers of Tensions in the Relationship." *Intelligence and National Security* 21:6 (2006): 999-1021.

Davis, Jack. "Paul Wolfowitz on Intelligence Policy-Relations." *Studies in Intelligence* 39:5 (1996): 35-42.

Davis, Jack. "A Policymaker's Perspective on Intelligence Analysis." *Studies in Intelligence* 38:5 (1995): 7-15.

Draper, Robert. *Dead Certain: The Presidency of George W. Bush.* New York: Free Press, 2007.

Duarte, José L., Jarret T. Crawford, Charlotta Stern, Jonathan Haidt, Lee Jussim, and Philip E. Tetlock, "Political diversity will improve social psychology." *Behavioral and Brain Sciences* (2015): 1-13.

Dujmović, Nicholas. "Tech Stars on the Wall: The Human Cost of Intelligence Technology." *International Journal of Intelligence and CounterIntelligence* 31:1 (2018): 126-138.

Dulles, Allen, *The Craft of Intelligence.* New York: Harper & Row, 1983.

Durbin, Brent. "Addressing 'This Woeful Imbalance:' Efforts to Improve Women's Representation at CIA, 1947-2014." *Intelligence and National Security* 30: (2015): 855-870.

Eriksson, Gunilla. "A theoretical reframing of the intelligence–policy relation." *Intelligence and National Security* 33:4 (2018): 553-561.

Feaver, Peter D. *Armed Servants: Agency, Oversight, and Civil-Military Relations.* Cambridge MA: Harvard University Press, 2003.

Feaver, Peter D., and Richard H. Kohn, ed. *Soldiers and Civilians: The Civil-Military Gap and American National Security.* Cambridge MA: MIT Press, 2001.

Fingar, Thomas. "New Missions, New Challenges, 2005-2008." In Hutchings and Treverton, *Truth to Power*, 133-156.

Fingar, Thomas. *Reducing Uncertainty: Intelligence Analysis and National Security.* Stanford CA: Stanford University Press, 2011.

Firehock, Raymond B., John A. Gentry, Julia W. Rogers, and James M. Simon, Jr. "Negotiating the Review Process: A Guide to Intelligence Analysis, 1970." *Intelligence and National Security* 33:5 (2018): 774-783.

Fischer, Benjamin B. "An Agency Insider's View of the World." *International Journal of Intelligence and CounterIntelligence* 28:2 (2015): 383-397.

Ford, Harold P. *Estimative Intelligence: The Purposes and Problems of National Estimating.* Lanham MD: University Press of America, 1993.

Ford, Harold P. "The US government's experience with intelligence analysis: Pluses and minuses." *Intelligence and National Security* 10:4 (1995): 34-53.

Freedman, Lawrence. "The CIA and the Soviet Threat: the Politicization of Estimates, 1966-1977." *Intelligence and National Security* 12:1 (1997): 122-142.

Freeh, Louis J. *My FBI: Bringing Down the Mafia, Investigating Bill Clinton, and Fighting the War on Terror.* New York: St. Martin's, 2005.

Gannon, John. "A New Global Agenda, 1997-2001." In Hutchings and Treverton, *Truth to Power*, 57-84.

Garthoff, Douglas F. *Directors of Central Intelligence as Leaders of the U.S. Intelligence Community, 1946-2005.* Washington: Potomac Books, 2007.

Gates, Robert M. "The CIA and American Foreign Policy." *Foreign Affairs* 66:2 (1987-88): 215-230.

Gates, Robert M. *Exercise of Power: American Failures, Successes, and a New Path Forward in the Post-Cold War World.* New York: Alfred A. Knopf, 2020.

Gates, Robert M. *From the Shadows: The Ultimate Insider's Story of Five Presidents and How They Won the Cold War.* New York: Touchstone, 1996.

Gates, Robert M. "Guarding against Politicization." *Studies in Intelligence* 36:5 (1992): 5-13.

Gawthrop, William. *The Criminal Investigator-Intelligence Analysts Handbook of Islam.* Parker CO: Outskirts Press, 2021.

Gelb, Leslie H., and Richard K. Betts, *The Irony of Vietnam: The System Worked.* Washington, Brookings, 1979.

Gentry, John A. "Belated Success: Soviet Active Measures against the United States." *American Intelligence Journal* 39:2 (2022): 151-170.

Gentry. John A. "The Cancer of Human Rights." *Washington Quarterly* 22:4 (1999): 93-112.

Gentry, John A. "Demographic Diversity in U.S. Intelligence Personnel: Is It Functionally Useful?" *International Journal of Intelligence and CounterIntelligence* 36:2 (2023): 564-596.

Gentry, John A. "Has the ODNI Improved U.S. Intelligence Analysis?" *International Journal of Intelligence and CounterIntelligence* 28:4 (2015): 637-661.

Gentry, John A. "An INS Special Forum: US Intelligence Officers' Involvement in Political Activities in the Trump Era." *Intelligence and National Security* 35:1 (2020): 1-19.

Gentry, John A. "The intelligence of fear." *Intelligence and National Security* 32:1 (2017): 9-25.

Gentry, John A. "Intelligence Learning and Adaptation: Lessons from Counterinsurgency Wars." *Intelligence and National Security* 25:1 (2010): 50-75.

Gentry, John A. *Lost Promise: How CIA Analysis Misserves the Nation.* Lanham MD: University Press of America, 1993.

Gentry, John A. "Managers of Analysts: The Other Half of Intelligence Analysis." *Intelligence and National Security* 31:2 (2016): 160-182.

Gentry, John A. "A New Form of Politicization? Has the CIA Become Institutionally Biased or Politicized?" *International Journal of Intelligence and CounterIntelligence* 31:4 (2018): 647-680.

Gentry, John A. "The New Politicization of the U.S. Intelligence Community." *International Journal of Intelligence and CounterIntelligence* 33:4 (2020): 639-665.

Gentry, John A. "Partisan Political Polemics: Wrecking One's Reputation." *International Journal of Intelligence and CounterIntelligence* 32:1 (2019): 170-178.

Gentry, John A. "The 'Professionalization' of Intelligence Analysis: A Skeptical Perspective." *International Journal of Intelligence and CounterIntelligence* 29:4 (2016): 643-676.

Gentry, John A. "Purges of Intelligence Services: Motives, Methods, and Consequences." *Journal of Intelligence History* 22:1 (2023): 77-97.

Gentry, John A. "Trump-Era Politicization: A Code of Civil-Intelligence Behavior Is Needed." *International Journal of Intelligence and CounterIntelligence* 34:4 (2021): 757-786.

Gentry, John A. "'Truth' as a Tool of the Politicization of Intelligence." *International Journal of Intelligence and CounterIntelligence* 32:2 (2019): 217-247.

Gentry, John A., and Joseph S. Gordon, *Strategic Warning Intelligence: History, Challenges, and Prospects.* Washington: Georgetown University Press, 2019.

George, Roger Z. "Reflections on CIA Analysis: Is it Finished?" *Intelligence and National Security* 26:1 (2011): 72-81.

Gkotzaridis, Evi. "'Who Really Rules this Country?' Collusion between State and Deep State in Post-Civil War Greece and the Murder of Independent MP Grigorios Lambrakis, 1958-1963." *Diplomacy & Statecraft* 28:4 (2017): 646-673.

Glennon, Michael J. *National Security and Double Government.* New York: Oxford University Press, 2015.

Goldberg, Bernard. *Bias: A CBS Insider Exposes How the Media Distort the News.* Washington: Regnery, 2001.

Golitsyn, Anatoliy. *New Lies For Old.* San Pedro, CA: GSG & Associates, 1984.

Gonzales, Mike. *BLM: The Making of a New Marxist Revolution.* New York: Encounter, 2021.

Gonzales, Mike. *The Plot to Change America: How Identity Politics is Dividing the Land of the Free.* New York: Encounter, 2020.

Goodman, Melvin A. *Whistleblower at the CIA: An Insider's Account of the Politics of Intelligence.* San Francisco: City Lights Books, 2017.

Goodman, Michael S. "Learning to Walk: The Origins of the UK's Joint Intelligence Committee." *International Journal of Intelligence and CounterIntelligence* 21:1 (2007): 40-56.

Grabo, Cynthia M. "Soviet Deception in the Czechoslovak Crisis." *Studies in Intelligence* 14:1 (1970): 19-34.

Grabo, Cynthia, with Jan Goldman, *Handbook of Warning Intelligence.* Lanham MD: Rowman & Littlefield, 2015.

Groseclose, Tim. *Left Turn: How Liberal Media Bias Distorts the American Mind.* New York: St. Martin's, 2011.

Gustafson, Kristian, and Christopher Andrew. "The Other Hidden Hand: Soviet and Cuban Intelligence in Allende's Chile." *Intelligence and National Security* 33:3 (2018): 407-421.

Handel, Michael I. "Intelligence and the Problem of Strategic Surprise." *Journal of Strategic Studies* 7:3 (1984): 229-281.

Hänni, Adrian. "When Casey's blood pressure rose: a case study of intelligence politicization in the United States." *Intelligence and National Security* 31:7 (2016): 963-977.

Hastedt, Glenn. "CIA's organizational culture and the problem of reform." *International Journal of Intelligence and CounterIntelligence* 9:3 (1996): 249-269.

Hastedt, Glenn. "The Politics of Intelligence and the Politicization of Intelligence: The American Experience." *Intelligence and National Security* 28:1 (2013): 5-31.

Hastedt, Glenn. "Public intelligence: Leaks as policy instruments—the case of the Iraq war." *Intelligence and National Security* 20:3 (2005): 419-439.

Hayden, Michael V. *The Assault on Intelligence: American National Security in an Age of Lies.* New York: Penguin, 2018.

Hayden, Michael V. *Playing to the Edge: American Intelligence in the Age of Terror.* New York: Penguin, 2016.

Hedley, John H. "The Intelligence Community: Is It Broken? How to Fix It?" *Studies in Intelligence* 39:5 (1996): 11-18.

Hegseth, Pete, with David Goodwin. *Battle for the American Mind: Uprooting a Century of Miseducation.* New York: Broadside, 2022.

Helgerson, John L. *Getting to Know the President: Intelligence Briefings of Presidential Candidates, 1952-2004*, 2d ed. Washington: Central Intelligence Agency, Center for the Study of Intelligence, 2012.

Helgerson, John L. *Getting to Know the President: Intelligence Briefings of Presidential Candidates, 1952-2016*, 3d ed. Washington: Central Intelligence Agency, Center for the Study of Intelligence, 2021.

Helgerson, John L. "The Trauma of 9/11: 2001-2002." In Hutchings and Treverton, *Truth to Power*, 85-104.

Helms, Richard, with William Hood. *A Look Over My Shoulder: A Life in the Central Intelligence Agency.* New York: Ballantine, 2003.

Herman, Michael. "Intelligence and the assessment of military capabilities: Reasonable sufficiency or the worst case?" *Intelligence and National Security* 4:4 (1989): 765-799.

Heuer, Jr., Richards J. *Psychology of Intelligence Analysis.* Washington DC: Center for the Study of Intelligence, 1999.

Hiam, C. Michael. *Who the Hell Are We Fighting: The Story of Sam Adams and the Vietnam Intelligence Wars.* Hanover, NH: Steerforth, 2006.

Hulnick, Arthur S. "Intelligence Reform 2007: Fix or Fizzle?" *International Journal of Intelligence and CounterIntelligence* 20:4 (2007): 567-582.

Huntington, Samuel P. *The Soldier and the State: The Theory and Politics of Civil-Military Relations.* Cambridge MA: Harvard University Press, 1960.

Husain, Aiyaz. "Covert Action and US Cold War Strategy in Cuba, 1961-1962." *Cold War History* 5:1 (2005): 23-53.

Hutchings, Robert. "America at War: 2003-2005." in Hutchings and Treverton, *Truth to Power,* 105-132.

Hutchings, Robert. "Introduction." In Hutchings and Treverton, *Truth to Power,* 1-23.

Hutchings, Robert, and Gregory F. Treverton, *Truth to Power: A History of the U.S. National Intelligence Council.* New York: Oxford University Press, 2019.

Immerman, Richard H. "Intelligence and Strategy: Historicizing Psychology, Policy, and Politics." *Diplomatic History* 32:1 (2008): 1-23.

Jamieson, Kathleen Hall. *Cyberwar: How Russian Hackers and Trolls Helped Elect a President.* New York: Oxford University Press, 2018.

Jarrett, Gregg. *Witch Hunt: The Story of the Greatest Mass Delusion in American Political History.* New York: Broadside, 2019.

Janis, Irving. *Victims of Groupthink: A Psychological Study of Foreign-Policy Decisions and Fiascoes.* Boston: Houghton-Mifflin, 1972.

Janowitz, Morris. *The Professional Soldier: A Social and Political Portrait.* New York: Free Press, 1960.

Jeffreys-Jones, Rhodri. *The CIA and American Democracy*, 2nd ed. New Haven: Yale University Press, 1998.

Jervis, Robert. "Reports, Politics, and Intelligence Failures: The Case of Iraq." *Journal of Strategic Studies* 29:1 (2006): 3-52.

Jervis, Robert. *Why Intelligence Fails: Lessons from the Iranian Revolution and the Iraq War.* Ithaca: Cornell University Press, 2010.

Jervis, Robert. "Why Intelligence and Policymakers Clash." *Political Science Quarterly* 125:2 (2010): 185-204.

Jervis, Robert. "Why Intelligence and Policymakers Clash Reexamined," in Gentry, "An INS Special Forum," 9-10.

Johnson, Loch K. "In Remembrance: Admiral Stansfield Turner, Naval Officer as DCI," *Intelligence and National Security* 33:4 (2018): 587-597.

Johnson, Thomas R. *American Cryptology During the Cold War 1945-1989; The Complete Declassified Official Four-Volume History of the NSA.* St. Petersburg FL: Red and Black Publishers, 1995.

Johnston, Rob. *Analytic Culture in the U.S. Intelligence Community: An Ethnographic Study.* Washington DC: Central Intelligence Agency, Center for the Study of Intelligence, 2005.

Jones, Christopher M. "The CIA Under Clinton: Continuity and Change." *International Journal of Intelligence and CounterIntelligence* 14:4 (2001): 504, 503-528.

Jones, David Martin. "Intelligence and the management of national security: the post-/11 evolution of an Australian National Security Community." *Intelligence and National Security* 33:1 (2018): 1-20.

Kalugin, Oleg. *Spymaster: My Thirty-Two Years in Intelligence and Espionage against the West.* New York: Basic, 2009.

Katz, Barry M. *Foreign Intelligence: Research and Analysis in the Office of Strategic Services, 1942-1945.* Cambridge MA: Harvard University Press, 1989.

Kendall, Willmoore. "The Function of Intelligence." *World Politics* 1:4 (1949): 542-552.

Kent, Sherman. "A Crucial Estimate Relived." *Studies in Intelligence* 35:5 (Spring 1964): 111-119.

Kent, Sherman. *Strategic Intelligence for American World Policy.* Princeton: Princeton University Press, 1949.

Kibbe, Jennifer. "Congressional Oversight of Intelligence: Is the Solution Part of the Problem?" *Intelligence and National Security* 25:1 (2010): 24-49.

Kimball, Roger. *Tenured Radicals: How Politics Has Corrupted Our Higher Education.* Chicago: Ivan R. Dee, 2008.

Kissinger, Henry. *White House Years.* Boston: Little, Brown, 1979.

Knorr, Klaus. "Failures in National Intelligence Estimates: The Case of Cuban Missiles." *World Politics* 16:3 (April 1964): 455-467.

Kohn, Richard H. "Out of Control: The Crisis in Civil-Military Relations." *The National Interest* 35 (Spring 1994): 3-17.

Kojm, Christopher. "Intelligence Integration and Reform: 2009-2014." In Hutchings and Treverton, *Truth to Power,* 157-179.

Kurtz, Howard. *Media Madness: Donald Trump, the Press, and the War Over the Truth.* Washington: Regnery, 2018.

Landon-Murray, Michael, and Stephen Coulthart. "Intelligence Studies Programs as US Public Policy: A Survey of IC CAE Grant Recipients." *Intelligence and National Security* 35:2 (2020): 269-282.

Leadbetter, Jr., Wyland F., and Stephen J. Bury. "Prelude to Desert Storm: The Politicization of Intelligence." *International Journal of Intelligence and CounterIntelligence* 6:1 (1993): 43-54.

Lefebvre, *Stéphane*. "The Difficulties and Dilemmas of International Intelligence Cooperation." *International Journal of Intelligence and CounterIntelligence* 16:4 (2003): 527-542.

Lillbacka, Ralf G.V. "Realism, Constructivism, and Intelligence Analysis." *International Journal of Intelligence and CounterIntelligence* 26:2 (2013): 304-331.

London, Douglas. *The Recruiter: Spying and the Lost Art of American Intelligence*. New York: Hachette, 2021

Lowenthal, Mark M. "Intelligence Analysis: Management and Transformation Issues." In Sims and Gerber, ed., *Transforming U.S. Intelligence*, chapter 13.

Lowenthal, Mark M. *Intelligence: From Secrets to Policy*, 7th ed. Los Angeles: CQ Press, 2017.

Lowenthal, Mark M. "Intelligence is NOT About 'Telling Truth to Power.'" *International Journal of Intelligence and CounterIntelligence* 34:4 (2021), 795-798.

Lucas, Scott. "Recognizing Politicization: The CIA and the Path to the 2003 War in Iraq." *Intelligence and National Security* 26:2-3 (2011): 203-227.

Lukianoff, Greg, and Jonathan Haidt. "The Coddling of the American Mind." *The Atlantic*, September 15, 2015, https://www.theatlantic.com/magazine/archive/2015/09/the-coddling-of-the-american-mind/399356/.

Mac Donald, Heather. *The Diversity Delusion: How Race and Gender Pandering Corrupt the University and Undermine Our Culture*. New York: St. Martin's, 2018.

Marangione, Margaret S. "Millennials: Truthtellers or Threats?" *International Journal of Intelligence and CounterIntelligence* 32:2 (2019): 354-378.

Marchetti, Victor, and John D. Marks. *The CIA and the Cult of Intelligence*. New York: Alfred A. Knopf, 1974.

Marrin, Stephen. "At Arm's Length or at the Elbow? Explaining the Distance between Analysts and Decisionmakers." *International Journal of Intelligence and CounterIntelligence* 20:3 (2007): 401-414.

Marrin, Stephen. "CIA's Kent School: Improving Training for New Analysts." *International Journal of Intelligence and CounterIntelligence* 16:4 (2003): 609-637.

Marrin, Stephen. "Evaluating the Quality of Intelligence Analysis: By What (Mis) Measure?" *Intelligence and National Security* 27:6 (2012): 896-912.

Marrin, Stephen. *Improving Intelligence Analysis, Bridging the Gap between Scholarship and Practice.* Abingdon UK: Routledge, 2011.

Marrin, Stephen. "Training and Educating U.S. Intelligence Analysts." *International Journal of Intelligence and CounterIntelligence* 22:1 (2008): 131-146.

Marrin, Stephen. "Why strategic intelligence has limited influence on American foreign policy." *Intelligence and National Security* 32:6 (2017): 725-742.

Mazzetti, Mark. *The Way of the Knife: The CIA, A Secret Army, and a War at the Ends of the Earth.* New York: Penguin, 2013.

McCabe, Andrew G. *The Threat: How the FBI Protects America in the Age of Terror and Trump.* New York: St. Martin's, 2019.

McCarthy, Andrew C. *Ball of Collusion: The Plot to Rig an Election and Destroy a Presidency.* New York: Encounter, 2019.

McCombie, Stephen, Allon J. Uhlmann, and Sarah Morrison. "The US 2016 presidential election & Russia's troll farms." *Intelligence and National Security* 35:1 (2020): 95-114.

McDermott, Rose. "Experimental Intelligence." *Intelligence and National Security* 26:1 (2011): 82-98.

McMaster, H.R. *Battlegrounds: The Fight to Defend the Free World.* New York: Harper, 2020.

McPhee, Justin T. *Spinning the Secrets of the State: Politics and Intelligence in Australia*. Melbourne: Monash University Publishing, 2020.

Mellers, Barbara, et al., "Identifying and Cultivating Superforecasters as a Method of Improving Probabilistic Predictions," *Perspectives on Psychological Science* 10:3 (2015): 267-281.

Mérieau, Eugénie. "Thailand's Deep State, Royal Power and the Constitutional Court (1997–2015)." *Journal of Contemporary Asia* 46:3 (2016): 445-466.

Miller, Bowman H. "Intelligence and Policy: The Case for Thin Walls as Seen by a Veteran of INR," *Studies in Intelligence* 62:2 (2018): 35-39.

Millick, Professor (pseudonym). *CIA 101: A Crash Course in Agency Case Officers*. Self-published, 2020.

Moran, Christopher. *Company Confessions: Secrets, Memoirs, and the CIA*. New York: Thomas Dunne, 2016.

Moran, Christopher. "Nixon's Axe Man: CIA Director James R. Schlesinger." *Journal of American Studies* 53:1 (2019): 95-121.

Muller, Jr., David G. "Intelligence Analysis in Red and Blue." *International Journal of Intelligence and CounterIntelligence* 21:1 (2008): 1-12.

Murray, Douglas. *The War on the West*. New York: Broadside, 2022.

Nance, Malcolm. *The Plot to Destroy Democracy: How Putin and His Spies Are Undermining America and Dismantling the West*. New York: Hachette, 2018.

National Intelligence Council, "Assessing Russian Activities and Intentions in Recent US Elections." Intelligence Community Assessment, January 6, 2017. https://www.dni.gov/files/documents/ICA_2017_01.pdf.

Ngo, Andy. *Unmasked: Inside Antifa's Radical Plan to Destroy Democracy*. New York: Center Street, 2021.

Nolan, Bridget Rose. "Information Sharing and Collaboration in the United States Intelligence Community: An Ethnographic Study of the National Counterterrorism Center." Unpublished dissertation, University of Pennsylvanian, 2013.

Nye, Joseph S. Jr. "Estimative Intelligence after the Cold War, 1993-1994." In Hutchings and Treverton, *Truth to Power*, 23-41.

Nye, Joseph S, Jr. *Soft Power: The Means to Success in World Politics*. New York: PublicAffairs, 2005.

Oakley, David P. *Subordinating Intelligence: The DoD/CIA Post-Cold War Relationship.* Lexington: University Press of Kentucky, 2019.

O'Brien, Alexa, and Luis E. Rodriguez. "By the Numbers: Former U.S. Intelligence Officials Discuss Personal Opinion versus Professional Obligation." *International Journal of Intelligence and CounterIntelligence* 33:2 (2020): 354-379.

Office of the Director of National Intelligence, "Annual Demographic Report: Hiring and Retention of Minorities, Women, and Persons with Disabilities in the United States Intelligence Community Fiscal Year 2016," at https://www.dni.gov/files/documents/Newsroom/Reports%20and%20Pubs/Annual%20Demographic%20Report%20-%202016.pdf.

Omand, David. "Reflections on Intelligence Analysts and Policymakers." *International Journal of Intelligence and CounterIntelligence* 33:3 (2020): 471-482.

Omand, David, Jamie Bartlett, and Carl Miller. "Introducing Social Media Intelligence (SOCMINT)." *Intelligence and National Security* 27:6 (2012): 801-823.

Omestad, Thomas. "Psychology and the CIA: Leaders on the Couch." *Foreign Policy* 95 (Summer 1994): 104-122.

Orwell, George. *1984*. Boston: Houghton Mifflin Harcourt, 1949.

Ott, Marvin C. "Partisanship and the Decline of Intelligence Oversight." *International Journal of Intelligence and CounterIntelligence* 16:1 (2003): 69-94.

Pacepa, Ion Mihai, and Ronald J. Rychlak. *Disinformation.* Washington: WND Books, 2013.

Page, Carter. *Abuse and Power: How an Innocent American Was Framed in an Attempted Coup Against the President.* Washington: Regnery, 2020.

Panetta, Leon, with Jim Newton. *Worthy Fights: A Memoir of Leadership in War and Peace.* New York: Penguin, 2014.

Park, Bill. "Turkey's Deep State." *The RUSI Journal* 153 (2008): 54-59.

Petersen, Martin. "What I learned in 40 Years of Doing Intelligence Analysis for US Foreign Policymakers." *Studies in Intelligence* 55:1 (Extracts, March 2011): 13-20.

Phillips, David Atlee. *The Night Watch: 25 Years of Peculiar Service.* New York: Atheneum, 1977.

Phillips, Katherine W., et al. "How Diversity Works." *Scientific American* 311:4 (2014): 42-47.

Pillar, Paul R. "Good Literature and Bad History: The 9/11 Commission's Tale of Strategic Intelligence." *Intelligence and National Security* 21:6 (2006): 1022-1044.

Prados, John. *The Family Jewels: The CIA, Secrecy, and Presidential Power.* Austin: University of Texas Press, 2013.

Prados, John. *Safe for Democracy: The Secret Wars of the CIA.* Chicago: Ivan R. Dee, 2006.

Priess, David. *The President's Book of Secrets: The Untold Story of Intelligence Briefings of America's Presidents from Kennedy to Obama.* New York: PublicAffairs, 2016.

Rid, Thomas. *Active Measures: The Secret History of Disinformation and Political Warfare.* New York: Farrar, Straus and Giroux, 2020.

Riebling, Mark. *Wedge: From Pearl Harbor to 9/11: How the Secret War Between the FBI and CIA Has Endangered National Security.* New York: Touchstone, 2002.

Roberts, Patrick S., and Robert B. Saldin. "Why Presidents Sometimes Do Not Use Intelligence Information." *Political Science Quarterly* 131:4 (2016-2017): 779-802.

Rogg, Jeff. "The U.S. Intelligence Community's 'MacArthur Moment.'" *International Journal of Intelligence and CounterIntelligence* 33:4 (2020): 666-681.

Rohde, David. *In Deep: The FBI, the CIA, and the Truth about America's Deep State*. New York: W.W. Norton, 2020.

Rosenberg, Daniel. "From Crisis to Split: The Communist Party USA, 1989-1991."*American Communist History* 39:1-2 (2019): 1-55.

Rovner, Joshua. *Fixing the Facts: National Security and the Politics of Intelligence*. Ithaca: Cornell University Press, 2011.

Rovner, Joshua. "Is Politicization Ever a Good Thing?" *Intelligence and National Security* 28:1 (2013): 55-67.

Rubin, Michael. "The Temptation of Intelligence Politicization to Support Diplomacy." *International Journal of Intelligence and CounterIntelligence* 29:1 (2016): 1-25.

Saldin, Robert P., and Steven M. Teles. *Never Trump: The Revolt of the Conservative Elites*. New York: Oxford University Press, 2020.

Schmidt, Michael S. *Donald Trump v. The United States: Inside the Struggle to Stop a President.* New York: Random House, 2020.

Shimer, David. *Rigged: America, Russia, and One Hundred Years of Covert Electoral Interference*. New York: Alfred A. Knopf, 2020.

Simon, James M., Jr. "Intelligence Analysis as Practiced by the CIA." *International Journal of Intelligence and CounterIntelligence* 26:4 (2013): 641-651.

Sims, Jennifer E. "Foreign Intelligence Liaison: Devils, Deals, and Details." *International Journal of Intelligence and CounterIntelligence* 19:2 (2006): 195-217.

Sims, Jennifer E., and Burton Gerber, ed., *Transforming U.S. Intelligence*. Washington: Georgetown University Press, 2005.

Smith, Lee. *The Permanent Coup: How Enemies Foreign and Domestic Targeted the American President*, New York: Center Street, 2020.

Smith, Michael. *The Anatomy of a Spy: A History of Espionage and Betrayal*. New York: Arcade, 2020.

Smith, Russell Jack. *The Unknown CIA: My Three Decades with the Agency.* New York: Berkley, 1992.

Snepp, Frank. *Decent Interval.* New York: Random House, 1977.

Snowden, Edward. *Permanent Record.* New York: Metropolitan, 2019.

Soukup, Stephen R. *The Dictatorship of Woke Capital: How Political Correctness Captured Big Business.* New York: Encounter, 2021.

Söyler, Mehtap. "Informal institutions, forms of state and democracy: the Turkish deep state." *Democratization* 20:2 (2013): 310-334.

Steinberg, James B. "The Policymaker's Perspective: Transparency and Partnership." In Roger Z. George and James B. Bruce, ed., *Analyzing Intelligence: National Security Practitioners' Perspectives.* Washington DC: Georgetown University Press, 2014, 93-101.

Stevens, Sayre. "The SAM Upgrade Blues." *Studies in Intelligence* 18:2 (1974): 21-35.

Strassel, Kimberley. *Resistance: How Trump Haters Are Breaking America.* New York: Twelve, 2019.

Strzok, Peter. *Compromised: Counterintelligence and the Threat of Donald J. Trump.* Boston: Houghton Mifflin Harcourt, 2020.

Sulick, Michael. J. *Spying in America: Espionage from the Revolutionary War to the Dawn of the Cold War.* Washington: Georgetown University Press, 2014.

Taylor, Stan A., and Daniel Snow. "Cold War Spies: Why They Spied and How They Got Caught." *Intelligence and National Security* 12:2 (1997): 101-125.

Tenet, George, with Bill Harlow. *At the Center of the Storm: My Years at the CIA.* New York: HarperCollins, 2007.

Tetlock, Philip E. *Expert Political Judgment: How Good Is It? How Can We Know?* Princeton: Princeton University Press, 2006.

Tetlock, Philip E. "Political psychology or politicized psychology: Is the road to scientific hell paved with good moral intentions?" *Political Psychology* 15:3 (1994): 509-529.

Tetlock, Philip E., and Dan Gardner. *Superforecasting: The Art and Science of Prediction*. New York: Crown, 2015.

Tetlock, Philip E., et al., "The Psychology of Intelligence Analysis: Drivers of Prediction Accuracy in World Politics." *Journal of Experimental Psychology: Applied* 25:1 (2015): 1-14.

Thomas, Evan. *The Very Best Men: The Daring Years of the CIA*. New York: Simon & Schuster, 2006.

Thompson, Terence J. "A Psycho-Social Motivational Theory of Mass Leaking." *International Journal of Intelligence and CounterIntelligence* 31:1 (2018): 116-125.

Treverton, Gregory. "From Afghanistan to Trump: 2014-2017." In Hutchings and Treverton, *Truth to Power*, 180-197.

Treverton, Gregory. "Conclusion: Looking to the Next Chapter." In Hutchings and Treverton, *Truth to Power*, 198-208.

Tromblay, Darren E. *The FBI Abroad: Bridging the Gap between Foreign and Domestic Intelligence*. Boulder CO: Lynne Rienner, 2020.

Tromblay, Darren E. "Information Technology (IT) Woes and Intelligence Agency Failures: The Federal Bureau of Investigation's Troubled IT Evolution as a Microcosm of a Dysfunctional Corporate Culture." *Intelligence and National Security* 32:6 (2017): 817-832.

Tromblay, Darren E. *Spying: Assessing US Domestic Intelligence since 9/11*. Boulder CO: Lynne Rienner, 2019.

Tromblay, Darren E. "The Threat Review and Prioritization Trap: How the FBI's New Threat Review and Prioritization Process Compounds the Bureau's Oldest Problems." *Intelligence and National Security* 31:5 (2016): 762-770.

Turner, Stansfield. *Secrecy and Democracy: The CIA in Transition*. Boston: Houghton Mifflin, 1985.

U.S. Government Accountability Office, *Intelligence Community: Additional Actions Needed to Strengthen Workforce Diversity Planning and Oversight*, GAO-21-83, December 2020, p. 3.

U.S. Government Accountability Office, *Intelligence Community: Actions Needed to Improve Planning and Oversight of the Centers for Academic Excellence Program*, GAO-19-529. Washington, DC, August 2019.

Usowski, Peter S. "Former CIA Officers Writing about Intelligence, Policy, and Politics, 2016-2017." *Studies in Intelligence* 62:3 (Extracts, September 2018): 1-14.

Warner, Michael. "The Use and Abuse of Intelligence in the Public Square." *Studies in Intelligence* 63:3 (Extracts, September 2019): 15-24.

Watts, Clint, and John E. Brennan. "Capturing the Potential of Outlier Ideas in the Intelligence Community." *Studies in Intelligence* 55:4 (Extracts, December 2011): 1-10.

Wege, Carl Anthony. "The Changing Islamic State Intelligence Apparatus." *International Journal of Intelligence and CounterIntelligence* 31:2 (2018): 271-288.

Weiner, Tim. *Enemies: A History of the FBI.* New York: Random House, 2013.

Wells, Luke Benjamin. "The 'bomber gap': British intelligence and an American delusion." *Journal of Strategic Studies* 40:7 (2017): 963-989.

Westerfield, H. Bradford. "Inside Ivory Bunkers: CIA Analysts Resist Managers' 'Pandering' - Part II." *International Journal of Intelligence and CounterIntelligence* 10:1 (1997): 19-54.

Wettering, Frederick L. "(C)overt Action: The Disappearing 'C'." *International Journal of Intelligence and CounterIntelligence* 16:4 (2003): 561-572.

Whaley, Barton. *Strategem: Deception and Surprise in War.* Boston: Artech House, 2007.

Whipple, Chris. *The Spy Masters: How the CIA Directors Shape History and the Future.* New York: Scribner, 2020.

White, Ismail K., and Chryl N. Laird. *Why are Blacks Democrats?* Princeton: Princeton University Press, 2020.

Wilder, Dennis C. "An Educated Consumer Is Our Best Customer." *Studies in Intelligence* 55:2 (Extracts, June 2011): 23-31.

Wilder, Ursula M. "The Psychology of Espionage and Leaking in the Digital Age." *Studies in Intelligence* 61:2 (Extracts, 2017): 1-36.

Wippl, Joseph W. "HUMINT With Spiritual Awareness." *International Journal of Intelligence and CounterIntelligence* 34:3 (2021): 614-621.

Wirtz, James J. "Intelligence to Please: The Order of Battle Controversy during the Vietnam War." *Political Science Quarterly* 106:2 (1991): 239-263.

Wirtz, James J. "The Politicization Paradox." *International Journal of Intelligence and CounterIntelligence* 25:1 (2012): 205-209.

Wirtz, James J. *The Tet Offensive: Intelligence Failure in War*. Ithaca: Cornell University Press, 2013.

Woodard, Nathan. "Tasting the Forbidden Fruit: Unlocking the Potential of Positive Politicization." *Intelligence and National Security* 28:1 (2013): 91-108.

Woodward, Bob. *Rage*. New York: Simon & Schuster, 2020.

Zegart, Amy B. *Spying Blind: The CIA, the FBI, and the Origins of 9/11*. Princeton: Princeton University Press, 2009.

ABOUT THE AUTHOR

JOHN A. GENTRY was for twelve years an intelligence analyst at the Central Intelligence Agency, where he worked mainly on economic issues concerning the Soviet Union and Eastern Europe. He also was senior analyst on the staff of the National Intelligence Officer for Warning in 1987-1989. In 1986 he experienced politicization from the political Right—efforts by CIA managers to make the Soviet Union and its allies look even worse than they clearly were. He approached the Senate intelligence committee about his concerns in 1991 during the confirmation hearings of Robert Gates to be director of central intelligence, recommending that Gates not be confirmed. Gates was head of CIA's analysis directorate in 1982-1986 and was, many CIA personnel then believed, responsible for the politicization. History indicates fairly clearly that politicization of all sorts is damaging in many ways, and Gentry has tracked the issue of politicization of intelligence by intelligence professionals closely ever since. The politicization since 2016 has been from the political Left, does the same kind of damage Gentry personally experienced, but is massive by historical standards and correspondingly is a much more important development in US intelligence and national political history.

After completing his Ph.D. in 2008, Gentry taught at several educational institutions, including the National Defense University, George Mason University, Columbia University, and from 2011 to 2015 at National Intelligence University—the educational arm of the intelligence community. Hence, he fairly recently was a member of the IC, dealing daily with personnel from virtually all IC agencies. He is now an adjunct professor with Georgetown University's School of Foreign Service. He teaches courses on intelligence subjects.

Especially after turning to teaching, Gentry has also written extensively on security-related subjects, especially in recent years on intelligence topics. He has published more than 30 articles on intelligence subjects, mainly in academic journals such as *Intelligence and National Security* and *International Journal of Intelligence and CounterIntelligence*. He is on the editorial advisory board of *International Journal of Intelligence and CounterIntelligence*. He has written three published books, two of which are on intelligence topics. His most recent book (with Joseph S. Gordon) is *Strategic Warning Intelligence: History, Challenges, and Prospects* (Georgetown University Press, 2019). He is a member of the International Studies Association, which has a vibrant intelligence studies section, and is well-known to intelligence studies scholars. He regularly serves as a peer reviewer for submissions on intelligence topics to academic journals and book publishers and periodically gives guest lectures at universities as an expert on intelligence subjects.

Gentry's writing on intelligence has attracted the attention of the press. He has spoken to radio interviewers repeatedly since the mid-1990s and appeared on television three times: ABC News, C-SPAN, and, most recently, with Tucker Carlson of Fox in 2019. He is periodically asked by print journalists for expert commentary, most recently by Bill Gertz of the *Washington Times*. He spoke in 2019-2020, before the pandemic broke, on the subject of this book to groups organized by: the Council on Foreign Relations in New York City; Ryerson University in Toronto, Canada; and the Association of Former Intelligence Officers (AFIO) in New York City. He spoke to another AFIO group in February 2023.

Gentry has published six journal articles that directly discuss aspects of the recent politicization of intelligence by intelligence professionals. Coverage and analyses evolved over time as the extent of politicization became clearer. The most recent three articles make some of the key points of the book but discuss only parts of the book. They amount to marketing for the book as well as scholarly contributions. The articles are: "The New Politicization of the U.S. Intelligence Community," *International Journal of Intelligence and CounterIntelligence* 33:4 (2020): 639-665 and "Trump-Era Politicization: A Code of Civil-Intelligence Behavior Is Needed," *International Journal of Intelligence and CounterIntelligence* 34:4 (2021): 757-786; and "Demographic Diversity in U.S. Intelligence Personnel: Is It Functionally Useful?" *International Journal of Intelligence and CounterIntelligence* 36:2 (2023): 564-596.

INDEX

D

F

G

H

I

L

M

N

O

P

R

S

U

V

W

Z